REALM OF THE RING LORDS

Also by the same Author

BLOODLINE OF THE HOLY GRAIL

GENESIS OF THE GRAIL KINGS

Laurence Gardner is an internationally known sovereign genealogist and historical lecturer. Distinguished as the Chevalier Labhràn de St. Germain, he is Presidential Attaché to the European Council of Princes, a constitutional advisory body established in 1946. He is also Prior of the Sacred Kindred of St. Columba, a Knight Templar of St. Anthony, a Fellow of the Society of Antiquaries of Scotland and Attaché to the Grand Protectorate of the Imperial Dragon Court, 1408. Formally attached to the Noble Order of the Guard of St Germain, founded by King James VII of Scots in 1692 and ratified by King Louis XIV of France, he is the appointed Jacobite Historiographer Royal.

REALM OF THE RING LORDS

The Myth and Magic of the Grail Quest

Laurence Gardner

le Chevalier Labhràn de St. Germain

FAIR WINDS
PRESS
GLOUCESTER, MASSACHUSETTS

Dedicated to
Julia, Richard and James

Fable should be taught as fable, myth as myth, and miracles as poetic fancies. To teach superstitions as truth is horrifying. The mind of a child accepts them and only through great pain, perhaps tragedy, can the child be relieved of them.
Hypatia of Alexandria, AD 370-415

First published in Great Britain in 2000 by
Multi MediaQuest International Ltd.,
PO Box 4, Ottery St Mary, EX11 1YR, England

First published in the United States in 2002 by
Fair Winds Press
33 Commercial Sreet
Gloucester, MA 01930

ISBN 1-55267-758-3

Typeset by MediaQuest

Jacket design by Adrian Wagner and Stephen Knight
Cover illustrations by Peter Robson

Printed and bound in Canada

CONTENTS

GENEALOGICAL CHARTS

Included in Appendix X

PLATES

FIGURES AND ILLUSTRATIONS

ACKNOWLEDGEMENTS

For their valued assistance in the preparation of this work, I am indebted to the good offices of the Sacred Kindred of Saint Columba, the Royal House of Stewart, the European Council of Princes, the Order of Knights Templars of Saint Anthony, the Noble Order of the Guard of Saint Germain and the Imperial and Royal Dragon Court and Order.

I would also like to thank those archivists and librarians who have aided my quest, especially those at the British Library, the Departments of Western Asiatic Antiquities and Egyptian Antiquities at the British Museum, Bibliothèque Nationale de France, Bibliothèque de Bordeaux, Devon County Library, Birmingham Central Library, the National Library of Scotland, Manchester City Art Galleries and the Royal Irish Academy.

My utmost gratitude is due to the directors and staff of MediaQuest, along with HRH Prince Michael of Albany for affording me privileged access to Household and Chivalric papers. I am also thankful to my wife Angela and son James for their forbearance during my time-consuming endeavour.

To those many friends and colleagues who have smoothed the path of this venture in one way or another I offer my appreciation. In particular, I am grateful to Helen Wagner, Stephen Knight, Chev. David Roy Stewart, Karen Lyster, Ron Saunders, Penny Stopa, Florence Hamilton, Jenny Carradice, Scarlett Nunn, John Baldock, Matthew Cory, Tony Skiens, Chev. David Wood, Angus McBride, Daniel Sewell Ward, Nicholas de Vere, Mike Simms, Dayle Sheridan, Julia Kerr, Prof. Elizabeth Miller, Chris Rosling, Sharon Lee, Dr. Beverly Whipple and Dr. Gary Schubach.

For their generous support in aiding my work internationally, my special thanks to Eleanor Robson and Steve Robson of Peter Robson Studio; to Duncan Roads, Ruth Parnell and Marcus Allen of *Nexus;* to Gretchen Schroeder and Laura Wagner of MediaQuest USA <http://www.mediaquestusa.com/index.html>; to JZ Knight and all at Ramtha's School of Enlightenment; to Christina Zohs of *The Golden Thread;* and to Nancy Simms of Entropic Fine Art.

My thankful recognition is due to Sir Peter Robson for his artistic liaison and for creating the inspired allegorical painting *The Portal of the Twilight World* (*see* also under Picture Credits). Similarly, to the composer Sir Adrian Wagner who, in his family tradition of such masterworks as *Lohengrin* and *Parsifal,* has endorsed this book with the release of his companion music album, *Realm of the Ring Lords* <http://www.mediaquest.co.uk/awrrl.html>.

Laurence Gardner
September 2000

PICTURE CREDITS

Thanks must go to those below in respect of the following photographic illustrations and copyright images

1, Courtesy of the The British Museum, London; 2, The National Gallery of Scotland, Edinburgh, and the Bridgeman Art Library, London; 3, 12, 13, 19, 22, Peter Robson Studio and Entropic Fine Art Inc. <http://www.entropic-art.com/> Ontario; 4, Museo Nacional Del Prado, Madrid, and the Ministerio de Educación y Cultura, Italia; 5, Sefton MBC Leisure Services Department, Arts and Cultural Services, Atkinson Art Gallery, Southport; 6, Reproduced by permission of the Royal Academy of Arts, London; 7, Illustration by Angus McBride from Men-at-Arms 137 The Scythians 700-300 BC. Reproduced by permission of Osprey Publishing Ltd. Copyright Osprey Publishing Limited; 8, Institut de France—Musée Jaquemart-André, Paris; 9, Courtesy of Cliché H Maertens—Musée des Beaux-Arts de Nantes, France; 10, Galleria Doria Pamphili, Rome; 11, Reproduced by permission of Manchester City Art Galleries; 14, 20, Private Collection; 15, National Gallery of Victoria, Melbourne, and the Bridgeman Art Library, London; 16, The Louvre , Paris, and the Bridgeman Art Library, London; 17, Palazzo Pitti, Florence, and the Bridgeman Art Library, London; 18, Musée d'Orsay and Agence photographique de la réunion des musées nationaux, Paris; 21, Museum zu Allerheiligen, Schaffhausen, Switzerland; 23, Courtesy of the Faringdon Collection Trust, Buscot Park, Farringdon, Oxfordshire. Illustrations relating to St Columba in Chapters 13 and 19, The Glencolumcille Heritage Centre, co. Donegal.

While every effort has been made to secure permissions, if there are any errors or oversights regarding copyright material, we apologise and will make suitable acknowledgement in any future edition.

PREFACE

THE MYTH AND MAGIC OF THE GRAIL QUEST

During these past years of my questing for the physical and spiritual aspects of the Holy Grail, it has become very apparent that the mythology and historical traditions of the Ring quest are equally compelling. Moreover, the time-honoured quests for the Ring and the Grail are, in essence, one and the same since they are both concerned with aspects of enlightenment and individual sovereignty. This similarity was commented upon in the 19th century by the poet Alfred, Lord Tennyson, and by the composer Richard Wagner, while in later times it has been supported by J. R. R. Tolkien, author of the popular trilogy, *The Lord of the Rings.*

Despite the observations of these noted researchers, however, it is a fact that the Ring and the Grail have generally been perceived to have separate identities and their individual traditions are rarely discussed as being in any way mutually supportive. It is, therefore, the purpose of this book to bring the two mysteries together for the first time in one arena and, in so doing, to shed new light upon the historical truths which lie behind these enigmatic relics of sacred heritage.

The Grail and Ring are each the subjects of their own mythologies and, from the earliest Arthurian romance to the recent tales of J. R. R. Tolkien, these are enveloped within the lore of Elphame—the magical world of elves and fairies. However, the myths are based upon no mere fantasy, for beyond the portal of this twilight world there exists an engaging history of real characters and events which have been strategically ignored by orthodox educational establishments. It is for this reason that the Grail and Ring are still perceived as the objects of ultimate quest, despite all attempts by Church and academic society to veil and suppress the truth of our heritage.

Subsequent to the 1996 publication of *Bloodline of the Holy Grail,* I have received an ever increasing number of supportive letters from readers, many of whom have provided some very useful information concerning my areas of research, while numerous others have asked some truly fascinating questions. I am most grateful for this correspondence and, for some time, was able to respond to all individual communications, even if with some delay. Nevertheless, the position now is that, with many thousands of letters arriving in the past year or so, the volume is somewhat overwhelming. Please be assured, however, that I do appreciate and read every item of correspondence. Meanwhile, I have endeavoured to answer many of the most frequently asked questions within the pages of this book, and shall continue to do so in others, while also making use of the newly introduced Web site <http:www.laurencegardner.com> in this regard.

One aspect of my writing which has prompted a certain amount of enquiry over past months, and which I introduced in *Genesis of the Grail Kings*, is the establishment of the Hungarian Order of the Dragon. In this respect I have imparted some further information in Chapter 18 (*see* also Internet <http://www.mediaquest.co.uk/RDCsite/RDChome.html>). By way of an extract from these sources, the position concerning the officers of this closed, non-joining fraternity is as follows.

The Order is currently registered at the High Court of Budapest as The Imperial and Royal Dragon Court and Order (*Ordo Draconis*)—Sárkány Rend, 1408. The Grand Chancellor is Chev. Dr. Gyorgy von varhegyi Lehr, Count of Oberberg, with Inner Court members including HRH Prince Michael of Albany, Head of the Royal House of Stewart, Grand Duke Peter Galicin of Carpathia and Baron Wodiank Zoltan Nemessary. Bishop Bela Csernak is the Grand Prior in Transylvania and Chev. Baron Andreas G. von Lehr the Grand Prior in Germany. Other notable members are Count Monsignor Laszlo Esterházy, Chev. Count Dr Janos szeki Teleki and Chev. Monsignor Laszlo von galantal Esterházy, Papal Chaplain, Provost Parochus of the Mariaremete Cathedral in Budapest. In Britain and the English speaking countries, the Order resides within the Protectorate of the Royal House of Stewart, with the Grand Prior being Dr. Andrew von Zsigmond, Baron de Lemhény, of the Hungarian Consulate.

Laurence Gardner

1

The Ring and the Grail

Eternal Quests

One Ring to rule them all,
One Ring to find them,
One Ring to bring them all,
And in the darkness bind them.[1]

J. R. R. Tolkien's *The Lord of the Rings* is one of the most enchanting and successful tales of all time. First issued in the 1950s, this famous trilogy[2] could just as well have emanated from the Dark Ages or medieval times, for it has all the qualities and attributes of the most ancient Grail and Ring traditions. This was made possible by the fact that Tolkien (an Oxford professor of Anglo-Saxon and English language) had the legendary wealth of ages at his fingertips and moulded his story accordingly. As a result, his masterwork became the most popular individual publication of the 20th century.

The Ring Quest has a history that dates far back into the mists of time—beyond the pyramids of Egypt and the walls of Babylon. It has lived on through the era of the pagan gods and has seen the rise of Buddha, Christ and Mohammed. Remarkably, its traditions and allegories remain alive and intact to this day, evoking the imagery of a long distant past. Despite the many centuries of Church and governmental indoctrination designed to sway us from the Quest, its enlightened truths draw hard upon our collective memory. Consequently, the difference between fiction and suppressed fact is inherently recognizable and the ancient lore sits very comfortably in today's environment having, as we shall see, a perpetual moral truth at its heart.

In considering the history of the Ring Quest, its parallel association with the Grail Quest becomes increasingly apparent, as do the origins of fairies, elves, pixies, sprites, gnomes and goblins. Ring lore is also deeply rooted in many of the best loved nursery tales and provides the essential facts behind numerous time-honoured characters of popular legend.

Grail stories are generally associated with Arthurian knights roaming the Wasteland in search of the sacred relic. But the genre also embodies many other questing tales, incorporating such characters as Cinderella, Robin Hood, Sleeping Beauty and Count Dracula. Each account holds its own separate mystery and fascination, but it is not generally understood that, in one way or another, they all stem from a common historical base which is rooted in the ancient culture of the Ring Lords. Even though some of the themes have their origins in very old lore, the majority of these tales were newly slanted from the Dark Ages onwards, when the Church set its sights against the Ring tradition. This was especially the case from medieval times when the persecution of heretics was in full swing, leading to the brutal Inquisitions which began in the 13th century.

From the earliest of Sumerian and Scythian times, over five thousand years ago, the abiding symbol of the Ring Lords was the Ring—a representation of wholeness, unity and eternity, often identified as an ouroboros: a serpent clutching its own tail. With a cross positioned beneath the Ring, it becomes the familiar device of the female: the Venus symbol. Alternatively, with a cross positioned above the Ring, it becomes the masculine Orb of sovereign regalia. With the cross positioned within the Ring, it symbolises the Holy Grail itself—identified as the *Rosi-crucis*: the Dew-cup or Cup of the Waters. Hence, as confirmed by Professor Tolkien, along with the poet Alfred, Lord Tennyson, and the composer Richard Wagner, the Grail and the Ring are closely affiliated and, in some measure, synonymous.[3]

The *Rosi-crucis* emblem is recorded as far back as 3500 BC in Mesopotamia and it has long been the distinguishing device of the *Sangréal* (the Blood Royal, or Holy Grail), whose supporters became known as Rosicrucians. Though traditionally referred to by the Church as the Mark of Cain,[4] this device is in fact the original and longest-standing mark of sovereignty. In Mesopotamia and Egypt, the early kings of the succession were called Dragons because they were anointed with the sacred fat of a large monitor called the *Mûs-hûs* or *Messeh* (see figure on page 7). From this derived the Hebrew stem *MSSH*, which gave rise to the verb *mashiach* (to anoint). Thus, the kings were also called Messiahs (*Meschiachs:* Anointed Ones). In the Gaelic world the overall Kings-of-kings were known as Pendragons (Head Dragons) and, from the earliest times, they were also styled Ring Lords by virtue of their Rings of office which symbolised divinely inspired justice.

Although the Messianic bloodline of the *Sangréal* is believed to descend from Jesus and his family, the fact is that the Grail dynasty began more than three millennia before the Gospel era. As an hereditary emblem, the *Rosi-crucis* represented the matrilinear blood of the Messianic succession held within the *vas-uterine* chalice (the womb) of the Grail Queen. The Dragon, being emblematic of wisdom, was the epitome of the Holy Spirit which moved upon the waters of time,[5] while the Grail was the perpetual blood of the succession. Originally called the *Gra-al* in old Mesopotamia, the maternal blood of the *Rosi-crucis* was said to be the 'nectar of supreme excellence' and the Greeks called it *ambrosia*.

Tolkien's Ring

For all practical purposes, the mythology of J. R. R. Tolkien's *The Lord of the Rings* can perhaps be seen as an intuitive parable of governmental suppression and of the combative quest for liberty and justice. It is essentially a tale of territorial lordship and of power vested in the wrong hands—a dark power which has to be destroyed in order to return the wounded Middle-earth to its former equanimity. In its own way, the story is entirely reminiscent of the central precept of Grail lore, which determines that only when the wound of the Fisher King is healed can the Wasteland be returned to fertility.

Tolkien's story begins with Bilbo Baggins, a hobbit who has acquired a magic Ring that can render its wearer invisible. Having bequeathed it to his heir, Frodo Baggins, Bilbo promptly vanishes on his eleventy-first (111th) birthday. Gandalf the wizard is concerned because he believes the Ring to have been made long ago by the evil Lord Sauron and that it is having a negative effect on the Middle-earth environment, where the once sublime forest of Greenwood the Great is beset by oppressive forces to become known as Mirkwood.

Bilbo had originally purloined the Ring from a strange underground creature called Gollum and, on testing it, Gandalf discovers that it is certainly the Ring of Sauron–the One Ring which binds various others within its ultimate power.[6] Meanwhile, the dark forces have been driven out of the forest by the elves, but they now gather to the east in Sauron's land of Mordor, where they plot to retrieve the Ring.

There is only one way to destroy the Ring of power, and that is to cast it into the fire in which it was forged on the Mount of Doom—and so Bilbo's young cousin Frodo and a few hobbits embark on the dangerous journey. Along the way, they are attacked by the Black Riders, but also meet with friendly elves and with Aragorn, King of Gondor, who conducts them to the White Council of Elves and Dwarves, where they learn about the great war against Sauron.

Frodo and the hobbits, forming a fellowship with Gandalf and Aragorn, pursue their course to dispose of the Ring, but Gandalf is soon lost to the abyss in a battle, leaving the group without their wizard. At this, a conflict ensues over who should be the leader and Frodo disappears with the Ring to the Land of Shadows. The others set out to find him, but they are now in dispute as to their purpose because the dark powers are working against them.

Various members of the fellowship are lost in a battle against the hostile Orcs, leaving only Aragorn and two others in the search for Frodo. Later, they meet again with Gandalf, who has returned from the Underworld to defeat his one-time chief, the wizard Saruman, who has joined forces with the Dark Powers and the Orcs. Meanwhile, Frodo and his colleague Sam have reached the land of Mordor, but Frodo is paralysed by Shelob the giant spider and seized by the Orcs.

In Aragorn's land of Gondor, the regent Denethor is preparing for war against the forces of Mordor, but Sauron's magic is too powerful and Gondor is overrun – saved only by the timely return of King Aragorn and his rangers. Sam, in the meantime, has managed to rescue Frodo from the Orcs and the pair make their way to the Mount of Doom with the Ring on Frodo's finger. But the Ring now has Frodo in its grasping power and he cannot hurl it into the hellfire. The strange Gollum, whom Bilbo had first encountered, then reappears to take back the Ring. He bites off Frodo's finger, but slips and topples headlong into the inferno. And so the Ring is finally returned to where it was forged, at which the Mount of Doom erupts in a final blaze of destruction and Sauron's dark land of Mordor is demolished for all time.

On returning home after a meeting with Gandalf and Aragorn, the hobbits Frodo and Sam find their Shire in the grip of the wizard Saruman, but he is soon overcome and the land is restored. With the great war and its era of darkness at an end, Frodo and Gandalf then join together for the last time as they leave Middle-earth and sail westward to the white shores beyond the sea.

The Ring of Justice

Historically, the Ring was a symbol of perpetually divine justice, which was measured by the Rod. In ancient depictions the Sumerian goddess Lilith and the Babylonian god Marduk are individually portrayed holding the Rod and Ring devices.[7] These are in keeping with other portrayals of Mesopotamian kings and queens as, for example, on the Stelae of Shamash and Ur-Nammu from the 3rd millennium BC. In some instances the Rod is clearly marked in calculable units (like a modern ruler)[8] and, in Babylonia, it was referred to as the Rule. The one who held the Rule was the designated 'ruler'—which is from where the governmental term derives.

From around 4000 BC, the Ring was a primary device of the Anunnaki gods, who were recorded as having descended into ancient Sumer and were responsible for the establishment of municipal government and kingly practice. In view of this, it is of particular relevance that, when Professor Tolkien was asked about the Middle-earth environment of *The Lord of the Rings*, he said that he perceived its setting to relate to about 4000 BC.[9] "The pot of soup (the cauldron of the story) has always been boiling", he said, "and to it have continually been added new bits". In this respect, the root of Tolkien's popular tale was (in accordance with his Anglo-Saxon scholarship) extracted directly from Saxon folklore and was not actually new in concept. Indeed, the early Saxon god Wotan (Odin)—the equivalent of the Sumerian god Anu—was said to have ruled the Nine Worlds of the Rings—having the ninth Ring (the One Ring) to govern the eight others.[10]

The contested ownership of the One Ring, as related in *The Lord of the Rings*, is little different to the enduring quest for the Holy Grail; they are both quests for the maintenance of sovereignty. But, in both fact and fiction, the Ring and the Grail are each seen to be misappropriated by those who perceive them as weapons of power. Hence, it has been imperative (in the respective stories) that access to the Grail is protected by difficult questions, just as it was essential to keep the One Ring from the evil Sauron of Mordor.

As the generations passed from ancient Mesopotamian and Egyptian times, the ideal of dynastic kingship spread through the Mediterranean lands into the Balkans, the Black Sea regions and Europe. But, in the course of this, the crucial essence of the old wisdom was lost and this gave rise to dynasties that were not of the original kingly race. Instead, many were unrelated warrior chiefs who gained their thrones by might of the sword.

The sacred culture of the ancients was, nevertheless, retained in the Messianic line of King David of Judah (*c*.1008 BC), whose significance (as detailed in *Genesis of the Grail Kings*) was in his pharaonic heritage, not in his generally portrayed descent from Abraham and the Shemite strain. It was because of this particular inheritance that David's son, Solomon the Wise, was enabled to create his Egyptian-style Temple project in Jerusalem. This led to a Holy Land revival of the pharaonic and one-time Mesopotamian *Rosi-crucis* movement at a time when Egypt was beset by foreign influences, first from Libya, Nubia and Kush, and then from further afield. Resultantly, the traditional marriage arrangements of the pharaohs and princesses gave way to diplomatic alliances.

Marduk with the Rod (Rule) and Ring of Divine Justice.
At his feet is the Mûs-hûs

Ring Lord at the Persopolis in Persia
From a stone relief of Ahura Mazda, associated with the Sumerian Enki

In 525 BC Egypt was conquered by the Persians, whose kings were subsequently ousted by Alexander the Great of Macedonia's army in 332 BC. This led to the Greek dynasty of the Ptolemies and the well-known Queen Cleopatra VII. Her liaison with the Roman general Mark Antony caused the final downfall of the pharaohs, and Egypt was subjugated by Imperial Rome shortly before the time of Jesus. At length, as the Roman Empire collapsed, Egypt fell to Byzantine governors and then, after 641, to the sway of Islam.

By that time, the Grail dynasty from David and Solomon had progressed into the West, notably to the Merovingian Kings of the Franks, while related branches established kingdoms in Ireland and Gaelic Britain.[11] These lines were linked through marriage to the parallel strains from the Old Testament characters Ham, Japhet and Tubal-cain (which had survived as the royal houses of Scythia and Anatolia), and the families had forged their own marital links with the early princesses of the Egyptian succession.

The first Pendragon (Head Dragon) of the Britannic Isle (*Pen Draco Insularis*) from this stock was King Cymbeline of the House of Camulot (*camu-lot* meaning curved light, whence Camelot), who was installed in about AD 10. The British Pendragons were not father-to-son successors in a particular descent, but were individually elected from reigning family branches by a druidic council of elders to be the overall Kings of Kings (*see* Appendix I). The last Pendragon was the Welsh King Cadwaladr of Gwynedd, who died in 664. At around that time much of Britain fell to the Germanic influence of the invading Angles and Saxons—hence Angle-land (England) was born, as distinct from Scotland and Wales.

This coincided with Byzantium's loss of Egypt to the Caliphs and, following the last Roman Emperor in AD 476, a whole new governmental structure had evolved in the West. Eventually, its ultimate overlords were the popes, and outside the preserved Gaelic domains they appointed kings, not by any right of heritage, but to suit the political motives of the bishops and the fast-growing Roman Church. In view of this, the staunch upholders of the Church's articles of dogma openly opposed the pre-papal concept of Grail kingship. These bishops pronounced the Arthurian romances heretical and blacklisted the *Prophecies of Merlin* in 1547 at the Council of Trento in Northern Italy. Everything that was magic to the ears, and all that was fresh air to the subjugated, became denounced as sinister and occult. The great enlightenment of the Grail Code of service was condemned in a series of brutal Inquisitions from 1203, and anything remotely connected with the female ethic was dubbed Witchcraft. In this latter regard, the Church became so fanatical in its opposition to the Ring culture that, in 1431, when Joan of Arc was sentenced to burning at the stake for her alleged sorcery, one of the main charges levelled against her was that she had used magical rings for curative purposes!

The Sacred Hallows

In all the Grail romances and in the tales of the Ring, the message is relentlessly clear: in the wrong hands, both the Ring and the Grail can bring disaster. The power of the Ring has to be withstood, otherwise it will enslave its master, whereas the Grail will retaliate with a vengeance if misused. Either way, the moral is the same in that, ultimately, power is self-destructive when achieved through selling one's soul. Consequently, the Ring can be a halo or a crown, but it can equally become a noose.

From the 1930s, Adolf Hitler's fanatical obsession with finding the Hallows of Grail Castle was a prime example of this misconceived notion of power. In his search for the Hallows, the Fuehrer of Germany obtained an ancient lance (said to have been used by Charlemagne), which he insisted was the spear of Longinus the centurion—the spear which pierced the side of Jesus at the Crucifixion. This, he reckoned, was the sacred Spear of Destiny, so revered in Grail lore. With this in his possession, Hitler was confident that his Empire (Reich) would be as strong as that of Charlemagne, but legend had it that, after many great victories, Charlemagne was doomed to defeat from the moment he lost the magical weapon. In Richard Wagner's opera, *Parsifal,* this powerful imagery is conveyed when the old knight Klingsor promptly disappears from the mortal plane on hurling the hallowed spear at Parsifal. And so it was that on 30 April 1945 (the very day when the American 7th Army, under General Patton, seized the lance from Nuremberg Castle)[12] Adolf Hitler, in the grip of such forceful and consuming lore, accepted defeat and shot himself. Today, the lance resides in the Hofburg Museum, Vienna.

In the 13th-century Grail romance, *Parzival,* by the Bavarian knight Wolfram von Eschenbach, the questing Parzival first sees the mysterious spear, dripping blood from its point, at a ceremony in Grail Castle.[13] The sight of it causes much consternation among the knights, who explain that it represents the forces which kill the higher spirit in man. Also, its appearance (when carried) signifies that the Grail Quest has not yet been fulfilled. Whether or not the spear of Charlemagne, eventually acquired by Hitler, was indeed the biblical spear of the Crucifixion has long been a matter of debate. That apart, it does seem to have an extraordinary history which, according to Liutbrand, a 10th-century Bishop of Cremona in Northern Italy, can be traced back to the ownership of Constantine the Great and to various other kings and emperors—to become known as the Imperial Lance.[14]

Tarot Magician with the sword, cup, pentacle and wand–representative of the Grail Hallows.

Whether applied in fact or fantasy, the concept of the Ring and the Grail was such that it inspired hope for the social and natural environments. The Grail Hallows the—Sword, Chalice, Platter and Spear—were traditionally regarded as tools of princely service but, when presumed to be weapons of power, they would always, one way or another, destroy the wielder from within.

These Hallows were represented in the four suits of the Tarot's *Minor Arcana* as the Swords, Cups, Pentacles and Wands—subsequently to become the Spades, Hearts, Diamonds and Clubs that are familiar in our playing-card decks today.[15]

Clearly, a major inspiration for Tolkien was the legendary tale of King Solomon's Ring which, although not mentioned in the Bible's Old Testament, appears in other traditional Hebrew writings. In the Talmud[16] Solomon is reckoned to have been the mightiest magician of his age, and his great wisdom and considered judgement as a sorcerer-king are directly attributed to his ownership of an enchanted Ring with which he summoned the demons of the Earth. This famed son of King David was the ancestral model for the Merovingians of Gaul,[17] who were themselves noted sorcerer-kings in the Ring Lord tradition.

In the same manner as King Solomon, Tolkien's Sauron used his One Ring to command the demons of the Earth, charging them to build the Tower of Mordor just as Solomon used his demons to build the Temple of Jerusalem. The Rings were also similar in that each had the power to corrupt and destroy its master. Solomon's Ring achieved his downfall through the agency of the demon Asmodaeus, whereas Sauron is presented as his own destructive demon. Along with the Rings, there are also story similarities concerning the possession of light-radiating jewels, with Solomon's being the *Schamir*, while that of Tolkien's Elf King Thingol (in *The Silmarillion*) was the *Silmaril*—each of which is said to be an heirloom of the respective king's race.

2

Legacy of the Damned

A Conflict of Interests

Prior to the year 751, kings of the Grail succession were priests in their own right; they were priest-kings, known as Fisher Kings.[1] But when their rights to priesthood were undermined by the Roman Church, the legacy was forsaken in all but the Gaelic realms. Before this, the representative substances of priest-kingship were gold (for nobility), frankincense (for priesthood) and myrrh (for knowledge). These were the very substances presented to Jesus by the ascetic Magi in the New Testament, thereby positively identifying him as a dynastic priest-king of the Grail bloodline. The significance of this magian presentation has been lost though, within a contrived fable of humble birth in a stable, which is not mentioned in any original Gospel. Yet, for some obscure reason, the Grail symbolism was retained by the Church in its Eucharist (Communion) sacrament, wherein the blood of the *Sangréal* is drunk from the sacred chalice of the *Rosi-crucis*. In this regard, the true symbolism of the ancient custom (originally called the Ritual of the Star Fire)[2] has been strategically veiled, while both Grail lore and Ring lore are denounced as unofficial heresies.

As related in *Bloodline of the Holy Grail*, the disputes between the Grail family and the Church establishment prevailed for centuries because of their conflict of interests.[3] From the 1st century, Imperial Rome had decreed that the Messianic heirs should be hunted down and put to the sword. Then, once the Roman Church was formally operative from the 4th century, the sacred dynasty was forever damned by the bishops.

It was this formal damnation which led to such events as the Albigensian Crusade in 1209 and the subsequent Catholic Inquisitions, for these brutal assaults by the papal machine were specifically directed against the upholders and champions of the original concept of Grail kingship, as against the style of pseudo-monarchy which had been implemented by the Bishops of Rome. In practical terms, Church kingship prevailed from the 8th century and has continued, through the ages, to the present day. But the fact is that, under the strict terms of sovereign practice, all such monarchies and their affiliated governments have been invalid.

So, what exactly is Church kingship? It is precisely that with which we have become so familiar. It applies to all monarchs who achieve their regnal positions by way of Church coronation by the Pope or other Christian leader (in Britain, by the Archbishop of Canterbury). In terms of true kingship, there was no necessity for coronation because kingly and queenly inheritance were always regarded as being 'in the blood'—to be precise, in the mitochondrial DNA of the *Sangréal*.

During the past few years, many readers have asked about the position of the *Sangréal* today, and of who might be descended in the line. In this regard it must be said that, although certain lines of the succession can be traced through the noble registers of Britain and Europe, all the branches have become substantially diluted by way of intermarriage with other families through the centuries. Also, if one were to consider any couple in, say, the 1st-century Gospel era, and to presume that two offspring emanated from that couple, with those offspring each responsible for producing another two—and so on—the calculation down to date amounts to 1,208,925,819,574,363,856,306,176 births in the year 2000.[4] As a measure of comparison against this theoretical (and obviously impossible) projection, the total number of people in the whole world at this time of writing is substantially fewer at around 6,107,035,302.

It can be seen, therefore, that there is neither any merit nor uniqueness in the fact that anyone today might be descended from a person that far back in time and eventually we all trace to common ancestors.

In the old scheme of things, *Sangréal* kingship was automatic because it was deemed to be an alchemical inheritance which had nothing to do with ruling over anyone or anywhere. It was actually rather more concerned with the maintenance of justice and the Grail Code of princely service. By virtue of an illegal dictate, however, monarchies were brought under Church control and the magical realm of the Ring Lords was supplanted by the material and territorial reigns of the papal kings. One might ask why this was allowed to happen. Why did no one stand up for the legacy of the Holy Grail? Well, the fact is that many did: the Cathars did, the Knights Templars did and the Rosicrucians did. Indeed, any number of gnostic groups and fraternities did, and it was this open support which led to the hideous tortures, executions and witch-hunts that persisted through so many generations.

By the Middle Ages, the Church controlled the majority of European monarchies—with Scotland being a notable exception, as a result of which King Robert the Bruce and the whole Scottish nation were excommunicated by the Pope.[5] The Church, therefore, influenced governments, parliaments and educational establishments, as it still does today. And, by implication if not by direct instruction, the military forces of the pseudo-kings operated at Church command.

The Church held such enormous financial, political and military power that the Grail adherents became an 'underground stream'—living in fear of their lives at every turn. They were not only proclaimed heretics, they were singled out for punishment as sorcerers (conjurors of sourced spirits) and necromancers (from *negro-mans*: black magicians). Also, since they did not conform to papal dictates, they were clearly satanists!

Additionally, the women were all reckoned to be whores—but this was nothing new; the Roman Church had forged this dogmatic classification at the time of its earliest constitution when the female ethic was so fearfully suppressed.

In order to understand the legacy of the Ring, we must look at how Church kingship was made possible in the first place by way of a document called the *Donation of Constantine*—a document which led to just about every social injustice that has since been experienced in the Christian world. All monarchical and governmental practice has, for centuries, been based upon the initial precept of this charter but, in reality, its precept is wholly invalid. When the *Donation* made its first appearance in the middle 8th century it was alleged to have been written by Emperor Constantine some 400 years earlier, although strangely never produced in the interim. It was even dated and carried his supposed signature. What the document proclaimed was that the Emperor's appointed Pope was Christ's elected representative on Earth, with the power to create kings as his subordinates since his palace ranked above all the palaces in the world, while the papal dignity was above that of any earthly ruler. The Pope was formally styled therein as the Vicar of the Son of God (*Vicarius Filii Dei*), with the distinction of 'Vicar' denoting a deputized or vicarious office (*see* Appendix II).

The provisions were put into operation by the Vatican in 751, whereupon the Merovingian Kings of the Grail bloodline in Gaul (France) were deposed and a whole new dynasty was supplemented by way of a family of hitherto mayors. They were dubbed Carolingians and their only king of any significance was the legendary Charlemagne. By way of this strategy, the whole nature of monarchy changed from being an office of community guardianship to one of absolute rule and, by virtue of this monumental change, the long-standing Grail Code of princely service was forsaken as European kings became servants of the Church instead of being servants of the people.

The fact is that over 500 years ago in the Renaissance era, proof emerged that the *Donation* was an outright forgery. Its New

Testament references relate to the Latin *Vulgate* Bible[6]—an edition translated and compiled by St Jerome, who was not born until AD 340, some 26 years after Constantine supposedly signed the document! Apart from this, the language of the *Donation*, with its numerous anachronisms in form and content, is that of the 8th century and bears no relation to the writing style of Constantine's day. The truly ridiculous aspect of this is that the *Donation's* overwhelming dictate, which cemented the Pope as the supreme spiritual and temporal head of Christendom, has prevailed regardless.[7]

The fraudulent *Donation of Constantine* (*Constitutum Constantini*) was specifically designed to strengthen the power of the Church and, in particular, the Roman See after the fall of the Western Empire.[8] It purported to be an Imperial Grant by Emperor Constantine of temporal power in the West to the papacy, and it thoroughly misrepresented the territorial status of the popes by vesting them with a great, but false, antiquity. It was said to be the document presented by Constantine to Pope Sylvester I (the first Imperial Bishop of Rome, AD 314-35) but, in historical terms, the key documentation of that era relates only to the Emperor's grant of the Lateran Palace and other benefits and buildings to the newly styled Church of Rome.

Even though implemented in 751, there is no official reference to the *Donation* until it was mentioned in a letter written by Pope Leo IX to Michael Cerularis, the Patriarch of Constantinople, in 1054. However, by the 12th century it had become the primary document of papal lordship over the whole of Christendom and its monarchs.

Kingship and Conspiracy

One of the greatest threats posed to the early Roman Church prior to 751 was the royal Merovingian dynasty of Gaul. They were male-line descendants of the Fisher Kings, with an ancestry tracing back to the family of Jesus and were named after their founder Meroveus, whom the Franks had proclaimed their Guardian at

Tournai in AD 448. The Merovingians reigned by an ancient tradition of Messianic right and inheritance passed down from generations of ancestors. In keeping with the Grail Code, they served as guardians of their people, rather than territorial overlords. Hence, they were styled 'Kings of the Franks', but never Kings of France.

When Meroveus's son Childeric died in AD 481, he was followed by his son Clovis, the most prominent of all the Merovingians and the traditionally reckoned founder of the French monarchy. At that time the Roman Church greatly feared the increasing popularity of the Arian religion[9] in Gaul (a Christian faith which did not subscribe to the divinity of Jesus), and Catholicism was dangerously close to being completely overrun in Western Europe. Clovis was, in practice, neither Catholic nor Arian and it occurred to the Roman hierarchy that the rise of Clovis could be used to their advantage. As it transpired, Clovis aided them quite inadvertently when he married the Burgundian Princess Clotilde.

Although the Burgundians were traditionally Arian in their beliefs, Clotilde was herself a Catholic and she made it her business to evangelize her version of the faith. For a time she had no success in promoting the doctrine to her husband, but her luck changed in AD 496 when King Clovis and his army were locked in battle against the invading Alamanni tribe near Cologne. For once in his hitherto illustrious military career, the Merovingian was losing and, in a moment of near desperation, he invoked the name of Jesus at much the same instant that the Alaman king was slain. At the loss of their leader, the Alamanni faltered and fell into retreat, whereupon Clotilde wasted no time in proclaiming that Jesus had caused the Merovingian victory. Clovis was not especially convinced of this, but his wife sent immediately for St Remy, the Catholic Bishop of Reims, and arranged for Clovis to be baptised.[10]

In due allegiance to their leader, around half of the Merovingian warriors followed Clovis to the font. Word soon spread that the high potentate of the West was a Catholic and this was of enormous value to Bishop Anastasius in Rome. A great wave of conversions followed and the Roman Church was saved from almost inevitable collapse. In fact, were it not for the baptism of King Clovis, the ultimate Christian religion of Western Europe might well now be Arian rather than Catholic. In this regard, the royal compliance was not a one-way bargain and, in return for the King's agreement to be baptised, the Roman authorities pledged an allegiance to him and his descendants, promising that a new Holy Empire would be established under the Merovingians.

Clovis had no reason to doubt the sincerity of the Roman alliance, but he became the unwitting instrument of a bishops' conspiracy, for they had a longer-term strategy in mind. Their plan was to usurp the Merovingians in due course, thereby leaving the Bishop of Rome (the Pope) supreme in Gaul.[11] In preparation for this, the key provinces of the Merovingian realm (Austrasia, Neustria, Aquitaine and Burgundy) were placed under the immediate supervision of appointed mayors, who were themselves closely allied to the Catholic bishops.

By 655, Rome was in a position to begin dismantling the Merovingian succession and, at that time, the Mayor of the Austrasian Palace (akin to a modern prime minister) was firmly under papal control. When King Sigebert II died, his son Dagobert was only five years old and Mayor Grimoald took the first step in the bishops' plan. To begin, he kidnapped Dagobert and had him conveyed to Ireland, to live in exile among the Scots Gaels. Then, not expecting to see the young heir again, Grimoald told Queen Immachilde that her son had died.

Prince Dagobert was educated at Slane Monastery, near Dublin, and he married the Gaelic Princess Matilde when he was fifteen. Subsequently, he went to York under the patronage of St Wilfred, but then Matilde died and Dagobert returned to France, where he appeared much to the amazement of his mother. In the meantime, Grimoald had placed his own son on the Austrasian throne, but Wilfred of York and others spread word of the mayoral treachery and the House of Grimoald was duly discredited.

Having married his second wife, Gizelle de Razès (a niece of the Visigoth king), Dagobert was reinstated in 674, after an absence of nearly twenty years, and the Roman intrigue was thwarted—but not for long. Two days before Christmas 679, Dagobert was hunting near Stenay in the Ardennes when he was confronted in the forest and lanced to death—impaled to a tree by a henchman of his own powerful mayor, Pepin the Fat of Herstal.

The Church of Rome was quick to approve the assassination and immediately passed the Merovingian administration in Austrasia to the ambitious Pepin. In due course, he was succeeded by his illegitimate son, the well-known Charles Martel, who sustained the Roman endeavour by gaining control of other Merovingian territories. When Martel died in 741, the only Merovingian of any notable authority was Dagobert's nephew Childeric III. Meanwhile, Martel's son, Pepin the Short, was the Mayor of Neustria.

Up to that point (except for the Grimoald affair), the Merovingian monarchy had been strictly dynastic, with its hereditary succession considered an automatic and sacred right—a matter in which the Church had no say whatsoever. But that tradition was destined to be overturned when Rome grasped the opportunity to 'create' kings by way of a spurious papal authority made possible by the *Donation of Constantine*.

In 751 Pepin the Short, in league with Pope Zachary, secured Church approval for his own coronation as King of the Franks in place of Childeric. The Church's long-awaited ideal had come to fruition, and from that time onwards kings were endorsed and crowned only by self-styled Roman prerogative. And so it was that, with the full blessing of the Pope, Pepin became King of the Franks and Childeric was deposed. The pledge of allegiance made by the Roman Church in AD 496 to King Clovis and his descendants was broken and, after two and a half centuries, the Church was suitably geared to usurp the ancient legacy of the Merovingian bloodline, thereby taking control of the Frankish realm by appointing its own kings. Childeric was publicly humiliated by the bishops, and his hair (kept long in the Old

Testament Nazarite tradition)[12] was cut brutally short. He was incarcerated in a monastery, where he died four years later, and thus began a new dynasty of French kings, the Carolingians—so named after Pepin's father, Charles (Carolus) Martel.[13]

A Fraudulent Donation

It was at that stage in 751 that the forged *Donation of Constantine* was brought into play by Pope Zachary, who saw his opportunity not only to depose the Merovingians of the Messianic strain, but to bring the kings and queens of Christendom under papal control for all time. In order to gain Roman Church supremacy in the spiritual domain, the *Donation* provided a security of mastership in the political arena. Various nations became subordinate to a Church which had designated itself to be the supreme Sovereign State.

There was no thought by anyone at the time that the document might actually be a contemporary forgery, while even the anti-papists who sought to criticise its content did not think to question its authenticity. The best they could do was to maintain that Emperor Constantine had no right to have signed away the Western Empire in this fashion. The fact was that, although the opening and closing sections of the *Donation* were cleverly constructed in the 4th-century style of Constantine's day, its more central themes, such as the descriptions of Imperial and papal ceremony, were representative of a much later era.[14] Also of particular significance was the fact that, at one stage of the document, the Byzantine city of Constantinople (named after Constantine) is cited as being in existence, whereas later in the text the idea of building this city is put forward as a future concept!

The *Donation* was first declared to be a forgery by the Saxon Emperor Otto III in the year 1001. Intrigued by the fact that Constantine had moved his personal capital from Rome to Constantinople, Otto recognized that this was actually a ruse to pre-empt any Merovingian ambition to perhaps centre their own kingly operation in Rome in opposition to the Imperial bishops. Although

Otto was a German, his mother was an East Roman who was well aware that this same fear had existed in the late Merovingian era, at which time the further deception of the *Donation of Constantine* was implemented.

Otto's pronouncement came as very unwelcome news to the prevailing Pope Sylvester II, but the matter was ignored and did not come to the fore again until the German theologian and philosopher Nicholas of Cusa (1401-64) announced that Constantine had never produced the said *Donation*.[15] However, although a doctor of canon law, who decreed that the Pope was actually subordinate to the members of the Church movement, Nicholas was somehow overawed by the bishops and subsequently took up a Cardinalate position in 1448, becoming a staunch supporter of the papacy!

The *Donation* was not publicly mentioned again until its authenticity was fiercely attacked by the Italian linguist Lorenzo Valla in the 15th century.[16] Valla (*c*.1407-57) was chosen by Pope Nicholas V to translate the works of Herodotus and Thucydides from Greek into Latin. But, Valla was not just an eminent scholar, he was an ardent spokesman for the reform of education and firmly believed that the spirit of Greco-Roman antiquity had been lost during the Middle Ages. Angered by the fact that the elegance of classical Latin had given way to a clumsy medieval language, as exemplified by the corrupted and largely incomprehensible style of Church Latin, he was highly critical of the Church's *Vulgate* Bible and its strategic errors in translation from the earlier Greek texts. This led other scholars of the Renaissance, such as the Dutch humanist Desiderius Erasmus (*c*.1466-1536), to revert their Bible studies to the more original texts. Resultantly, in 1516, Erasmus issued his own Latin translation of the Greek New Testament, thereby exposing the *Vulgate* as a cleverly mistranslated document, which he called a 'second-hand' account.

The outcome of Lorenzo Valla's investigation into the *Donation of Constantine* was that he discovered it to be an outright forgery compiled some four centuries after Emperor Constantine's death. In his related *Treatise*, he wrote, "I know that for a long time now men's ears are waiting to hear the offence with which I charge the Roman pontiffs. It is, indeed, an enormous one".[17] Yet it was this very Donation which facilitated the final move in overthrowing the Merovingians so that the Church could implement its new style of papal kingship with the Carolingian dynasty. It was the device by which the Roman Church reverted political power to itself after the collapse of the Roman's Western Empire, enabling the bishops to introduce the newly styled Holy Roman Empire under the control of the Pope.

Notwithstanding the debates which ensued from Valla's findings in 1450, the Church managed to survive the Renaissance era of enlightenment, branding many of the great thinkers of the time as heretics. And so Valla's report (known as the *Declamatio*) was conveniently lost within the Vatican Archives. It was not discovered for more than a hundred years until it was once more revealed by the priest Murator who worked in the Vatican Library in the 17th century. Subsequently, the spurious nature of the *Donation* was discussed anew by the Anglican minister Henry Edward Manning (1808-92)[18] but, in the footsteps of Nicholas of Cusa, he too was swayed from his original Church to become a Vatican Council member, a Cardinal and Catholic Archbishop of Westminster, publishing his *The Temporal Power of the Vicar of Jesus Christ* in 1862.

The task of exposing the fraud was then taken up by Christopher B. Coleman, a director of the Historical Commission and Historic Bureau at the Indiana State Library from 1924, who produced an updated commentary on *The Treatise of Lorenzo Valla on the Donation of Constantine*.[19] In the event, the very fact that this work came out of America, and not out of Britain or Continental Europe, made it easy enough to contain—as a result of which very little, outside the occasional encyclopaedic reference, has been written concerning the *Donation* during the past century. But the fact remains that it still exists as the very document which has enabled the Church to maintain control of monarchical, political, military and educational affairs for well over 1200 years.

3

The Shining Ones

Elves and Anunnaki

Prior to the Grail's formal subjugation by the Church Inquisition in the Middle Ages, the victimised heterodox Christians (or 'heretics' as they were called) included the Cathars—the Pure Ones of the Languedoc region in the South of France. The Cathars were fully conversant with the Ring Lord culture and, in accordance with tradition, referred to the Messianic bloodline as the Elven Race, venerating them as the Shining Ones.

In the language of old Provence, a female elf was an *albi* (*elbe* or *ylbi*), and Albi was the name given to the main Cathar centre in Languedoc. This was in deference to the matrilinear heritage of the Grail dynasty, for the Cathars were supporters of the original *Albi-gens:* the Elven bloodline which had descended through the Grail queens of yore such as Lilith, Miriam, Bathsheba and Mary Magdalene. It was for this reason that, when Simon de Montfort and the armies of Pope Innocent III descended upon the region in 1209, it was called the Albigensian Crusade.

Through some thirty-five years, tens of thousands of innocent people were slaughtered in this savage campaign,[1] all because the inhabitants of the region were upholders of the original concept of Grail kingship, as against the inappropriate style of monarchy which had been established by the papal machine. But the Cathars were rather more than the lowly apostate cult which propagandist histories would have us believe. In contrast to the prevalent subjugative climate in Western Europe, Languedoc society was markedly more tolerant and cosmopolitan.[2] As pointed out by Yuri Stoyanov of the Warburg Institute in *The Hidden History of Europe,* Languedoc was actually a prominent centre of a 12th-century 'renaissance', being the cradle of Troubadour lyric poetry and Courtly Love which had flourished under the patronage of the Counts of Béziers, Foix, Toulouse and Provence. In the course of this, the Counts of Toulouse were actually admonished by the papacy for affording Jews positions of public office.

The concept of calling the princely race of the Grail the 'Shining Ones', while also defining them as Elves, dates well back into ancient Bible times and can be traced into Mesopotamia (Iraq) and Canaan (Palestine). Some of the best modern research into the etymological roots of the long distant BC years has been conducted by the writers Christian and Barbara Joy O'Brien. Christian, who read Natural Sciences at Christ's College, Cambridge, subsequently spent many years as an exploration geologist in Iran, where he was involved in the discovery of the Tchoga Zambil ziggurat. Since 1970 he has concentrated his research into many enigmas of prehistory, and the O'Briens have some excellent books to their credit.[3] In *The Genius of the Few* they explain that the ancient word *El,* which was used to identify a god or lofty-one (as in El Elyon and El Shaddai) actually meant 'Shining' in old Mesopotamian Sumer. To the north in Babylonia, the derivative *Ellu* meant 'Shining One', as did *Ilu* in Akkad, and the word spread across Europe to become *Ellyl* in Wales, *Aillil* in Ireland, *Aelf* in Saxony and *Elf* in England. The plural of *El* was *Elohim,*[4] the very word used in old Bible texts to denote the gods, but strategically mistranslated to conform to the Judaeo-Christian 'One God' image. Interestingly, in Gaelic Cornwall, South West England, the word *el* was the equivalent of the Anglo-Saxon *engel* and the old French *angele* which, in English, became 'angel'.

The Shining Ones of the Elohim (as indicated in Sumerian writings from as far back as the 3rd millennium BC) were identified with the skies or with a high place described as *An* and often translated to mean Heaven (or the heavens). In this context, the great gods and overlords of ancient Sumer were called the Anunnaki (*Anun-na-ki* meaning 'Heaven came to earth'). Alternatively, they were the Anannage (*An-anan-na-ge*), the 'Fiery great sons of heaven', and it was from this Anunnaki royal strain that the Grail line ensued. For this reason, it was traditionally referred to as the Elven Bloodline or the dynasty of the Shining Ones.

Quite who these Anunnaki overlords were is a matter of continuing debate and the extant Sumerian texts, which talk of their 'coming down' or 'coming from the heavens', have led many to conclude that they were an alien race from another planet. Indeed, prominent and respected writers such as Zecharia Sitchin, a scholar of the Sumerian language, have written extensively in this regard.[5] This very plausible concept is convincingly supported by some of the unearthly portrayals of the era, as for example a statue of the goddess Nîn-khursag from the first half of the 3rd millennium BC. In this depiction, Nîn-khursag, the great mother of the Grail bloodline and surrogate mother of the *Adâma* (the Earthlings)[6] Atâbba and Kâva (better known as Adam and Eve), is shown with distinctly alien features.

There is, though, another school of thought which supports the notion that the Anunnaki were the remnant of an advanced earthly race which had persisted from very early times, with their 'coming down' relating rather more to a geographical high place (perhaps a more mountainous or more northern country) rather than from the skies. The fact is, nevertheless, that both concepts are possible and neither should be discarded out of hand in favour of the other, for the solution seems to lie in the chronological timing of events in those far off days, and the chances are that both conclusions are correct.

It is becoming ever more clear that the Anunnaki were not confined to the Mesopotamian region; neither did they make their only appearance in the Sumerian culture, as we shall discover later in our investigation. If they were of alien origin, as appears to be the case, then their arrival appears to have been rather more distant in history—some time before the Sumerian era, which began in around 5500 BC.

Dragons and Merlins

In ancient cultural lore the dragon was emblematic of wisdom. Dragons were thought by the Greeks to be the benevolent conveyors of enlightenment, while the Gaels considered them to be representative of sovereignty and the Chinese saw dragons as bringers of good fortune. It was in the Judaeo-Christian tradition that dragons became customarily regarded as sinister and meddlesome, but this was directly due to the fact that the Hebrew and Christian faiths were suppressors of learning, rather than champions of it. On that account, the dragon—the symbolic keeper and bringer of wisdom—was designated superfluous to requirement and sidelined into a dark realm of heresy.

The English word 'dragon' comes to us via the Latin *draco*, but more specifically from the Greek *drakon*, said to mean 'serpent'. The word is apparent in *edrakon*—an unqualified past tense of *derkesthai*: 'to see clearly'—and is equivalent to *nahash*, the biblical Hebrew for 'serpent'. However, this Semitic word (from the consonantal stem *NHSH*) actually related to a threshold of understanding and meant to 'decipher' or 'find out'.[7] The serpent was, therefore, one who saw clearly—and it was held that clarity of vision engendered wisdom. Thus, the serpent was considered to be a wise seer. It was precisely this *nahash* definition which applied in the Genesis story of Eve, when the wise serpent correctly advised her that, contrary to what she had been led to believe, she would not die by eating from the Tree of Knowledge.[8]

In human terms, the great seers of the Gaelic realms were the Merlins of the royal courts—the seers to the High Kings. They were a class of druid priests alike to the classical philosophers or magi, and their tradition derived from an ancient priestly tribe known in Indo-Europe as the Wise Ones. In Latin they were called the *Noblis,* from *gnoblis* and the Greek verbal root *gno,* meaning 'to know'—hence, 'noble' (*gnoble*) and 'gnosis' (knowledge).

Traditionally and consistently the symbol of both wisdom (Greek: *sophia*) and healing was the serpent—and the emblem is still used today by medical organizations around the world.[9] Spiralling serpents are also prominent in allegorical fine art—featuring in such paintings as Sébastien Bourdon's *Moses* and John Collier's *Lilith.* These and other similar portrayals are significant in that the characters are associated not just with wisdom, but with noble wisdom—the far-seeing druidic wisdom of the dragon.

Single and double spiralling serpents as used by medical organizations worldwide

The ancient Mesopotamian dragon, the *Mûs-hûs,* was a four-legged monitor or sacred crocodile, but in subsequent early heraldry the dragon was depicted as a serpent with the wings of a swan—or sometimes the wings of a bat. Also, as we have seen, Messianic kings and queens were themselves called Dragons or Pendragons and were reckoned to uphold the sexual prowess, the warrior fearlessness and the ultimate wisdom of the intrepid beast. Often their armour was scaled and their robes would display serpentine emblems, while the gnostic transcendence of their *noblis* was symbolised by shamanic swan-feather cloaks.

This wing-like garb also became relevant to the artistic portrayal of angels, so as to identify their ability to transcend human normality, while the titular distinction 'Merlin' was similarly indicative of a high-flying, far-seeing falcon.

There exists in Iran (Persia) and the Canary Islands a large plant called the dragon tree (the *dracaena draco*). This plant is of the genus *lillaceae*, or 'lily', and its resin is known as dragon's blood. The red extract was used as a ceremonial dye in the East,[10] where it was referred to as *lac* (the derivative 'lake' pigment being found in the paint colour Scarlet Lake). It is easy to recognize, therefore, why the blood of the dragon was associated with the essence of the lily.

In *Genesis of the Grail Kings*, we saw how the early Mesopotamian kings of the Grail bloodline were supplementally fed with the lunar essence of the matrilinear Dragon Queens—a menstrual extract of the Anunnaki goddesses, which became known as Star Fire.[11] This was said to be the 'nectar of supreme excellence' since it carried the essential elements of what we now define as mitochondrial DNA, while also embodying endocrinal substances which could heighten the recipients' qualities of awareness and perception. Additionally, it was noted that the queens of the line were likened to lilies (or lotus flowers), with names such as Lily, Lilith, Luluwa, Lilutu and Lillet. It is from this very tradition that the family name of du Lac became prominent in Arthurian lore—as for example in Lancelot du Lac. This was translated into English to become Lancelot of the Lake, but its more correct representation was Lancelot of the dragon blood.

Alongside this, the Grail dynasty was also variantly styled the House del Acqs, meaning 'of the waters', from which came the queenly tradition of the Ladies of the Lake. As previously cited, the *Rosi-crucis* (Cup of the waters, or Dew-cup) emblem of the Holy Grail was itself identified with the Messianic blood, held within the sacred chalice of the maternal womb. It can, accordingly, be seen that the styles of *du Lac* and *del Acqs* are entirely synonymous, as are the historical traditions of the

Dragon and the Grail. These conjoined traditions are especially significant in the story of the blood and water which flowed from Jesus's side at the Crucifixion (John 19:34) – being emblematic of the fact that he was truly a kingly dynast of the Shining Ones.

In the Old Testament's *Song of Solomon*, the lost bride of the king relates, "I am the rose of Sharon and the lily of the valleys".[12] In due course, we shall discuss the lily and the rose symbolism but, at this stage, it is worth mentioning that in the traditional lore of the Grail maidens – those styled *du Lac* (of the dragon blood), alternatively *del Acqs* (of the waters) – the whole culture was brought together within the monthly rites of the Temple goddess. These were the sacred blood and water rituals of the time-honoured Ladies of the Fountain, romantically epitomised by such characters as Nimuë and Mélusine, to whom we shall return. These ceremonies, with their said pagan magical origins, were denounced long ago by Church doctrine, which defined them as satanic or vampiric along with the Grail heresy in general. To the enlightened champions of the *Albi-gens*, however, they lodged at the very heart of the Courtly Love tradition of the medieval troubadours. In this context, these rites held the ultimate secret of the divine Star Fire priestesses – the Scarlet Woman whom the Greeks called *hierodulai* (sacred women), but whose prestigious legacy the Christian bishops undermined, denigrating them as whores.

Fate of the Fairies

The concept of fairies (the fair folk) was born directly from Dragon and Ring Lord cultures, being a derivative of *fey* (Old French: *faerie*) and relating especially to 'fate'. In the Gaelic world, certain royal families (especially those of the Pendragons) were said to carry the fairy blood – that is to say, the fate or destiny of the Grail bloodline and of humankind at large – while the Elf-maidens of the *Albi-gens* were the designated guardians of the earth, starlight and forest. It is for these reasons that fairies, elves and leprechauns have so often been portrayed as shoemakers and lamplighters, for the fairy cobblers made the shoes which measured the steps of life, while the Shining Ones of the elven race were there to light the way.

In national terms, although fairies present a widespread image, they are particularly associated with Ireland, where they are epitomized by the ancient people of the *Tuatha Dé Danann*. This formidable king tribe was, nevertheless, mythologized by the Christian monks, who rewrote the majority of Irish history to suit their own Church's vested interest in Eire. From a base of the monastic texts, which arose onwards from medieval times, it is generally stated that these people were the supernatural tribe of the pre-Achaean agricultural goddess Danaë of Argos,[13] or perhaps of the Aegean Mother-goddess Danu. But their true name, rendered in its older form, was *Tuadhe d'Anu*. As such, they were the people (or tribe) of Anu, the great sky god of the Anunnaki.

It is often said that, in strategically mythologizing the heritage of this noble BC race, the Christian Church was responsible for dubbing them 'fairies', but this is not strictly true. The *Tuadhe d'Anu* were always fairies in the Ring Lord tradition, but what the Church did was to redefine the meaning of the word 'fairy'.

In life, when confronted with a seemingly insurmountable problem, one can either submit to the stress and pressure that it causes or, alternatively, one can mentally diminish the problem. This does not mean that the problem goes away, but it can appear less harassing and more controllable. That was precisely what the Church did with the *Tuadhe d'Anu*; they reduced the problem by diminishing the nominal significance of this ancient king tribe and, in so doing, portrayed them as minute little figures who were moved into the realm of mythology. Because of this, the miniaturizing of their figures caused a parallel diminution of their history, and their proud legacy was lost from the stage of Western education.

Onwards from the year 751, the Church sought all possible measures to diminish the status of any royal strain emanating from the original Ring Lords so that the fraudulent *Donation of Constantine* could be brought into play. Henceforth, only the subjugative Church could determine who was and was not a king, while the elves and fairies of the *Albi-gens* were manoeuvred from the forefront of history into a realm of apparent fantasy and legend. In this regard, it is significant that the Elves in Tolkien's *The Lord of the Rings* are quite unlike the cute little characters of many fairy tales; they are actually larger and more powerful than average mortals. They are also endowed with greater powers of wisdom; they ride magical horses and closely resemble the ancient king tribe of the *Tuadhe d'Anu*.

Settling in Ireland from about 800 BC, the noble *Tuadhe d'Anu* hailed from the Central European lands of Scythia,[14] the Black Sea kingdoms which stretched from the Carpathian mountains and Transylvanian Alps, across to the Russian River Don. They were strictly known as the Royal Scyths and their classification as fates or fairies occurred because they were masters of a transcendent intellect called the *Sidhé* (pronounced 'Shee'), which was known to the druids as the Web of the Wise. Druid (*druidhe*) was itself a Gaelic word for 'witch'—an English form of the Saxon verb *wicce* (feminine) or *wicca* (masculine), meaning to bend or yield, as do willow and wicker. The druids were also said to yield to the consummate *Sidhé*, a word which eventually became a colloquial term for fairy. Interestingly, the Scythian warlords of the *Sidhé* were also called the *Sumaire* and, in the language of old Ireland to where many of the caste migrated, the word *sumaire* was related to a coiled serpent.

In the Sanskrit holy language of India, the wisdom derived from attaining the highest state of transcendent consciousness was called *Siddhi*, while the powers said to manifest themselves as a result of that achievement have been dubbed *siddhis*—a term which, once again through Church intervention, has become associated with sinister magic and Witchcraft. Thus, it can be seen that *Sidhé* and *Siddhi* are one and the same, while the Scythian *Tuadhe d'Anu* were the original fairies of history. They were considered to be the world's most noble race, alongside the early dynastic pharaohs of Egypt, and it was by virtue of two particular Scythian-Egyptian royal marriages that the Scots Gaels of Ireland emerged. The first occurred in about 1360 BC, when Niul, Prince of Scythia, married the daughter of Pharaoh Smenkhkare (also called Akenkheres or Cinciris).[15] By virtue of this, the daughter, Merytaten-tasherit, became a Princess of Scythia (nominally styled Princess *Sco-ta* = Ruler of people). The second Princess Sco-ta (or Scota, as became more familiar) was the daughter of Pharaoh Nekau (Nechonibus, *c.*610-595 BC). She married Prince Galamh of Scythia (a descendant of the earlier Scota marriage) and their son, Eire Ahmon, was the ancestral forbear of the Scots Kings of Ireland, a branch of which eventually founded Scotland in the North of Britain.[16]

One of the strangest things about fairy lore is not that these historical Ring Lords became portrayed as miniature figures of the twilight realm, but that in the public imagination they have become identified with friendly little winged flower creatures—but this was not the way the Church portrayed them. In fact, quite the reverse was the case and, for the longest time, their orthodox image was strictly malevolent; they were actually said to be vampiric. In Scotland it was common practice to leave a bowl of water available in the house at night, since it was reckoned that fairies would suck the sleepers' blood if there was no water to quench their thirst. In Ireland the wasting disease consumption was said to be the work of the fairies who would steal away one's soul. To combat this, wreaths of oak and ivy were kept for protection and the afflicted were tied to stakes by holy wells, 'to end them or mend them'. Such was the power of Church propaganda that numerous Christian charms were used to ward off the fairies who, it was claimed, were ready to abduct or consume anyone straying from the clerical doctrines.

> Up the airy mountain, down the rushy glen,
> We daren't go a-hunting for fear of little men;
> Wee folk, good folk, trooping all together;
> Green jacket, red cap and white owl's feather.
> *William Allingham* (1824-89)

The Lost Bride

As the Church rose to power following the 8th-century implementation of the *Donation of Constantine,* so the 'underground stream', which supported the true *Albi-gens,* found strategic methods of preserving the old culture of the royal bloodline. In the course of this, and based upon a traditional principle of folklore and legend, the fairy tale concept was born—stories which were not unlike many of the parables inherent in the New Testament Gospels. They were likewise contrived 'for those with eyes to see and ears to hear', while others among the uninitiated would perceive them simply as fanciful children's entertainment.

A key focal message built into these fairy tales was an understanding of the importance of perpetuating the family line of the *Sangréal,* regardless of the power of the bishops and the Church's puppet kings. The whole scenario was presented, time after time, as if it were a struggling nightmare, wherein the female (the Elf-maiden who carried the essential mitochondrial DNA) was out of reach of the Grail prince, so that his torturous quest to find her was akin to the quest for the Holy Grail itself. Consequently, many of the tales which emanated from this base were stories of lost brides and usurped kingship, based upon the Church's subjugation of the Grail bloodline.[17] The fairy tale ideal was essentially geared to relate the truth of these persecutions. They were allegorical accounts of the predicament of the Messianic family—the Ring Lords of the *Sangréal,* whose fairies and elves (having been manoeuvred from the mortal plane of orthodoxy and *status quo*) were confined to a seemingly Otherworld existence.

They emerged as tales of valiant princes who were turned into frogs; of Swan knights who roamed the Wasteland and of Grail princesses locked in towers, or put to sleep for hundreds of years. In the course of their persecution, the Elf-maidens

The Tower (House of God) card from the Tarot's Major Arcana

were pricked with bodkins, fed with poisoned apples, subjected to spells or condemned to servitude, while their champions swam great lakes, battled through thickets and scaled mighty towers to secure and protect the matrilinear heritage of the *Albi-gens*. These romantic legends include such well-known stories as the Sleeping Beauty, Cinderella, Snow White and Rapunzel. In all cases, the underlying theme is the same, with the princess kept (through drugging, imprisonment or some form of restraint) out of reach of the prince, who has to find and release her in order to preserve the dynasty and perpetuate the line.

For the most part, the establishment of the Mother Church was symbolized by a malevolent stepmother, an evil witch or some other jealous female with an opposing vested interest. Always, the stories are reminiscent of the lost bride in the Bible's esoteric *Song of Solomon,* while their content also embodies the forlorn aspect of Mary Magdalene, the bride of Jesus whose royal heritage and maternal legacy were so thoroughly undermined by the Christian bishops.[18]

An interesting feature of many classic fairy tales is that they truly are very old stories. The tale of *Cinderella,* for example, is often attributed to the Brothers Grimm or Charles Perrault. However, these men were not writers of original tales as is commonly thought; they were compilers, amenders and interpreters of traditional tales. The story of *Cinderella* can actually be traced back to the Carolingian era, with its first known version appearing in the year 850. It appears to have been modelled upon a Chinese tale about foot-binding and the noble aspect of women with tiny feet. Perrault published his well-known French edition in 1697, while Jacob and Wilhelm Grimm produced their German version in 1812. It was during the period of France's Carolingian dynasty (the dynasty of Emperor Charlemagne), which began in 751, that the seeds of most of these popular stories were planted, and it is because of the inherent truths which lie behind the stories that we find them so naturally appealing. Some academics argue that fairy tales survive and thrive because they are often based upon a rags-to-riches doctrine, but this is not the case. They survive because deep within the Western psyche is an inherent, inbred awareness that the Grail (symbolised by the Lost Bride) has to be found if the Wasteland is to return to fertility.

At the same time, there is often an apparent contrary aspect to the stories and, despite our obvious support for the champion in his endeavour, we can also see a reason for the predicament of the princess—especially when there is a tower involved, as is the case with Rapunzel. The tower (sometimes in the form of a chessboard castle or rook) was a long-standing symbol of the del

Acqs female line, being expressly connected with Mary Magdalene in *la Légende de Sainte Marie Madeleine* by Jacobus de Voragine, 13th-century Archbishop of Genoa.[19] The very name Magdalene (or Magdala) stems from the Hebrew noun *migdal*, meaning 'tower', and was used to denote a high titular station of guardianship, as portrayed by the *Magdal-eder* (Watchtower of the flock) in the Old Testament book of Micah 4:8.[20] It is also represented in the Tower (or House of God) card of the Tarot's *Major Arcana*, which is traditionally referred to as a Magdalene card. With its tower struck by lightning, or otherwise mysteriously assaulted, this card symbolized the plight of the esoteric Grail Church in the face of the merciless Roman establishment, and was introduced in France and Northern Italy by the 'underground stream' of Grail adherents following Pope Gregory IX's Catholic Inquisition of 1231.

The *Rapunzel* story relates that, in order to function as an effective seer, Rapunzel was confined to a tower by an enchantress as a measure of protection against the world at large—in essence to preserve her maidenly virtue and the supernatural power related to that virtue. By maintaining her virginity, Rapunzel was symbolically endowed with the overlordship of the *Magdal-eder* and was kept apart from the mundane environment. Hence, as in all similar stories, although the lost bride has been confined (whether by fair means or foul), she always emerges in a fit mental and physical state for the Grail prince. The concept of a tower being representative of female virtue is very well defined in the early Renaissance painting, *The Allegory of Chastity*, by the 15th-century Flemish artist Hans Memling.

Another important facet of the desired virginal portrayal, as evident in the tale of *Rapunzel*, is the allegorical symbolism of long hair. Rapunzel's golden locks are presented as being plaited into a lengthy braid which the prince used to scale the tower. Before eventually being freed, however, Rapunzel's hair was cut off by the enchantress, thereby implying the release of the maiden's chastity to the wilderness. The importance of very long hair was that it afforded an appropriate veil of modesty even when in a naked state. Although perhaps physically or metaphorically divested of clothes (as symbolised by the willing or compulsory subordination to another), the Elf-maiden with tresses was never vulnerable; her dignity was always preserved and neither her body nor soul was ever bared until the appropriate time.

It is for this reason that Mary Magdalene was so often depicted with very long hair that enveloped her form as in the Renaissance carvings of Donatello and Riemenschneider, or in the Sforza *Book of Hours* portrayal of Mary arriving in Provence. The Church's official Magdalene image was that of a wanton harlot, but enlightened artists were often quick to establish the reality of her modest bridal estate. They were equally willing, on occasions, to relate the fact of her flight and pregnancy,[21] with the most telling of all paintings in this regard being Caravaggio's stunning *Mary Magdalene* portrait at the Galleria Doria-Pamphili in Rome. In this seated portrayal from 1595, the contemplative Magdalene, with her customary long reddish hair, wears the white bodice of purity and the green dress of fertility. While making her gravidity very apparent in an abdominal nursing pose, the scene is completed by a shell-designed chalice upon the front of her skirt. No painting could be more forthright in its Grail representation of the expectant Messianic queen.

4

The Ring Cycle

Ring of the Dwarf Lord

The oldest complete version of the Ring Cycle comes from the Norse mythology of the *Volsunga Saga*. This was described by the English poet and designer William Morris (1834-96) as "The great story of the North which should be to all our race what the tale of Troy was to the Greeks".[1] Compiled from more than forty separate legends, the 13th-century Icelandic tale relates to the god Odin, to the kingdom of the Nine Worlds and to a dark forest called Mirkwood—a name later repeated by Tolkien in *The Lord of the Rings*. It also tells of how Prince Sigmund of the Volsung dynasty is the only warrior able to pull the great sword of Odin from a tree in which the god had driven it to its hilt—as replicated in the Arthurian story of the sword and the stone. We also learn of the Water-dwarf Andarvi, whose magical One Ring of red-gold could weave great wealth and power for its master—precisely as depicted in all related Ring legends.[2]

The hero of the *Volsunga* action is Sigmund's son Sigurd, who inherits the magical sword of Odin and defeats the dragon who (reminiscent of Tolkien's dragon, Smaug, in his tale of *The Hobbit*) guards the golden hoard of the Dwarf Lord. Having slain the dragon, Prince Sigurd gains the Ring of Andarvi and sets out on his travels, but the Ring carries with it a dreadful curse. At length, in the land of the Franks, he finds a sleeping beauty in a mysterious tower. On awakening her, he discovers that she is Brynhild, a Valkyrie battle-maiden of Odin who once carried the souls of heroes to the land of Valhalla. She, in true fairy-tale fashion, had been pricked by a sleep-thorn and shut away in the turret, surrounded by a ring of fire.

The two become lovers and Sigurd places the Ring on Brynhild's finger, whereupon she returns to sleep, bound to him forever, while Sigurd rides to the Rhineland of the Nibelung dynasty. There, he is given an enchanted drink to rob his memory of Brynhild so that he can marry the Princess Gudrun, but the magic of the Ring is too strong and he is eventually drawn back to the Valkyrie. On hearing of the royal marriage, but knowing nothing of the potion, Brynhild presumes that Sigurd has deceived her and swears revenge, in consequence of which Sigurd is murdered—but on learning the truth, Brynhild then kills herself in order to sleep with her hero for ever. The Ring of Andarvi is subsequently inherited by Princess Gudrun but, in the final event, she is compelled to return it to the realm of the Water-dwarf. And so, with the Ring on her finger, she fills her apron with stones and leaps from a cliff into the sea.

Contemporary with the *Volsunga Saga* was a very similar tale which appeared in and around Burgundy in the 1200s: a Middle High German epic called *The Nibelungenlied*. In this account, which follows a similar path, the hero is called Siegfried and the tale is given a knightly gloss of the Gothic era, while unfortunately losing some of the pagan enchantment of the Northern legend.

A Golden Age

Six-hundred years later, and some while before Tolkien, came William Morris and the German composer Richard Wagner, working separately but similarly pulling the essence of the two traditions together—one for an epic poem and the other for a grand opera. The main difference between the emergent works is that, while Morris sat more squarely with the Northern legend of Sigurd and Brynhild, Wagner was more inclined to the Western

European version, calling his principal characters Siegfried and Brunhilde. The main themes are actually very much the same and both were inspirational to J. R. R. Tolkien. Indeed, in 1914, when he won the Skeat Prize for English from Exeter College, Oxford, at the age of twenty-two, he used five pounds of the proceeds to purchase copies of William Morris's translated *Volsunga Saga* and its related work *The House of the Wolfings*[3] (*see* Appendix III).

William Morris was associated with the renowned Pre-Raphaelite Brotherhood of painters, whose emergent movement in the Golden Age of Victorian art produced so many wonderful Grail-related images. The *Briar Rose* series by Sir Edward Coley Burne-Jones[4] is especially significant in this regard, as is Dante Gabriel Rossetti's *Attainment of the Sangréal*, which features Morris's immortalized wife Jane. During this same era, the English poet Alfred, Lord Tennyson, produced his series of Arthurian legends, entitled *Idylls of the King*, and it would appear that against the general political toils and social hardships of the time there was a widespread movement in Western European culture that was keen to revive the time-honoured legacy of the *Albi-gens*.

No musical composer has done so much to preserve the legacy of Ring lore as Richard Wagner (1813-83) whose renowned opera, *Der Ring des Nibelungen* (*The Ring of the Nibelung*), was largely drawn from the Burgundian folklore of *The Nibelungenlied* and, to some extent, from the *Volsunga Saga*. The opera had its first complete performance in 1876 at Wagner's newly founded and specially designed festival theatre of Bayreuth in Bavaria. Prior to this, Wagner's grand work concerning the Swan Knight *Lohengrin* (composed while he was conductor of the Dresden Opera House) had been produced at Weimar in 1850 by his colleague and fellow composer Franz Liszt. This was followed by the Arthurian tale of *Tristan und Isolde* (Sir Thomas Malory's *Tristram and Isoud*), first performed at Munich in 1865 while, after *The Ring* and *Die Meistersinger von Nürnberg*, Wagner's last masterwork, the Grail opera *Parsifal*, was produced at Bayreuth in 1882.

It is of particular relevance that, irrespective of noted earlier works such as *The Flying Dutchman* and *Tannhäuser*, Wagner found the Grail and Ring quests so compulsive once embarked upon. Moreover, it is doubtless not coincidental that, in that same year of 1876 when *The Ring* was launched, William Morris published his poetic translation of the epic Ring Cycle, *Sigurd the Volsung*.[5] Both Wagner's opera and Morris's poem were debated at length by the Irish dramatist and critic George Bernard Shaw (1856-1950),[6] who perceived them not only as relics of traditional lore, but as being wholly representative of the social conflicts of the prevailing era. Prior to his death, Richard Wagner had commenced writing an article entitled *The Feminine Element in Mankind* and, interestingly, more than a hundred years afterwards, Richard's great-great-grandson, the composer Sir Adrian Wagner, Knight of the Swan, has also written his own essay under that very same title,[7] whilst sharing the same continued enthusiasm for the eternal Quest.

In Wagner's *Der Ring des Nibelungen*, the warrior Siegfried obtains the golden Ring of the Rhinemaidens, which had been stolen from them by Alberic the Nibelung, Dwarf Lord of the Underworld. He had lost it to the sky-god Wotan (the Anglo-Saxon equivalent of Odin), following which Siegfried won it by killing a dragon. The Ring (forged from the enchanted flat-stone of the Rhinegold) had the power to afford its master the lordship of all the world, but only at the cost of forsaking love and selling his soul to the Ring's awesome power.

At the top of a mountain, surrounded by a ring of fire, Siegfried discovers the sleeping Brunhilde and awakens her with a kiss (a familiar scene in the *Sleeping Beauty* story of Briar Rose). Brunhilde, it transpires, is the daughter of Wotan—a Valkyrie goddess turned mortal for angering her father. Having been released by her earthly hero, Brunhilde dutifully swears her love and allegiance to Siegfried, who gives her the golden Ring as his pledge before continuing his adventures into the Rhineland. At the Court of the Gibichungs he is given a potion which makes him forget Brunhilde and fall in love with Princess Gutrune, but when the Valkyrie discovers this she pursues a course of vengeance and masterminds Siegfried's death. Afterwards, however, she realises her error and throws herself upon Siegfried's funeral pyre to be with him in eternity. The magical Ring that Siegfried gave to Brunhilde is retrieved from the ashes by the Rhinemaiden guardians of the gold and, by virtue of this along with Brunhilde's self-sacrifice, a hitherto curse placed upon the Ring by Alberic the Nibelung is lifted.

Upon the final cleansing of the Ring by the Rhinemaidens, Wotan perishes, together with his dream kingdom of Valhalla—and with the Ring now back in its rightful hands, the world is redeemed and the Cycle is complete. And so, once again the traditional Ring lore is apparent—just as in Tolkien's *The Lord of the Rings*—for the Ring is finally seen to destroy whoever holds it without the right of affinity.

The Serpent's Ring

Over the years, many people have likened Tolkien's wizard, Gandalf, to Merlin of the Arthurian tales. At the same time, Tolkien's Aragorn has been likened to King Arthur but, as Tolkien himself pointed out (in a letter written in 1967),[8] there was really a closer similarity between Aragorn and the historical Charlemagne.

The challenge which faced Charlemagne in the 9th century (having been charged by the Pope to establish a viable Empire from various disunited kingdoms) was not unlike that which confronted Aragorn, who reunited the divided kingdoms of Middle-earth in *The Lord of the Rings*. But there was a marked difference in practice, for Aragorn was far more like Arthur in having an advisory wizard, whereas Charlemagne did not because the Church would not consent to royal counsellors outside its own appointees. Aragorn's was, therefore, more of a Gaelic-style environment, with his enemy being the evil Sauron of Mordor. Charlemagne, on the other hand, was supposedly a champion of the Roman Church whose adversaries were the supporters of the unlawfully ousted Merovingian establishment—an establishment to which Aragorn would personally have been well suited.

The difficulty one has in understanding Charlemagne is that, for all the apparent Carolingian attachment to the Vatican, he does not seem to have been wholly committed to the Roman ideal and clearly inherited a strong contrary legacy from his mother, who was a daughter of the Merovingian Princess Blanche Fleur. Undeterred by the *Donation of Constantine,* which had enabled his father, King Pepin, to usurp the Merovingian throne, Charlemagne retained advocates of both the Grail Church and the Roman Church at his Court.[9] He was not even too keen on the idea of becoming Holy Roman Emperor but, on Christmas Day in the year 800, while in the Roman Basilica of St. Peter's in the company of several bishops, Pope Leo III crept up behind him and placed the Imperial crown on his head without warning![10]

From that moment, Charlemagne forsook his previous reserve and took up his appointed cause with vigour, to become the most forceful destroyer of the cult of Odin (Wotan) to which the Ring lore of the period was essentially linked. But, for all that, and despite the Church's hatred of the Ring tradition, Charlemagne remained the willing subject of his own mythology. Just as Tolkien's Aragorn carried the magical sword *Andúril,* forged by the smith Telchar, so Charlemagne carried *Joyeuse,* a magical sword said to have been forged by the smith Wayland. In *The Lord of the Rings,* Aragorn uses the enchanted herb *athelas* to cure the Black Breath, while in the Carolingian stories, Charlemagne used the herb *sowthistle* to cure the Black Death. In such respects, it is understandable that Tolkien likened Aragorn to Charlemagne since it is apparent that the Emperor was a partial model for Tolkien's fictional hero. Even Aragorn's betrothal to the Elf Princess Arwen is reminiscent of Charlemagne's betrothal to the Elf Princess Frastrada[11]—a betrothal which supported its very own legend: the tale of *The Serpent's Ring.*

The tale relates that, on the royal wedding day of Charlemagne and Frastrada, there appeared among the guests at Court a great serpent with an enchanted golden ring in its mouth. The serpent dropped the ring into the Emperor's wine goblet, whereupon Charlemagne, recognizing what he thought to be a good omen, placed the ring on Frastrada's finger. But, from that moment, the Emperor's love for his bride increased to the point of obsession and he knew he could never be parted from her, being bound for all time to whoever held the ring.

Some years later, following Frastrada's death, the ring's power did not abate and Charlemagne refused to have her buried. He had her laid upon a table, where he kept his vigil day and night, not leaving Frastrada's side for many weeks while the Empire was falling to ruin. Then, one night while the Emperor slept, a bishop removed the ring from the bridal finger and, when Charlemagne awoke with his obsession released, he sanctioned the burial of the Queen. Bishop Turpin then had the ring, and Charlemagne was thereby bound in love and duty to him. On recognizing this unfortunate state of affairs, the bishop wondered how he could release the spell, for if he were to part with the ring it would fall into the hands of another to whom the Emperor would become enslaved. So he threw it into a forest pool—at which point the Emperor's infatuation for him subsided, but the ring's power called out to Charlemagne, compelling him to the forest glade, where he was promptly filled with a yearning desire for the crystal pool. And so he built a great palace at the water's edge, and remained there for the rest of his life.

This, according to the story, is how Aix la Chapelle became the capital of Charlemagne's realm, but there was a particular significance to the name Aix because, as given in the *Legenda Aurea* (Golden Legend) of Jacobus de Voragine,[12] the similarly named Aix en Provence was the original European centre of Mary Magdalene. Also, as detailed in the medieval *Chronica Majora* of Matthew Paris, Aix en Provence was where the Magdalene died in AD 63. Originally the old Roman town of Acquae Sextiae,[13] it was the hot springs at Aix (Acqs) which had given rise to its name—*Acqs* being a medieval derivative of the Latin word *aquae* (waters). In the Languedoc tradition, Mary Magdalene is remembered as *la Dompna del Aquae*: the Mistress of the Waters, and the Grail dynasty was variantly styled the House del Acqs.

Sirens and Water Nymphs

Traditionally, the *Albi-gens* has been identified with water—a concept that can be traced back some five millennia to Tiâmat the Dragon Queen. Her Akkadian name actually means 'Salt waters' and had its equivalent in the Hebrew *tehôm* (plural, *tehômot*), as used in Old Testament references to 'the deep' (e.g. Genesis 1:2).[14] Psalm 74 (verses 13-14) explains that God 'didst divide the sea ... and ... breakest the heads of the dragons in the waters'. In this account, the dragon of the *tehôm* is called the Leviathan (a Canaanite term), as it is also named in the book of Job (41:1). Elsewhere in the Old Testament, the formidable sea-dragon is called Rahab, as in Psalm 89 (verses 9-10): 'Thou rulest the raging of the sea...Thou hast broken Rahab into pieces'. Also, in the book of Isaiah (51:9): 'Awake ... O arm of the Lord... Art thou not it that hath cut Rahab and wounded the dragon'.

It was a common theme in the writings of the Mesopotamians, Canaanites and Hebrews that the foremost accomplishment of their respective deities was the calming of the wild ocean deep. Even in the *Origin of the World* document of the Alexandrian Gnostics,[15] the great 'first father', Yaldaboath, was brought forth from the depths by the Holy Spirit, who was called Sophia (from the Greek *sophia*: wisdom). She was said (just as related in Genesis 1:2) to have 'moved upon the face of the waters' but, in this regard, the Semitic word *ruah*, which was translated in Genesis to 'spirit', actually meant 'wind'.[16] Hence, Sophia was a wind-spirit which, in Akkadian-Assyrian, was called *Lilutu*—whence derived the names of Lilith, Luluwa and others associated with the lily (or lotus flower) wisdom culture of the Star Fire maidens.

The name 'Mary', which is associated with the Messianic line (as in the Blessed Mary, Mary Magdalen, etc.), was itself linked to the sea (Latin: *mare;* French: *mer*) and with water in general. It is an English form, based upon a Greek variant of the Hebrew *Miriam* along with the Egyptian *Mery,* meaning 'beloved' (as in Merytaten: Beloved of Aten). For this reason, in some conventual orders, the nuns still use the titular style of Mary in front of their baptismal given names: Sister Mary Louise, Sister Mary Theresa and the like. In respect of the water symbolism, Mary Magdalene's own dignity as *la Dompna del Aquae* or *Marie de la Mer* is no better preserved than in the painting *Marie of the Sea* by Sir Peter Robson, whose inspired allegorical artwork continues to uphold the emblematic Grail tradition of the Renaissance era.[17]

Alongside the Mary Magdalene movement in 1st-century Provence was that of her colleague Mary Jacob. She was the New Testament wife of Cleophas (John 19:25) who had accompanied the Magdalene to Gaul in AD 44,[18] as detailed in *The Acts of Magdalene* and the ancient MS *History of England* in the Vatican Archives. St. Mary Jacob was a Nazarene priestess, who became better known in Europe as Mary the Gypsy or Mary the Egyptian. In England her cult was widespread in medieval times and her Oath of Wedlock was referred to as the *Merrie.* Probably the verb 'to marry' derives from this, as does the tag applied to 'Merrie Englande'. Often depicted with a fish-tail, Mary the Gypsy was an original *Merri-maid* (mermaid),[19] and she was given the attributive name Marina in the Middle Ages. She is portrayed as such alongside Mary Magdalene in a window at the Church of St Marie in Paris, and her memory is preserved in Maid Marian and the Merrie Men of the Robin Hood legends.

In the early days of Christianity, Emperor Constantine banned the veneration of Mary the Gypsy,[20] but her cult persisted in France, Spain and England, where she was identified with the goddess Aphrodite, who was said to have 'risen from the sea foam'.[21] Mary's most significant emblem was the scallop-shell, depicted so effectively, along with her Aphrodite status, in the famous *Birth of Venus* paintings by Sandro Botticelli and Adolphe

Bouguereau. Mary the Gypsy—sacred harlot and love cultess—was ritually portrayed by the Anglo-Saxons as the May Queen, while in Cornwall they called her Merrow, and her dancers (Merrow's Men) still perform their rites under the corrupted name of 'Morris Men' in English rural festivities.

Just as in the story of Charlemagne and *The Serpent's Ring*, pools, lakes, springs, wells and fountains abound in fairy tale and Grail romance—as do sea sirens, water nymphs and mermaids. In the mythology of ancient Greece, the nymphs were even classified by habitat: Potimids inhabited the rivers and streams, Niads the brooks, Crenae and Pegae the springs, and Limnads were the nymphs of still waters.[22] One of the best known stories from this genre is that of Hylas, a member of Jason's *Argo* expedition in search of the Golden Fleece, who went ashore to find fresh water. On discovering a suitable fountain spring, Hylas met with the water nymphs, who were so charmed by his beauty that they carried him to the depths of their watery abode. In the way that the Christianized version of the story is told, one might imagine that this was bad news for Hylas, since it is implied that he met his untimely death by virtue of pursuing the 'heresy' of the Golden Fleece. In reality, it is beyond any imagining that Apollonius of Alexandria (when writing his Homeric-style *Argonaut* epic in about 250 BC) might have guessed and purposely flouted the rules of a Church that was not to emerge for another 600 years! Nevertheless, along with much else that was colourful and romantic, sirens, water nymphs and mermaids were proclaimed heretical in the Church's suppression of pagan doctrines since they were reckoned to be emblematic of the hideous 'sin' of the *femme fatale*.

In practice, the tale of Hylas has an abiding Grail significance, which was astutely portrayed by the Pre-Raphaelite artist John William Waterhouse in his 1896 painting of *Hylas and the Water Nymphs*. The Waterhouse nymphs, bathing amid the water-lilies, wear the sacred *Nymphaea Lotus* flowers in their hair—whose significance we shall recognize later when considering the Lady of the Lake rituals of the Lily and the Rose—while Hylas is cleverly portrayed wearing the red belt of the Cathars of Languedoc. This latter item, called the 'red thread', was a relic of old Jewish lore and was said to represent the sins for which the people atoned. It relates to the Old Testament book of Isaiah 1:18 which states, 'Though your sins be as scarlet, they shall be as white as snow; though they be red like crimson, they shall be as wool'.[23] To the more spiritual gnostic groups, the 'red thread' was a symbol of the very heresy which they upheld—the heresy of the *Albi-gens*: the quests for the Golden Fleece and the Holy Grail which were perceived as loathsome by the orthodox believers.

In gnostic terms, entry into the depths of a sacred pool (as was the case with Hylas) did not constitute the death of the person, simply the death of ego and desire. It was regarded as an entry through the *daleth*—the doorway of Light—beyond the portal of the twilight world into the land of Elphame, where all that mattered was revealed.

From the earliest of times in Palestine, Phoenicia and Syria, mermaids were associated with the moon and the sea. The Syrian moon goddess Atargatis was often depicted as a mermaid for this very reason. Sacred pools also had lunar significance, just as the original 'Moon' card of the Tarot's *Major Arcana* included a pool of still water. In this regard, there is also an astronomical significance to the tale of Hylas since his name (from *Helios*) means Sun, and the sun's submission to the moon is emblematic of a total eclipse, where those on the earthly side are left in darkness, but those beyond the moon's shadow can see the Light.

The name Mary, quite apart from its ancient Egyptian origin, has another root in the old Indo-European *Mari*, with the *mar* element relating to a mere or a pool. The addition of *an* (as in Marian) denotes a fire-alchemy status, as we saw with the Shining Ones of the *An-anan-na-ge*—the 'Fiery great sons of heaven'. Thus, Marian, in its original form, meant 'Pool of fire'—the equivalent of the Dew-cup of the Star Fire: the *Rosi-crucis* which, in the Old Testament's highly esoteric *Song of Solomon* (4:15), is called the 'well of living waters'.

The definition 'siren' comes from a Greek root meaning 'to bind or attach'[24] and, in this regard, sirens were seductive enchantresses who, with their lyres and plaintive song, were said to lure sailors into oblivion. Though perhaps not unlike the freshwater nymphs, they were rather more akin to the Irish fairy called the *Leanhaun Sidhé* (Faerie Mistress), whose dangerous beauty caused mortal men to be bound to her charms. If they refused, she became their slave, but if they succumbed to her beguilement, they became hers.

Unlike the somewhat malevolent sirens, the mermaid tradition is that of a love goddess who rises from the sea like Venus or Aphrodite. Her popular image is that of a beautiful muse with long hair and a fish-tail, often vainly portrayed with a comb and mirror, together with scallops and periwinkles as her aphrodisiacs. Perhaps the best known mermaid depiction in the world today is *Den lille Havfrue*—the monument to the *Little Mermaid* of Hans Christian Andersen's nursery tale—which graces Copenhagen Harbour in Denmark. However, the most important historical character dubbed with mermaid significance is the Lilithian Princess Mélusine, the Lady of the Fountain, with whom we shall meet in due course.

5

Dawn of the Dragon Queens

The Rule of Nine

In ancient Egypt it was common practice for the pharaohs to marry their sisters in order to progress their kingship through the female line.[1] These wives were often the pharaohs' half-sisters, born of their mothers by different fathers, for it was the mitochondrial DNA of the matrilinear succession that was important to the dynasties. (Although mitochondria is inherited from mothers by both sons and daughters, it is only passed on by the daughters, since this DNA resides within the female egg cells.)[2] It can be seen from plotted genealogical charts of the era that, although Egypt had many successive kingly dynasties, these houses were only renamed and renumbered when a pharaoh died without a male heir. The important thing was that his queen had a female heiress, and it was upon that daughter's marriage into another male line that a new dynasty began.

It can also be seen from the charts that many pharaohs had a number of strategically chosen wives and often married into various strains of the original royal blood of Mesopotamia from which the early pharaonic dynasties were themselves descended. In such cases, the crown princes would marry the daughters of their fathers' second or junior queens, thereby perpetuating an apparent patrilinear descent, but in fact heightening the female blood of their line in favour of successive generations.

The story of matrilinear royal descent traces back thousands of years to the very dawn of recorded time when the great Anunnaki Lord of the Sky was Anu. He is documented on clay tablets and cylinder seals from the 3rd millennium BC, discovered in the Sumerian delta eden[3] of the Persian Gulf. His queenly consorts were his sisters: Antu, Lady of the Sky, and Ki, the Earth Mother. Anu had two sons: Enlil (whose mother was Ki) and Enki (whose mother was Antu). Enki had two wives, one of whom was his half-sister Nîn-khursag, the Lady of Life. By the same token, Enlil similarly had two wives, including Nîn-khursag who was, therefore, consort to each of her brothers. This deiform family had descended from the great Mother Goddess Tiâmat—described in the *Enûma elish* (the original Creation account which preceded the writing of the Old Testament's book of Genesis by more than 2000 years) as 'She who bore them all'.[4]

Tiâmat appears to have no particular place in recorded time, but she was wholly associated with the eternal ocean deep. She was likened to a mighty sea-serpent, who rode upon the waters like the Holy Spirit at the opening of the book of Genesis and, as such, she was venerated as the Dragon Queen.[5] The Holy Spirit, by whatever name in whatever culture, was always associated with feminine wisdom (*sophia*), and on that account, wisdom and the serpent became forever synonymous.

The rule of kingly descent through the senior female line appears to have been established from the outset when a dispute over entitlement arose between the brothers Enki and Enlil. The Anunnaki overlords were said to have governed by way of a Grand Assembly of nine councillors who sat at Nippur. The nine consisted of eight members (seven males and a female), who held the Rings of divine justice, along with their president, Anu, who held the One Ring to bind them all. Not only does this conform with the nine kingdoms of the *Volsunga Saga*, which cites Odin (Wotan) as the ultimate presidential Ring Lord, but it is also commensurate with the seven archangels of Hebraic record along with their two supervisors, the Lord of the Spirits and the Most High (equivalent to Anu).[6] As the original god-kings of Mesopotamia, this Assembly was said to have introduced kingly practice which, according to the *Sumerian King List* (dating from before 2000 BC)[7] was 'lowered from heaven'.

In the fields of Gematria and scientific Numerology, the number '9' (as associated with the nine Rings) is considered especially magical since it has many fascinating calculable properties and can be used to create a variety of very curious patterns.[8] To the ancient Greeks, nine was the *Ennead*: the great outer heaven of the universe, and they introduced the nine Muses of which Terpsichore, Muse of the Sacred Dance, is the ninth and most potent. In Norse mythology, Odin hangs in the 'world tree' for nine days and nine nights, learning nine songs. In William Shakespeare's *Macbeth* the three witches use the Charm of Nine, and the 'ninefold strength' was a healing ritual in Western Europe from Germany to Scotland. Nine is the number of compassion, divine will, invocation, dragons and the oceans, while also being the symbolic number of Merlin.

An especially interesting feature of 9 is that the digits in its multiples always add up to itself— e.g. 9 x 2 = 18 (1 + 8 = 9); 9 x 3 = 27 (2 + 7 = 9). Hence, nine is the eternal number—the optimum number of the 360 degree Ring (3 + 6 + 0 = 9) and the supreme superlative. As recently stated in a report entitled *The 9 in Sacred Geometry*, by the physicist Daniel Sewell Ward, "Of all the single digit numbers, nine (9) may be the most profound. Composed of three trinities (3 x 3), nine represents the principles of the sacred Triad taken to their utmost expression".

Goddess of the Fire-stone

The Anunnaki fraternal dispute arose when Anu resigned his presidency of the Grand Assembly, at which point his elder son Enlil became the apparent candidate. His brother Enki challenged this on the basis that, although he was younger than Enlil, he was the senior son and royal successor because his mother, Antu, was Anu's senior sister, whereas Enlil's mother, Ki, was Antu's junior. Therefore, claimed Enki, "I am the great brother of the gods. I am he who has been born as the first son of the divine Anu". As such, it was his mother Antu who held the primary office of queenship, and among her variously recorded titles, the later Kassite Kings of Mesopotamia (from around 1750 BC) called her the Lady of the Fire-stone, granting her the name Barat-Anna. This derived from the Kassite royal stem *BRT* and from the Akkadian *An-na* (meaning Fire-stone).[9] Barat-Anna (Barati to the Phoenicians) was the Great Mother of the Air and Sea, the Goddess of Light and Fire who was later identified with Diana of Ephesus (Diana of the Nine Fires). Her symbol was the *Rosi-crucis* (the Cup of the waters)—a cross within a circle which, as we have seen, was the original emblem of the Grail bloodline from the 4th millennium BC.

Barat-Anna and the Rosi-crucis on an Anatolian coin of the 3rd century AD From Iconium (modern Konya in Turkey)

On early Phoenician coins, it is significant that Barat-Anna is portrayed sitting upon the water with the *Rosi-crucis* emblem beneath her chair. This very same image was transported by the Kassites into the Gaelic realms of Europe and, eventually, found its way onto the coins of Britain, where Barat-Anna was redefined as Britannia and given a torch to signify her fire-alchemy status. From the 17th century, when Frances *la belle* Stuart (the daughter of Lord Blantyre) modelled for the updated Britannia image used on British pennies until modern times, the *Rosi-crucis* emblem was enlarged and adapted to become a Union Jack shield, but it remained a rounded device. Also, the torch of fire was replaced by a separate lighthouse and Britannia was given a trident but, in all other respects, this supposed unique symbol of Britain's tribal goddess is not British at all; it is ancient Phoenician.[10]

In order to placate the Anunnaki brothers, it was determined that Enki should govern the Waters, while Enlil governed the Air, and they would jointly govern the Earth. After a couple of generations, the matrilinear heritage fell to Enlil's granddaughter, Erish-kigal of the Netherworld, and subsequently to her daughter, the legendary Lilith who, while representing the unyielding ethic of female opportunity, has posed a problem for the male-dominated Judaeo-Christian Churches to this very day. Indeed, it was from Lilith, who became another young consort of Enki (known to the Hebrews as Samael—from *Sama-El*: Lord of Sama in northern Mesopotamia), that the more direct line of royal succession evolved, for she was the mother of Luluwa, the sister of Kalîmath (Kali) and wife of the biblical Cain, who was so maligned by the writers of the Hebrew scriptures. This was done in their endeavour to support a junior parallel descent from Cain's brother Seth in order to promote a patrilinear succession in place of the matrilinear reality (*see* Chart: 'Anunnaki and the Dragon Queens').

The Serpent Lady

Back in 1918, translations were made at the University of Philadelphia Museum of a series of related tablets and cylinder seals from Nippur in the 3rd millennium BC. They have become known overall as the *Kur-sag Epic* (*Epic of the Enclosure*).[11] The account relates: 'At Kur-sag, where heaven and earth met, the heavenly assembly, the great sons of Anu, descended—the many wise ones'. In the context of these tablets, Nîn-khursag is specifically referred to as the Serpent Lady, thereby denoting her position as the prevailing Grail Queen. Similarly, the male Anunnaki are also referred to in the *Kur-sag Epic* as princes and 'splendid serpents'.

Some extant statuettes from the ancient Ubaid culture of Southern Mesopotamia (the culture which preceded the Sumerians) portray their gods and goddesses with distinctly serpentine facial characteristics.[12] But this does not mean they were shapeshifting reptilian creatures, who had come from another planet to take over the world as some would have us believe. It is not even certain that these supposed deiform figures represent the Anunnaki at all, for their later Sumerian portrayals were quite different, with more generally human features.[13] The Ubaid depictions were probably no different in concept to the symbolic beaked and bull-faced figurines of the Vinca culture of the Balkans from the same era,[14] or to the variously masked falcon, jackal and fish-headed renderings of ancient Egypt.

Just as all creatures were dubbed with particular significance, the serpent represented the self-energizing, creative force of the supreme spirit.[15] It is comparable with the Indian concept of the *Kundalini*—a divine cosmic energy, symbolised by a coiled serpent which lies dormant at the base of one's spinal column. When energized, the serpent is said to rise through the body's chakras (Yogic centres of spiritual power) to ultimately join in union with the supreme universal soul. It is because physical and spiritual healing were recognized as emanating from an energized force that serpents were associated with medicine from the earliest times. The book of Enoch, which was excluded from the Old Testament canon, refers to a Watcher (angel) called Kashdejan, who explained to men the dangers of sickness and disease, citing that he was the assistant of a serpent named Taba'et.[16] This is of particular significance since the physician to the *Tuadhe d'Anu* fairy kings in Ireland was said to be Diyan Cecht (Dejan Kash), a reversal of Kashdejan.[17]

The Kundalini representation is apparent in the familiar medical emblem of the two coiled serpents, spiralling around the winged caduceus of the messenger-god Mercury. In this instance, the central staff and serpents represent the spinal cord and the sensory nervous system, while the two uppermost wings signify the brain's lateral ventricular structures. Between these wings, above the spinal column, is shown the small central node of the pineal gland.[18] The combination of the central pineal and its lateral wings is traditionally referred to as the Swan, being emblematic of the fully enlightened being. This is the utmost realm of Grail consciousness achieved by the medieval Knights of the Swan, epitomized by such chivalric figures as Perceval and Lohengrin.[19]

Overall, the Anunnaki-related Sumerian sojourn, with its preceding Ubaid culture, appears to have lasted about 3500 years, from *c*.5500 BC to a little after 2000 BC when the plains of Eden were invaded by foreigners from the north, west and east. It was at this time, in around 1960 BC, that the biblical family of Abraham was said to have left the Sumerian capital, Ur of the Chaldees, to travel northwards to Haran in the kingdom of Mari. The Sumerian records from that same year state, 'The gods have abandoned us like migrating birds'.[20] However, the Anunnaki heritage of the Ring Lords prevailed, sweeping across Europe into other lands, having already been apparent in Egypt from about 2800 BC.

In the succession from the hereditary Queens, Erish-kigal, Lilith, Luluwa and her daughter Awan (the wife of Enoch) arose King A-kalem of Ur (the biblical Lamech). His daughter Lilith-Naamâh was mother-in-law to her own brother, the famed metallurgist Tubal-cain (Genesis 4:22), who is still remembered in modern Freemasonry. In descent from him and Queen Nîn-banda came Nimrod the mighty hunter (Genesis 10:8-12), whose grandson Boethos founded the 2nd pharaonic dynasty of Egypt. At length, the 3rd, 4th, 5th and subsequent dynasties followed (each time by virtue of a daughter of the line marrying into another family) and this continued until *c*.1335 BC when, following the death of young Tutankhamun and a short period of reign by a couple of his relatives, the 18th dynasty expired. With the installation of Ramesses I (who was not of the immediate royal blood,[21] neither married into the original line), the mitochondrial succession moved from Egypt into the Royal House of Scythia, where the Black Sea princes were known as the Lords of Anu.

The diversionary link occurred when Niul, Lord of Capacyront (an Egyptian region by the Red Sea), married the daughter of Pharaoh Smenkhkare (Tutankhamun's uncle and predecessor) in about 1361 BC.[22] This daughter became known as Princess Scota (*Sco-ta)*, and her son by Prince Niul was Gadheal Glas, the ancestor of the Scots Gaels of Ireland.

A Violent Outrage

Alongside the 751 *Donation of Constantine,* which ensured the suppression of the Grail and Ring traditions, was another equally hideous Church outrage, perpetuated through violence some 360 years earlier. But, on this occasion, it was not only dynastic custom that was assaulted, it was the very essence of recorded enlightenment—the great archive of history, science and philosophy held within the Library of Alexandria.

The City of Alexandria, which had been founded in the North of Egypt in 331 BC by Alexander the Great of Macedonia, was the most important cultural centre of the ancient world. It was an academic focus for the greatest scholars, scientists, doctors, mathematicians and philosophers, who travelled from far and wide to study the largest collection of arcane documents ever amassed in one arena. But, one day in the year AD 391, a fevered Christian mob, led by the Roman-appointed Bishop Theophilus, marched upon the Serapeum where the library collection was held.

Close to the harbour, this majestic building, with its marble steps, columned halls and magnificent gardens, had been a centre of Egyptian worship for seven centuries, as well as being an inspired foundation of Greek learning, housing many hundreds of thousands of valuable papyrus and parchment texts, together with fine statues, tapestries and other works of art. To this truly cosmopolitan academy came Egyptians, Macedonians, Greeks, Anatolians, Italians, Arabians, Persians, Indians and Jews—but according to Bishop Theophilus and his Christians it was a satanic and sinful place, full to bursting with historical records that were superfluous to Imperial requirement and contrary to the newly devised Church teaching. Emperor Theodosius of Rome (AD 385-412) therefore brought to bear the Council Creeds of Nicaea (AD 325) and Constantinople (AD 381), demanding that orthodox Christianity must be imposed upon Alexandria and that the contents of the Serapeum should be destroyed.

Once inside the great Library, the angry mob, acting upon the Emperor's instruction, smashed everything to pieces and burnt every written text they could find—more than half a million irreplaceable documents representing the finest minds of the ancient world. Resultantly, in that one day the vast wisdom of ages was lost for all time, leaving the Church free, henceforth, to make up its own history, to interpret its own science and to establish its own philosophy.

Following this atrocity, while under the leadership of Cyril, the Patriarch of Alexandria, the clerics then turned upon the scholars themselves—especially the women, who were said to have no place in the academic arena! They pursued them for years, hounding and slaughtering, until the last of them was hacked to death on Lenten Day in March AD 415. She was Hypatia, a professor of philosophy, a noted authority on the works of Plato and a teacher of algebraic mathematics. But, in the eyes of the Church, Plato was a heretic and Hypatia was a witch who must be dealt with accordingly.[23] On being wrested from her carriage, she was disrobed and dragged naked to the churchyard of Caesarium by a group of Christian monks. There, undergoing death by torture at the age of forty-five, she had the flesh scooped from her bones with sharp tiles and oyster shells before her remains were scattered as a public warning in the streets of Alexandria.

Hypatia, daughter of the Greek geometrician Theon, wrote a renowned work called the *Astronomical Canon* and a commentary on *The Conics of Apollonius* (a student of Euclid who, in the 3rd century BC, first introduced the now familiar terms *ellipse, parabola* and *hyperbola*).[24] She invented and perfected many devices for calculating astronomical measurement, including the Planesphere and, in particular, the Astrolabe—an instrument used to measure the height of stars above the horizon.[25] Once set, astrolabes would identify the entire sky (whether visible or invisible) and they became widely used for maritime navigation. Another of Hypatia's inventions was the Hydroscope, which determined the specific gravity of liquids. To the Christian bishops, however, she was a sorceress and when, many centuries later, the Italian Renaissance artist Raphael (1483-1520) painted his masterwork *The School of Athens*, he was instructed to remove Hypatia from the scene in order to make his work acceptable to the Bishop of Rome.

Fruit of the Womb

Early in the 1960s, a now often cited work from Morton College, Oxford,[26] stated that the 5th to 8th-century Merovingian Kings of the Franks considered their blood to be such that, in perpetuating their line, 'it could not be ennobled by any match, nor degraded by the blood of slaves'. The fact is that, although this is a widely held view of the academic establishment, the names and families of the mothers of Merovingian kingly successors are very difficult to trace and, where they are known, many (such as Clotilde of Burgundy, Basina of Thuringia, Brunhilde the Visigoth, Immachilde of Swabia and Gizelle de Razès) certainly do have noble origins. What the Merovingians did not do was to select their mating partners (be they wives or mistresses) in accordance with any aristocratic code that would have been recognized by the Roman Church. It is because of this that orthodox history records these royal mothers of the Goth, Visigoth and Ostrogoth nobility as being barbarians of contemptible blood.

It was, in fact, a part of all Messianic kingly tradition that a man could not be a king without a queen, for only upon anointing by his bride did he achieve Messianic (Anointed) standing—as in the all-important anointing of Jesus by Mary Magdalene at Bethany.[27] This established custom of a king's required marital status applied in the world of Gaelic royalty and is made particularly apparent in the ancient Vedic *Satapatha Brahmana* of India, which states: 'Therefore as long as he does not find a wife, so long is he not born; for so long he is not complete. But in finding a wife he is born, for then he becomes complete'.[28]

Not only could a man not become a king without a queen, but the queen had to be of the royal blood.[29] This marital regulation arose because the queen (as were women in general) was reckoned to represent Mother Earth and had, accordingly, to be consort to the king if he were to reign upon that Earth. The symbolism for this union is found in the most archaic of Mesopotamian times, wherein the queen was regarded as a goddess, just as the king was himself considered godly. Hence, Queen = goddess = earth = matter = body, while King = god = sky = spirit = soul. It was by virtue of their Earth Goddess representation that women did not have to be bothered with the responsibilities of owning land and property in law, for it was deemed an impossibility to gain access in law to that which was already theirs by natural right. The fact that the later Roman Church and its governments strategically misappropriated this sacred custom in its eventual subjugation of women's rights to property ownership is a different matter altogether, and latter-day sexist regulations cannot be aligned with ancient custom in this respect.

On occasions where, for one reason or another, a king was hurriedly installed before his marriage, wedding ceremonies were held soon afterwards. At that time, the queenly consort would also be crowned and the other key reason for the union would then be announced: the reason of perpetuating the dynasty. In this regard, the coronation of the queen was accompanied by the words, 'Grant that thy handmaid enter with mercy into a worthy and sublime union with our King. May she deserve to be made fruitful with the fruit of her womb'.[30] In the general scheme of things, therefore, and irrespective of the propagandist nonsense which academic history teaches about the Merovingian Fisher Kings, the mothers of royal heirs were very carefully chosen within the realm of the true *Albi-gens*.

6

Warlords of the Pict-sidhé

The Kings of Edom

The Kassites of Mesopotamia, who venerated the goddess Barat-Anna, were kin to a line descended from the biblical Esau. The book of Genesis explains that Esau had a number of wives, one being a princess of the old line called Bashemath, by whom he had two prominent grandsons: Nahath, Lord of Edom (Idumaea), and Shammah-si, also Lord of Edom (Genesis 36:13). Despite their listing in the Bible (only to be sidestepped in favour of pursuing a junior course from Esau's brother Jacob), the powerful Lords of Edom are still given an amount of temporary prominence, being cited as 'the kings that reigned in the land of Edom [north-east of Sinai] before there reigned any king over the children of Israel' (Genesis 36:31).

Scholars of Hebrew literature make the specific point that, in listing the legitimate Lords of Edom, the Genesis compilers defined twelve individual dukedoms, equivalent in number to the twelve tribes of Israel.[1] Also that Esau's Edomites were destined to inherit the kingdom of Edom as the dragons and owls of eternity, in accordance with the book of Isaiah (34:13-17): 'They shall possess it for ever; from generation to generation shall they dwell therein. The wilderness and the solitary place shall be glad for them, and the desert shall rejoice and blossom as the rose' (Isaiah 35:1). The fact is that such a retrospective prophecy was not a problem for the eventual writers of Isaiah, nor even for Isaiah himself, to cite more than 1100 years after the event. By that time it was a matter of recorded history that the Edomites had risen to greater fame than ever achieved by the Israelite House of David. It is within their history that we find another root of the Elf distinction, for the members of this influential king-tribe were described in old biblical Hebrew as *Elefs*.[2]

Not only did the family of Esau inherit Edom, but they became Kings of Assyria and Lords of the Babylonian Sea Land from around 1780 BC. Later successors of the line were the Hyksos Kings of Egypt: the shepherd-guardians who reigned in the Nile Delta simultaneously with the 17th pharaonic dynasty of Thebes.

During that same era, from about 1750 BC, their cousin line of Kassites governed Greater Mesopotamia,[3] bringing a return to law and order after some 200 years of turmoil since the departure of the Anunnaki overlords. Subsequently, from *c*.1600 BC, they ruled more specifically in Babylonia and Sumer for another 500 years. The Kassites came to Mesopotamia from the Persian Zargos region now known as Luristan, and they were noted horse rearers. The first horse-drawn chariots in Mesopotamia were Kassite, introduced at much the the same time (*c*.1700 BC) that the related Hyksos Kings introduced them into Egypt.

What emerges from these coextensive tribal histories is that there were common Sumerian roots in Anunnaki times between the Kassites and the biblical family of Esau which, as Genesis explains, descended from the patriarchs of Ur. Their mutual interest in horse-drawn vehicles is also significant since it pulls the families back beyond Sumerian times to the Kurgan race of Scythia and the Russian steppe-lands who originated the concept. In recent times there have been some astonishing discoveries in this regard—discoveries which prove that Sumerian was not the first written language as is commonly portrayed, and that the Sumerian culture (generally held to be the earliest cradle of civilization) had an older origin of its own. Indeed, the Ring Lord culture and the notion of earthly kingship did not begin in ancient Sumer; it began long before in the Balkans, specifically in Transylvania and the Carpathian regions.

Since these discoveries are especially relevant to the fairy lore of the *Tuadhe d'Anu* and the druidic *Sidhé*, we shall consider them at a more appropriate later stage of our investigation. Meanwhile, in preparation for this, we should continue our journey with the Kassites. These people gained their name from the word *Kassi* (or *Cassi*), which meant 'Place of Wood' — the place in question being a sacred royal mound dwelling, variantly called a *Katti* or *Caddi*. By virtue of this, the Kassites were designated Wood Lords.

Following their time in Babylonia, the Kassite culture moved across Syria and Phoenicia into Europe and, eventually, to Britain where they established many great kingdoms within which the remnant of their name survived: the Welsh King Cadwallan, for example, and the earlier British King Casswallan, who reigned at about the time of King Herod the Great. In each of these names the 'wallan' aspect is also important since *Wallan* was also the distinction of a Wood Lord — again with Mesopotamian roots. The original Wallans were called *Yulannu*, and it was from their ancient culture that the Winter solstice Yuletide festival derived before moving into Scandinavia.

The most important aspect of the early Grail successions was the conjoining of their various lines of primary descent at around the time of Moses. Not only did the two key parallel lines from Esau join through marriage but, when the emergent Prince Niul of Scythia married the heiress of Egypt in about 1360 BC, the resultant family was the most prestigious in all history to date. They were the Royal Scyths of the *Albi-gens* — the line which spawned the fairy kings of the *Tuadhe d'Anu*. In time, their descendants were the High Kings of the Irish, Picts and Scots, with their legendary links to the Merovingian Fisher Kings and the enchanted dynasty of the Elf Kings. This, as we shall see, was the magical family of the fairy Mélusine — the family of Robin Hood and of Shakespeare's Oberon who, in spite of their apparent fictional portrayals, were all founded upon characters of historic reality.

Fairy Writing

Subsequent to the library destruction in Alexandria, similar atrocities were carried out in the Gaelic realms and other parts of Europe. Thereafter, history was rewritten and taught anew by the bishops and monks in compliance with the self-styled Christian doctrines. By virtue of the Church's removal of recorded evidence from these early times, this period became known as the Dark Ages, but few clerics of the 4th century were to know that one day other libraries would be discovered—archives of even older record which had been lost beneath the desert sands long before the sacking at Alexandria. Among these, perhaps the most notable were the Egyptian archives of Pharaoh Amenhotep III, who reigned in about 1400 BC, and the great Mesopotamian library of King Ashur-banipal of Assyria (668-631 BC), discovered at Nineveh in 1845 by Britain's foremost Assyriologist, Sir Henry Creswicke Rawlinson.

In this regard, Rawlinson's most important discovery (as far as our present investigation is concerned) was that which he discussed in his 1853 address to the Royal Asiatic Society. This talk concerned various ancient Babylonian and Assyrian scripts which he had been deciphering, in the course of which Rawlinson announced that he had found an even older written language—a non-Semitic type, which he determined was probably Scythian.[4]

This notion was quickly disputed by other scholars since the world's oldest written language, they said, was Sumerian—as it is still generally portrayed today. They decided to call the newly discovered text 'Akkadian' (Akkad being the older name for Babylonia) but, as Rawlinson pointed out, the Scythians were the early occupiers of Akkad and, therefore, "may be assumed to have invented cuneiform writing". In defiance of Rawlinson's known expertise with linguistic syllabaries, historians have since ignored his considered opinion, but it transpires that he was absolutely correct. Pre-Sumerian text has now been found over 1500 miles north-west of Mesopotamia in the Carpathian mountain region of Transylvania—the land made so famous by the legendary tales of Count Dracula and the cult of the vampire.

The very earliest type of Mesopotamian writing, which preceded the strictly wedge-shaped Sumerian cuneiform, is known to be a little more than 5500 years old (from around 3500 BC). It was found at Uruk in Sumer and at Jemdat Nasr, between Baghdad and Babylon, where the Oxford Assyriologist, Stephen Langdon, made numerous important discoveries in 1925. But, as reported at length in the *Scientific American* journal of May 1968, a more significant find was subsequently made in the Balkans. Beneath the ancient village of Tartaria in the Transylvanian region of Romania were found clay tablets inscribed with a form of script which Carbon-14 dating and strata positioning have revealed to be a good deal older than the earliest Sumerian tablets—perhaps by more than 1000 years. But that was not the only surprise, for some of the Tartarian symbols were practically identical to those which emerged later in Mesopotamia. The very name of Ur (the capital of Sumer and the city of Anu) came from the Scythian word *Ur*, meaning 'Lord'.

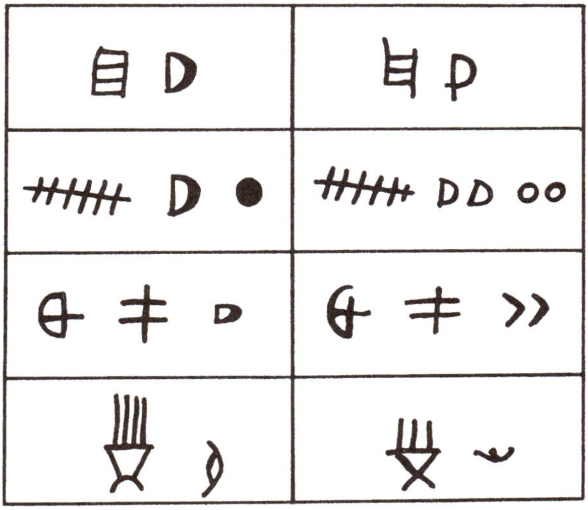

Comparison of the ancient pre-cuneiform Mesopotamian writing of Nemdat Nasr (left) with the much earlier writing (right) from Tartaria in Transylvania

Tartaria, which sits on the Maros River, seventy miles south of the Transylvanian city of Cluj, was famous in classical times for its rich gold deposits, and its culture in those far-off days was essentially of a Vinca style.[5] The people lived in huts constructed with a framework of poles and walls woven from thin branches daubed with clay. It is generally classified as a Neolithic culture, which gives a somewhat primitive image of an age when the use of metals was unknown. However, as determined by the writings and numerous artifacts discovered in the 20th century, the Tartaria culture was actually quite advanced and, in many ways, compared with the later Bronze Age environments of other countries. In fact, the people are now known to have had axes and tools made of copper.[6] This possibility would have been discounted not so long ago, regardless of the fact that the Greek chronicler Hesiod wrote, in around 700 BC, that the Scythians were the historical inventors of bronze working—with bronze, of course, being an alloy of copper and tin.

The truly important fact about this region is that its culture was that of the Scythian Wood Lords—the Transylvanian fairy race who spawned the *Tuadhe d'Anu* king tribe. Their wood and earth dwellings were called *tepes* (pronounced 'tepesh'—akin to the American Indian *tepees*) and their settlements were continually built each on top of the last as their previous habitations deteriorated and collapsed. Thus, for the most part, they lived upon mounds of the compacted encampments of ages, thereby retaining beneath their dwellings the spirits of their ancestors, who were also buried within these and other mounds called barrows or *kurgans*. These were the forerunners of the Gaelic royal seats known as *Raths* (the Irish high seat on the Hill of Tara, for example). The people of the Tartarian region were the progenitors of many aspects of the emergent Sumerian culture—even of the original concept of tribal kingship—and their fairy writing is proof enough that in this regard they were ahead of the Sumerians by at least a thousand years.

To write the number '10' the Sumerians pressed the end of an upright round stick into the clay, making a circular impression.

Then to make other numbers they added semicircular marks by pressing the stick at an angle, using both small and large semicircles. As can be seen from the comparison diagram, the earlier Scythian process was much the same. To denote the two nominal syllables for the god Enki (*En-ki*), the Sumerians used a long line crossed with short dashes, linked to a grid symbol with several parallel bars. These *En-ki* graphics each have their equivalents on the Tartaria tablets. There are actually many similarities, one of the most striking being a common sign shaped like a candelabra, together with the fact that both the Transylvanians and later Sumerians customarily separated their groups of signs with vertical and horizontal dividing lines.

The odd thing about the Uruk and Jemdat Nasr Mesopotamian texts is that, prior to this style of writing, there were only crude pictographs in the region, with nothing to justify the apparently sudden change. But this would be explained by the arrival of the Scythians who brought their culture and fairy writing with them. Subsequently, this writing style evolved to become the disciplined cuneiform text which emerged in later Sumerian times.[7] In the Tartaria district of the Balkans no preceding pictographs have been found and the tablet inscriptions are seen to be a unique phenomenon—the original form of what afterwards became a transient written language. It is also apparent that, when the fairy script arrived in ancient Sumer, so too did the gold culture—a direct inheritance from gold-rich Transylvania. The first secreted gold in Sumer came to light in the royal graves at Ur, dated to around 3500 BC and unearthed by the British archaeologist Sir Charles Leonard Woolley and his Anglo-American team in the 1920s.[8]

Of particular importance when tracing the southward movement of the Scythians into Mesopotamia is the fact that these mighty warlords of the transcendent *Sidhé* were also called the *Sumaire* which, as we have seen, was an old Gaelic word for a coiled serpent. It is, therefore, perhaps not surprising that their *Sumairian* fairy language was the root of the later dubbed 'Sumerian' tongue, from which the very place name of Sumer derived,[9] supporting a wholly new culture from soon after 4000 BC. It is also of interest that the Anunnaki gods were as much a part of the *Sidhé* heritage as they were of the emergent Mesopotamian tradition. The main settlement of the sky god Anu was not in Sumer where one might expect to find it, but hundreds of miles to the North on the Caspian Sea. Similarly, the ancient centre of Scythopolis was not in the land generally regarded as Scythia; it was in Galilee, thereby denoting a migration route from the Black Sea country down into the delta plains of the Sumerian eden. The Syrians called Sythopolis *Beth-Shean*: the House of Power—i.e. the House of the *Sidhé* (*Shean* being the equivalent of *Sidhéan*).

Tombs of the Ring Lords

Among the priceless Scythian treasures unearthed to date in Romania and Russia are magnificent bronze weapons, ceremonial silver battleaxes, silver spears, alabaster mace heads, wonderfully designed gold bracelets, necklaces, earrings, pendants and a great 21-carat golden dagger weighing three pounds (*c*.1.36kg.).[10] Indeed, many of the collected artifacts from the Black Sea region are considered among the most valued treasures of the State Hermitage Museum in St. Petersburg. More than two-hundred of these exquisite golden objects, including platters with distinctive Scythian animal designs, were once the property of Tsar Peter the Great (1672-1725), having been discovered in Western Siberia. But for all this prestigious wealth, the most significant discovery has been made high in the Altai Mountains between Siberia and Mongolia. There, preserved by the severe cold since the distant BC years, was found a Scythian burial mound—a *kurgan* where the bodies of ancient chieftains, together with their horses, clothing and possessions had all been remarkably preserved from decay.[11] Once again, the contents of the individual tombs display a quite remarkable sensitivity and sophistication in artwork, albeit these Royal Scyths of the *Tuadhe d'Anu* were among the most intimidating warriors of all time.

These were the people who, in the Black Sea steppe lands, first domesticated the horse in about 4000 BC. Consequently, the extent of their subsequent travels through the centuries and their influence on the various indigenous cultures is most impressive. It ranges geographically from Hungary and Romania, north into the Russian steppes and Siberia, eastwards across the Ukraine and Anatolia (Asia Minor/Turkey), south into Syria and Mesopotamia, and still further east to Mongolia, Tibet and the Chinese border country.

Digging first commenced at the Altai site in 1927, with some measure of success, but it was not until 1947 that the richest mound containing six separate tombs was discovered and the various bodies found. They were preserved not only by the extreme cold of the region, but also by skilled embalming. There was hair on their heads, but their brains had been removed, along with other internal organs (just as in Egyptian mummification).[12] Even certain muscles had been cut or extracted so that the bodies would retain their shapes and positions. The men were extensively tattooed, mostly with animal depictions, but the most astonishing aspect of this decoration was the appearance of ring-tailed lemurs (*lemur catta*). Ring-tailed lemurs, we are led to believe, are native to, and restricted to, Madagascar and the Comoros Islands off Mozambique—but these depictions were found thousands of miles to the North (where we are told that lemurs never were) embellishing the bodies of historical Ring Lords.

It has been known for some time that there was once a great continent, inhabited by a formidable king-tribe, which was noted for its lemurs—and for this reason it has long been dubbed Lemuria. For many decades enthusiasts have searched for the sunken whereabouts of Lemuria beneath the Atlantic, Pacific or Indian Oceans—and maybe concealed territories do exist in these regions. Of far more importance, however, is the fact that the mightiest Lemurian land tract was never lost. It was the great mainland continent which still exists today—stretching across eastern Europe through the one-time USSR, being once linked in its far Asian reaches to North America. In essence, these conjoined continents could all have been aptly styled Lemuria.

This was the original realm of the great warlords of Anu before they migrated and battled their way to warmer regions in the ever cooling climate of the last Ice Age. Undoubtedly, at some stage before the Altai chieftains were interred, the environment was very warm in their northern homeland. This is proved by the fact that the lemurs must subsequently have followed the sun, and then travelled about as far southwards as they could possibly go before Madagascar and the Comoros Islands broke away from the African mainland. In the same way, it is very likely that

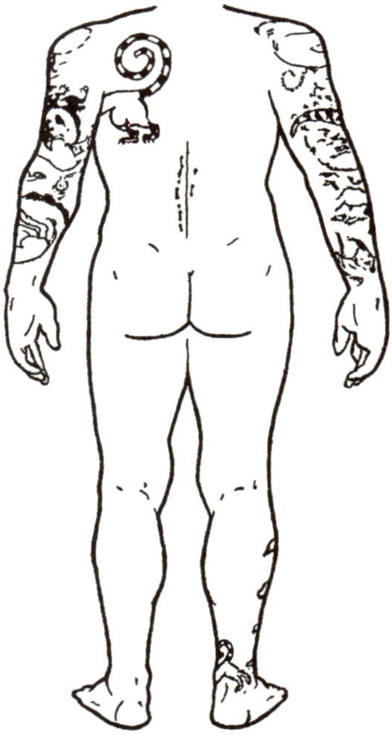

Scythian tattoos of ring-tailed lemurs (shoulder and ankle) as discovered at Altai
From a mummified figure as discussed in the Scientific American, *May 1965*

certain of today's South American creatures will be discovered to have once inhabited the Alaskan and Canadian North.

The men of Altai wore narrow trousers made of soft chamois-like leather, felt stockings and high boots. Upon their backs were loose tunics with long sleeves, while their headgear was a felt hat with leather-covered ear flaps. The women wore a similar style of tunic, perhaps embroidered with beads and an additional bib. They too had felt stockings, along with dress boots made of leopardskin, and their general apparel (as with the men) included many gold and silver adornments. Their horses, with neatly clipped manes and bobbed or plaited tails, were more richly adorned than their owners, with remarkably designed trappings, ornate headpieces and wonderfully soft saddles, like pillows, padded with deer hair.

Some way south of the Altai site, in the northern foothills of the Himalayas, are the centres of Hami, Loulan and Churchen. It was close to these places, nestling in the Tarim Basin below Mongolia and to the north of Tibet, that a number of similar discoveries were made as recently as 1994. Unlike the intensely cold climate of the Altai Mountains, this lower region of the Central Asian desert is quite different, as a product of which the various bodies were preserved by the perfectly dry air, coupled with the moisture-absorbing, underground salt beds[13] and, again, expert mummification. Dated at something around 4000 years old, these interred men, women and children have undermined all the established history teaching of the area, which previously stated that no one of their type arrived there until about 120 BC. But there they were, in true Scythian fashion, from 2000 years earlier at the time of Abraham, when Egyptian pharaohs such as Tutankhamun and Ramesses the Great were more than 500 years into the future.[14] These mummies (now housed in the nearby regional capital Museum of Ürümchi), although contemporary with the mummies of ancient Egypt, are actually far better preserved.

Like the Tartaria mummies, they are of impressive stock, with light skin, auburn hair and pale eyes. The leather and woollen clad men stood at least 6ft. 6ins. (2 m.) and upwards, while even the women were over 6ft. tall. Undoubtedly, these forebears of the Gaelic High Kings were among the most fearsome lords of their time, and their use of finely woven tartan cloth (which is also wonderfully preserved) serves as identifiable proof of the plaid designs which they eventually brought into Ireland and Scotland. Interestingly, their headgear, while not too dissimilar to that of the Altai chieftains, was classically Phrygian (like the Phrygian caps used as an expression of liberty in the 18th-century French Revolution). These caps positively identify their origin in the Black Sea steppe lands to the east of Hungary—the Scythian home territory of the magical *Tuadhe d'Anu* before the Phrygian branch migrated into Thrace and Anatolia in the early Iron Age.[15] For obvious historical reasons, a version of this cap became the recognized headwear of the pixies of popular mythology.

Perhaps the best known Phrygian king, remembered in Greek mythology, is Midas (*Meide-Asa*, son of King Gordius of Phrygia) who, as the outcome of a wish granted by the god Dionysus, turned all that he touched into gold. Interestingly, the Midas Monument which occupies the face of an immense cliff at the source of the Sangarious river near Ankara in Turkey, displays nine large *Rosi-crucis* emblems on its facade.[16]

Kingdom of the Pixies

A primary feature of the traditional folklore related to the Ring and Grail quests is that it embodies a nominal terminology that was historically applicable to the Messianic dynasts. As cited, the terms 'fairy' and 'elf' each related to certain castes within the succession of the Shining Ones. But there were others—notably the 'pixies'—who were of the utmost importance within the overall structure of the princely bloodline. Having the same *Sidhé* heritage as the historical elves and fairies, their familiar name derived from the description *Pict-sidhé*.

Along with the royal *Tuadhe d'Anu* (often called the *Daoine-sidhé* = fairy-folk), the sovereign warlords of the *Pict-sidhé* (the Pixies) also have an identifiable tradition and a traceable genealogical structure. They were the ultimate custodians of law and culture, and their female counterparts were called the *Behn-sidhé* (Banshee) which, in old Irish, meant 'wise women'.

As already discussed, the three key lines of Egyptian and Mesopotamian royal descent drew together in marriage towards the end of the 14th century BC, to progress as a single royal house in Scythia, commencing with Gadheal Glas, the ancestor of the Scots Gaels. By about 1100 BC the line had split into three, with each separate line destined, in time, to reign in Ireland. The first was a line from Gadheal's grandson Prince Eibhear Scot (sometimes called Partolon I), which descended to a dynasty called the Milesians. The second line, from Eibhear's brother Prince Tait, diverged after a few generations to become the fairy king tribe of the *Tuadhe d'Anu* on the one hand, while in parallel emerged the priestly race of the *Fir Bolg*.

The definition *Fir Bolg* is generally said to mean 'Bag men' (*Fir* = men; *Bolg* = bag: i.e. a bulge or knapsack), and it is reckoned that they carried the earth of their homeland around in little pouches as did many emigrant Scots refugees after the 18th-century Highland Clearances. Within their overall Scythian strain, they adopted the culture of the old *Yulannu* Wood Lords (or Wallans) and were, in essence, priest kings or druid kings. Their formidable cousins of the *Tuadhe d'Anu* succession were, by way of contrast, warrior kings. The totem animal of the *Fir Bolg* was the Blue Boar, while the *Tuadhe d'Anu* favoured the Stag. (In a symbolic combination of these totems, the *Fenian Cycle* of Irish folk tales introduced a boar-headed stag to carry heroes to the Otherworld.)

In time, by about 650 BC, following the legendary Battle of Mag Tuireadh, the succession of *Fir Bolg* kings gave way to the *Tuadhe d'Anu* kings in Ireland.[17] This dynasty, which guarded the sacred *Lia Fáil* (a precursor to the *Saxum Fatale*: Stone of Destiny), included such famed characters as Eochaid Ollathat (called the *Daghda Mór*: Great God), whose cauldron, it was said, would cook only for heroes. Also Lugh Lamhfada, famed for his magical spear which won every battle, and the sacred sword of his ancestor Nuhadu. Soon afterwards, the parallel Milesian line from Gadheal Glas inherited the Irish kingship, leading to mighty dynasts such as Ugaine Már, Conaire Mór and, ultimately (from the 6th century AD), to the Kings of the Dalriadan Scots and the foundation of Scotland.

In the course of this, from about 600 BC, a newly styled line evolved from Bruithné (sometimes given as Cruithné), the brother of the Lugh Lamhfada in the *Tuadhe d'Anu* succession, and they were the *Pict-sidhé* (pixies)—or as they became better known, the Picts. Within a short space of time, the Picts were reigning in Pictavia (later Anjou, in France) and in the far North of Britain, which they called Caledonia (from *Caille Daouine:* Forest People). It is perhaps not a generally considered aspect of the Picts that they were kings in France as well as in Caledonia. However, as confirmed in the *Chronicle of the Picts and Scots* and the Irish *Book of Ballymote*, the Picts actually founded the centre of their kingdom at Poitiers, south of Tours.[18]

If there was an ultimate high-point in the successive separating and conjoining of families in the lines of Grail descent, it is fair to say that this occurred with the emergence of the druidic Pictish kings. Meanwhile, another family branch from Bruithné founded the Royal House of Gwynedd in Wales, while in Cornwall, in the West of England, they were revered as the sacred Gentry (the Cornish 'piskies').

For more than three centuries the Gaelic Scots of the Milesian strain governed the Western Highlands and the Scottish Isles, while the Picts reigned in the Caledonian North of what was later to become incorporated into Scotland. These separate dynasties of the Scots and Picts prevailed until the year 844, with the last individual King of Scots being Alpin (839-41). But Alpin was also a matrilinear heir to the kingdom of Caledonia through his mother, Princess Unuisticc of the Picts—and Alpin's son Kenneth duly became King of the newly unified nation of Scotland after defeating King Bruide of the Picts at the Battle of Scone.[19] It was recognized, nevertheless, that in accordance with all the established custom of ages, a kingly descent should rightly be a matrilinear succession—just as had been operative with the pharaohs of old. For this reason, it was determined that the descending Kings of Scots would marry Pictish princesses, thereby conjoining and preserving the time-honoured legacy of the Shining Ones and the family ties of their mutual ancestor, Gadheal Glas, from over 2000 years before.

Unfortunately, the oldest complete history of Ireland to survive was not written until the early Middle Ages, by which time (as a result of the Church destruction and suppression of historical records which began with the burning of the Library of Alexandria), much of the truth had conveniently been Christianized. In the course of this, the fairies of kingly tradition had been literally diminished in status and stature, while being removed into the realm of mythology. The *Tuadhe d'Anu*, it was claimed by the monks who wrote the medieval *Lebor Gabála* (Book of Invasions, *c*.1300),[20] came down from the skies in an obscure cloud and subsequently lived in underground burrows! The transcendent *Sidhé* (the druidic Web of the Wise) became reclassified as the Web of the Weird and was portrayed as a strange netherworld fantasy, while the priestly *Fir Bolg* seemingly wandered around aimlessly, gathering peat for their little bags!

When not depicted in this patronizing manner, the Church scribes have often referred to the *Fir Bolg* as vampires, compelled to carry their native earth around with them. Even the intimidating leprechauns of Scythian tradition were sidelined into becoming cute little shoemakers, with the definition 'leprechaun' said to be an Irish word emanating from *luchorpan*, meaning 'small body'. But it actually stems from *lepracorpan*—wherein 'lepra' (as in leprosy) means scaly—hence 'scaly body'. It relates to the scale-like armour—made from a multitude of small metal plates stitched to leather bands to facilitate ease of movement—as worn by the later Scythian warriors and their legendary successors, the Sarmatian cavalrymen. In accordance with the derivative leprechaun image, the Scythian warriors also wore armoured helmets that were distinctly Phrygian in shape and the little pointed elven caps of mythology replicated this design.

Despite the Church's propagandist teachings, and having now established the historical origins of the elves, fairies and pixies by following a line of Ring Lord descent from Mesopotamia and Egypt, through Scythia and into Ireland, it is apparent that we have not yet determined any obvious link with the Bible's Royal House of Judah. This is the Albigensian strain of David, Solomon, Jesus and the Merovingians which constitutes, in the minds of many, the more apparent line of the *Sangréal*. In fact, this line has been running in parallel all the way through our story to date, having emerged from the same beginning with Eve, the Lady of Life. It is now time to pick up this line again for, with the Picts of Caledonia and Anjou, a new link is forged with this succession. This leads us directly into a merging of the fairies, elves and pixies with the mermaid strain of the Ladies of the Waters—and our link in this chain is the most enchanting mermaid of all historical tradition—the mysterious Mélusine.

7

The Fount of Mélusine

The Paradox

In Transylvania, a little to the north of the Romanian citadel of Bucharest—founded by Prince Vlad Tepes of Wallachia in the 15th century—stands Castle Bran, often incorrectly associated with Count Dracula. After an extensive restoration programme completed in 1993, the castle is in splendid condition and is now a museum of history and feudal art, as well as having operative residential quarters. Within the confines of Castle Bran, one of the most captivating paintings on display is a 15th-century depiction of the tutelary Grail fairy Mélusine, complete with her legendary serpent's tail and bat's wings.

Princess Mélusine, like Lady Lilith of Mesopotamia, has a strangely paradoxical tradition in that she is often described as a demonic succubus on the one hand while, on the other, various noble and royal families have gone to great lengths to attempt a validation of their descent from her. In just the same manner, a similar fascination prevails in putting forward royal descents from the House of Dracula. Even Britain's late Sir Iain Moncrieffe, Her Majesty's Albany Herald of Arms, made a point in 1982 of stating with regard to Charles, the prevailing Prince of Wales, that "Today, perhaps the most famous of HRH's Romanian relations is Prince Vlad Dracula the Impaler, an ancestral uncle who took the surname of Dracula because his father Prince Vlad Dracul was proud to be a Knight of the Dragon".[1]

In this same work, when dealing with the ancestry of Diana, Princess of Wales, Sir Iain also featured a descent from Mélusine's House of Lusignan—the dynasty of the Kings of Cyprus and Jerusalem in the Middle Ages. By this strategy a Mélusine tradition was provided for the future Royal House of Windsor through Princess Diana's son, Prince William, who was born to her and Prince Charles that year. In this particular instance Mélusine is romantically presented rather more as an ancestral spirit but, that apart and in accordance with many similar genealogical instances, the historical 8th-century Mélusine has been deliberately ignored so that another more conveniently situated female could be dubbed with her name and mystery. In reality, the woman in question with respect to the House of Lusignan was not actually Mélusine at all, but Melisende, the 9th-century wife of Hugh the Hunter, Sire de Lusignan.

Another Melisende often wrongly credited with the Mélusine name was the 11th-century wife of Hugues de Rethul, whose son Baldwin du Bourg became Crusader King of Jerusalem in 1118. They had a daughter also named Melisende (later spuriously dubbed Mélusine). She married Foulques, the succeeding King of Jerusalem from whom Britain's Angevin House of Plantagenet subsequently descended—the dynasty of Richard the Lionheart and Henry V. These are examples of three historical Melisendes said to be the matrilinear progenitors of royal houses, but none was the true fairy Mélusine. Indeed, the line from Foulques to the House of Plantagenet was not born from his second wife Melisende anyway, it emerged from his first wife Aremburg of Maine.[2] In the light of this, Mélusine is sometimes said to have been a wife of Foulque's father (known as Foulques the Quarreller),[3] even though his real wives and their offspring are well enough recorded.

The intriguing fact about all this genealogical chicanery is that one wonders why these royal houses should wish to prove, against all historical evidence, that they were descended from a woman who, in the eyes of the Church, might just as well have been the daughter of Satan! Mélusine was, according to all orthodox propaganda, a shapeshifting dragon, a malevolent fairy like the *Leanhaun Sidhé*,[4] a seductive mermaid and very often a vampire. So why would eminent heralds and archivists go to such lengths to claim their individual patrons' descents from someone who, on the face of it, is perhaps better ignored by the orthodox establishment? What is the enigmatic secret of the Grail fairy Mélusine that is seemingly so important?

To answer these questions we have only to revert once again to the detrimental effect upon the office of kingship which resulted from the spurious *Donation of Constantine*. From the moment of its implementation in 751, European kings were 'created' by the Pope, in consequence of which many new dynasties evolved which were not of the true *Albi-gens*. Charlemagne was a perfect example of a king who was not totally happy about his contrived position. He knew that, by way of his own Merovingian maternal grandmother, he had enough personal entitlement to kingship, but he could not say the same about his father with whom the Carolingian dynasty had begun, for his father was a usurper. In this regard, Charlemagne held his kingly office by default, as did many other kings of various emergent successions. Even so, there was perhaps a way for the Church's puppet-kings of later times to justify their untenable positions if only they could find some way to substantiate a descent from a legitimate Elf Queen. Better still, a descent from the last prominent female of the Ring Lord bloodline from the Picts and the Royal Scyths of the *Tuadhe d'Anu*. She was, of course, not difficult to find for the senior prevailing Elf Queen at the time of the fraudulent 751 *Donation* was none other than Princess Mélusine.

The problem was that very few, except the line which had prevailed as the Albigensian Elf Kings in any event, could prove a descent from Mélusine. But there were some convenient Melisendes around, whose names could be strategically manipulated to comply—no matter if they were a century or two out of historical context!

The Mermaid and the Rings

In 1387 Jean, Duc de Berry of the Valois House of France, commissioned his secretary Jean d'Arras to write a history of the family of Lusignan. He duly complied, producing le *Noble Hystoire de Lusignan*,[5] within which was included the *Chronique de Mélusine*. There is no doubt that this account was meant to be romantic in style but, beyond its fairy tale element, the story had a firm factual base. Indeed, d'Arras admitted that he had discovered an older version of the text written in Italian by a certain William de Portenach.[6]

In the wake of this French account of Mélusine (published in Paris, Troyes, Lyons and Toulouse), numerous translations were made and, between 1478 and 1838, the tale became popular by way of editions from Geneva, Copenhagen, Prague, Augsburg, Strasbourg, Heidelberg, Nuremberg, Leipzig and Antwerp. Not only was Britain's House of Plantagenet quick to realize the importance of concocting and promoting a Mélusine descent, but other royal and noble houses (such as those of Luxembourg, Rohan and Sassenaye) soon altered their genealogies in order to claim this illustrious pedigree.[7]

Since, in all versions of the story, the accounts of Mélusine begin in Caledonian Scotland and Northumberland before moving to France, the best version for our purpose is perhaps the English-language translation prepared by Sir Algernon Tudor-Craig,[8] which tells the story as follows:

Once there was a King of Albany (Scotland) named Elynas who, while hunting after the death of his first wife, heard angelic singing when he approached a fountain to quench his thirst. The singer was a beautiful woman, quite unknown to him, who explained that her name was Préssyne and that she was amusing herself while her servants rested. Elynas was enchanted by her and, in due time, they planned to marry—but there was a condition. Préssyne would only consent to this marriage if the

King would solemnly promise never to attempt to see her birthing or feeding their eventual children—an undertaking to which Elynas dutifully agreed.

The couple lived happily together until Préssyne gave birth to three lovely daughters; they were named Mélusine, Mélior and Palatyne. But the King already had a son called Nathas by his first wife. Nathas hated his step-mother and managed, in his intrigue, to persuade his father to visit Queen Préssyne and his daughters in their nursery. Breaking his marriage vow, Elynas entered the chamber where Préssyne was lying with the infants, whereupon she chastised him and immediately disappeared with the children, never to be seen again by the King. Elynas was greatly distressed and lamented for seven years, to the extent that the people of Albany thought he was going mad and made Nathas their King in his stead.

Meanwhile, Préssyne had gone to the lost Isle of Avalon, where she raised her daughters, and every morning until they were fifteen she took them to a high mountain to show them the Caledonian land of their birth. On being questioned by Mélusine, Préssyne told the story of her father's breach of faith, at which the girls decide to punish Elynas for the sorrow he had caused. They had him seized and imprisoned high on a mountain in Northumberland, but when they told Préssyne what they had done, she reprimanded them for their shabby conduct and dealt out her punishments.

Being the eldest and most at fault, Mélusine's punishment was to be the most severe and she was to have the lower part of her body turned into a serpent's tail every Saturday. Then, when she eventually married, her husband would have to promise never to see her on those days, or she would be condemned for eternity.[9]

After living for many years on the mountain, King Elynas died and was buried by Préssyne, who erected a richly decorated tomb in his memory. The tomb bore his statue, along with a gold plate inscribed with the family's unfortunate story, and a giant named Grymault was appointed to guard the site for ever. Prior to this, Mélusine had removed to France, where she was soon destined to meet her future husband Raymond, the son of the Earl of Forez.

Having been adopted from his father by Aymery, Earl of Poitiers, Raymond accidentally killed Aymery one day when they were out boar hunting, at which he became struck with grief. He rode aimlessly about in the area until coming, quite unwittingly, to *la Fontaine de Soif* (the Fountain of Thirst) at the place called Lusina. Préssyne's three daughters were there at the fountain, but Raymond, in his state of sorrow, took no heed until Mélusine approached him. Thereupon, he gained her pardon and began a friendship just as Elynas and Préssyne had done at the fountain in Albany.

In a repeat of the previous events, the couple agreed to marry, but Raymond had to vow that he would never attempt to see Mélusine on a Saturday. She then urged him to visit the new Earl of Poitiers and to ask him, as a boon, for as much land as could be enclosed by a hart's skin. The gift was duly granted, and the deed signed and sealed, at which Raymond returned to the fountain. There, Mélusine had the hart skin sliced into a multitude of long thin strips that would enclose a large tract of land, and it was upon this ground that she built the great Château de Lusignan.

After many years of happiness and the births of a few sons, Raymond was somehow persuaded by a jealous rival that Mélusine had secret meetings with other men on Saturdays. And so, breaking his vow just as Elynas had done before him, Raymond stole into Mélusine's quarters as she lay in her bath, only to discover that on Saturdays his wife was a mermaid with a serpent's tail. Mélusine said she would forgive his intrusion so long as he agreed to keep her secret. But some time afterwards, on learning of a dispute between two of their sons, Raymond blamed Mélusine and, in a moment of rage, called her a 'serpent' before an assembled company.

Mélusine was horror-struck at Raymond's disloyalty, whereupon she gave him two Rings, saying that as long as he or his heirs had one of them they would never be defeated in law or killed in battle. Having done this, she wished him farewell and flew out of the window in the form of a blue and gold dragon. She then passed three times around the castle uttering a mournful and terrible cry—the famous Cri *de Mélusine,* said to have been heard thereafter whenever one of her descendants was about to die.

Lady of Lusignan

The key symbolic aspects of this tale are the facts that Mélusine is depicted as a serpentine mermaid, while also being a Ring guardian. In these respects the essence of her Albigensian heritage is clearly identified as being of the senior matrilinear succession of Serpent Ladies—the line from Tiâmat, Erish-kigal, Lilith, Bashemath and the other great queens of yore down to Préssyne. In this regard, she was an hereditary Lady of the Lake or, as the story portrays, a fountain fairy, as was her mother. It is, therefore, hardly of any wonder that those of various other reigning and royal families sought to attach themselves, however tenuously or spuriously, to the Mélusine Grail bloodline.

The main feature of the story that was strategically altered (so as to comply with the House of Lusignan and Duc de Berry requirement to literally split the line in their favour) is that Raymond is described as being the son of the Earl of Forez and the adopted son of Amery de Poitiers. In historical reality, there was only one character in this regard, for Amery de Poitiers was himself the Earl of Forez. To be more precise, he was the Prince-Comte de Forez.

Commencing our ancestral trace in Caledonian Scotland, where the story itself begins, it transpires that Elynas of Albany and his wife Préssyne were, historically, Elinas, King of Albha (Northern Argyll) and the Pictish Queen Bruithina (Pressina). Elinas, the son of Maelusthain of Dalriada, has sometimes been referred to as the *Gille Sidhean,* meaning Elf Servant, and he was descended from Loarn of Argyll (a contemporary of the Merovingian King Clovis) and the Milesian High Kings of Ireland.

Pressina's early ancestry was of the *Tuadhe d'Anu*, descending through the Pictish Kings of Caledonia. Thus it was that, from the time these two lines had split with the Scythian brothers Eibhear Scot and Tait in about 1200 BC, Mélusine emerged as the senior heiress of the two finally conjoined lines of succession.

To complete the picture and to bring the Picts of Caledonia back into a union with the Picts of Pictavia (Poithou), from whom they had separated in about 650 BC, all that remained was for Mélusine to marry the senior heir of the Poitiers succession in France. This heir would be the son of Aymeri, Prince-Comte de Forez, which is precisely the man to whom the *Chronique de Mélusine* refers.

Consequently, the husband of Mélusine from about 733, was Raymond of Pictavia, known more fully as Rainfroi de Verrières en Forez. The region of Verrières en Forez was about 170 miles east-south-east of Poitiers in the Loire Valley near St. Étienne. It sat to the south of Burgundian Avallon, the seat of the 6th-century Albigensian House del Acqs (or *du Lac*)—the Ladies of the Lake.[10] Although Mélusine's tradition was closely allied to this royal house, the mystical Avalon referred to in the *Chronique de Mélusine* (from where Préssyne and her daughters had gazed from the mountain at their distant homeland) was clearly in Britain's Cumbrian North Country. It would most likely have been the high ground which rises at Cross Fell to over 3000 feet (*c*.920 m.) above sea-level near Penrith. From this site there are good northerly views of the present Northumberland National Park. Also, the site is very close to Appleby in Westmoreland, and the Avalonian 'otherworld' was often likened in literature to an *Insula Pomoru* (Isle of Apples).[11]

The background to the dispute between Mélusine's parents, Elinas and Pressina, concerned Pressina's father King Brude mac Bile who, on 20 May 685, waged war upon King Eacgfrid of Northumberland at the *Bellum Duin Nechtan* (Battle of the Hill-fort of Nechtan), where Eacgfrid was slain.[12] As determined in the *Chronicles of the Picts and Scots*, Brude's mother was Eacgfrid's first cousin,[13] hence this was a family dispute (essentially over entitlements in Ireland) in which various relatives took their respective sides.

In this regard, it rather looks as if Elinas elected to support Eacgfrid, thereby betraying his wife's queenship in the Pictish line—as allegorically portrayed in the *Chronique de Mélusine*. In a similar manner, Raymond clearly betrayed this same heritage when siding against Queen Mélusine in the dispute between their sons. According to the Lusignan *Chronique*, one of the sons, Fromont, had become a Christian monk against Mélusine's wishes, and Raymond undermined her motherhood by supporting Fromont against her.

The Caledonian North of Britain was heavily wooded in those times (as was the French region of Verrières en Forez) and the Picts established their fortified community settlements within this environment to become the *Caille Daouine* people of the forest. In such surroundings they were able to appear and disappear as if by magic. They had completely confounded Britain's Roman invaders, who eventually built great walls across the country[14] to separate these seemingly enchanted elves from the controllable and more predictable southern lands which they had managed to conquer and subdue. It was precisely this woodland aspect of the fairy culture that eventually found its way into the Robin Hood tradition which was directly related to the lifestyle and kingly customs of the Albigensian Wood Lords.

The Fount of Mélusine was said to be located deep within a thicket wood at Verrières en Forez in a place called Lusina (meaning 'light bringer'), while Anjou was first apparent as a district name in ancient Babylon.[15] The German equivalent was Anschau[16] and the word denoted a 'Revelation'—as applicable to the transcendent consciousness of the *Sidhé*. In the Arthurian and Magdalene traditions of the Ladies of the Lake, therefore, Mélusine was a fountain fey—an enchantress of the underwood, whose magic spring was called *la Fontaine de Soif*.

Knight of Love

Once upon a time, over 500 years ago, there was a man of good report who was titular King of Hungary, Sicily, Aragon, Valencia, Majorca, Sardinia and Jerusalem. He was the Duke of Anjou, Calabria and Lorraine. He was the Count of Bar, Provence and Guise. He was a renowned artist, writer and chivalric warrior. He rode at Joan of Arc's side at the Siege of Orléans, and he gave Christopher Columbus his first ship's commission.

Such an impressive opening would be a fine introduction to any fairy tale—but this was no character from the pages of mythic romance. This man was King René d'Anjou (born in 1408), Grand Master of the navigational Order of the Crescent, whose sister Maria was married to King Charles VI of France, and whose daughter Margaret was the wife of King Henry VI of England. René d'Anjou introduced the famous double-barred Cross of Lorraine, which became the lasting symbol of Free France and was the emblem of the French Resistance during World War II. He was the qualified author of *The Manual for the Perfect Organization of Tournaments,* along with *Battles and the Order of Knighthood, and the Government of Princes.* The latter exists today in the translation of the *Rosslyn-Hay Manuscript* in the library of Lord William Sinclair at Rosslyn Chapel, near Edinburgh in Scotland, and it is the oldest work of Scottish prose in existence.[17]

Few men in history have been so talented, influential, illustrious and popular—but very little, if anything, is taught about King René d'Anjou in our schoolrooms. Why has this been the case? Because, despite all his fame and importance, René became the victim of a contrived and purposeful literary Inquisition. The Church perceived René as the epitome of all that it detested in terms of the Grail tradition of the *Albi-gens.* Worst of all he was a close friend, confidant and military ally of Joan of Arc who, at the auspices of England's Duke of Bedford and

France's Bishop of Beauvais, was burned alive in the Old Market Square at Rouen on 30 May 1431 because she was supposedly a witch (*see* Appendix IV). As for King René, he was strategically removed from Church-approved history teaching. The great irony of this is that, as recently as 1920, the Church reconsidered Joan of Arc's case and, in the light of hypocritical hindsight, she was not only pardoned, but canonized!

Among René d'Anjou's most popular manuscript works, which he also illustrated with wonderful paintings and illuminations, was his allegorical romance of the intrepid Knight of Love, entitled *le Livre du Cueur d'Amours Espris*. Written in 1457, the story tells of the chivalric Cueur who, in the company of his page Desire, embarks on a perilous journey of courtship to liberate Sweet Grace (*la Dame Doulce-Mercy*) who is being held captive in the Fortress of Resistance by the three enemies of Love, namely Denial, Shame and Fear.

One night in the course of their travels, Cueur and Desire come across an upright marble slab with a water spring at its base and a brass cup upon a chain. On drinking the magic water, some is accidentally spilled upon the marble, whereupon a great storm erupts and they discover an inscription on the slab which explains that this is the Fountain of Fortune—emanating from the enchanted Spring of Chance from which flows the Stream of Tears. This meandering water, it transpires, is to become the pathway of Cueur's questing journey—just as all life's journeys are carried along like the flow of a stream. But if, with the aid of Hope, he can negotiate the stream correctly beyond the Hill of Despondency, and can cope along the way with the hostile forces of Wrath, Sloth, Trouble and Sorrow, he will ultimately liberate Sweet Grace and live in a state of love for ever.

An interesting fact about springs and fountains as they are presented in such tales is that the tradition of their magical property stems directly from the old Pictish lands of Caledonia.[18] Even the well-known tales of Merlin and the Spring of Barenton in Brittany, France, have their origins in the ancient lore of the Caledonian Wood (*Cat Coit Celidon*) to the north of Carlisle—the very same Cumbrian region of Britain where the literary Préssyne took her daughters. In the 12th-century French Grail romance of *Ywain, le Chevalier au Lion* by Chrétien de Troyes, the hero's journey takes him from Carlisle into the Scottish Lothians, where he encounters a fairy fountain beneath a magical spring attended by a beautiful maiden: a water-fey. Geographically, this is the mineral spring known as Hart Fell Spa. At this place, the historical Merlin Emrys took refuge in 574 after the great Battle of Arderydd, where his patron, King Gwenddolau of the North, was defeated by King Rhydderch of Strathclyde.[19]

In Brittany, the enchanted Spring of Barenton is also still to be found within the Forest of Brocéliande, a little to the west of Rennes. It was here that Merlin taught Queen Viviane the very spell by which she was able to charm him to her side. Nearby, is the Valley of No Return, where Morgan le Fay was said to have confined her lovers. In parallel with King René's tale of le Cueur d'Amours, there was also a marble slab featured beside the Spring of Barenton—the famous Stone of Merlin called the *Perron*.[20] Similarly, in the *Roman de Rou*—a late 12th-century work by the Jersey poet Robert Wace—this spring is described as rising from beneath the stone, and the text continues: 'There too fairies are seen and many other wonders happen'. A little later, in the 14th century, came an anonymous poem entitled *Chanson de Geste de Brun de la Montaigne*, which told of the brave Brun who met with the fairies at this same beguiling place. Ring lore is also apparent here, for one of the fairies presented Brun with a golden ring as a pledge of her lasting protection.

Hence (in a similar manner to the symbolic towers of virtuous guardianship), forest springs and fountains play very important roles in fairy lore and Grail romance. However, they have a far greater alchemical significance than any other aspect of the conjoined traditions, as we shall discover when later considering the ultimate del Acqs symbolism of the Lily and the Rose.

8

The Round Table

Excalibur and the Red Dragon

As we have seen, the Ring Lords of the Royal Scyth were the root stock of the *Tuadhe d'Anu* Kings of Ireland and of various Sumerian, Hittite, Mitannian, Phoenician and Phrygian cultures. The 7th-century Byzantine Emperor Justinius II of Constantinople (685-695) referred to them as being among 'the most ancient races in the world—older than the Egyptians'. Over 1000 years before that, the Greek historian Herodotus (*c*.484-425 BC) had written at length about the Scythians,[1] explaining that, by his time of writing, a particular area of the Black Sea lands of Scythia had become known as Sarmatia.

The Sarmatians were very much akin to the Scythians, being a noble cousin race who had returned to their homeland after some centuries in the Mesopotamian and Persian regions. As related by Herodotus, their language was very similar, as were their dress and expert horsemanship, but unlike the Scythians they had both male and female warriors. The Sarmatian body armour was constructed from small scale-like plates of bronze, which tarnished to a greenish colour, giving the warriors the appearance of lizards or, as the 2nd-century Greek geographer Pausanias referred to them, dragons.[2]

In the main, the Sarmatian cavalry consisted of formidable horse archers and spearmen, but they were also the upholders of a ritualistic sword culture developed by the Scythian iron-working tribe of the Kalybs, from which derived the name of

King Arthur's legendary sword Caliburn (*Kalyburn*) or Excalibur (*Ex-Kalyburn*). One of the best known tales of Scythian sword mythology tells of the hero Batradz who, having received his death wound, asked his companions to throw his sword into a lake. Twice they pretended to do so, but Batradz knew they had failed to comply, whereupon they conceded to his wish, at which the water turned blood red and became very turbulent.[3] In Sir Thomas Malory's famous 1485 *Morte d'Arthur*, it is the knight Bedevere who twice disobeys King Arthur in the same manner, but when eventually casting Excalibur into the water, the sword is mysteriously caught by the Lady of the Lake.

The original military banner of the Sarmatians was a dragon, whose bearer was called the Draconarius,[4] but this emblem was subsequently purloined by the Roman legions of Emperor Marcus Aurelius following a victory over the Sarmatians of Hungary in AD 175. Afterwards, many captives were transported to Britain, where they were seconded to the Roman forces of Lucius Artorius Castus, becoming the first heavy cavalry unit in the Imperial army.[5] Then, following the Romans' withdrawal from Britain in AD 410, regional leadership reverted to tribal chieftains, one of whom was the Welsh king, Vortigern of Powys. Having assumed full control in the region by AD 418, Vortigern was elected Pendragon of the Isle *(Pen Draco Insularis)* seven years later, reintroducing the Sarmatian banner device which has since become the famous Red Dragon on the national flag of Wales.[6]

King Arthur of the Britons

Because of the similarity of Arthur's name with the middle name of Lucius Artorius Castus, it has been suggested by some that a possible third-generation successor and Cornish-born namesake of Castus could perhaps have been the historical King Arthur. Such a premise is based upon the notion that the name 'Arthur' derives from the Latin *Artorius*, but this is a complete misconception of a type which is persistently fuelled by those who endeavour to diminish the heritage of the native Britons against that of the temporary Roman overlords.

During the latter days of the British Empire it became common practice to uphold and proclaim the concept of Imperial regimes at a time when some twenty-five percent of the world's area and population were under British dominion. Hence, although the conquest of England by the troops of the Roman Empire was an unwelcome and hostile invasion, it became portrayed (especially from Victorian times until very recently) as a classic high-point of cultural classroom teaching, as if it were something to be admired. Similarly the earlier Macedonian Empire of Alexander the Great (356-323 BC) was upheld as a positive landmark in world affairs. To cement this Imperialist dogma firmly into place, students in British schools were indoctrinated with the classical works of Homer and Virgil in their prerequisite studies of old Greek and Latin languages, while music and all else of any cultural worth was said to have emanated from ancient Greece, Macedonia or Rome. Today, of course, we know better but, during this extended period of Imperial teaching, numerous characters such as King Arthur and even Jesus were put forward as having been the sons of Roman officers.

In contrast to what is so often written, the Arthurian name was far from having a Roman origin and it certainly did not derive from the Latin *Artorius* (meaning 'bear like'). The name was wholly Irish, emerging from the Scythian-Milesian 'Artúr'. The 3rd-century sons of King Art, for example, were Cormac and Artúr. The Romans never conquered Ireland and Irish names were not influenced in any way by the Romans. In fact, the root of the name Arthur can be found as far back as the 5th-century BC, when Artur mes Delmann was King of the Lagain. It was long afterwards that Augustus Caesar established the Roman Empire in 44 BC and, by AD 476, the Empire had crumbled to extinction in the West, nearly a hundred years before King Arthur of the Britons was born.

In a previous chapter we saw how the *Volsunga* story of the heroic pulling of Odin's sword from a tree found its way into Arthurian romance, just as did the Sarmatian legend of throwing Batradz's sword into the lake. From these two sequences alone, it can be seen that the popularized stories of King Arthur were compiled from various aspects of traditional lore. In the same way, the literary character of Arthur was also a composite, fashioned from the deeds of numerous historical figures. This has led many enthusiasts to home in on these individuals in their competitive endeavours to portray each of them in turn as the historical King Arthur. Not only has the great-grandson of the Roman, Lucius Artorius Castus, been cited in this regard, but so too has Arthun, son of the Roman governor Magnus Maximus (*c.*AD 400), along with the Welsh lords Owain Ddantgwyn of Powys (*c.*AD 500) and Athrwys ap Meurig of Gwent (*c.*540), while even the 6th-century Saint Armel of Brittany is now on the list of presumed Arthurs. The fact remains, however, that the best way to find an historical king called Arthur is to look for an historical king called Arthur—not to latch on, without justification, to someone with a vaguely similar name and to claim that some chronicler must have changed that name in telling the story.

The subject of King Arthur is dealt with at length in *Bloodline of the Holy Grail*,[7] wherein it is explained that, in spite of all the literary speculations as to whose name might perhaps have been changed to Arthur by the romancers, and notwithstanding all the regional tourism propaganda of today, the fact is that there were actually two royal Arthurs recorded by that very name in the 6th century.

One was Arthur, Prince of Dyfed,[8] who was installed by St. Dubricius in the year 506 even though he and his forebears were hated enemies of the native Welsh people. He was descended from disinherited Déisi royalty, who had been expelled from Ireland in the late 4th century. When the Roman troops left South Wales in AD 383, the Déisi leaders came across from Leinster to settle in Dyfed. This Arthur features as a notorious tyrant in *The Lives of the Saints* (in the tales of St. Carannog and others) and he is generally portrayed as a troublesome regional interloper who often battled with the indigenous kings and led incursions into Gwynedd and Powys. Doubtless this was the Arthur to whom the 10th-century *Annales Cambriae* (Annals of Wales) and the 15th-century *Red Book of Hergest* (a collection of Welsh folk-tales) refer when relating their account of the Battle of Maes Camlann. This was fought in 537 south of Dinas Mawddwy, and was the battle in which the Welsh Arthur apparently died.

What is certain is that, in the year 600, another royal Arthur fought at the subsequent Battle of Camelyn, west of Falkirk in Scotland—a battle which is detailed in the *Chronicles of the Picts and Scots*. This other Arthur was undoubtedly the famed king of the Grail stories. Not only was he proclaimed High King and Sovereign Commander of the Britons in 574, but he was the only recorded Arthur ever born as the son of a Pendragon. He was Prince Arthur of Dalriada, the son of King Aedàn mac Gabràn of Scots, and his mother was Ygerna d'Avallon whose own mother, Viviane del Acqs, was the recognized Lady of the Lake. Born in 559, he was the only royal Arthur with a son named Modred and a sister called Morgaine (referred to in Royal Irish Academy texts as 'Muirgein, daughter of Aedàn in Belach Gabráin'),[9] just as related in the Grail legends. Arthur's primary seat was at Carlisle—the City of the legion (Caer leon)—from where he controlled the military defence of the English-Scottish border country. Arthur mac Aedàn is cited in St. Adamnan of Iona's 7th-century *Life of St. Columba*; his kingly installation by the druid Merlin Emrys is recorded in the *Chronicle of the Scots*; his legacy is upheld by the Celtic Apostolic Church of Scotland, while famous conflicts (including the Battle of Badon Hill)[10] with which he is traditionally associated are recorded in the *Chronicles of Holyrood* and of *Melrose*, the Irish *Tigernach Annals* and the *Books of Leinster* and *Ballymote*.

The Pendragon Deceit

Because of King Arthur's senior descent in the Albigensian lines of the Milesian Scots and the Grail House of Avallon del Acqs,[11] his tradition suffered in just the same way as that of Mélusine, with various kingly dynasties claiming their fictitious descents from him. Arthur's father was Aedàn mac Gabràn, the 18th Pendragon of Britain, who was dubbed the 'Terrible Pendragon' (the *Uthir* Pendragon) by the Welsh cleric Geoffrey of Monmouth in his 1135 *Historia Regum Britanniae* (*History of the Kings of Britain*). In compiling this work, Geoffrey was commissioned and funded by Robert, the Norman Earl of Gloucester, with an express requirement to cement High King Arthur into the English tradition even though, being Scottish, he did not feature at all in the *Anglo-Saxon Chronicle* of England. And so, with Geoffrey's strategic restyling of King Aedàn, the new and very convenient fictional character of Uther Pendragon was introduced into a supposed historical account.

It was known that, prior to her marriage to Aedàn, Ygerna del Acqs had been the wife of Gwyr-Llew, Dux (warlord) of Carlisle—and so Geoffrey literally spirited this man to England's West Country, calling him Gorlois, Duke of Cornwall, whose castle was said to be at Tintagel. The fact that there was no castle at Tintagel until the first was built by Richard, Earl of Cornwall, in the 1100s was ignored in the intrigue; as was the fact that there were no dukes in 6th-century England (this territorial title first came into England with William the Conqueror). In the context of Geoffrey's *Historia*, the Norman purpose was well served with Arthur of Tintagel perceived as a champion against the Saxons, whose King Harold had actually been ousted by William of Normandy in 1066.

The next significant mention of Uther Pendragon did not occur for more than 300 years when, quite suddenly, he had a second useful purpose for yet another dynasty. From 1154 the

Norman kings had given way to the House of Plantagenet in England and, since this house was a junior offshoot of the royal *Pict-sidhé* of Anjou, their heritage was seemingly on a firm enough footing—at least as far as they were concerned, even if the senior Anjou branch did not agree. However, in 1485 the Plantagenets were usurped by the son of the Earl of Richmond who, as King Henry VII, established the new reigning House of Tudor. The problem was that, although having gained the throne of England from Richard III by might of the sword at the Battle of Bosworth Field, Henry's only justification for kingship extended, via his mother, through four generations to a son of Edward III Plantagenet (1327-77), and there were many contenders with far less tenuous claims.

In preparation for this, two plans had been actioned some years before to cement a better legacy for the Tudors, whose family were originally from Wales. In the first instance Henry's English mother, Margaret Beaufort of Somerset, had commissioned a notorious Warwickshire rogue called Thomas Malory to write up a new version of the tales of King Arthur, while Henry had set the second plan in motion by making substantial financial and land grants to a certain Welshman called Richard of Mostyn. What Henry required in return was a new, specially concocted family genealogy—a comprehensive chart which showed his descent from the ancient Kings of Wales: a table so stirring that it would outstrip the heritage of the House of Plantagenet.

As it transpired, Malory (who spent the better part of his life in various prisons for theft and conspiracy) died in Newgate debtors' gaol before his Arthurian work, the masterpiece *Morte d'Arthur,* was printed in London by William Caxton in 1485. By that time, the extensive Welsh family tree had also been prepared—a thoroughly spurious set of documents which are still tactically used by some today, and which have become known as the *Mostyn Manuscripts.*[12] Although the *Mostyn's* given key line of Tudor descent is essentially in order, it is surrounded by invention on all sides, embracing every impressive name in the book, including King Arthur and the wholly fictional Uther Pendragon. The absurd thing is that the manuscript sections were not properly cross-referenced, as an outcome of which they actually disagree with each other. One section, for example, gives Uther as the son of Emrys ap Gwertheuyr, while another shows him as the son of Kustenhin Goronog. In one succession Uther supposedly has a Welsh father, while in the other his father is reckoned to be Cornish! Regardless of these discrepancies and the deceitful nature of the overall document, the *Mostyn Manuscripts* are held in high regard by many who strive to keep all eyes away from the historical Arthur of Scots Dalriada. They prefer, for the sake of regional tourism or other vested interests, to maintain his contrived tradition in South-west England or Wales.

To compound the duplicity of the Tudor supporters, a further chart emerged in 1604 with Uther Pendragon in a prime position as the son of the Welsh King Constantine the Blessed (AD 433) and cousin of Emyr Llydaw, Prince of the Bretons. This was yet another expensive commission but, although purposely fabricated, it has been used on many occasions in the most illustrious works. Even latter-day Manuscript Society professors have been seduced by this genealogy because it seemingly emanated from a source of such high authority. This chart in its multi-page format was issued in the form of a book by a cleric styled 'King's Advocate' ,[13] but what the public were not told was that it was actually commissioned by the late Queen Elizabeth I Tudor's Secretary of State, Sir Robert Cecil, Earl of Salisbury.

The Rings of Camelot

In 1542 King Henry VIII Tudor's antiquary, John Leland, identified an Iron Age fort in England's West Country as the Arthurian Court of Camelot. His vague justification for this was that the South Cadbury site was near to the conveniently named

River Camel in Somerset but, previously, according to Malory's writing, Camelot had been located some distance to the east at Winchester in Hampshire. To this very day, an 18-foot (5.5 metres) Arthurian-style Round Table hangs at Winchester Castle Hall. It has been Carbon-14 dated to about the middle 1200s, but its symbolic paintwork is an addition from Tudor times.

Latter-day excavations at Cadbury during the 1960s unearthed the remains of a Dark Age feasting-hall but, appealing as it was to the tourist industry (and it has been well used in this regard), there was absolutely nothing to associate the camp with King Arthur. Indeed, more than forty constructions of a similar age and type have been found in the immediate area, and there are many more elsewhere in the country.[14]

The first mention of Camelot as the Royal Court of King Arthur was in the tale of Lancelot: *le Chevalier de la Charrette*, produced by Chrétien de Troyes in about 1135. Historically, the place first recorded as Camelot—or more correctly Camulot (Camulodunum to the Romans)—was the ancient city of Colchester in the East of Britain, and the name derived from *camu-lot* meaning 'curved light'. This was the seat of the very first Pendragon of Britain, King Cymbeline (AD 10-17), who governed the Catuvellauni and Trinovante tribes from the most impressive hill-fort in the land. In the writings of Chrétien de Troyes, King Arthur had an alchemical Court of curved light (*camu-lot*) at Carlisle in the Cumbrian North Country. Likewise, the 13th-century *High History of the Holy Grail* (sometimes known as *The Perlesvaus*) refers specifically to Carlisle, which also features in the French *Suit de Merlin* along with the British tales of *Sir Gawain and the Carl of Carlisle* and *The Avowing of King Arthur*.

Carlisle (often called Caruele or Cardoil in the old Scots records) was the historical military base of Arthur mac Aedàn. It was also located just south of the Caledonian Wood, where Préssyne took Mélusine and her sisters in the 8th century to gaze upon the homelands of the *Pict-sidhé*, while the ruin of a later Pendragon Castle stands nearby at Kirkby Stephen.

The British Pendragons (Kings of Kings) were not successive heirs in any particular family, but were appointed from an overall Gaelic royal stock by a druidic council of elders. In descent from the Sovereign Wood Lord, Beli Mawr, the office fell to his great-grandson Cymbeline, and then to his son King Caractacus (AD 46-54).[15] Subsequently, the position was held by various regional kings including Caradawc of Gwent, Coel Hen of Carlisle and Maelgwyn of Gwynedd until, after more than six centuries of tradition, Cadwaladr the Blessed of Wales (654-64) was the last Pendragon.[16]

Throughout the centuries, much has been made of the harmonious concept of King Arthur's Round Table, and many thousands of people travel from all over the world to see the replicated specimen at Winchester, albeit just a wonderfully conceived ideal. Notwithstanding this, the true legacy of this Arthurian tradition lies not in the table itself, but in the knights who sat at the table, for these noble emissaries represented the most important aspect of ancient lore by presenting themselves as a living, iron-clad Ring.

In all representative custom of the fairy culture, from the earliest Scythian kings and lords of the *Tuadhe d'Anu*, their social structures were firmly centred upon designated seats of assembly which became known as Fairy Rings. These royal seats, from Scythia to Ireland, were known as *Raths*, which denoted 'round' or 'circular'. On that account, the Round Table of Arthurian romance was designed to symbolize this Fairy Ring concept and, in accordance with traditional Ring lore, the land fell into waste and chaos when the power of the Ring was usurped by virtue of Queen Guinevere[17] being unfaithful to Arthur with Lancelot. Resultantly, from that moment when the unity of the Ring was severed, Arthur's knights were destined to roam the Wasteland in search of the wound-healing Holy Grail. Thus it is that, although not generally portrayed as such, the Arthurian mythos (along with the *Volsunga Saga* and *Der Ring des Nibelungen*) presents one of the most powerful of all Ring Cycles.

There are, in fact many similarities between the Arthurian, Volsunga and Nibelungen traditions—similarities which occur also in Tolkien's *The Lord of the Rings*. Treating the heroes Sigurd and Siegfried as one for the sake of comparison, it is first apparent that Arthur, Sigurd and Aragorn are all rightful heirs to kings who are slain in battle, and they are each deprived of their heritable entitlement.[18] All three, through some circumstance of childhood, are raised in a fostered and protected situation while, during their individual periods of youthful upbringing, they each skilfully achieve some notable feat which brings them to the attention of unwitting onlookers, thereby paving the way to their future prominence. In the course of their stories, all three are connected with the magical sword culture wherein their weapons are not only enchanted but named—Arthur's sword being *Caliburn/Excalibur*, Sigurd's being *Gram*, and Aragorn's being *Narsil/Andúril*. Similarly, Arthur, Sigurd and Aragorn each have ageing, supernaturally empowered mentors in the forms of Merlin, Odin and Gandalf.

In romantic terms, we have Arthur and Guinevere, Sigurd and Brynhild, Aragorn and Arwen. But, as pointed out by David Day in his fascinating study of *Tolkien's Ring*, each of these women is a tragic heroine. A clear fact about Ring Cycles is that, unlike most children's nursery tales, they do not have happy endings because a 'cycle' cannot, in practice, have an end of any description. Guinevere becomes a nun and dies in a convent having lost her queenly status; Brynhild commits suicide after losing her godlike Valkyrie powers, and Arwen dies a mortal death, having sacrificed her elven immortality. The moral of each of the stories is, in essence, the same since the awesome creative power of the Ring is such that it also carries an inherent destructive curse which becomes operative, without mercy, when a trusted guardian confronts it with a lie.

What actually transpires in the Arthurian tale to make it somewhat unique is that it conjoins the fates of two separate Rings, with each being reliant upon the other. In the first instance, as mentioned, we have the iron-clad Ring of Knights who sat at the Round Table to provide the Fairy Ring of Assembly. However, this Ring is wholly dependent upon the sanctity and security of the golden ring with which Arthur was married to Guinevere. This was the Ring of Arthur's original quest and, to win his Queen, he had to prove himself in physical and strategic contest against fearsome opponents. Having become a worthy suitor, Arthur pledged the golden ring, in return for which Guinevere's emblematic dowry, granted to the Court of Camelot, is the iron-clad Ring with its Knights swearing their allegiance to the royal marriage. And so, the Rings become interdependent and the power of either one must fail if the other fails, for the marital and knightly oaths are part of the same compact.

The irony of the tale is that neither Ring is actually the first to break, as would have been the case if Guinevere's infidelity were conducted with an outsider. What transpires is that Lancelot breaks the iron Ring of which he is an integral part, while he and Guinevere simultaneously break the golden Ring. Thus, each sacred Ring is immediately destroyed by the breaking of the other.

9

The Land of Elphame

Spirit of the Wise Ones

Apart from the fairies, pixies, elves and leprechauns of history, there are others of the Shining Ones who are also said to inhabit the magical Land of Elphame; they are the sprites, goblins and gnomes.

The definition 'sprite' means no more nor less than a 'spirit person'—one of the transcendental realm of the *Sidhé*. The original Sprites were the ancient Scythian ghost warriors, who painted their bodies grey-blue to look like corpses when they entered the battlefield. In Shakespeare's *A Midsummer Night's Dream*, Puck is described as a sprite and is identified with a certain Robin Goodfellow who, in traditional English wood lore, was said to be a mischievous goblin. In the Teutonic doctrine of old Germany, forest sprites were called *hodekins*[1]—the 'hod' syllable of which was a root of the legendary name Robin Hod, Hode or Hood.

The 'goblin' description stems immediately from the Germanic word *kobelin*, and kobelins were mine-workers or those who worked underground. In the context of the Ring culture, goblins were attendants of the Raths (the royal seats, or sacred mound dwellings), wherein they were custodians of the wealth and wisdom of the ages, being essentially treasurers and archivists. It was their role as guardians of the treasures which led to their nominal distinction being used in association with banking, as in the Gnomes of Zurich. The word root is in the

Greek equivalent of *gno,* from which we derive 'gnosis' (knowledge) and 'gnoble' (noble). The gnomes and goblins were, in practice, a branch of the noble fairy race who performed specific duties as stewards or wardens and were venerated as the Wise Ones. They were held to be the champions of the ancient *gnosis,* and it was by way of this noble (or *gnomic)* distinction that the fairy race in general was referred to as the Gentry. This was particularly the case with the druidic castes of the *Pict-sidhé* (the pixies) and the *Behn-sidhé* (the banshee) who were the ultimate custodians of law and society.

The land of Elphame is, in essence, that same realm to which Hylas was transported by the water nymphs, and it is figuratively entered by way of a sacred pool which constitutes the *daleth*—the doorway to the Light. The process is likened to a form of death (the demise of ego and desire, which are primary aspects of the mortal plane) from which one is effectively born again, so as to become focussed in a different dimension. In the earliest Nazarene philosophy (before Rome began to subjugate the original Albigensian believers) Elphame was likened to the kingdom of heaven, with Jesus stating (John 3:3), 'Except a man be born again, he cannot see the kingdom of God'.

In the Qabalistic tradition, *daäth* (whence, death) represents the higher knowledge,[2] while in ancient Egyptian lore, the terms equivalent to 'tomb' and 'womb' were considered interchangeable and mutually supportive as routes to that knowledge.[3] Hence, the Elphame state is one of residing 'within this world', but not being 'of this world' by virtue of one's higher spiritual and intellectual achievement. It is not the same as being dead, but it is beyond the normal state of life in a gnostic dimension which came to be known as 'undead'. This was the intuitive realm of the fairy gold and, as we shall see, of the enigmatic vampire.

Since water was reckoned to mark the boundary between Elphame and the mortal world it has long been the instrument of baptism, similarly representing the conjunction of Heaven and Earth. Streams and rivers often formed the boundaries between camps and kingdoms, thereby becoming paramount in folklore as places of conflict or confrontation where champions would battle for passage across a ford or bridge as, for example, in the meeting of Robin Hood and Little John. The apocryphal story of Saint Christopher carrying Jesus across a river is also echoed in the tale of Robin Hood and Friar Tuck, when each demands to be carried through the water by the other. Eventually, after some carrying and mutual dunking, Robin emerges by grasping a broom tree, while Tuck pulls upon a willow. Allegorically, the broom was the tree of Mélusine (the *planta genista,* from which derived the name Plantagenet), and the willow was representative of druidism, while both had Witchcraft connotations associated with the elven race, as in the willow cult of Wicca and the Witches' broom.

The colour associated with the transcendent state was always green: the colour of Nature and of Robin's Greenwood garb. It was the paramount colour of the elves and of the stag of the *Caille Daouine,* while also being the Gaels' colour of death. Green is additionally associated with the goddess Venus and with fertility, which is why it is not ritually used by a Christian Church establishment that places itself and its God above Nature. It is the colour of wisdom and the colour of Elphame, both of which are inaccessible to the uninitiated, but are envied and sought by them, as a product of which green has become the traditional colour of envy. In Church doctrine, it is perceived that the abiding fairies of Elphame were once the proud Queens of the Gauls (the House of Viviane del Acqs) who 'carried on dancing' and were wickedly impertinent in the face of Christ and the Apostles.[4] On that account, these princesses of the *Albi-gens* were designated as sorceresses and, by bishops' decree, are apparently doomed until the Day of Judgement!

The Elf King

Returning now to Mélusine, the Lady of the Fountain, we can see how the Elphame (fairyland) tradition which exists within her recorded history became so much a part of Shakespeare's *A Midsummer Night's Dream*, and how it was that the playwright's Oberon, King of the Fairies, was drawn from this very same family history.

According to the *Oxford English Dictionary*, the word 'over' evolved from the Middle Teutonic *ober*. This, in turn, stemmed from the Old European *ubar*, which derived from the Scythian *uper*. The word 'reign' (as related to a king or queen) similarly emerged from *rgn* (ron). Hence, *Ober Rgn*—as in Oberon—is a derivative style for Over Reign. Alternatively, as *Ober On* it would relate to Over Light. These are the equivalents of *Ard Rí* (High King) or *Albe Rí* (Shining—or Elf—King).

In the Gaelic and Pictish tongues, the two names which derived from these titular distinctions were Arthur and Albrey. As we saw earlier, *albi* (as in *Albi-gens*, from the language of old Provence) relates to the elven race of the Shining Ones, in consequence of which the Shining King is also the Elf King. Shakespeare's choice of Oberon was, therefore, an apt name, as would have been the equivalent Albrey or its variants Alberigh, Alberic or Aubrey. Indeed, the Dwarf Lord of the *Nibelungenlied* Ring Cycle was called Alberic, and a medieval French romance entitled *Huan de Bordeaux* similarly features the Dwarf King Alberon.[5]

The significance of all this is that a prominent 11th-century descendant of Princess Mélusine and Rainfroi de Verrières en Forez (whom she married in about 733) was Aubrey the Elf King, from whom sprang fourteen generations of Court Chamberlains to the Kings of England.

To begin, we should first consider the *Plantagenet Chronicles*[6] and the publication entitled *Ex Libris Comites Oxensis*[7] which concerns England's Earls of Oxford. This work relates to Maelo, Duc d'Angiers (the son of Mélusine and Rainfroi), commander-in-chief of Charlemagne's Imperial Army and the husband of Charlemagne's half-sister Berthelde. Their son in succession was Maelo II, Comte de Guisnes d'Anjou.

From the very fact of these two generations alone, we can immediately see why Charlemagne was uncertain about his kingly office, for here during his own lifetime was a very apparent senior line of succession. The only difference was that Charlemagne had the Pope and the spurious *Donation of Constantine* on his side, while the elven line of Verrières en Forez did not.

Charlemagne's father, King Pepin was, as we have seen, a usurper, who happened to marry the daughter of a Merovingian princess, thereby cementing Charlemagne's own position. But, as confirmed by the Duc de Castries of the Académie Française,[8] Charlemagne was actually born illegitimately and he was not legalized until his father's marriage to Princess Bertha some time afterwards. As Charlemagne knew only too well, kingship was carried in the matrilinear blood (the mitochondrial DNA) of the female line and his half-sister Berthelde (a daughter of the deposed Merovingian King Childeric III and a bloodline princess in her own right) had married into a succession with more seniority than the Merovingians themselves. She had married into the *Pict-sidhé* strain—the line of Mélusine and Préssyne, with its direct descent from the *Caille Daouine* and the Scythian Lords of the *Tuadhe d'Anu*. From that moment in time, it would not matter who was married to whom in the generations to follow; what mattered was that Charlemagne's military commander had more right to be King of France than Charlemagne had himself. It is hardly any wonder that he was reluctant to accept the Imperial crown and that Pope Leo had to foist it upon him without warning.

While the Carolingian dynasty of Charlemagne persisted as Kings of France, the generations of Prince Maelo and Princess Berthelde continued in parallel as Counts of Anjou and Guisnes. By 987, however, the Carolingian line had expired and a new dynasty reigned in France, bringing its Capetian kings more than ever under papal control with a new Oath of Allegiance sworn more fervently to the Church and its bishops.[9]

Soon after that, Maelo's eighth generational descendant, Aubrey the Elf King, was in England, where he built Castle Hedingham in Essex by way of a land grant from William the Conqueror. He also became Lord of Kensington, establishing his Earl's Court where London's current Earls Court exhibition and conference centre now stands. Then, by 1110, he was styled King's Chamberlain to Henry I of England, thus beginning a stunning reign of generational Chancellery that was to continue for more than 500 years through the successive Norman, Plantagenet, Tudor and Stuart reigns.

The Celtic Myth

By studying the roots of various words in common use today, it can be seen that the details of our past are not just drawn from recorded history, but also from etymology and linguistic semiology. In many instances this provides a more honest approach since words are more understandably derivative, whereas written or artistically portrayed history is generally produced by its victors and is, therefore, always a matter of opinion and interpretation. Tudor artists, for example, added a spinal hump to the portrayals of the Plantagenet King Richard III,[10] who was defeated and usurped by their own King Henry VII—a thoroughly fictitious disfigurement which has now become generally accepted as a fact. Such is the nature of recorded history, with each successive dynasty telling the 'authorized' story of the former, while the Church's monks and clerics have shrouded everything beneath their own contrived veil of dogmatic vested interest.

Words, on the other hand, do not often suffer for their own sake; they simply evolve into their different forms, with their varying phonetic adjustments as certain letters and syllables receive greater or lesser emphasis in different regions, with *dd* becoming 'th', for example, or *ph* becoming 'f'. The word 'fairy' is a very good example of such an adjustment. Generally speaking, it conjures an image of a tiny, gossamer-winged sprite—but this is a late interpretation based upon a determined propagandist teaching. If we trace the word back into ancient time, we discover that it emanates from *phare*, which has precisely the same root as *pharo* (pharaoh), meaning a Great House and being specifically identified with a kingly dynasty.

Another much misused description, tossed around at will today, is the word 'Celtic', which is used as if it applied to a cohesive cultural group who lived in some long lost era of wondrous achievement. This is a modern age myth. The Celtic definition springs from *keltoi* or *celtae*—Greco-Roman words which meant 'strangers'—any strangers. In Latin records, it was applied to non-Latin speaking Italians, Spaniards and the Gauls—but it was never used for the people of Britain, who were simply called Britons.[11] Neither would any people of Britain ever have called themselves Celts because they were obviously not 'strangers' to themselves and each other. It was not until as recently as the 18th century that certain French writings began to refer to the Bretons, along with the Cornish, Irish, Manx, Welsh and generally Gaelic speaking peoples, as Celts—thereby enveloping them into a fanciful society that had never existed in history.

When Britain was entrenched in her Industrial Revolution, a whole new burgeoning middle-class of *nouveau riche* emerged—a breed of employers who spared nothing to equate their newly acquired chieftainship with an imaginary past Golden Age. They immersed themselves in a romantic Celtic illusion, while venerating the one-time tribal priestess Britannia in their attempts to cement some worthwhile ancestral status and to justify their dominant labour intensive regime. It was during this period that the true nature of Gaelic and ancient British culture became rudely idealized to the point that we have now inherited a thoroughly fictitious Celtic myth.

Fortunately, modern archaeology and a more realistic approach to knowledge acquisition has now revealed a picture of Gallo-British society which is far more satisfactory. We now know that the popular image of the noble Celt—the tall blonde, blue-eyed warrior or the flaxen-haired maiden—is not Celtic at all. This demeanour is of a Nordic and Caucasian stock, while the red-haired, green or pale-eyed Gaelic types were of noble Scythian origin. They were the fairies of the *Tuadhe d'Anu* who, as confirmed by Herodotus, were identified as the Royal Scyths. Since they perceived themselves as a kingly race overall, they operated an egalitarian caste system wherein they had levels of active function but no levels of individual class distinction—and it was from this that the Scottish Clan system evolved.

Fairy Magic and a Garter

Fairies are generally associated with an ability to perform magic of one sort or another, and this too had its historical base in the culture of the *Tuadhe d'Anu* priests and kings. Their magic was essentially geared to outstanding gifts of perception, along with their ability to access the wisdom of Elphame. In this regard, the maintenance of a pure blood stock was very important to the Scythians, and intermarriage with those outside the fairy caste was forbidden—doubtless, often lamented. There are many stories which relate to the love of fairy princesses for mortal men, thereby portraying the forlorn aspect of this tradition. From this custom we also inherit the tales of the 'changelings'—fairy children who were said to have been stealthily substituted for identical mortal children in order to progress the fairy blood into the outside world—or in order that the fairy princesses might bring some mortal blood into their own fold.

Changeling stories were especially prevalent in the Highlands of Scotland, where any number of family ills and misfortunes were blamed upon innocent children who were suspected of being malevolent changeling fairies. To test for such infiltrators, the home-fires were piled high with burning peat, and children were suspended over the flames in metal baskets. If a child was truly a changeling, it was thought that he or she would escape up the chimney.[12] But if this did not happen (which it never did), then the youngsters emerged with horrific burns that supposedly made everyone happy! It was said that cobblers, on the other hand, looked forward to the possibility of receiving a changeling child since they felt that fairies were very good shoemakers!

A well-known locational aspect of the fairy culture (particularly among the druidic caste) was the stone circle or Fairy Ring. This was, in practice, how the concept of local churches began, as against the more majestic style of city temple. The very word 'church' stems from *circe*, meaning a 'ring', having the same root as circus, circle and circuit. The common use of the stone circles fell into decline, though, when those of the pagan fraternities who identified religion and spirituality with Nature, were denounced as witches by the Roman Church. Being very much of a woodland stock, the majority of the denounced Scythian types took even more purposefully to the hills and forests in medieval times, to live as custodians of the Greenwood in the *Caille Daouine* fashion.

In their pursuit of farming, the fairy race operated a system of settled agriculture centred upon at least four Raths in a region, whose lands were farmed in rotation. This was rather like today's crop rotation programmes, but instead of moving from field to field, or from strip to strip, the Scythian method was to rotate between whole Rath-centred districts, with each one in turn supplying produce to the others. As each district's farmland was vacated for the next, the farmers would move in unison at certain times of the year. In Ireland it is still claimed that these trooping fairies can be seen, riding in stately sunset processions, especially on the eves of Beltane and Samhain.[13]

Often associated with pagan stone circles and fairy rings is that other, often cutely portrayed, item of the elven domain: the mushroom. There are, in fact, two types of mushroom with the fairy distinction, the first of which is that called the *Mousseron* or Fairy Ring. This is the attractive little parasol topped mushroom which tastes as good as it looks and is one of the first to appear in springtime.

The other, though wildly colourful and often used in fairy depictions, is somewhat less acceptable at the table because of its uncomfortable hallucinogenic effects. This is the Fly Agaric or *Amanita Muscaria*—the familiar red-topped fungus with the white warty protuberances. These are generally regarded as being extremely poisonous, but are actually used (in accordance with certain controlled recipes) in North-eastern Asia, just as wine and various stronger intoxicants are used in other lands. The narcotic effect of the protuberances on these mushrooms is somewhat violent, producing an amount of dizziness and nausea in the early stages, coupled with some vomiting within the first hour. Subsequently, the hallucinogen moves into a calmer operation and was often used in tribal ceremonies, being largely responsible for many emergent stories of people flying or shapeshifting into animals and birds. This particular mushroom was reckoned to be a divine instrument of immortality and was very much a part of the Scythian fairy culture.[14]

It is said that many things are exaggerated while under the influence of the *Amanita Muscaria* and that a person stepping, say, over a straw would react as if stepping over a log. Thus, it was felt that any person or warrior who was able to confront and combat the mentally determined obstacles presented by this hallucinogen, would find the real trials of life minimal in comparison. It was, they figured, a method of mental cleansing which enabled one to depose unwanted demons, resulting in a free and uncluttered mind. Certain amphibians such as the cane toad exude a very similar chemical from nodes situated beneath their skin. The fables concerning princesses kissing frogs and toads, which turn into handsome princes, are representative of a profound change in perception caused by the creature's highly potent, mind-deceptive intoxicant. The *Amanita Muscaria* are, therefore, called 'fairy mushrooms' not because the fairies sat on them, but because they ate them to demolish fears, complexes and inhibitions.

Despite the Church's hatred of the Albigensian fairies, the bishops' demeaning propaganda could never overcome the fact that people clung tightly to the notion that they were wondrous to behold. They called them the 'fair folk' and their grace was often associated with that of the swan, while the image of the Grail maiden was always one of beauty and poise, even if she were perceived as seductively dangerous like the *Leanhaun Sidhé*. It was precisely this concept which the English poet John Keats (1795-1821) used in his famous poem, *La Belle Dame Sans Merci*. On first meeting the beautiful damsel, the poem's knight relates,

> I met a lady in the meads,
> Full beautiful—a faery's child.
> Her hair was long, her foot was light,
> And her eyes were wild.

But, having then ridden off with the fairy maid to rest upon the hillside, the knight's story suddenly begins to chill as the truth of his seduction is realized:

> I saw pale kings and princes too;
> Pale warriors, death pale were they all.
> They cried, 'La Belle Dame Sans Merci
> Hath thee in thrall'.

So powerfully evocative was this beguiling twelve-verse poem that four artists of the subsequent Pre-Raphaelite movement, Sir Frank Dicksee, Frank Cadogan Cowper, John W. Waterhouse and Arthur Hughes, made paintings with the very same title.

Within the priestly orders of the fairy society, various forms of garment (now generally associated with Witchcraft) were worn to signify status and accomplishment. The most magical of these, when worn by a woman, was reckoned to be the garter. These, in lace or other coloured materials, were worn upon the leg and were confidentially displayed at weddings, where the competitive status of brides' garters (still a custom of bridal apparel today) often caused women to come to blows.[15] The significance of the garter was that it was a personally secreted item of the Fairy Ring tradition, the design of which denoted the wearer's status in pagan society.

The garter tradition is especially significant in England where, from 1348, the nation's most auspicious sovereign order was founded upon it: The Most Noble Order of the Garter. Popular tradition has it that King Edward III noticed some of his courtiers laughing when the Countess of Salisbury dropped her garter in their presence. Apparently, Edward picked up the item and affixed it to his own leg, saying, '*Honi soit qui mal y pense*' (Shame to him who sees wrong in it). From this small beginning emerged the Noble Order, taking the King's chance comment as its motto (sometimes alternatively translated as 'Dishonoured is he who thinks ill of it'). Edward, whose jousting tournaments became widely renowned, selected twenty-four knights with whom to inaugurate the Order along with himself and his son, the Prince of Wales. The romantic tradition of King Arthur's Round Table was Edward's model for knightly equality, and the chivalric code was based upon the premise that the knights would protect and do honour to ladies.

A knight visits a fairy house
From a 16th-century woodcut

Although a charming story, it hardly provides a good enough base upon which to found a sovereign order and the account, as it stands, makes very little sense. It gives no reason why the courtiers should 'think ill' or 'see wrong' in the fact that the Countess wore a garter. The true importance, however, was in the very existence of the garter itself, not in the Lady's embarrassment at losing it, as the tale seems to convey. What the garter proved was that the Countess was not only a member of the old religion, but a high priestess of her Order (or as the Church might call it, her coven). With her fairy garter unintentionally revealed in public she was, therefore, in imminent danger from the bishops whose reign of persecution and execution of heretics was well under way. Edward's presence of mind, in donning the item himself, might have made light of the immediate situation, but by forming twelve knights for himself and twelve for the Prince of Wales, he effectively created two sovereign covens of the required thirteen each to protect the Countess thereafter. He then had 168 garters attached to his mantle which, together with the one on his leg, totalled 169, knowing full well that 13 x 13 covens under the auspices of the King of England was more than any superstitious Church bishop would ever dare to challenge.

It is very doubtful that any Garter Knight of today would give a thought to the fact that he belonged not to an originally Christian Order, but to a contrived witches' coven. It is even less likely that he would be very happy to consider himself a deputy fairy but, in practice, that is the truth of it.

10

The Lily and the Rose

Living Waters

In the Old Testament's *Song of Solomon*—a series of esoteric love Canticles between a lost bride and her king—the bride, while lamenting for her husband, relates that she is 'the rose of Sharon and the lily of the valleys'.[1] In order to get the best from this English passage, it is necessary to understand that there were no roses in biblical Palestine; the word (*chabazzeleth*) which became 'rose' in translation actually meant a 'bulb'—described in the *Oxford English Dictionary* as 'a fleshy, leaved storage organ'.[2] The rather more romantic 'rose and lily' symbolism (said by the Church to represent beauty and purity) was, nonetheless, later applied to Jesus's mother and to other princesses of the Grail bloodline.

The theme returns in the *Sleeping Beauty* nursery tale of Briar Rose who, in the same manner, is lost to her prince, while the lily (in its *fleur de lis* form) was introduced as the royal emblem of France by the 5th-century Merovingian Fisher Kings.

Apart from the flower representations, there are various other allegorical remarks in the *Song*, because of which there have been centuries of debate in both Jewish and Christian circles as to the canonical merit of this particular lyric poem. Some, such as the 2nd-century Rabbi Akiba, considered it 'a most holy work', while others reckoned it was too erotic for religious comfort. There have also been disputes as to who the bride and groom of the *Song* might have been. Jewish opinion has long favoured them as emblematic of Jerusalem and Jehovah, while the orthodox Christian view (in spite of the wholly inappropriate time frame) nominates the Church and Jesus. The more traditionally held belief is that the couple in question were undoubtedly King Solomon and one of his many wives (as featured in 1-Kings 11:1-3). However, given that the *Song's* authorship is uncertain, and since the style is reminiscent of the sacred marriage texts of the goddess Inanna and her shepherd-king Dumuzzi in old Mesopotamia, it could well have a far more ancient origin.[3]

Following the lily and rose entry, the *Song of Solomon's* bride states, 'My beloved is mine, and I am his: he feedeth among the lilies'. To which the king responds,[4] referring to his queen as 'a fountain of gardens, a well of living waters'.

The queens of the Grail succession were often likened to lilies, which are themselves bulbous plants. For this reason, the *Song's* bride (herself a 'lily' of the Lilithian strain) relates that she is the 'bulb' (storage organ) of Sharon, whose husband 'feedeth among the lilies'. Additionally, we have the familiar fountain association which, in the Old Testament language of Leviticus (20:18), is directly associated with menstruation.

In ancient times, the Sharon definition related to a dimensional plane called the Orbit of Light (*Shar On*),[5] a realm of advanced enlightenment associated with the alchemical science of Star Fire gold—a lunar extract of the Anunnaki goddesses. Now, we can see a more direct connection with the enticement of 'living waters', while the Plane of Sharon appears very similar to the more lately defined land of Elphame. This was the magical realm into which Hylas was drawn by the seduction of the water nymphs who were portrayed among the water lilies.[6] We are, therefore, once again in the esoteric dimension of the *Rosi-crucis*—the Dew-cup or Cup of the waters (*Calice del Acqs)*, while also in the *du Lac* Star Fire realm of the matrilinear bloodline of the Shining Ones.

The Essence of Kali

The original Star Fire nectar of Mesopotamian times (often called the Plant of Birth) was fed to the kings of the early Grail bloodline until about 1960 BC. From that time the Anunnaki goddesses were replaced by high priestesses called *hierodulai* (Greek: sacred women), a word which, when transposed via medieval French into English, became 'harlot'. The menstrual flow-er (she who flows)[7] was the designated 'flower', customarily represented as a lily or lotus—and she was the 'bulb' (the storage organ—or biblical 'rose') of the essential essence.

Menstruum, contains the most valuable endocrinal secretions, particularly those of the pineal and pituitary glands which heighten the qualities of intuition, awareness and perception. In this regard, the lunar extract was dignified as being the ultimate *Ritu* (Truth)—the rich food of the matrix. Indeed the very word 'ritual' stems from this Sanskrit definition of the ancient Star Fire ceremony, while the word 'secret' has its root in this same science of glandular *secret*ions.[8]

Sanskrit was the ancient holy language of India, dating back in the Vedic (divine knowledge) tradition to about 2000 BC. Hence, it is apparent that there was a cultural migration between India and Mesopotamia (present-day Iraq) in those far distant times, with Persia (Iran), the home of the original Zoroastrian Magi, doubtless included as well. Whatever the case, it is the Sanskrit words which survive in relation to the Lily and Rose customs, and this has happened by virtue of the long-prevailing esoteric art known as Tantra (meaning 'continuity'). This art is regarded not just as mystical, but as magical, and it is often aligned with Yogic practice although being historically much older, dating back several millennia.[9]

In the old Tantric environment, the Goddess (or *Shakti*) was considered to be the major source of spiritual power—a power held within her transcendental fluids, called the *Rasa*.

Interestingly, this same word was used by alchemists in much later medieval times to describe the 'first matter' of the alchemical process, and has also been used as a descriptive term for the emotive sentiments aroused by music and art.[10]

There is, to some measurable degree, a recognizable Tantric revival taking place in the West today, but many of the books compiled in western languages are remarkably silent with regard to certain aspects of the truly ancient traditions.[11] This has resulted in a significant downplaying of the Goddess culture in an environment which, for all its supposed New Age freedoms, is apparently restrained by the prevailing one male God establishment. And so, as with all things seemingly based upon old lore, a type of acceptable pseudo-Tantra has evolved in much the same way as the Celtic myth emerged in the 19th century.

A primary key to the original Tantric practice was undoubtedly the *Shakti* ritual of the Divine Mother: the power of consciousness and spiritual evolution. This was the magical province of the *Suvasini* priestesses—the Fragrant Ladies who were the sacred flow-ers or lilies (lotus flowers). They were the equivalent of the Star Fire maidens who produced the menstrual *Rasa*—the designated Vehicle of Light.

This lunar essence was rich in endocrinal secretions such as melatonin and serotonin—hormones that are mirrored in some of the supplements provided by today's organo-therapy establishment. The difference is that today's supplements are obtained from the desiccated glands of dead animals and, as pointed out some while ago by Kenneth Grant, Outer Head of the Ordo Templi Orientis, they lack the truly important elements which exist only in live human glandular manufacture.[12] By the same token, the secretions obtained from the temple priestesses for kingly ingestion were mundane by comparison with the original Anunnaki Star Fire, but they were clearly held in high esteem until the practice finally expired at around the time of King Solomon.

The secretions collected from the sacred priestesses (or goddesses) in the Temple of the Divine Mother, were called *Kalas* (units of time),[13] while the womb (the *Kalana*) was regarded as a measurer of lunar time. In this regard, the goddess of time, seasons, periods and cycles was Kali, who was said to be 'black but beautiful'—a description used of herself by the bride in the *Song of Solomon* (1:5). The English word 'coal' (denoting 'blackness') stems from her name via the intermediate words *kuhl, kohl* and *kol*. Even the word 'alcohol' comes from this root, being originally *al-kuhul*—a rectified substance used in medieval alchemy. The monthly Kalas were also responsible for the derivation of the word 'calendar' *(kalandar)*.

In the Hebrew tradition, the heavenly Bath-kol was called the 'daughter of the voice', and the voice (*vach* or *vox*) which called from the blackness was said to originate during a female's puberty. The womb was resultantly associated with the voice (the *qoul* or *call*) and Star Fire was said to be the oracular word of the womb, with the womb itself being the utterer or *uterus*.[14] In the earliest schools of mysticism, the symbol of the 'Word' (or the Logos) was the serpent: a venerated emblem of the Holy Spirit that moved upon the face of the waters.[15]

In the British Museum collection is a fallopian-designed Mycenean Star Fire chalice from the 13th-century BC,[16] and the Kala practice appears to have still been operative in the days of King David of Judah (*c*.1000 BC). Even the Bible's book of 1-Kings (1:3-4), in reference to David, mentions the Shunammite *Suvasini* priestess Abishag, who 'cherished the King, and ministered to him, but the King knew her not'. The Shunammites (or Shulamites) were from the border town of Shunem (alternatively Sölam) in the Valley of Jezreel, and it is to this same Abishag that the *Song of Solomon* (6:13) refers, saying, 'Return, return, O Shulamite; return, return, that we may look upon thee'.[17] Thus, although the tradition of the *Song* is undoubtedly of greater antiquity than Solomon's era, its text was certainly contrived to suit the Tantric sentiments of that age.

The Fountain of Youth

Something which becomes very apparent in the Tantric writings is that the Kalas collected from the Suvasini (or *hierodulai*) are discussed in the plural and, therefore, relate to rather more than the Star Fire menstrual extract alone. They are mentioned in relation to various chakra centres of spiritual power, but appear to fall into two distinct classifications: the first associated with blood (the Star Fire) and the second related to water.[18] In essence, they were the traditional equivalents of the previously cited *du Lac* and *del Acqs* traditions in Grail lore—with the first related to the rose (or bulb) and the second to the lily (or lotus). As defined in Tantric teaching, it is the lotus which collects the dew; consequently the Grail is represented by the *Rosi-crucis*: the Dew-cup.[19]

The realm of the water maidens—those designated mermaids or ladies of the fountain such as Mary Jacob and Mélusine—is truly the enlightened land of Elphame, and these priestess-queens of the waters were generally portrayed in an environment featuring scallop shells (as, for example, in the *Birth of Venus* paintings mentioned earlier). It was not uncommon for scalloped edges (known as 'engrailing') to be used on Albigensian devices. This symbolism is prominently used, for instance, in the Grail Cup skirt design of Caravaggio's *Mary Magdalene* portrait. The open cup-like shell was extremely important in the Kala tradition since it was directly associated with the collection of a Suvasini fluid which the Sanskrit mystic song of the *Sama Veda* (*c.*2000 BC) refers to as *Amrita*—a divine nectar of sacred waters known as the 'fountain of youth'.[20] In ancient India the receptacle for collecting Amrita was not a shell, but a curled triangular bhurja (birch) leaf.[21]

The fact that some women, when sexually excited, produced the Amrita fluid was recorded by the Greek philosopher Aristotle in about 350 BC.[22] It was subsequently mentioned by the famed

2nd-century Greek physician Galen; then later by the 16th-century Roman anatomist Renaldus Columbus and the 17th-century Dutch physician Regnier de Graaf.[23] In the early 20th century, the English psychologist and biologist Henry Havelock Ellis wrote in his *Studies in the Psychology of Sex* about female secretions which contained certain values from cerebral-spinal fluid and from the endocrine glands, especially from the pineal and pituitary bodies.[24] However, owing to the austere climate of the post-Victorian era and the subsequent World Wars, the matter was ignored until Amrita was investigated again in 1950 by the German obstetrician Ernst Gräfenberg. Since then, various eminent doctors have pursued this area of research, which was brought to the fore on a global scale at the 1997 World Congress of Sexology in Valencia, Spain.

Amrita, the once highly valued but long neglected 'ambrosia of immortality', was said, in the fairy tale tradition, to be manifested by the Grail princess when she was 'awakened' by her prince (as symbolized in such stories as those of Briar Rose and Brunhilde).[25] According to modern laboratory study and immuno-histochemical research, the fluid appears to be produced in part by the urethral Skene's glands, which have often been likened to the male prostate.[26]

But why is the Amrita Kala in particular a traditionally designated 'fountain of youth'? This is a term often used today in relation to the enzymes which build, heal and detoxify the body. Without enzymes, seeds would not sprout, fruit would not ripen, and life would not exist.

In recent years, the PSA protein (secreted by the epitheliel cells of the male prostate gland, and also found in Amrita fluid[27]) has revolutionized the world of prostate cancer research. It is produced by normal and abnormal prostatic tissue, but it is especially relevant since normal and benign cells produce different PSA levels than are evident in malignant tissue.[28] The PAP antigen is similarly used to determine the extent of carcinoma. An interesting fact about cancerous cells is that they contain the enzyme known as *Telomerase*, which is itself reckoned to be the 'enzyme of immortality', identified in the *Science* journal of January 1998 as the Fountain of Youth.[29]

Studies at the University of Texas Southwestern Medical Center, along with separate corporate research findings, have determined that Telomerase has unique anti-ageing properties conducive to active longevity.[30] Healthy body cells are programmed to divide many times during a lifetime, but this process of division and replication is finite, so that a non-dividing state is ultimately achieved, and this is a crucial factor of ageing. The division potential is controlled by caps at the end of DNA strands (rather like the plastic tips on shoelaces), and these caps are the *telomeres*. As each cell divides, a piece of telomere is lost, and the dividing process terminates when the telomeres have shortened to an optimum and critical length. There is then no new cell replication and all that follows is deterioration.

Laboratory experiments with tissue samples have now shown that application of the genetic enzyme Telomerase can prevent telomere shortening upon cell division and replication. Thereby, body cells can continue to divide far beyond their naturally restricted programming (just as do cancer cells, which can achieve immortality through being rich in this substance). Telomerase is not usually expressed in normal body tissue but, apart from being present in malignant tumours, it is also apparent in germline cells and in mature male and developing female reproductive cells.[31] It seems, then, that somewhere within our DNA structure is the genetic ability to produce this anti-ageing enzyme, but the potential has somehow been 'switched off'. As recently mentioned by Robert F. Newbold of the Department of Biology and Biochemistry at Brunel University, "Isolation (molecular cloning) of this gene will enable its fine structural integrity to be determined in a wide variety of human malignancies and, therefore, its role as an important target for inactivation in human cancer development to be established".[32]

Clearly, the sciences of DNA study and genetic research in general are very much the emergent projects of recent times, while specific investigation of the Telomerase enzyme is a development of the last few years. On that account, when specific Amrita analysis tests were conducted from 1981 to 1997, Telomerase was not on the list of tested-for substances. Shortly before the publication of this book, two of the eminent doctors concerned with the ongoing research stated, respectively, "I have never heard of it in connection with this subject", and "No one has ever tested for this to my knowledge". Nevertheless, given that Amrita is a part-product of the Skene's glands (the said 'female prostate'), with some identifiably male characteristics, and since Telomerase is evident in mature male reproductive cells, perhaps the time is now opportune to test for this particular enzyme.

It has already been suggested by scientists that, if Telomerase can afford immortality to malignant tumours, then its introduction into normal human cells could well have the effect of extending life-span. No fewer than ten current genetic researchers, to the author's knowledge, have agreed that "The ability to extend cellular life-span, while maintaining the diploid status,[33] growth characteristics and gene expression pattern typical of young normal cells, has important implications for biological research, the pharmaceutical industry and medicine".[34]

In the Tantric tradition, Amrita—the dew of the lily and nectar of the goddess—has been called 'the ambrosia of immortality' and the 'fountain of youth'. Telomerase, seemingly a recent discovery, has been called precisely the same. Perhaps they are indeed one and the same. Modern science has a way of following a long and arduous path to finally catch up with things that were common to ancient knowledge, albeit the reasoning and technical understanding might be different. What we perceive today as scientific technology might once have been considered magic but, whatever the label, the magic remains. What was lost for so long to a world overwhelmed by logic was the ultimate simplicity of the unpretentious spiritual art.

Grail of the World

Gradually, throughout the Eastern and Mediterranean regions, the Star Fire and Amrita traditions drew to a close, ceasing to be general aspects of the kingly culture. There appear to be no references in this regard onwards from about 900 BC, but that is not to say the perpetuation of a lost ideal did not live on in ceremonial and ritualistic custom. In Mesopotamia and Egypt, a new logic had begun to prevail from around 1960 BC—a logic based upon the premise that instead of taking hormonal supplements from an outside source, one might do better to ingest substances that made one's own glandular system work overtime. By this method, heightened powers of awareness, perception, intuition and the general qualities of leadership were individually controllable by activating specific endocrinal glands, thereby absorbing self-made secretions into the bloodstream. The primary ingested substance which made this possible was monatomic (single atom) high-spin gold, which has a distinct effect upon the pineal gland and was known to the Sumerians as *shem-an-na* or 'highward fire-stone'.[35]

A normal atom has a screening potential around it—a positive screening produced by the nucleus—and the majority of electrons going round the nucleus are within this screening potential, except for the very outer electrons. The nucleus goes to the highward or high-spin state when the positive screening potential expands to bring all of the electrons under the control of the nucleus.

These electrons normally travel around the nucleus in pairs—a forward-spin electron and a reverse-spin electron. But when these come under the influence of a high-spin nucleus, all the forward-spin electrons become correlated with the reverse-spin electrons. When perfectly correlated, the electrons turn to pure white light and it is quite impossible for the individual atoms in the high-spin substance to link together. On that account, they cannot naturally re-form as metal, and the whole remains simply a white powder. This is created by striking metallic gold, under strictly controlled conditions for a pre-calculated time, with a designated high-heat. In modern laboratory research this is done by means of a DC (direct current) arcing process.

Barat-Anna, the goddess of light and fire who, from around 1750 BC, was known to the Kassites and Phoenicians as the Lady of the Fire-stone, was identified with Diana of the Nine Fires. Her symbol was the *Rosi-crucis*—a red cross within a circle—which formed the original base for the British Union Jack flag some time after she became known in the West as Britannia.

The tradition of the Fire-stone goddess was later superficially adopted in Rome, where the Vestal Virgins (six at a time) served for individual periods of thirty years before the days of Roman Christianity. The word *vesta* derived from an old oriental stem meaning 'fire'—hence, matches are today still called 'vestas'. Vesta was originally a Trojan goddess of fire[36] and burning tapers were used in the veneration of her eternal flame, kept alive by the Virgins within the temple. It was this custom which, in time, the Roman Church subverted to become the familiar candle-lighting ritual of modern 'churchianity'. The taper rituals of Vesta were closely linked to the old torchlight procession of Persephone of the Underworld which prevailed especially in the South of France. Even today, the harbour at Marseilles, by the ancient Basilica of St. Victor, gleams for a night every February as the people gather in ceremony with their long green candles of fertility.

And so the ancient tradition of the physical Star Fire—the Vehicle of Light and the Rose of Sharon—gave way to the symbolism of torchlight, just as Barat-Anna was portrayed holding her torch of fire on the early Phoenician coins. The Lily symbolism of the Waters of Amrita remained, however, and it was Persephone, daughter of the goddess Demeter, who provided the cultural cross-over in Greek mythology. Springs, wells, streams, fountains and all water sources emanating from below ground are associated with the tears of Persephone. It was she who, on her return from the Underworld, brought new life and springtime to the barren waste of winter, enchanting the land with the bulbous (*chabazzeleth*) flowers: the crocuses of the field and lilies of the valley.

Today, Marseilles continues its vestige of the old heretical customs, even if now conducted beneath a veil of approved Christianity to appease the *status quo*. Not only was the South of France steeped in the traditional lore of Mary Magdalene, who was resident there from AD 44 until her death in AD 63,[37] but the official language of Marseilles was actually Greek until the 5th century.[38] In both the Persephone and Grail traditions, Mary gained the title *la Dompna del Acquae* (Mistress of the Waters), with her descendants becoming the House del Acqs.

From the time that Chrétien de Troyes wrote his 12th-century tale of *Ywain and the Lady of the Fountain*, in which the Lady corresponds to *la Dompna del Aquae*—the heritage of *del Acqs* (with its Amrita 'lily' symbolism) has persisted in Arthurian literature. The legacy remained central to the theme and was always directly related to the Magdalene image, as was the alternative heritage of *du Lac* (with its Star Fire 'rose' affiliation). By a natural course of events, in the 15th-century writings of Sir Thomas Malory, the two styles were assimilated to become 'Lady of the Lake' and various Magdalene descendants, such as Nimuë and Viviane d'Avallon, the mother of Lancelot, were dubbed with this significance.

Returning now to the *Song of Solomon*, and bearing in mind the lily and rose symbolism that prevailed through the centuries, we can see how the lost bride of the Old Testament *Song* is directly comparable to the New Testament character of Mary Magdalene.

The *Song of Solomon* is itself reminiscent of the ancient Sumerian marriage texts and it specifically contains the bridal refrain: 'While the king sitteth at his table, my spikenard sendeth forth the smell thereof' (1:12). This alludes to the sacred marriage rite of the *Hieros Gamos*, whereby the Messianic bride prepared her royal bridegroom's feast and anointed him, while he sat at the table, with the ointment of spikenard—a fragrant root oil from the Himalayas.

When compared with the Gospel texts of Matthew 26:6-7, Mark 14:3 and John 12:1-3, it can be seen that precisely this marital act is repeated in accordance with the old custom. Quoting from the Gospel of John, we read:

> Then Jesus six days before the passover came to Bethany. ... There they made him a supper, and Martha served, but Lazarus was one of them that sat at the table with him. Then Mary took a pound of ointment of spikenard, very costly, and anointed the feet of Jesus, and wiped his feet with her hair; and the house was filled with the odour of the ointment.

In both the Matthew and Mark accounts, it is further explained that while Jesus was at the table, Mary also anointed his head with the spikenard. There is absolutely no doubt whatever that, in keeping with the time-honoured ritual, the Bible tells us in no uncertain terms that Jesus and Mary Magdalene were married on that auspicious day in Bethany.[39] By all reckoning then, whoever the said bride of the original *Song of Solomon* might have been, Mary Magdalene was (from that moment in AD 33) the designated rose of Sharon and lily of the valleys—to be subsequently referred to by the medieval troubadours of Provence as the Grail of the World.

11

Robin of the Greenwood

Herne the Hunter

There is an old tale goes that Herne the hunter,
Sometime a keeper here in Windsor forest,
Doth all the winter-time, at still midnight,
Walk round about an oak, with great ragg'd horns;
And there he blasts the tree and takes the cattle
And makes milch-kine yield blood and shakes a chain
In a most hideous and dreadful manner:
You have heard of such a spirit, and well you know
The superstitious idle-headed eld
Received and did deliver to our age
This tale of Herne the hunter for a truth.

The tale of Herne the Hunter, referred to here in Shakespeare's *The Merry Wives of Windsor,*[1] relates back to the Plantagenet era of King Richard II (1377-99) when he was resident at Windsor Castle in England's royal county of Berkshire.

At that time, the King's Master of the Hunt was said to have been Herne and, while he and the King were in the Royal Forest one crisp morning, they came upon a noble white stag in a clearing. Instead of running though, the stag turned to face the huntsmen and their hounds, charging forward at Richard's horse and throwing the King to the ground. Perceiving his lord's danger, Herne rushed between the animal and the King, whereupon he was severely injured by the stag's antlers before he could make the kill with his blade. So badly damaged was

Herne that everyone knew he must die. But then a stranger on a black horse appeared from the woods, announcing that he was Philip Urwick, a wise man with the power to heal the ailing hunter. Urwick then affixed the stag's antlers to Herne's own head and carried him away.

At length, Herne returned to the Windsor Court, where he was given treasures and a royal apartment, but this made his fellow huntsmen jealous to the extent that two of them claimed that, while in the wise man's custody, Herne had become an exponent of evil magic. So convincing were their lies that King Richard was obliged to dismiss the hunter, who was discovered later that night hanging from a large oak tree. By the morning, though, the oak had been struck by lightning and Herne's body was gone.

It was said that, from that day forth, the ghost of Herne appeared at each midnight in the winter-time, riding his steed through the lanes of Windsor Forest, with the stag's antlers upon his head. Meanwhile, the King's other huntsmen became quite incompetent without their Master, at which they consulted the wise Urwick. He advised them to go to Herne's Oak with horses and hounds, where they could join with Herne once more, to ride forever in the night skies, hunting the souls of the dead.

Following Shakespeare's reference to Herne in 1598, the tourists flocked to Windsor, where a suitable tree was established as Herne's Oak. Then, in 1893, the great and aged tree fell during a storm, but all was not lost because it was cut into thousands of small pieces that were sold as souvenirs. Later in 1906, King Edward VII planted another, which grew to become the Herne's Oak which exists today.

Diana and the Wild Hunt

The hounds which accompany the phantom Herne in his search for souls across the sky have often been called Gabriel Hounds because in old lore it was said to be the archangel Gabriel whose task it was to summon souls to judgement.[2] Gabriel and Herne are figuratively equated in a 13th-century stone relief portrayal by the church door at Stoke Gabriel in South Devonshire.

In the days before Herne, there were others who were said to lead the Wild Hunt, including the Norse god Odin and the legendary French Hellequin,[3] whose name derived from the Danish Ellerkonge, a variant of Elverkonge, meaning Elf King. The classic leader of the Hunt, however, was always the goddess Diana, whose night-riders were called the Furious Horde. Diana, in the Kali tradition, was another moon deity, whose sacred animal was the deer but, in strict terms, from her apparent origin in the 6th century BC, she was rather more of a wood nymph than a goddess. Her culture was consistent with the early *Caille Daouine* forest people of the *Tuadhe d'Anu* Ring Lords and, being of the fairy strain, she came under severe attack from the later Roman Church. Diana even fell victim to Vatican Law in 1140 when her said practice of 'flying without licence from God' was criticised in the *Concordance of Discordant Canons*!

Subsequently, her followers were hideously persecuted by the witch-finders after the 1486 publication of the *Malleus Maleficarum* by the Dominican friars Heinrich Kramer and James Sprenger. With regard to Diana the Huntress, this evil work (better known as *The Hammer of Witches*)—obtaining its information from the *Concordance* and from an earlier 9th-century regulation called the *Canon Episcopi*—stated:

> It is also not to be omitted that certain wicked women, perverted by the devil and seduced by the illusions and phantasms of demons, believe and profess that they ride in the night hours on certain beasts with Diana, the heathen goddess, and an innumerable multitude of women, and in the silence of the dead of night do traverse great spaces of the earth.[4]

It was actually from the Dianic cult of the Wild Hunt, along with the Church's many allusions to the women sky-riders of the night, that the concept evolved of witches riding on familiar animals or broomsticks.[5] In the *Tuadhe d'Anu* tradition of the Fairy Rings of Assembly—as mentioned in connection with King Arthur's Round Table—the followers of Diana were associated with a particular Ring dance, with a designated leader who took the swirling Ring every which way. This was based upon the dance in which Apollo led the nine Muses of Greek mythology, and it is from this ritual that the common expression 'Ring-leader' derives.[6]

Prior to Inquisitional times in the Middle Ages, Diana the Huntress was never regarded as a witch, but she did represent the self-empowered woman, which was reason enough for the Church to condemn her tradition. She was the designated Lady of the Wildwood and her lunar aspect was directly related to the customary rites of the moon-dew, celebrated every twenty-eight days. As pointed out by the great master of the goddess culture, Robert Graves, moon-dew was a magical definition associated with menstruation.[7] Hence, Diana's true heritage was essentially that of the lily and rose culture of the Tantric *Shakti*.

Diana was the personification of the positive aspects of lunar forces in the ancient *Suvasini* tradition, but to the bishops of the Christian establishment she was a nocturnal temptress. In the late 15th century, the brutal Dominican Grand Inquisitor Tomâs de Torquemada declared Diana to be the emissary of the devil, calling her the Goddess of the heathens.[8] Because of her supposed night-riding with the Wild Hunt, she was said to be a Lilithian succubus who would take sexual advantage of men in their sleep. In those days a seductive succubus of the *nyghte* was called a *maere* and Diana was said to be a man's worst *nyghte-maere,* from which derives the English word 'nightmare'.[9]

From the distant era of the Dark Ages, Diana was reckoned to rule all the wild forests of Europe and, in England, she was the recognized Mistress of the Greenwood. Because of this, with her quiver of arrows always to hand, her cult became firmly embodied in the legends of Robin Hood.

The Horned One

The fact that Robin Hood was himself a designated Ring Lord and historical Elf King of the *Albi-gens* is something which we shall discuss in due course. Meanwhile, it is appropriate to consider his newly perceived connection with Herne the Hunter—a modern perception which was popularized in the British 1980s TV series *Robin of Sherwood*. In this series, Robin, seemingly in the 12th-century days of King Richard the Lionheart, was impossibly portrayed as a son of the stag-headed Herne, who supposedly did not exist until the 14th-century! The tradition portrayed here, however, is not that of Herne, but of the far more ancient stag-god Kerne, or Cernunnos, known as the Horned One.

The legacy of Cernunnos was prevalent in Gaul and Gaelic Britain where, as a god of fertility, abundance and the Underworld,[10] he was said to be born at each winter solstice, to marry the Moon Goddess at the Maytime Feast of Beltane, and to die at the summer solstice. Thus, he represented the continuing cycle of birth, death and rebirth—a base culture of all pagan belief which also found its way into the birth, death and resurrection faith of the Christian religion. A particularly fascinating depiction of Cernunnos, at the Cluny Museum in Paris, is carved upon an old altar-stone and shows the Horned One with a Ring-torc (neck bracelet) hanging from each of two short antlers to signify his noble status.

In Inquisitional Europe, Cernunnos was, as might be expected, vilified by the Church along with Pan, the Arcadian god of the shepherds. Pan was usually portrayed with certain features of a goat and was another designated Horned One (horns and antlers being physical characteristics which the bishops and friars associated directly with the devil). For this reason, both stags and goats were regarded as being satanic.

The stag was the totem animal of the *Tuadhe d'Anu*, while the goat was originally symbolic in ancient Egypt as Khem of

Capricorn. In about 2800 BC, the zodiacal goat was introduced by the 2nd-dynasty Pharaoh Raneb in the Nile delta city of Mendes.[11] Khem is, therefore, sometimes referred to as Khem of Mendes, whose emblem was an inverted pentagram, reckoned to be a truly magical device. And so, both the goat and the five-pointed star became figures of demonology to the medieval Christian Church.

In the esoteric tradition, the pentagram was indicative of enlightenment and was associated with the pre-Jewish Sabbath, a ritualistic period of reflection and experience outside of general toil. For this reason, Khem of Mendes was called the Sabbatical Goat, from which derives today's use of the word 'sabbatical' in academic circles. In representation, the two uppermost points of the star are the horns of the goat. The two downward-sloping side-points represent the ears, while the single base-point is the chin and beard.[12]

Khem of Mendes: the Pentagram and the Sabbatical Goat

From Genisis–The First Book of Revelations, *courtesy of Chevalier David Wood*

When a pentagram is seen in this inverted (male) position, Khem is personally identified by an emerald jewel set centrally at the meeting of the horns. When turned about, the pentagram achieves its female status with the uppermost single point becoming the head in a Goddess representation. The horizontal side-points are now arms, while the twin points (once the horns) are now at the base, being the legs of the goddess, with the emerald jewel established in the vulval position. Sometimes, the inverted Khem representation is shown with flames rising (between the horns) from the sacred jewel; these flames are called Astral Light. But when established in the Goddess position, the uterine flames are identified as Star Fire, the universal lunar essence of the Tantric *Kala*.

The Legend of Robin Hood

Along with King Arthur in Britain's legendary popularity, and equally sought after by countless researchers, is Robin Hood—the 12th-century outlaw and lord of the Greenwood, who robbed from the rich and gave to the poor. Robin's romantic adventures have survived the centuries as ballads, plays, books, poems and films, while his story has endured any number of adaptations and literally expanded versions from what might appear, as so many have concluded, to have been an original May Day tale. Despite all the unsuccessful research and speculative authorship, however, the reality is that, just like King Arthur, Robin Hood is not difficult to discover.

As far as can be ascertained from extant texts, Robin Hood was first mentioned by that name in 1377, when the English writer William Langland wrote an attack against corruption within the State and Church entitled *The Vision of Piers the Plowman*. In this work, he stated: 'I kan noght parfitly my Paternoster as the preest it syngeth, but I kan rymes of Robyn

Hode and Randolf Erl of Chestre' (I cannot perfect my Lord's Prayer as the priest sings it, but I can rhymes of Robin Hood and Randolph, Earl of Chester).

Subsequently, stories of Robin and Little John emerged from the woodwork, while Friar Tuck first appeared in a tale known as *Robyn Hode and the Munke*, from about 1450. Then, while related plays were being performed around Britain, various written and remembered accounts from the early 1400s were conjoined at the English press of Wynkyn de Word to become the famous *Geste of Robyn Hode*.[13] This was published in about 1500, commencing:

> Lythe and listen, gentlemen,
> That be of frebore blode,
> I shall tell of a gode yem
> His name was Robyn Hode.

By this time Much, the Miller's son, and Will Scarlett (originally, Will Scarlock) had joined the company, and Maid Marion made her first appearance in a Whitsuntide play of around 1500, passing into the traditional May Games where she and Robin were entwined as King and Queen of the May. This liaison was based upon a French pastoral play from about 1283, entitled Robin and Marian.[14] It is from these May Games that Robin's stag association can be seen to emerge. Also, the stag dons his red summer coat in May and the staghorn moss is sometimes called Robin Hood's Hatband.[15] Another connection was the Abbots Bromley Horn Dance, which originated in Staffordshire.[16]

The May revels, with their maypoles and ritual courtship, began on 1 May as spring became summer, progressing through the fertility Sabbat of Beltane (the Bale-fire) on 5 May. This was the festival of Mary the Gypsy, 1st-century mermaid, sacred harlot and love cultess, in whose Marian representation the May Queen would be united with the Horned One: the Lord of the Greenwood,[17] known to the *Pict-sidhé* as the Forest King of the *Caille Daouine*. In all this, as might be expected, a principal deity

Robin of the Greenwood

was Diana of the Moon—the Huntress Queen of the Wildwood and a fertility goddess in her own right.[18]

By the late 1500s, William Shakespeare had joined the Robin Hood fraternity, with a passing mention of Robin, John and Scarlett in *Henry IV* and a more romantic allusion to the popular Robin of the Greenwood in *As you Like It* (Act 1, Scene 1) which relates, in reference to a banished duke:

> They say he is already in the forest of Arden, and a many merry men with him; and there they live like the old Robin Hood of England: they say many young gentlemen flock to him every day, and fleet the time carelessly, as they did in the golden world.

Prior to the *Geste*, in stories such as *Robyn Hode and the Munke*, Robin was portrayed as a somewhat violent fellow in a series of blood-and-thunder adventures, but his image mellowed as time went by, along with which his apparent benevolence increased. In the *Geste*, however, Robin's place of residence is confusing, being cited firstly in Barnsdale, Yorkshire, and then in Sherwood Forest, Nottinghamshire—a discrepancy which is explained by the fact that at least two quite separate legends were conjoined for this particular account. It was also in this lengthy tale that the Sheriff of Nottingham appeared as Robin's primary enemy, along with the corrupted men of the Church:

> These bishoppes and these archebishoppes,
> Ye shall them bete and bynde.
> The hye sherif of Notyingham,
> Hym holde ye in your mynde.

When referencing the various stories, Robin seems to have belonged to many parts of England, from the northern Scottish Borders down to Exeter in the South West. Even his apparent time frame was confusing in the various plays and texts until 1521 when the Scottish historian John Major, who had spent many years at the University of Paris, stepped into the arena. Returning to teach at the University of Glasgow, he presented his *History of Greater Britain* which announced that Robin's era was indeed the late 12th-century Plantagenet period of King Richard I and King John. It also became apparent in Major's *History*, which had been compiled in France, that Robin Hood was a chieftain of some standing, with the text referring to him as a 'Dux' (noble warlord).[19] Later, Richard Grafton, King's printer to Edward VI in 1549, also referred to Robin's noble dignity in his *Chronicle at Large*, styling him Earl Robert, while also mentioning the confiscation of his lands by the Crown.

Subsequently, in two Elizabethan tragedies written in 1598, Shakespeare's contemporary, Anthony Munday, cited Robin as the rightful Earl of Huntingdon, establishing him once again in the reigns of Richard I Plantagenet and his brother John.[20] Some time after this, Dr. William Stukeley (1687-1765), a Lincolnshire member of the Royal Society and the Society of Antiquaries, maintained that Robin, Pretender to the Earldom of Huntingdon, had also been known as Robert Fitz Odo (Fitz Oath or Fitzooth), but in endeavouring to discover his lineage, he assigned Robin to the wrong family, as a result of which many have sought to discredit Stukeley's original discovery. This was most unfortunate for, in fact, his initial finding was entirely relevant.

Later, a principal player in the Robin Hood saga was Sir Hans Sloane (1660-1753), a physician, naturalist and antiquary, whose document collection was among those upon which, at his death, the British Museum in London was founded by Act of Parliament. Among the now famous *Sloane Manuscripts* is one from around 1600, which not only confirms Robin's date of birth as being in the year 1160, but also associates him with a place called Locksley.[21] It does not explain where Locksley was, although it has long been generally accepted that such a spelling from around 1600 would more likely relate to a 'Loxley' spelling of later times. And so, with the 18th-century awareness of this *Sloane Manuscript*, the old Yorkshire tradition came back to the fore since there was a village by that name just north-west of Sheffield.

It was not until 1864 that the truth of Loxley became known when it was discussed by the historian, playwright, Somerset Herald and Pursuivant of Arms, James Robinson Planché. The Loxley of Robin Hood, he wrote, was not in Yorkshire; it was the village of Loxley in Warwickshire—very near to William

Shakespeare's home at Stratford-upon Avon. Moreover, the 1196 Register of Arms (during the reign of Richard I, the Lionheart) stated that 'Fitz Odo of Loxley is no longer a knight'.

The Historical Robin

In tracing the historical Robin Hood, it should be borne in mind that Robin is an alternative for the name Robert, while the Hood definition (originally Hod, Hodd or Hode) is an elfin style related to the Teutonic sprite Hodekin, who is associated in English lore with Robin Goodfellow (or Puck, as featured in *A Midsummer Night's Dream*).

The questions which immediately arise are: Was there a nobleman called Robert who was at odds with King John (1199-1216) and who would fall into the category of being a Wood Lord or Elf King? If so, was this nobleman somehow connected with Loxley in Warwickshire? Was he the legal Pretender to the Earldom of Huntingdon, a declared enemy of the established Church, and might he have legitimately used the name Fitz Odo or Fitzooth? The answer to each and all of these questions is 'Yes'.

Loxley lies a little south-east of Stratford-upon-Avon, close to the old Warwickshire-Oxfordshire border. Although the Earls of Warwick and Oxford appeared to get along well enough, border territories were always subject to some dispute in matters of management and general administration, while the Earls of Warwick and Oxford both had houses in each other's domain.[22]

The Earls of Oxford from July 1142 were the senior-line descendants of Princess Mélusine and Rainfroi de Verrières en Forez, beginning with Alberic, the son of Aubrey the Elf King and Comte de Guisnes. Alberic's second son became the 3rd Earl of Oxford in 1214 after the death of his elder brother—and this 3rd Earl's name was Robert, who had under wardship the lands and person of a certain William Fitzoath.[23] Robert's own family name of de Verrières en Forez had been shortened by that time to de Vere.

Cokayne's Complete Peerage (under 'Oxford') explains that in 1142 Robert's father had been granted a choice of royal charters by Empress Matilda (the mother of King Henry II Plantagenet), who expressed her preference that he should become Earl of Cambridge. However, located within this newly perceived Cambridgeshire territory was the minor-shire Earldom of Huntingdon which, at that time, was temporarily held by King David of Scots, who was not happy to become a vassal of the House of Vere. Resultantly, as a diplomatic expedient, Alberic elected to become Earl of Oxford instead.

The story of the Earldom of Huntingdon began in Saxon times with Harold Godwinson of Wessex, who later became King Harold II and died at the Battle of Hastings in 1066. (Too lengthy perhaps to detail in this Chapter, the Earldom's history is recounted in Appendix V, while Appendix VI explains the relevance of Robin's traditional Lincoln green.) The fact was that from 1090 Huntingdon was the heritage of the Flemish House of Vermandois (to which the family of Vere was related),[24] with King David of Scots becoming a joint trustee by way of marriage in 1114. At that time there were fierce conflicts between the Scots and English, as an outcome of which David saw his opportunity to claim Huntingdon for Scotland when his son Henry came of age before the young heir of Vermandois.

What Robert de Vere recognized after his father's death in 1194, was that Empress Matilda's 1142 offer concerning the Earldom of Cambridge had been very cleverly worded, even though his father had chosen not to act upon it. As detailed in the Register, Matilda had offered Cambridgeshire to Alberic 'unless that county were held by the King of Scots'—which of course it was not. The Scots claim applied only to the inherent Earldom of Huntingdon. On that account, when Alberic died (leaving his elder son, Aubrey, to succeed as the 2nd Earl of Oxford), Robert—not realizing that Oxford might become his one day when his brother died without a son—claimed his legal right of pretension to the Earldom of Huntingdon.

In the course of this, Robert's elder brother Aubrey, the 2nd Earl, was made Sheriff of Essex by King John but, while he was away in Ireland, England came under interdict of the Church and the King was excommunicated. All Aubrey's worldly goods, including his family's Hedingham Castle in Essex were confiscated, while the bishops (to whose doctrines King John had refused to submit) denounced Aubrey as 'an evil counsellor of the King'.

King John, unlike his crusading Catholic brother Richard I, was not prepared under any circumstances to cater to the whims of the clergy and their puppet barons, who were levying extortionate taxes from the people. Meanwhile, John endeavoured to hold the Plantagenet reins intact, maintaining his own courts of justice outside the Norman-implemented feudal structure, and this made him very unpopular with the feudal lords. In the event, after a row with the Pope over who should be Archbishop of Canterbury, John fell foul of that very document which bound the monarchy beneath the Pope whether he liked it or not—the *Donation of Constantine*. Consequently, the Church finally won the day at Runnymede on 15 June 1215, when John was obliged to sign the *Magna Charta* (Great Charter), formally vesting the powers of his kingship in the Church and the Norman barons.

The *Magna Charta* is probably the most devastating document ever to be thrust upon the people of England for it removed, for all time, the protection of their King and his officers, establishing a positive Church-fronted, feudal class system with no room for manoeuvre. But, this whole course of events has been wrapped in the usual veil of strategically portrayed Christian history, so that King John enters our schoolrooms as one of the nation's 'bad guys', while his hooligan brother, Richard I, who spent hardly any time in England during his supposed ten-year reign, is portrayed as a champion of virtue!

What happened after Aubrey de Vere lost his inheritance to the Church, and subsequently died, was that his brother Robert was left to fight for reclamation—not only of the Oxford title and

Castle Hedingham, but also for the forest lands settled within the Sheriffdom of Essex, which were under the stewardship of the family of Fitzoath. In this regard, *Cokayne* reports that on 23 and 24 October 1214, the castles of Canfield and Hedingham were restored to Robert, and that he paid 1000 marks for the return of his brother's lands and for the land and heirs of William Fitzoath.

For some reason which is not made clear in the records, Robert became one of the Charter Guardians after the King's signing at Runnymede—but his involvement in this was probably the price of his family's reinstatement. After signing the *Magna Charta*, however, King John issued a writ against Robert, charging him with treachery, whereupon Robert sought assistance from Prince Louis of France, urging him to wrest the Crown of England. But, along with the other twenty-four Charter Guardians (who were then dispensable), Robert was promptly excommunicated by the Pope since King John's actions were now sanctioned by the *Magna Charta* itself.[25] At this, John seized Robert's lands in Buckinghamshire, along with Castle Hedingham and the Oxfordshire estates,[26] leaving the depleted nobleman simply as Robert of Fitzoath.

It was at this stage in 1216 that, as the Register of Peerage relates,[27] the excommunicated Robert (Robin—descendant heir of Aubrey the Elf King, Steward of the Royal Forest, Heritor of Fitzoath of Loxley and claimant to the Earldom of Huntingdon) took up arms against King John, having been divested of his family entitlements by the Crown.

12

The Witches' Ring

Pagan Heritage

According to Christian Church doctrine, the cult of Wicca (generally dubbed Witchcraft), in conjunction with all ancient pagan beliefs, was 'satanic'. This, however, is quite impossible since, as we shall see, the demonic Satan was a 4th-century Christian invention and, even though the now general use of the word Wicca was itself a late arrival (reintroduced for the Witch Craft by Gerald Gardner of the Hermetic Order of the Golden Dawn in the 1940s),[1] the said pagan cults were operative long before Christian times. This is proven by the fact that, even though the Old Testament obviously makes no mention of Satan as an Antichrist, it does contain numerous references to witches and Witchcraft.

Even King Saul of Israel was reckoned to have consulted the wise Witch of Endor on the eve of the Battle of Gilboa (1-Samuel 28:7-25). The virtues of magical potions are also commonplace, as in the Genesis (30:14-16) story of Jacob (father of the Tribes of Israel), which relates that his wives made use of mandrake as an aphrodisiac love-philtre. Strictly speaking, the English Bible's use of the word 'witch' is incorrect and a better translation would have been 'woman of the oracle' but, notwithstanding this, the concept of women with talismans and special powers was clearly around long before Satan the Antichrist was invented.

As the Bible story progresses from its more ancient accounts to the period of the prophets in the 1st millennium BC, it becomes clear that sorcerers, wizards, witches, necromancers and the like were anathema to the emergent One God religion—not because they were satanists, but simply because they upheld the notion of natural forces and other gods, while performing magic without licence from the 'chosen' God. There were any number of gods and goddesses to venerate in those days; the Old Testament names many of them, as for example in the story of King Solomon's own style of multi-faith worship (1 Kings 11:5-7). It was the much later Christian Church which enveloped all these pagan deities into one wrap and called them Satan.

Gradually, within the Jewish and Christian cultures, the old ways were forsaken as Jehovah became ever more rationalized as an individual absolute—a unilateral overlord of all things. The perception of Jehovah also became totally abstract, so that all physical connection with humankind was lost. In pagan thought, the earth and heavens were a reflection of the majesty of Nature, of which the people were themselves a part. But to the Jews and Christians, Nature as a whole (including the sun and the heavens) was seen to be a servant of God, who was said to have created everything: 'The heavens declare the glory of God, and the firmament sheweth his handiwork' (Psalm 19:1).

Jehovah was said to transcend even Nature herself and, because of this, the true harmony between humankind and Nature was forfeit. In contrast, the pagan believers maintained that the inexplicable divine was manifest within Nature, which enveloped both the gods and society. This belief was shattered for all time by the orthodox establishment when natural harmony was discarded in favour of subservience. Hence the balance of relationship between humankind and the phenomenal world was destroyed, and what was ultimately lost was integrity.

Within the rites of pre-Christian Wicca, the principal male deity was not Satan, nor even singular. There were, in practice, twin fairy-gods called the Oak King (represented by a robin) and the Holly King (represented by a wren).[2] The Oak King (also called Robin Redman or Robin Redbreast) was the designated Lord of the Greenwood and was depicted with antlers, being the wiccan 'horned one' and the true nominal ancestor of Herne the Hunter who died upon the Windsor oak tree. Thus, the Oak King provides the essential link between Herne and the Robin Hood legend, whereas the Holly King (undeterred by all the Church propaganda concerning St. Nicholas) provides a true elfin original for Father Christmas. The traditional Greenwood goddess was always Diana. It is for this reason that in 1921 the noted anthropologist Dr. Margaret Murray defined Witchcraft as the 'Dianic cult',[3] making it quite plain that it was the dark, oppressive side of Christianity that was truly satanic by virtue of the bishops' very acceptance that the fabricated Satan character actually existed.

Today, there are a number of annual events within the Christian festive calendar, but the two most obvious are Christmas on 25 December—celebrating the birthday of Jesus—and Easter (on a variable spring date)—celebrating the resurrection of Jesus. But where do these festival dates come from? They are both hijackings of pre-Christian pagan festivals and were each designed to eclipse festivities which had long been established.

The birth-date of Jesus is not openly given in the Bible or in any other authenticated document—and for over 300 years from the event no one ever celebrated Jesus's birthday as a public affair. It was certainly not in the pre-Roman Christian calendar. The date of Christmas was actually determined by Emperor Constantine the Great who, in the 4th century, established Christ's Mass Day as 25 December so as to coincide with the Eastern pagan *Sol Invictus* sun festival which followed the winter solstice on 21 December. In the Western tradition, though, Christmas strategically overshadowed the traditional winter solstice festival of Yuletide (the ancient feast of the *Yulannu* Wood Lords).

The annual timing of Easter is rather more complex, having a number of variable dates between 22 March and 25 April but, in essence, it is the first Sunday after the first full moon which occurs after the vernal equinox. Initially, it can be said to have emanated from the Jewish Passover, which, as given in the Old Testament book of Leviticus,[4] falls on the 14th day of the (March-April) month of Nisan, being the first full moon after the equinox. Nevertheless, the Christian bishops were adamant that Easter should always fall on a Sunday, which meant that, unlike Christmas, a specific date could not be set to apply every year. That apart, and despite arguments over the competitive lunar and solar calendars, the date of Easter in England—along with the very name of Easter itself—was finally settled in Yorkshire at the Synod of Whitby in the year 664. At this Council a deal was struck to enable the Roman bishops to overwhelm and usurp the name of the customary festival of Eostre, the Goddess of Spring.

In practical terms, the Roman strategy was not entirely successful, for many popular symbols of the original celebrations remain—mistletoe at Christmas and bunnies at Easter, for example—neither of which has anything to do with the Christian tradition. Nor, for that matter, do holly, ivy, fir trees, Yule logs, fruit puddings, hot-cross buns or Eostre eggs have any connection whatever with the birth, crucifixion or resurrection of Jesus.

The Holly and the Ivy

The term 'Sabbath' (*Shabbat*) is now generally associated with the familiar Jewish reference to Saturday, the seventh and last day of the week said to represent God's day of rest in the Genesis Creation account, as formally established in Exodus 16:23 and 20:8-11. In practice, the Mesopotamian *Shabattu*, from which the custom derived, had a much older origin, being the monthly feast of the full-moon in ancient Akkad.[5] By virtue of this, Sabbaths (essentially periods of rest from general toil, and not normally associated with the seventh of anything) have never been a Jewish prerogative and have been preserved in many cultures for socially festive occasions.

Calendars prior to Roman and Hellenic intervention were generally lunar, rather than solar, in concept—being based upon months rather than years. The moon's waxing and waning were easy for all to see, while New Moons and Full Moons were very discernible as well as being regular. Everything to do with time was lunar based, as a result of which Kali became the goddess of time, seasons, periods and cycles, while other goddesses such as Diana were representative of the moon, with the moon's orbit being used as a measuring device for earthly time. Also ostensibly regulated by the moon, as emphasised by the periods of Kali, were the menstrual cycles of women, and these were measured in 28-day sequences. For this reason, in the strict lunar calendar of the monthly *Kalas*, there were thirteen cycles to the year, not twelve months as in modern calendars.

Throughout the ages, calendars have been shown in a variety of forms which, in one way or another, are generally tabular. But the wiccan calendar was, and still is, denoted as a continuous and perpetual cycle called the Witches' Ring or Pagan Wheel. Just like the Ring Lord symbol of wholeness, unity and eternity, so the Wheel of the Year keeps on turning, while having within it thirteen designated lunar periods. Further denoted within the cycle are eight specified Sabbats, the solar holy days (holidays)—including those of Yule and Eostre—which mark the passage of the natural seasons.[6] In many respects, these Sabbats are not just relics of the past, but are colourfully and genuinely adhered to today. For this reason, therefore, the present tense is mainly used in the following descriptions.

Samhain (Halloween) – 31 October

The 31 October Sabbat of Samhain (pronounced *Sow-en)* was so named from the old language of Britain, meaning 'summer's end'. More importantly, it marks the end of the old year upon the Eve of All Hallows, with the wiccan New Year's Day on 1 November in the northern hemisphere. It is the time when crops are harvested for the last time in preparation for the coming winter, and a time for honouring ancestors and the souls of the dead, to whom ritual fires and candles have long been a customary mark of respect. They also serve to repel unwanted evil spirits (hence, the Jack o'Lantern tradition). Additionally, it is an occasion for offering food and winter supplies to the needy—and to the lately departed who might perhaps seek retribution if ignored (from which comes the modern game of Trick or Treat). [In the southern hemisphere the Samhain date corresponds to the northern feast of Beltane].

There was no particular event with which the Christian Church could eclipse the Samhain festival of All Hallows, and so the concept of All Saints Day was contrived for 1 November[7] in favour of all those saints who did not have a recognized feast day at any other time of the year.

Yule (Midwinter)—from 21 December

The winter solstice festival of Yuletide marks the longest night of the year; the turning point from when the days become longer and the Holly King is said to give way to the Oak King for the next six months. The Yule-log (customarily of oak) or an ash faggot is venerated and burned in the sacred fire, while evergreens are lit with candles. Also, puddings of fruit and grain (commonly, but incorrectly, now called Christmas puddings) are made to celebrate the fertile richness of the earth. Along with the oak and the ash, the general revelry of food and song includes fertility symbols such as holly, ivy, mistletoe and pine-cones at a time when the goddess is said to be giving birth again to the sun. At this festival the Holly King makes his final appearance of the year as old Father Winter, distributing gifts while the new season's king, the Oak King, is reborn. [In the southern hemisphere the Yuletide date corresponds to the northern feast of Midsummer].

It was because of the 'newborn king' aspect of Yuletide that the Roman Church bishops elected for 25 December (the feast day of the *Sol Invictus* sun cult at the end of the solstice festivity) to be an appropriate official birthday for Jesus. In the Christian tradition, therefore, the concept of the Bethlehem Nativity and a collection of related carols have been added to the general scene, but in all other respects it is the ancient feast of Yuletide that is still celebrated.

Imbolc (Oimelc) – 2 February

Imbolc (In the belly) was essentially a torchlight festival to celebrate the coming of springtime, and is associated with Persephone and various goddesses of fire such as Vesta, along with Brigid, a goddess of fire and inspiration. At a time when bulbs are sprouting and the days begin to lengthen, the goddess is now expectant again with the Holly King who will soon be reborn. Imbolc (which comes from *oimelc*: ewe's milk) is a time for preparation and renewal, for the light of the sun is now returning. [In the southern hemisphere the Imbolc date corresponds to the northern feast of Lammas].

This is the festival which was usurped as Candlemas by the Christian Church, to be established in favour of the Virgin Mary and the purification of Christ in the Temple. The candles, it is said, represent the arrival of Jesus as the Light of the World.

Eostre (Ostara) – c.21 March

The vernal equinox is a time when both day and night are equal. It is the time when the Holly King is reborn; when Eostre, the Goddess of Spring appears in the vines as the ultimate representative of fertility, to present the Eostre egg. Her symbol (from a rabbit image perceived in the moon) is the Eostre bunny, and she is generally portrayed within an abundant array of spring flowers. Coloured eggs, charged as talismans, are given as presents; curative fires are lit at dawn; seeds are planted for new grains; homes are spring-cleaned, *Rosi-crucis* buns with solar cross decorations (hot crossed buns) are baked, and baskets are woven just as the birds have made their nests. It is by way of Eostre (Ostara) that we obtain the name for the female hormone oestrogen. [In the southern hemisphere the Eostre date corresponds to the northern feast of Mabon].

Beltane (Bale-fire) – 1 May

The feast of Beltane (essentially the fire of Bel the Shining One) is associated with the May Day revels which herald the summertime. In readiness for Beltane Eve, fires of various woods are lit and the farm herds are driven between them for purification. Beltane, with its general frolicking, fire-jumping and maypole dancing, celebrates the full return of life when the 'horned one', the Oak King, begins to make way for the reign of the Holly King. It is also the time for ritual weddings in the *merrie* (marriage) month of May and, at one time, for trial marriages (known as 'handfastings') which lasted for a year and a day until the next *merrie* Maying. This custom was based upon the first and second wedding ceremonies of the ancient *Hieros Gamos*, whereby a trial period was allowed before any formal commitment, and the ceremony was led by the appointed King and Queen of the May. [In the southern hemisphere the Beltane date corresponds to the northern feast of Samhain].

Of all the wiccan festivals, Beltane, with its particular aspect of trial marriage and associated sexual freedom, was thoroughly detested by the Christian Church. There was, in fact, nothing the bishops required or desired from a revelry they felt was best ignored. Instead, the early May period became unusually packed with special prayer meetings in an attempt to draw the crowds from the hillsides and village greens into the churches.

Midsummer (Litha) – c.21 June

Falling at the summer solstice, with the sun at its zenith, this is the longest day of the year. It marks the preparatory period before the harvest season at a time when the Holly King takes over from the Oak King until Yuletide. The moon at Midsummer is known as the Honey Moon (whence 'honeymoon') and was especially associated with mead (made from fermented honey), the aphrodisiac wedding drink of the Beltane handfasters. It is seen as a time of passion and dreams, when fairies are at their most playful and all growing things flourish. Again, although in summertime, it is a fire festival when fragrant herbs are cast into the embers to purge disease and heal the sick as the season moves towards a waning sun. Sitting midway between Beltane and Lammas, it is the time of abundance and beauty—a time for glow-worms and for the God and Goddess to display their treasures, the spear and the cauldron—equivalent to the blade and chalice of the Grail tradition. [In the southern hemisphere the Midsummer date corresponds to the northern feast of Yule].

Being directly opposite to Yule on the Witches' Ring, and since the Midsummer revels sat between 20 and 23 June, the Christian Church elected to make 23 June St. John's Eve. This was designed to weigh the Christmas balance by honouring the baptiser and herald of Jesus, establishing his birthday on 24 June. To some extent, this strategy has failed since many pagans are quite happy to accept John the Baptist as a druid in his own right, thereby including him as a welcome character in the Midsummer festivities.[8]

Lammas (Lughnasadh) – c.1 August

Lammas, which marks the beginning of the harvest season, represents the wake of the sun-king, Lugh Lamhfada of the *Tuadhe d'Anu,* who is said to die when the grain is reaped. A primary feature of Lammas is the gathering of bilberries, whose crop is reckoned to determine the potential strength of other crops in the season. Like Bel, Lugh was also a recognized Shining One and became particularly associated with athletic feats, games and craft fairs. Lammas is a time for honouring the union of the Goddess and the Oak King, when corn-dollies are made of braided straw to preside over the coming harvest, and Catherine Wheels (tarred, straw-clad wagon wheels) are set ablaze and rolled down convenient hillsides. [In the southern hemisphere the Lammas date corresponds to the northern feast of Imbolc].

Correctly called Lughnasadh (pronounced *Loo-nus-uh*), this festival actually gained its other name, Lammas (Loaf Mass), from the medieval Christians who baked bread as altar offerings from the first grain. Also, since the Church, for some inexplicable reason, elected to canonize Catherine of Alexandria (the legendary protectress of wheelwrights, spinners and millers),[9] it was automatically caught up with Lammas despite feverishly moving Catherine's feast day around in an attempt to sever the pagan connection.

Mabon (Alben Elfed) – c.22 September

Once again, at Mabon, day and night become equal as summer disappears, giving way to autumn (fall) and the winter months ahead. This autumn equinox is a time of thanksgiving for the rewards of the harvest, but also a time of sadness as the old year winds towards its close at Samhain. The celebrations are concerned with the divine child Mabon ap Modron (the son of the mother), who disappears to the land of Elphame as night begins to conquer day, but emerges in time as a true Shining One. It is a time of symbolic death in preparation for new birth as the Wicker Man, constructed to honour the last gathered sheaf, is sacrificed in representation of John Barleycorn, the eternal spirit of the fields. [In the southern hemisphere the Mabon date corresponds to the northern feast of Eostre].

Since the Mabon equinox varies a little with regard to its precise timing, the Christian Church selected 25 September (now 29th) for the feast of St. Michael and all the Angels—generally known as Michaelmas Day.

* * * * *

Inasmuch as history is mostly written by its winners, so too do conquerors generally regard the religions of the vanquished as being devilish and mightily powerful in terms of magic. This has the effect of heightening the perceived powers of the conqueror's own belief—a perception which can then be reinforced by continued successful persecution and the expropriation of that other religion's articles of faith. And so, the god of the overwhelmed faith is portrayed as a devil by the victors. This was, in practice, precisely how Christianity rose to Inquisitional supremacy against the Wiccans who actually kept very much to themselves, so that most of what we think we know about Witchcraft actually comes from strategically contrived Christian propaganda.

It is important to recognize that, although the word 'propaganda' has moved into general usage, it was in fact first introduced by the Roman Church as a specific aspect of dogma. The word originated from Church Latin, akin to the propagation of plants—i.e. 'breeding like or cloned specimens from a parent stock' and first appeared in the *Congregatio Propaganda Fide*: the Congregation for the Propagation of the Faith. In 1662 Pope Gregory XV established the College of the Propaganda of Cardinals, whose job it was to enforce Church doctrine in places other than Rome. Hence, the Church not only practices propaganda—it invented it.

Clearly, the most visible aspects of old pagan lore were its regular festivals. But, no matter what steps the Church might have taken to overawe and suppress these, they were undoubtedly destined to persist and, in so doing, would remain visible and popular. To cope with this the bishops hit upon the clever plan of usurping these festivals by superimposing their own self-styled calendar, to the extent that today we still celebrate many of the important days of ancient Witchcraft without necessarily realizing it. Similarly, the emblems of a pre-Christian heritage are still very apparent—for the holly, ivy, mistletoe, robins, pine-cones and decorated trees of Christmas, along with the familiar Easter eggs, bunnies, baskets, flowers and hot cross buns, all emanate from their pagan originals.

Ring Dancers

Of all the ritual practices which the Church condemned, the Ring Dance was among the most detested. Witchfinder Henry Boguet likened the dancing of witches and gypsies to the hideous revels of the fairies, whom he called in his *Discourse des Sorciers* 'devils incarnate'.[10] This type of dance was essentially based upon that of Apollo and the Muses, but actually had a much firmer tradition within the ancient Egyptian healing community of the Therapeutate, which dated from before the time of Moses.[11] Later, when the Egyptians moved their culture into Judaea, a branch of this ascetic fraternity became allied with the Essene community of Qumrân, to which Jesus's own Nazarene sect was attached. Irrespective, therefore, of the Roman Church's hostile attitude towards the Ring Dance in the Middle Ages, it was very much a custom of the Gospel era and of the early Christians.

One of the most respected theologians of the Church soon after the time of Emperor Constantine was St. Augustine of Hippo (*c.*AD 354-430), as distinct from the later St. Augustine of Rome. Famed for his numerous epistles and philosophical writings, Augustine wrote about a Ring Dance that was directly attributed to Jesus and his Apostles.[12] He recorded every aspect of the dance and its related chant, from start to finish, as it had appeared in the 2nd-century Acts of John. Sections of the ritual were then subsequently read at the Church's Seventh Ecumenical

Council in Asia Minor—the Second Council of Nicaea—in the year 787, shortly before King Charlemagne became Holy Roman Emperor. An extract reads as follows:

> He [Jesus] gathered all of us together and said, 'Before I am delivered up unto them let us sing an hymn to the Father, and so go forth to that which lieth before us'. He bade us therefore make as it were a ring, holding one another's hands, and himself standing in the midst he said, 'Answer Amen unto me'. He began to sing an hymn and to say 'Glory be to thee Father'. And we, going about in a ring, answered him, 'Amen'.[13]

Ring revels of the satyrs
From a woodcut dated 1555

From that point, the dance continues through a lengthy sequence of chanting between Jesus in the centre and the others going around him in a Ring. Whether or not this apocryphal portrayal is historically factual or not is of no consequence; its importance lies in the fact that such dances were performed in that region in those days, as had been recorded by St. Augustine who knew that the tradition had been continued by the early Christians. What subsequently happened to annoy the Church was that, since Roman Christianity evolved as a hybrid of various faiths and customs, it grew ever further away from any form of Christianity that might have been recognized by the immediate followers of Jesus, Peter or Paul. Many of the original Nazarene rituals (the Ring Dance being one of them) became far more apparent outside the Roman movement and were continued by groups which, by the Middle Ages, the Church had designated heathen and heretical.

It was not so much that the Wiccans and various moon cultists had taken over an originally Christian tradition, but rather more that the cultures had all grown in parallel, with similar rituals from early times. It was the Roman Church which had changed the rules from the time that Emperor Constantine first established a pseudo-style Christian faith which had very little to do with the customs and conventions of the religion whose name it purloined. In many respects, the original Christians were far more like the later Wiccans than they were like the emergent Christians of the Imperial religion. As such, when the Ring Dance was performed in medieval times with Puck or Robin Goodfellow at its centre, it was perceived as a wholly pagan exercise by the unenlightened bishops of the day. It was seen to be representative of a witches' coven because there were thirteen participants in all, with one in the centre and twelve in the Ring. What never occurred to the Inquisitors was the fact that, as laid down in the Nazarene tradition (which we now know from the *Community Rule* document found among the Qumrân Dead Sea Scrolls)[14] and as given in the New Testament Gospels, Jesus and his immediate fraternity constituted their own coven of himself and the twelve delegate Apostles. These groups of thirteen were not invented by medieval witches, as the Inquisitors imagined, they were a part of the time-honoured lore of many kindred cultures.

The similarity between Witchcraft and the style of religion practised by the early Christians was actually far closer than has ever been openly publicised. Thus, when Emperor Constantine founded the Roman faith in the 4th century, it truly was a new religion, having very little to do with the ritualistic belief structure that it replaced. The unfortunate Christians who were tortured, persecuted and thrown to the lions by the Imperial regime from the time of Emperor Nero (AD 54-68) to Diocletian (AD 284-305) were, in practice, Ring dancers and followers of a faith with a deep-rooted mythological tradition. To them, Jesus was neither a godhead, nor the founder of their culture, but a particularly active member of it by virtue of his dynastic Christos (kingly) status in the manner of the ancient Ring Lords. The fact that he was sentenced to be crucified was recognized and this, in any event, appears in the Roman annals, but amid all the wall-drawings in the hundreds of miles of Christian catacombs webbed beneath the streets of Rome, there is not one single image of the Resurrection which became so important to emergent Catholicism. This apparently supernatural event was something quite unknown to them since it was not added to the Gospels until the bishops made their strategically designed interpolations in the 4th century. In referring to the Crucifixion, all Senator Cornelius Tacitus (born *c.*AD 55) stated when compiling the 1st-century *Annals of Imperial Rome* was: 'In spite of this temporary setback, the deadly superstition [Christianity] had broken out afresh, not only in Judaea where the mischief had started, but even in Rome'.[15]

In view of the early attachment between Witchcraft and original Christianity, Jesus always retained an acknowledged position within the structure of the former, much to the distaste of the Catholic and Protestant Churches. This was borne out as late as 1584 in a witch-debunking work entitled *The Discoverie of*

Witchcraft that published the details of numerous secret ritual processes. From one of its recorded witching ceremonies comes:

> By all the characters that be in the firmament, and by the King and Queen of the Fairies, and their virtues, and by the faith and obedience that thou bearest unto them ... by the blood that ran out from our Lord Jesus Christ crucified, and by the opening ... I conjure thee O Sybilla, O blessed and beautiful virgin, by all the royal words aforesaid, to appear in that circle before me ... adorned and garnished most fair.[16]

In one of its forms, the Ring Dance developed into maypole dancing, whereby the pole took the place of the central figure. In a like manner, it was common for such dances to be conducted around other such monuments, particularly town and market crosses. One of the most famous of these was England's Banbury Cross in Oxfordshire which was torn down by the Puritan witch-hunters in about 1650 (the present cross having been erected in Victorian times). A seemingly odd chord is struck, however, by the fact that the original Saxon cross was a Christian monument demolished by ardent Christians! Why? Because it was accepted by the pagan folk as being representative of the original Christian religion which was far closer to their own Elder Faith. At the Maytime festival, an elected girl, representing the Earth Goddess and decorated with magical rings and bells, would gallop her white horse through the fields in the hope of increasing their fertility. She would then complete her ride at the Cross, being led into town amid music and general merrymaking.

> Ride a cock horse to Banbury Cross,
> To see a fine lady upon a white horse.
> Rings on her fingers and bells on her toes,
> She shall have music wherever she goes.

This is not the only witches' song to survive as a modern children's nursery rhyme, for many of these popular party songs have wiccan derivations, especially the best known Ring Dance which swirled around the tree that bore the most sacred fruit of the Moon Goddess—the Mulberry.[17]

Here we go 'round the mulberry bush,
The mulberry bush, the mulberry bush.
Here we go 'round the mulberry bush,
So early in the morning.

This particular dance was of a special imitative variety, usually performed by children who would enact certain physical functions as they swung around the tree. Today, the words have all been changed beyond the first verse, with references to washing clothes and sweeping floors, but the original words and actions were far from such innocence, for this Ring Dance was an unabashed fertility rite.

Dances played a most important role in the fertility culture and, used in conjunction with the Sabbats, they varied in accordance with the precise fertility requirement—whether related to crops, animals or community.[18] Ring dances were usually performed around some central object or figure—perhaps a standing-stone, a tree, a cross or a person who often represented the Horned One himself (either as the Oak King, Cernunnos or Khem of Mendes). Crop fertility was, for example, willed by a jumping dance to emulate upward growth. Animal fertility generally required the donning of animal disguises, while the dance for community fertility left little to the imagination. The children were, however, raised with all these as a part of their normal way of life within what seems, in hindsight, to have been a very open and natural environment.

In addition to the Ring Dances, there was also another called the Round Dance in which stone circles were used, along with Fairy Rings which appeared from nowhere, as if by magic, like large circular shapes in the grasses. These, which seem remarkably like today's mysterious Crop Circles, are featured in the 17th-century *Antidote Against Atheism* by Dr. Henry More of Christ's College, Cambridge.[19]

A fact of primary interest concerning such ritual dancing is that it has survived in one form or another in defiance of all attempts to suppress its hold upon the collective psyche. In the wiccan culture, its high-point with the maypole persists today at the Beltane and May Day festivals—with May being the time for the handfasting *Merrie* (marriage); also for *Merrie's Men* (Merrow's men or Morris men) and for *Merrymaking* in general. These, as previously detailed, are all associated with the love cultess Mary the Gypsy, the companion of Mary Magdalene and Mary Salome—together known as *les Saintes Maries de la Mer* (the Marys of the Sea).

Along with Pan-pipes and other instruments, the main time-keeping percussion for Ring Dances was generally the timbrel (tambourine), while the European names Mary, Marie and Merrie derived from the Egyptian *Mery* and the Hebrew *Miriam*. In this musical regard, it is significant that a particular ritualistic function of the sacred Marys (the Beloved Ones) remained the same from the oldest of times. We read in the Old Testament book of Exodus (15:20) that Miriam, the prophetess and nursing-sister of Moses, 'took a timbrel in her hand, and all the women went out after her with timbrels and dances'. Hence, it is not difficult to understand why it was that, apart from a few vague references, the fascinating high-priestly story of Miriam was wholly omitted from the Bible, while other books that were excluded from the Old Testament feature her as 'She to whom the people bowed and the afflicted came'.[20] Historically, it was she, Mery-amon (Miriam) of Egypt, who held the original style of Mary the Gypsy or Mary the Egyptian (from which the word 'gypsy' derived).

13

Satan and the Yuletide Elf

A Diabolical Fantasy

It is an apparent fact that Satan, in the popularly conceived role of being a fiendish demonic figure, does not appear anywhere in the Bible's Old Testament. Even in other ancient scriptures he does not exist as Western Christendom has come to know him.[1] The Christian perception of Satan is that of an evil imperialist whose despicable horde wages war upon God and humankind—but this devilish character was an invention of the post-Jesus era, a fabulous myth with no more historic worth than any figment of a Gothic novel.

Satans, though rarely mentioned in the Old Testament, are generally portrayed as obedient servants or sons of God who perform specific duties of strategic obstruction. The Hebrew consonantal root of the definition is *STN*, which defines an opposer, adversary or accuser, whereas the Greek equivalent was *diabolos* (from which derive the words diabolical and devil), meaning no more than an obstructor or slanderer. Until Christian times, the term 'satan' had no sinister connotation whatever and, in the olden tradition, members of a straightforward political opposition party would have been called 'satans'.

In the Old Testament, Satan is seen as a member of the heavenly court—an angel who carries out God's more aggressive dictates. In the book of Job (1:6-12, 2:1-7) for example, Satan is sent twice by God to tease and frustrate Job, but with the express instruction that he should not seriously harm the man—an instruction which is duly obeyed. In 1-Chronicles 21:1 Satan suggests that King David should count the number of the Children of Israel. He receives a passing mention in Psalm 109:6, and appears again in Zechariah 3:1-2 siding with the Israelites who have returned from Babylonian exile in their endeavour to re-establish their traditional family stations in Jerusalem. That, in fact, is the extent of it. These are the only four satanic mentions in the whole of the Old Testament and in no instance is anything remotely dark or sinister implied.

The menacing horned figure of Christian mythology (sometimes called Lucifer, Beelzebub or Belial) emerged mainly through the onset of medieval Christian Dualism—the concept of two opposing and equally powerful gods.[2] According to different traditions, Satan was either the brother or the son of Jehovah, or was even the competitive and aggressive aspect of Jehovah himself. In essence, the said Jehovah-Satan conflict was representative of the ancient pre-Christian tradition of the symbolic battle between Light and Darkness as perceived by the Persian mystics, but this had nothing to do with any Antichrist figure in an era long before Jesus Christ was born.

So, from what original concept or Bible entry was the modern Christian image of Satan born? In the Old Testament book of Isaiah is a section dealing with the prophesied fall of Babylon and, in referring to the city and its despotic king, Isaiah 14:12 says, 'How are you fallen from heaven, day star, son of the dawn. How are you fallen to earth, conqueror of nations'. Many centuries after this was written, the image of the fallen day star (Venus) was redefined as 'light-bearer' and, when translated into Latin with a proper-noun connotation, it became 'Lucifer'. Likewise, Lucifer appeared in this Venus context in St Jerome's 4th-century *Vulgate* Bible, to become associated with an evil satan some 1400 years later[3] in John Milton's *Paradise Lost*:

> Of Lucifer, so by allusion called,
> Of that bright star to Satan paragon'd.

Today, the Isaiah verse in authorized Christian Bibles retains the Latinized Lucifer entry which emanated from the Christian Church's creation of its own Satan mythology during Roman Imperial times. The Roman faith was based wholly on subjugating people at large to the dominion of the bishops, and to facilitate this subordination an anti-God/anti-Christ figure was necessary as a perceived enemy. This enemy was said to be Satan, the 'evil one' who would claim the souls of any who did not offer absolute obedience to the Church.

With Satan as the perceived adversary, Roman Church domination was established on the back of a statement made by St. Paul in the New Testament Epistle to the Romans (13:1-2):

> Let every soul be subject unto the higher powers. For there is no power but of God; the powers that be are ordained of God. Whosoever therefore resisteth the power, resisteth the ordinance of God; and they that resist shall receive to themselves damnation.

It then remained only for the Church to become its own self-nominated bridge between God and the people. This was done by granting the vicarious office to the Pope (as in *papa* = father), alternatively styled the Pontiff (= bridge-builder), who became the Vicar of Christ, as eventually enforced by the *Donation of Constantine*.

For this scheme of threat and trepidation to succeed, it was imperative for people to believe that the diabolical Satan had existed from the beginning of time, and there was no earlier story with which he could be associated than that of Adam and Eve. The only problem was that Genesis made no mention whatever of Satan—but there was the inherent account of Eve and the wise serpent, and so it was determined that this story could be rewritten to suit the desired purpose. The original text was, after all, a Jewish version and Christianity had become quite divorced from Judaism, even from the westernized Judaism of Jesus.

In those days there was no understandable translation of the Bible available to Christians at large. The Jews had their Hebrew, Aramaic and Greek versions of the Old Testament, while the primary Christian Bible existed in an obscure form of Church Latin, translated from Greek by St. Jerome in the 4th century. Outside the immediate Roman Church of the West, there were enthusiastic Eastern Christian branches in places such as Syria, Egypt and Ethiopia, and it was mainly from these regions (where the Jewish competition was stronger) that the new Genesis accounts emerged for the Christian market.

Among these was an Egyptian and Ethiopic work called *The Book of Adam and Eve* (subtitled *The Conflict of Adam and Eve with Satan*), which was produced sometime in or after the 6th century AD.[4] This lengthy book not only features Satan as a central character, but even goes so far as to say that the cross of Jesus was erected on the very spot where Adam was buried!

A Syriac work entitled *The Book of the Cave of Treasures* is a compendium of earthly history from the creation of the world to the crucifixion of Jesus. It appears to have been compiled in the 4th century AD, but the oldest extant text comes from the late 6th century.[5] Once again, this book introduces Satan as the constant protagonist of evil, setting the scene for the dark and sinister element that flourished in the Church-promoted Gothic tradition which evolved as a product of the brutal Church Inquisitions. In one instance, Adam and Eve are seen to be dwelling in a cave when Satan comes fourteen times to tempt them, but each time an angel of God puts the demon to flight. The book even maintains that orthodox Christianity was in place before the time of Adam and Eve and the emergent Hebrews!

Another volume which upholds a similar notion is *The Book of the Bee*,[6] a Nestorian Syriac text from about 1222 compiled by Bishop Shelêmôn of Basra, Iraq. Its title is explained by virtue of the fact that it 'gathered the heavenly dew from the blossoms of the two Testaments, and the flowers of the holy books', thereby applying Christian doctrine to the traditional Jewish scriptures which it reinterpreted.

The satanic myth is, therefore, no more than a fictional fable, concocted long after Bible times and designed to undermine historical record while intimidating Christians into compliance with the dogmatic and subjugative rule of the Church bishops.

Horns and Hooves

In contrast to Imperial Christianity, Witchcraft was about a belief in the old gods and the forces of Nature. It was about harvests and home-fires, superstition, weather, husbandry and divination. It incorporated chants, spells, potions, music, dancing, ritual, masquerades, magic and an amount of apparent promiscuity. It was about the realities and hardships of life; about pastoral existence and, in essence, about procreation and survival—but it was certainly not evil. Nevertheless, in December 1484 Pope Innocent VIII issued a Bull which called Witchcraft an 'heretical depravity' in which people 'give themselves over to animals', causing children, herds and harvests to be ruined and perish.[7]

Plainly, since most members of the rural class were in some way connected to Witchcraft in those times, there must surely have been good and bad in their number as in any widespread community. However, the one thing that none would ever dream of doing was to cause purposeful harm to those very aspects of their lives that were so important: the children, herds and harvests. In this respect, therefore, Pope Innocent's official pronouncement was wholly inaccurate. What, then, was the Church's problem? It was, quite simply, one of fanatical authoritarianism, with the bishops being quite unable to accept that there were those who disagreed with their dogmatic theology—especially those of a fraternity that was more ancient than the Church itself, with as many active members.

Those were the days of a feudal regime which operated at Church command, backed by such documents as the *Donation of Constantine* and the *Magna Charta*. This regime had the effect of nailing everyday families to the soil and their trades, preventing mobility, while at the same time offering a high degree of uncertainty as to the continuance of existing conditions. Indeed, the feudal lords always retained the Right of Prehension—a privilege whereby they could carry away any animal or crop, or daughter for that matter, for their own benefit if desired.[8] Because of this, a man was never sure in what state he might find his home, family, workshop or farmstead at the end of a day!

Since this oppressive, self-righteous feudal system survived within a Christian Church structure by way of authority from the Pope and the bishops, it is not surprising that the rural folk and tenant farmers perceived Christianity itself to be an evil regime. They considered the Christian God to be the devil, for he appeared to be an obstructive force (a *satan*) as far as they were concerned. He did not represent them or their dignity in any way, for he was the friend of tyrants and warmongers who lived in fine palaces and stone-built castles. By virtue of this, they were reliant on their own age-old gods for support within a subjugated environment in which natural forces were their perceived route to survival. Fine things were never sought, but good weather was. Gold and riches were never attainable, but a rich harvest and enough surviving children might be possible if the gods of Nature were lenient.

Since the biblical Satan carries no physical description, he was generally considered in early artwork to look like any other angel (albeit a fallen one according to emergent lore). It was not actually until the beginning of the 7th century that Pope Gregory I (590-604) made his announcement concerning the devil's characteristics, thereby establishing the base satanic personality which has been perpetuated from that time. Satan has horns and hooves, said Gregory, and powers to control the weather.[9]

Henceforth, horned animals (in particular stags and goats) were considered to be devilish, while the pictorial imagery of Satan became ever more exaggerated with the addition of a tail, bat's wings and a variety of bodily characteristics based upon the satyrs of Greek mythology. Resultantly, many of these devil depictions were not unlike the familiar portrayals of Pan, with his goat's horns, ears and hooves. But, as the traditional guardian of flocks and herds, Pan was of some significance to the Wiccans. They also continued one of the most ancient of customs related to the Oak King in their ritualistic donning of stag's antlers—something which had been an apparent practice from the days of prehistoric cave painting before 5000 BC, as is evident at the Caverne des Trois Frères at Ariège in the French Pyrenees.[10]

Trois Frères at Ariège cave painting of a man in stag disguise from before 5000 BC

In Britain, Pope Gregory I is best remembered for the fact that in 597 he sent the Benedictine monk, Augustine, to England in order to Catholicise the nation after the death that year of Britain's key Church leader, St. Columba of Glencolumcille, Co. Donegal. His form of Christianity (eventually dubbed the Celtic Church) had been based upon pre-Roman, Nazarene principles, but Gregory and Augustine considered the Columban Kindred to be pagan and heretical. This was the era of King Arthur (559-603), whose Gaelic Britons of the Elder Faith[11] were manoeuvred into Cornwall, Wales and Scotland, while the Roman Church established itself in England (Angle-land).

The boyhood of St Columba
A stone relief from his birthplace in Co. Donegal

St. Augustine began his mission in the South East, where the wife of the Saxon King Aethelbert of Kent was already a confirmed Catholic. Then, in 601, Augustine was proclaimed the first Archbishop of Canterbury, moving England's centre of Church activity to Canterbury from London, where a Latin plaque above the vestry fireplace at St. Peter's, Cornhill, reads:

> In the year of our Lord 179, Lucius, the first Christian king of this island now called Britain, founded the first church in London, well known as the Church of St. Peter in Cornhill; and founded there the archiepiscopal seat, and made it the metropolitan church and the primary church of his kingdom. So it remained for the space of four hundred years until the coming of St. Augustine.... Then, indeed, the seat and pallium of the archbishopric was translated from the said church of St. Peter in Cornhill to Dorobernia, which is now called Canterbury.

The archiepiscopal seat of the Anglican Church remains at Canterbury today after nearly 1400 years. However, despite the fact that it broke away from Rome in the 16th century, Canterbury serves as a constant reminder that its ties with the first Inquisitional act in Britain remain embedded in the nation's Christian culture. This occurred very soon after Augustine's era, when Pope Gregory's horned definition of Satan came to the Britannic Isle—added to which was a rule implemented in France by the 6th-century Catholic Council of Auxerre, condemning those who masqueraded as stags.

It was not in the Middle Ages, as might be thought, but as early as 668 that Archbishop Theodore of Canterbury, under the auspices of Pope Vitalian, issued the first legislation against England's witches. This document, called the *Liber Poenitentialis*, actually referred to the donning of animal horns or skins as being a 'transformation', thereby implying that there was some form of personal shapeshifting involved—a concept which served the Church well when the Wiccans were hunted down like animals in later times. Meanwhile, the Canterbury penance for anyone found wearing stag's horns from 668 was 'three years because this is devilish'.[12]

The Burning Times

In 1229, while the Cathars of Languedoc were suffering their twentieth year of persecution, the Church formalized its related doctrine at the Synod of Toulouse, which established an ecclesiastical tribunal that was specifically charged with the suppression of heresy.[13] Subsequently, the Inquisition (or Holy Office) was formally implemented by Pope Gregory IX in 1233. Initially, the courts were manned by bishops, but the task soon fell to the Dominican Black Friars and Franciscan Grey Friars. Their power was considerable and they gained a terrible reputation for their cruelty. Torture was granted papal sanction in 1252 and the trials were all held in secret. Victims who confessed to heresy were imprisoned, then strangled or burned, while those who made no such confession were given exactly the same punishment for their disobedience.

By the 15th century, the Inquisition had lost some of its momentum, but new impetus was gained in Spain from 1480, when the wrath of the Spanish Inquisition was largely directed against Jews and Muslims. The Grand Inquisitor was the brutal Dominican Tomâs de Torquemada, senior confessor to King Ferdinand II and Queen Isabella. A few years after its implementation, the Inquisition set its sights towards the cult of Wicca, and the resultant oppression (within which tens of thousands were slain) was to last for more than two centuries—not only in Spain, but throughout Christian Europe. The unsuspecting prey were described as 'the most diabolical heretics who ever conspired to overthrow the Roman Church'.

It was then, in December 1484, as mentioned above, that Pope Innocent VIII issued his official Bull concerning the 'heretical depravity' of witches—a Bull (entitled *Summis Desiderantes Affectibus*) which removed any hitherto restrictions that might have limited the Inquisitors' powers in this regard. Subsequently, two years later, the Dominicans, Heinrich Kramer and James Sprenger, published the *Malleus Maleficarum* (commonly known as the *Hammer of Witches*)—an evil but imaginative work which gave full details of the hideous threat posed by practitioners of what was now being called 'satanic magic'. It also stipulated the Inquisitorial powers in a manner which left no doubt that enforced confessions were allowable and that execution was inevitable:

> The method of beginning an examination by torture should be begun in this way: First, the officers prepare the implements of torture, then they strip the prisoner. The reason for this is lest some means of Witchcraft may have been sewed into the clothes—for they often make such instruments, at the instruction of devils, from the bodies of unbaptized children that they may forfeit the vision of salvation.
>
> And when the implements of torture have been dispensed, the judge, with other honest men zealous in the faith, tries to induce the prisoner to confess the truth freely; but if the prisoner refuses to confess, the judge bid attendants make the prisoner fast to the strappado or some other implement of torture. The attendants obey forthwith, yet with feigned agitation, appearing to be disturbed by their duty. Then, at the earnest request of someone of those present, the prisoner is loosed again and is taken aside and

> once more persuaded to confess, being led to believe that by this means there can be an escaping of the death penalty.[14]

In addition to that, another new scenario was then brought to bear. Since the Inquisitors were all men, it was determined that Witchcraft must be a form of depravity linked to 'the insatiable wantonness of women' and, from a point in the text when this concept was determined, the witch references quite suddenly change from 'he' to 'she'.

The document also states that it is reasonable for a judge to promise a witch that her life will be spared, but then he can later excuse himself by passing her to another judge who has not made such a promise! Then, having established the fact that the carnal desires of women are responsible for the downfall of men in this regard, it is conceded that the gullible men must be punished as well, thereby bringing the 'he' definition back into the equation.

Three witches burned at Derneburg
From a woodcut of the event dated October 1555

To put the Roman accusations against witches into historical perspective, it is worth considering some extracts from another Roman persecution text, while at the same time trying to imagine which seemingly despicable sect is being discussed in this document:

> And now, as wickeder things advance .... those abominable shrines of an impious assembly are maturing themselves throughout the whole world. Assuredly this confederacy ought to be rooted out and execrated.
>
> They know one another by secret marks and insignia.... Everywhere also there is mingled among them a certain religion of lust.... they adore the head of an ass, that basest of creatures, consecrated by I know not what silly persuasion .... Some say that they worship the genitalia of their priest and adore the nature, as it were, of their common parent ....
>
> The initiation of young novices is as much to be detested as it is well known. An infant covered over with meal, that it may deceive the unwary, is placed before him who is to be stained with their rites. This infant is slain by the young pupil, who has been urged on as if to harmless blows on the surface of the meal, with dark and secret wounds. Thirstily—O horror!—they lick up its blood; eagerly they divide its limbs. By this victim they are pledged together; with this consciousness of wickedness they are covenanted to mutual silence. Such sacred rites as these are more foul than any sacrileges....
>
> On a solemn day they assemble at the feast, with all their children, sisters, mothers, people

> of every sex and of every age. There, after much feasting, when the fellowship has grown warm, and the fervour of incestuous lust has grown hot with drunkenness, a dog that has been tied to the chandelier is provoked ... and thus the conscious light being overturned and extinguished in the shameless darkness, the connections of abominable lust involve them in the uncertainty of fate.[15]

These extracts are not taken from an Inquisitional document issued by Christians, as might be supposed, but from an earlier Roman assault upon Christians![16] The work, entitled *The Octavius of Marcus Minucius Felix*, was compiled *c*.200 AD in the days before Christianity became acceptable as the State Religion under Emperor Constantine. It provides a good example of the way in which the Christians were portrayed by the Imperial overlords prior to the 4th century. In that era the Romans were themselves of a pagan persuasion, worshipping many gods, and so Christianity was portrayed as being base and evil. Subsequently, when the Romans had themselves become Christians, the tables turned and precisely the same type of vilifying nonsense was levelled at those with other beliefs! What this proves, therefore, is that it is not just history which is determined by its winners, but that religion and belief systems are also governed by the same rules. There is always the 'recognized faith'—the faith of those in positions of power who wield national authority and seemingly represent society. Meanwhile, those of other faiths, even if not persecuted, are made to feel in some way inferior.

The position of the Wiccans was, therefore, little different to that of the early Christians before them.[17] The only noticeable difference was that, instead of being sent to the lead mines or thrown to the lions, they were hanged, drowned, burned at stakes or roasted on spits during a period which has become known as the 'Burning Times'. From the Inquisitors' perspective, however, the wonderful thing about Witchcraft was that just about anybody could be caught in the ever widening net, and the charge of sorcery became an expedient substitute for criminal and political indictments. The flexible accusation was often used to circumvent courtroom trial altogether—sometimes being used against some very influential figures in England where Witchcraft could be ranked as an offence against the monarch and, therefore, said to be treasonable. Also, it was the perfect back-door mechanism to use against the Grail guardians and supporters of the *Albi-gens*. Even in the early 1300s when the Knights Templars were hounded, executed or banished by the Inquisition, some of the bizarre charges levelled against them were necromancy, blasphemy and the black arts.[18]

In England there were laws related to Witchcraft (including death penalties in some instances) from the 9th-century Saxon days of King Alfred the Great, but it was not until 1566 that the first major trial was held at Chelmsford in Essex. This was a particularly important landmark in Britain for it established the legality of accepting unsupported evidence from well-rewarded children, along with the notion of said Witches' Marks—physical attributes by way of which a Wiccan might be recognized.

One of England's key characters in all this was Matthew Hopkins, the puritanical, self-styled Witchfinder General. He began his notorious career under cover of the Civil War in 1644, earning his money from local authorities by promising to free their communities of satanists. Hopkins used the well-tried notion of witches having familiar animals to great advantage, concentrating his effort very largely on laying charges against elderly women with pets! Also, since witches were said not to bleed when pricked, Hopkins made good use of his spring-loaded, retractable knife. Eventually, though, his days were numbered when his methods were exposed in 1646, subsequent to which Hopkins wrote a pamphlet entitled *The Discovery of Witches* and then disappeared from the scene, with no one knowing quite what became of him.

Father Christmas

In considering the character of Santa Claus, and given that he is so closely associated with elves and antlered reindeer, the question has often been posed as to whether there is a Witchcraft connection here. Also, is the name Santa perhaps a play on Satan (being a straightforward anagram), or does Santa Claus really emanate, by phonetic corruption, from Saint Nicholas as we are led to believe?

As we have seen, the concept of Father Christmas (with the customary holly-sprig in his cap) is a direct representation of the gift-bearing Yuletide Holly King, sometimes called Father Winter or Grandfather Frost. His one-time pagan image was brought into line with the Christian festival in the 17th century, whereas Santa Claus first appeared by that name in America as late as the middle 1800s. And then, of course, there is the Kriss Kringle portrayal. Are they all the same character and, if so, how can an historical Christian bishop possibly equate with the jolly, pipe-smoking Yuletide Elf?

Back in the very earliest days of the Roman Church in AD 325, one of the bishops at Emperor Constantine's Council of Nicaea was a certain Nicholas of Myra from Asia Minor (modern Turkey), who claimed to have a personal dialogue with Jesus and an angel. At this Church conference the bishops were debating the nature of the Holy Trinity—the Father, Son and Holy Ghost—and of how Jesus was not simply the Son of God, but was also God incarnate. There were, nonetheless, some bishops of the pre-Roman school who opposed this new Imperial dogma and averred that Jesus was the Son as created in the flesh by God—but he was not himself God. The leading spokesman for this opposition faction was an aged Libyan priest of Alexandria named Arius, but when Arius rose to address the Council in this regard, Nicholas of Myra punched him in the face—an event which paved the way for the emergent Nicene Trinity Creed.

Other than that, very little is recorded about Bishop Nicholas (AD 271-343) until a fictitious biography was written by the Greek missionary Methodius in the 9th century.[19] Then, as a direct outcome of this, schoolboys, pawnbrokers, sailors, prostitutes, merchants and apothecaries all claimed the violent bishop as their patron saint! Methodius reported in his text that Nicholas had given a bag of gold to each of three girls to save them from prostitution—whence, apparently, the three golden balls used as a sign by pawnbrokers, although the connection is difficult to comprehend. He was also said to have the power to calm the seas, while the story which established his traditional link with children claimed that Nicholas successfully restored to life three boys who had been cut into pieces and preserved in brine by their innkeeping parents!

Father Christmas with a wassail bowl in the Holly King tradition, riding a goat
From the 1888 Book of Christmas

Following these reports, Nicholas became the elected patron saint of Greece, Apulia, Sicily, Lorraine and Russia—becoming especially popular with the Eastern Orthodox Church. Then, based upon the 'bags of gold' story, a new tradition grew in and around The Netherlands to the effect that St. Nicholas would return each year to bring gifts for well-behaved children on the eve of his 6 December feast day—a tradition which has long been acted out in places such as Denmark, Holland and Belgium.[20]

The origin of the modern Santa Claus story is often attributed to 17th-century Dutch settlers in America (in New York to be precise, which was called New Amsterdam until the 1700s).[21] They are said to have taken the St. Nicholas tradition across the ocean with them, but this is completely untrue. The Dutch colonial settlers were, in fact, members of the Protestant Dutch Reform Church, who had no empathy whatever with Catholic saints. Santa actually emerged from a character introduced to Pennsylvania by the German settlers—a character called Pelznichol (meaning Furry Nicholas)[22] and sometimes referred to as Old Nick. He was reckoned to be a mischievous hobgoblin (akin to Hodekin and Robin Goodfellow) and by 1827 he was firmly established in the Philadelphia Yuletide festivals.[23]

Reminiscent of Enkidu in the old Mesopotamian legend of Gilgamesh,[24] Pelznichol was a somewhat wild, hairy individual who was noted for playing tricks on people once a year—a tradition which was transformed into gift giving. The Dutch of Pennsylvania, along with various other settled families, became attached to the custom of Pelznichol (alternatively Belsnickle), but they gave his gifts a Christian flavour by relating them specifically to children and calling them *Krist-kindle* ('Christ-kind'). By the 1840s this definition was adapted for Pelznichol himself, who became known in some communities as Kriss Kringle.[25] Alternatively, from around 1823, it was reckoned that Kriss Kringle actually was the Christ child who, with no real explanation, appeared as an old bearded twin of Santa Claus. To differentiate between the two, it was said that, while Santa came down the chimney, his Christian twin came in through the keyhole.[26]

To discover the true identity of Santa Claus, we shall return again to Pelznichol. Meanwhile, though, we should take a look at some other events which established the character in the guise that we know him. In doing this, we can go back to early 17th-century England, where we discover the first use of the Father Christmas name in connection with the Holly King tradition. This occurred in the year 1610 when Father Christmas, in a tall hat bedecked with holly, made his first ever appearance by that name in the *Christmas Masque* production of William Shakespeare's colleague, the playwright Ben Jonson. Making his stage entry at the same time with a group of children was Cupid – a name eventually used for one of Santa's reindeer.

In 1822 the next major step came when the American writer Clement Clarke Moore penned a Christmas poem for his own children. It drew upon various traditions, especially that of the Russian Grandfather Frost, who had a sleigh and a reindeer (unlike St. Nicholas who always rode a white horse). It related also to the fur-clad German Pelznichol, whose signature was said to be Thunder (Donner) and Lightning (Blitzen), which provided two more reindeer names for Moore's poem – along with Cupid, Dasher, Dancer, Prancer, Vixen and Comet. (Rudolph did not appear until as recently as 1939 in a story by Robert L. May.) In spite of the anomalies, Moore's poem was entitled *A Visit From Saint Nicholas* – soon to become widely known in publication as *The Night Before Christmas*, which begins:

> 'Twas the night before Christmas, when all through the house
> Not a creature was stirring, not even a mouse.

Not only were the now famous reindeer introduced in this poem, but it established the first known link with stockings and chimneys, while also giving a description of the newly developing Yuletide Elf character:

> He was dressed all in fur, from his head to his foot,
> And his clothes were all tarnished with ashes and soot;

A bundle of toys he had flung on his back,
And he looked like a peddler just opening his pack.

His eyes—how they twinkled! His dimples how merry!
His cheeks were like roses, his nose like a cherry.
His droll little mouth was drawn up like a bow,
And the beard of his chin was as white as the snow.

The stump of a pipe he held tight in his teeth,
And the smoke it encircled his head like a wreath.
He had a broad face and a little round belly
That shook when he laughed like a bowlful of jelly.

He was chubby and plump, a right jolly old elf,
And I laughed when I saw him, in spite of myself.

Thus, the modern Santa was beginning to evolve, although one would hardly recognize him from the strange little fellow depicted in the 1848 edition of Moore's poem. In 1869 a colour edition was released, with pictures by an unknown artist, which brought the character a little closer to today's image. Oddly, though, this chubby elf with the red bobble-hat and pipe was still called St. Nicholas in the poem, although being as far removed from the historical bishop as one could possibly stray. But nowhere yet was this character called Santa Claus.

The magazine *Harpers Weekly* had, by that time, commissioned the political cartoonist Thomas Nast to produce a series of drawings of the popular elf for the annual covers of their Christmas editions, and these developed the character still further, making him a little larger and less elfin. Meanwhile, the separate Father Christmas (looking more like a druid with holly in his hair) was pursuing his own rather more wiccan career in England, appearing in 1888 in Thomas K. Hervey's *The Book of Christmas* not with reindeer, but riding on the back of a goat and carrying a wassail bowl.[27]

To complete the picture of Santa in America, along came Haddon Sundblom who (from 1931 to 1964) created a new representation each Christmas for the Coca-Cola advertisements which appeared worldwide in *The Post* and *National Geographic* magazines. And so the familiar modern Santa portrayal finally emerged in true Disney style—but why was he suddenly called Santa Claus? And why were the folk in Denmark now calling their one-time Sint Nicolaas by the new name of Sinterklaas? Had some other tradition perhaps become interpolated during the early decades of the 20th-century? It certainly had. In fact two other traditions had become merged with that of the American Yuletide Elf—the first being England's own druidic Holly King, Father Christmas. More importantly, though, was the re-cementing of the original Pelznichol culture—by then widely recognized as that of Kriss Kringle—for it was actually Pelznichol, the wild hobgoblin (a counterpart of Hodekin and Robin Goodfellow, or Puck) who carried the alternative name which became Santa Claus.

To understand how this transpired, we need to go back in history again to Europe, where Pelznichol was so called because he was a *nick* (a sprite). Consequently, one of his familiar names was Old Nick.[28] So, from the moment that Clement Clarke Moore's Christmas character appeared, 'dressed all in fur, from his head to his foot', the beginning of a merger was apparent between his St. Nicholas and the other Furry Nicholas.

Old Nick, meanwhile, had been the very figure most associated with Pope Gregory I's description of the devil, taking over totally from the earlier fallen angel depictions in medieval times, so that the devil was (and still is) often referred to as Old Nick. Where did this devil live? Apparently, he lived in the far North according to the churchmen who quoted the Old Testament book of Jeremiah (1:14): 'Then the Lord said unto me, Out of the north an evil shall break forth upon all the inhabitants of the land'. So the legendary Old Nick (Pelznichol) supposedly came from the North Pole, just as Santa does today—having no geographical relevance whatever to the historical St. Nicholas.

The rest of the story follows from this very root, and from the appearances of Pope Gregory's Satan (Old Nick) character in European Passion plays from the 12th century.[29] It is, however, from the writings of Jacob Grimm (of the Brothers Grimm fairy tale fame) that the puzzle is finally pieced together. In his comprehensive research work entitled *Teutonic Mythology* Grimm explains that, in the course of the Christmas plays of the Middle Ages, it was common for a famous saintly bishop (generally St. Nicholas) to develop a split personality within the plot.[30] While the traditionally benevolent saint would remain in character, his alter ego would degenerate into an additionally scripted figure of opposition akin to Pelznichol—a wild satanic creature called Claus.

And so it was that, when the Holly King, St. Nicholas, Father Christmas, Kriss Kringle and Pelznichol finally merged into the one all-embracing character, it was the Old Nick alter ego from the Christmas plays who finally reigned supreme. It was he who determined the Yuletide Elf's name for all time—for he was the 'Satan Claus', or as he has become better known (by way of a strategic anagrammatical switch from the original satanic definition to a more acceptable saintly style), Santa Claus.

14

The Faerie Queen

Red Cross Knight

From among the most enterprising works of the Elizabethan era comes Edmund Spenser's epic poem *The Faerie Queen*—a personal title which, in a letter to Her Majesty's Lieutenant Sir Walter Ralegh dated 23 January 1589, Spenser attributed to Queen Elizabeth herself.[1]

The central character of *The Faerie Queen* is Prince Arthur in the days before his Round Table kingship, while the Fairy Queen (also called Gloriana, as was Queen Elizabeth) does not actually feature except as a focus for the tale's inherent quest. Spenser described this quest as a 'continued allegory' which functions on several levels at the same time—a search for honour and enlightenment in the nature of all Grail romance, with the same emphasis on the merits of service.

In a similar fashion to the cast of René d'Anjou's *le Livre du Cueur d'Amours Espris*, Spenser's characters are representative of certain virtues such as holiness, chastity, truth, love, temperance, honour, friendship, justice, courtesy, faith, hope and charity—with the poem making the point, for example, that holiness cannot be attained without the knowledge of truth. Of particular importance is the fact that all these virtues are perceived in the poem as being the qualities of true Christianity, although the greatest evil presented by Spenser, and therefore the great adversary of that truth, is the dogma of the Church of Rome.

Based upon the philosophical themes of Aristotle and Arthurian legend, *The Faerie Queen* (the longest poem in the English language) begins with the adventures of the Red Cross Knight, who symbolizes holiness and fights against pride. At the request of the Fairy Queen and in the company of a dwarf, he rides to the aid of the maiden Una, whose parents and their nation are being oppressed by an evil dragon. In the course of their travels, Red Cross meets and slays a malevolent creature called Error, but then encounters the magician Archimago, who deceives the knight into leaving Una with him since she is not the virtuous damsel he thought her to be. Without Una at his side, Red Cross is seduced by the treacherous Duessa, who whisks him off to the House of Pride. There, he is confronted by Queen Lucifera and her attendants, Idleness, Gluttony, Pride, Lechery, Avarice, Envy and Wrath—the seven deadly sins—by whom he is spiritually weakened and thrown into a dark dungeon.

Meanwhile, having made her escape from Archimago, Una is befriended by a lion who becomes her protector, but the magician (disguised for a while as Red Cross) joins them, following which the lion is killed and Una takes shelter with a rusty knight and a band of satyrs and wood nymphs. At length, they met with the dwarf who informs them of the imprisonment of Red Cross, whereupon they seek the aid of Prince Arthur, whose army promptly storms the House of Pride to secure the knight's release.

Red Cross, although reunited with Una, then falls into a deep despair for being so gullible in the face of the magician's wiles. But the maiden (in the manner of a true fountain fey) takes him to the House of Hope where, with the supplemental aid of her 'well of life', he regains his composure and emerges to engage and defeat the wicked dragon.

Secret Agents

In 1517, during the Church's expensive years of Inquisitional persecution, the Dominican monk Johann Tetzel had introduced a lucrative scheme to replenish the Vatican coffers from the pockets of the Church's own members. The scheme concerned the forgiveness of sins, which had generally been expiated by means of penances such as fasting, repetition of the rosary and other acts of sincere repentance. Tetzel's concept, however, replaced these traditional penalties with Indulgences—formal declarations of guaranteed absolution which were available for cash, with the scale of monetary donation determining the extent of forgiveness! Approved by papal decree, the sale of Indulgences was very popular with the bishops and soon became a source of considerable revenue for the Church.

For centuries before this, the orthodox clergy and its associated monastic Orders had suffered a series of outrageous measures imposed by an avaricious hierarchy that was becoming ever more corrupt. Through it all they had, nonetheless, upheld successive Vatican dictates with as much loyalty as they could muster, but the trading of Christian salvation for cash was more than some could tolerate and the practice was openly challenged in October 1517. At the forefront of this challenge was Martin Luther, an Augustinian monk and professor of theology at the University of Wittenberg, Germany, who nailed his written protest to the door of his local church. When he received a papal reprimand, he publicly set fire to it and was excommunicated for his pains. In the event, though, Luther's act of formal objection was destined to split the Western Church permanently in two—giving rise to a large scale Reformation movement and the establishment of an alternative Christian structure outside Vatican control—a structure which, being named after Luther and his fellow 'protesters', became known as the Protestant Church.

In the course of this Lutheran Reformation, the year 1570 was a major turning point in the religious history of England for, on 15 February of that year, Queen Elizabeth I Tudor was excommunicated by Pope Pius V (*see* Appendix VII). The Catholic Church had long prevailed in England from the time of St. Augustine, but Elizabeth's father, King Henry VIII, had separated the English Church from Roman control to aid his divorce from Catherine of Aragon and to acquire Church property in England for himself. He did not become a Protestant as is so often incorrectly reported; he simply made himself Head of England's branch of the Catholic Church. But his daughters took the family in two opposite directions for they were severely at odds in matters of religion: Mary Tudor (known as Bloody Mary) being a convinced Catholic, while Elizabeth was a committed Protestant. This manner of division was prevalent throughout the realm but, on succeeding Mary as Queen in 1558, Elizabeth endeavoured to unite the dissenters by creating the separate Anglican Church—a Protestant version of the Roman episcopal concept. In this regard, she implemented her *Thirty-nine Articles* of the English doctrine in 1563 and was duly denounced by the Vatican seven years later.

At that time both France and Spain remained officially Catholic and, since England was so influential on the world stage, there were two courses open to the respective Kings. Either one of them might arrange a marriage alliance with Elizabeth in order to bring England back under Vatican control, or they could take the alternative measure of open warfare. In this regard, the French suggested that Elizabeth should marry King Henri III's brother, the Duc d'Anjou, but this plan was strategically forced out of play by Robert Dudley, Earl of Leicester, and his powerful War Against Catholics party. Meanwhile the Spanish remained especially hostile since Elizabeth had actually rejected a marriage proposal from their King Philip II in 1559. It was, therefore, not long before the English people (to whom Elizabeth was a popular monarch) turned the tables on their Augustinian past and decided that, even among their own number, to be a Catholic was to be an enemy of England.

It was during the ensuing religious and political intrigue that the Elizabethan Court established what was to become England's key Intelligence network: the Secret Service. Placed in charge of this as Ambassador to France from 1570 was Sir Francis Walsingham, a hitherto Protestant field agent.[2] It is his 1587 paper concerning the impending Spanish Armada, entitled *The Plot for Intelligence out of Spain* (now held within the *Sloane Manuscripts* at the British Museum), which is regarded as the formal inaugural document of the Secret Service Department.

Early in his Intelligence career, Walsingham established a team of espionage agents to work with him, one of the earliest of whom was the noted astrologer, mathematician and Dudley collaborator John Dee (1527-1608). He was placed in charge of affairs in Poland, being responsible for reporting on intrigue between the Vatican and Spain.[3] A few years earlier, in 1562, Dee had discovered a book entitled *Stenographia* by Johannes Trithemius, the Benedictine Abbot of Sponheim (1462-1516), and from this he learned a good deal about codes and ciphers, producing his own explanatory work on the subject for Walsingham's spy network.[4] Subsequently, numbers were used by the Secret Service to denote the agents themselves, along with other people and places: England was number 39, Holland 96, Germany 70, the Queen of Spain 55 and Mary, Queen of Scots 3. As for Secret Agent John Dee, he was numbered 007.[5]

The Magic Circle

Apart from his Government activities, Dr. Dee was Queen Elizabeth's appointed astrologer and a practising alchemist under royal licence. He was also famed for his *Liber Mystorium*, which is often said to concern Enochian magic because of its inherent 'angelic conversations'. But the work (now at the British Museum) was actually compiled as a record of conversations concerning Vatican Intelligence presented in a heavily coded form with the help of Dee's lawyer confederate Edward Kelly.[6] The Catholics, in their attempt to discredit Dee's reports, were quick to invent a heap of propaganda suggesting that he was some kind of black magician who consorted with the angel Uriel in a strange alien language, and Dee used this to good advantage by playing upon his supposed links to the spirit world.

Eventually, some decades later, Dee's encrypted writings were made perfectly clear to the Stuart Royal Society by Dr. Robert Hooke (inventor of the spirit-level and marine barometer). Yet there are still plenty of books produced today which naively centre upon the Church-promoted counter-intelligence concerning the presumed occult nature of John Dee's activities.

That apart, there is good reason to place Dr. Dee in the category of being a magician, since there are many things that we might refer to today as science, but which in the 1500s would have been considered magic. It was a word often used to define something which could not be understood or was considered irrational—for example, if some unconventional method of healing were apparent in the skill of a gypsy or foreigner. The Christian churchmen were surrounded by their own crucifixes and rosary beads, but if someone of another superstition were seen with a charm or talisman it was automatically perceived as a dark and sinister device. Since the Christian bishops considered all other faiths to be devilish, they assumed their own privilege to conduct exorcisms, but if someone of another belief system dared to use similar mumbo-jumbo to ward off evil spirits, this was regarded as satanic Witchcraft! Such was the arrogance of a Church that was itself steeped in the most evil sacrificial ritual, as proved by the savage death-cults of the Catholic Inquisition and the Puritan witch hunts.

The followers of the *Malleus Maleficarum* had stated with all certainty that such interests as astrology, divination, alchemy and numerology were forms of hideous magic, and even the ancient *Prophecies of Merlin* were formally blacklisted by the bishops at the 1545-47 Council of Trento in Northern Italy. Such attitudes were of enormous use to international agents such as John Dee, who made very good use of the convenient cover. Dee was everything the Roman Church despised—an astrologer, alchemist, diviner and numerologist, but above all he was a chief adviser to Queen Elizabeth and a valuable Court field operative. In his Preface to *Euclid*, however, Dee did see fit to complain about having his mathematical skills classified as 'conjuring', while Gabriel Naudé (the renowned French librarian for Cardinals Richelieu and Mazarin) made a rather more forceful comment in this regard.[7] In his 1623 *Instruction a la France sur la verité de l'histoire des Frères de la Roze-Croix*, Naudé stated in reference to John Dee:

> All that is said about his marvellous works should be ascribed to his knowledge of nature and mathematics, rather than to a commerce with demons, which he never had .... I must fill this gap so that the good name of this English Franciscan, who was a doctor of theology and the greatest chemist, astrologer and mathematician of his time, may not remain perpetually buried and condemned among the crowd of sorcerers and magicians to which he most certainly did not belong.

Interestingly, among John Dee's primary students we discover Edward de Vere (1550-1604), 17th Earl of Oxford, a descendant of Aubrey, the 11th-century Elf King, and of Robert, 3rd Earl of Oxford, whom we met as the model for Robin Hood. Apart from being yet another Great High Chamberlain of his line, Edward was a respected writer and poet, renowned for his patronage of the arts and called by many a 'friend of the Muses', being a leader of the Elizabethan romantic movement.[8] Much of his historical work was based upon *The Chronicles of Englande, Scotlande and Irelande*, published in 1558 by Raphael Holinshed, whose research was also used by Edward's contemporary, William Shakespeare.

Another prolific writer of the era was the astrologer and philosopher Francis Bacon (1561-1626), who was later knighted and created Viscount St. Albans by Elizabeth's successor, James VI Stuart of Scots (James I of England). Bacon also became King James's Attorney General and Lord Chancellor, as well as being a Grand Master of Rosicrucians as had been Dr. John Dee before him. These men—William Shakespeare, Edward de Vere and

Francis Bacon—along with notable writers such as Philip Sydney, Christopher Marlowe, Ben Jonson, John Fletcher, Edmund Spenser and various others, all moved in the same circles, while some were associated with the Secret Service and with the Rosicrucian movement.

The most celebrated writer of the group to work for the Secret Service was Christopher Marlowe, who was first recruited by Walsingham as a Cambridge student in 1580. His most active period, according to the records, appears to have been between February and July 1587, when he was sent under-cover to Reims to be entertained by King Philip of Spain's leader of the Catholic movement, the Duc de Guise.[9] In such company, Marlowe duly accepted the predetermined role of a double-agent, thereby learning of plots against Queen Elizabeth.

On 30 May 1593, however, Marlowe was stabbed to death at a London meeting-house in Deptford, where Robert Poley, the espionage attaché and steward to Walsingham's daughter, was staying.[10] Also there, as given in the Coroner's report, were Poley's assistant Nicholas Skeres and the Walsingham secretary Ingram Fritzer. Precisely which of the men committed the murder is still a matter of debate. Fritzer was imprisoned after the event, but was conveniently released with a Queen's Pardon within the month. What is clear is that Marlowe had been arrested on the previous Sunday, 20 May, and charged with heresy, but had been released on bail pending trial by the Star Chamber—a bail which actually expired on the day of his murder.[11] It seems likely, therefore, that his killing was an in-house, politically motivated affair in order to prevent him from giving away State secrets in court.

Given the close proximity and mutual fraternity of the various Court writers, there is an amount of content and style similarity in some of their work, especially when it comes to relating Grail subject matter in some veiled form. Resultantly, there has been an amount of debate over the past couple of centuries as to who might actually have written what for whom. Many have suggested that the works of Shakespeare were actually penned by Bacon or de Vere. In endeavouring to prove a case one way or another since 1781 (when a clergyman first cast doubt on Shakespeare's expertise), the Stratfordians, Baconians and Oxfordians still pursue their respective claims today, with each group having its own operative society.[12]

Others have suggested that Christopher Marlowe or William Stanley, Earl of Derby, was the real William Shakespeare but, with the 'alternative author' theories falling well short of their individual objectives, there is no reason on earth to suppose that anyone but William Shakespeare wrote the works of William Shakespeare. All the records of the era support this fact, no matter what the latter-day protagonists might care to suggest. There is, nevertheless, no doubt that from the time of John Dee there was a very apparent and well organized syndicate of Court poets and playwrights. Many of these were of a Rosicrucian leaning and would have been interested, if not directly involved, in scientific and spiritual matters which the Church would have considered magic.

Recently, the present Charles Vere posed the question as to why the Shakespeare debate is coming to such a head of resolution in Shakespeare's own favour at the turn of the millennium. In answering his own considered question in relation to the *Oxford de Vere Files*,[13] he concludes that the writings of William Shakespeare must be recognized for the wisdom they contain, since they 'can furnish mankind with the key to its future development'. In complete accord with the sentiments of the Grail Code of the Ring Lords as expressed at the outset of this book, Charles Vere maintains that so long as calculating self-seekers like Shakespeare's Edmund in *King Lear* hold sway in this world, 'power remains purely pragmatic, rather than being a sacred force, and both man's relationship with language and his relationship with the land cease to be organic'.

It is a fact that many of the political issues which preoccupy today's society also concerned those of Elizabethan times. In this context, Shakespeare's plays encompass much which relates to the conflict between commercial capitalism and spiritual exchange, with the playwright's own inherent message constantly supporting the importance of the latter. We seem now to be at a turning point, Charles Vere suggests, when people are reassessing their fundamental values. Shakespeare was not heeded in his day, as a result of which 'men took the mercenary route', but now is a time for his true message to be heard and understood. It is not for no reason that his plays have survived in the popular psyche for some 400 years, for we have always instinctively known they are a 'force of revelation'. What is important now is to recognize the man for precisely who he was. In so doing, we should also acknowledge and heed his uniquely penned philosophy which, at all times, identifies that nobility of birth and appearance do not guarantee nobility of the soul—for whether a leader or a follower, true nobility is to be found in the honourable code of service.

Mary Stuart

The Royal House of Stuart (originally 'Stewart' in Scotland) emerged from its Scots-Gaelic and Breton roots as one of the primary Grail successions in the Ring Lord culture.[14] In descent from the 5th-century King Erc of Irish Dal Ríata in one line, and from the Fisher Kings of Gaul in another, this was Europe's longest reigning dynasty, maintaining the throne for more than three centuries from 1371—first as the Stewart Kings of Scots and then, from 1603, as the Stuart Kings of Britain.

Earlier, we saw how Elizabeth's House of Tudor had no prior right to the crown of England, gaining it simply by might of the sword at the Battle of Bosworth Field in 1485 from the House of Plantagenet. Elizabeth's aunt, Margaret Tudor, had nonetheless married King James IV Stewart of Scots to become the grandmother of Mary Stuart, whose unfortunate story, like that of Joan of Arc, has made her one of history's most loved tragic heroines.

From the age of six in 1548 (while Scotland was under constant threat from Elizabeth's father, Henry VIII of England), James V's daughter Mary was educated in France by Diane de Poitiers, the influential mistress of King Henri II. (It was while Mary was in France that the 'Stuart' spelling of her family name was introduced since there was no 'w' in the French alphabet.) When she was sixteen, Mary was married to François the Dauphin and, by way of this alliance, she was not only Queen of Scots (her father having died in 1542), but soon became Queen of France as well. However, François died shortly afterwards, whereupon Mary returned to Scotland in 1561.[15] At that time, her cousin Elizabeth Tudor was formulating plans for the Protestant Church of England, and the austere John Knox (a one-time chaplain to the Tudor Court) had established the Presbyterian Kirk in Scotland. Prior to that, the Kings of Scots had never shown any particular religious allegiance, and they were certainly not Catholic since the whole nation had been excommunicated in the 14th century because King Robert the Bruce had antagonized the Pope.

What Mary Stuart discovered, though, was that there was no longer any acknowledged religious tolerance in Scotland for, in her absence, the narrow-minded Knox had laid down new rules. These came very hard upon Mary because, through absolutely no choice of her own, she had been raised in a Catholic environment at the French Court and knew nothing different. Then, to cap it all, Knox announced that according to God's law, no woman was capable of ruling the kingdom! In the light of this, Mary's Protestant half-brother James, Earl of Moray, decided to claim the crown of Scots for himself, raising an army against Mary's troops in 1565. His attempt was unsuccessful, though, and he was subsequently exiled to England.

In that same year Mary married her younger kinsman Henry Stewart, Lord Darnley, who had a strong claim to the crown of England through his grandmother Margaret Tudor (the widow of James IV) and her second husband the Earl of Angus. Meanwhile, from a safe distance, Moray fed information through his agents to the gullible Darnley, insinuating that Mary was rather too closely involved with her personal secretary David Riccio, whereupon Darnley had the Queen's confidant dragged from her presence and stabbed to death.

Soon afterwards, on 19 June 1566, their son (later King James VI) was born at Edinburgh Castle. But then a new character appeared on the scene: James Hepburn, Earl of Bothwell, Great Admiral of Scotland. With the support of the Privy Council he suggested that Mary should divorce Darnley because of his involvement in the Riccio murder, but Mary refused and so an alternative plan was put into action. In the early hours of 10 February 1567, Bothwell and his henchmen blew-up the Kirk o'Field House where Darnley was sleeping. As it transpired, Darnley escaped through a window, but met immediately with a quite separate group of enemies who killed him on the spot. Following this, Bothwell took Mary to his castle in Dunbar, where she remained for ten days and, within a few weeks, they were married.

Subsequently, a rebellion of jealous nobles erupted and Bothwell's army was defeated at Carberry Hill in 1567. Mary was taken hostage to the island-castle of Lochleven, where she was illegally compelled to abdicate under duress in favour of her one-year-old son. At this, the scheming Moray then emerged once more to be proclaimed Regent of Scotland, but Mary was rescued from Lochleven and duly raised her army, only to be defeated by the forces of Moray. It was at that point, on 13 May 1568, that the final chapter of Mary Stuart's sad story began for, on escaping from Scotland in a fishing-boat, she elected not to go back to Catholic France where she had money, friends and property. Instead, she sailed to England, seeking protection from her kinswoman Queen Elizabeth I—only to find herself perceived as a threat, at which she was confined under house-arrest at various locations for nineteen years.

The problem was that, not only was Mary Stuart the lawful Queen of Scots and the Queen Dowager of France, she was also deemed to be Elizabeth's closest living relative and, since

Elizabeth had neither married nor borne any children, Mary was heiress-presumptive to the English crown. For this reason, although she had been manoeuvred from Scotland, she could still emerge as the next Queen of England—a prospect that was quite unacceptable to the newly-styled Anglican clergy because of Mary's Catholic upbringing.

Given Mary's defenceless position, various attempts were made by the Elizabethan Court to implicate her in treasonable actions, and these attempts became ever more desperate as Queen Elizabeth grew older. To begin, Darnley's murder was laid at Mary's feet, and letters were produced at Court (the so-called *Casket Letters*) suggesting that she had been Bothwell's mistress before the event. It transpired, however, that the letters proved absolutely nothing except their own dubious origin.

Ultimately, a *Bill of Attainder* was passed against Mary in 1572, denying her any rights of accession to the English throne—but it was not as if she had ever made any claim in that direction and she was hardly capable of doing so in her contained situation. In protesting her innocence time and time again, all Mary ever stated was, "I came to England on my cousin's promise of assistance against my enemies and my rebel subjects, and was at once imprisoned". She begged Elizabeth to believe that the *Casket Letters* had been forged, and asked even to be banished to France rather than "consume away in tears and regrets at receiving this evil when I came in request of aid". But her pleas were ignored.

Plainly, the unfortunate Queen of Scots had landed in an enemy nest from which there was no escape, while typically Tudor-style plots and counter-plots evolved around her. The most famous of these was the Babington Plot which led to Mary's execution. Quite unbeknown to Mary, the Englishman, Anthony Babington, had organized a scheme with members of Elizabeth's household to assassinate the English Queen, but the plan was foiled by the Secretary of State—the Head of the Secret Service, Sir Francis Walsingham.

After nineteen years of virtual imprisonment Mary, Queen of Scots, was brought to trial following Babington's arrest; she was convicted of treason, and sentenced to be beheaded at Fotheringay Castle, near Peterborough, on 8 February 1587, with her death warrant signed by her cousin Queen Elizabeth of England. In preparation for the event, Mary had her ladies-in-waiting make her a blood-red dress, along with similarly dyed petticoats and hose. Then, on the appropriate morning, dressed in her red attire, Mary was conducted to the Castle Hall, having tucked her little dog inside her bodice to gain courage from the animal's warmth. Letting her cloak fall to reveal the red gown as she reached the dais, she announced, "You may take my blood against my will, but I shall not show it to you". And so Mary's head went to the block, but as it fell, having taken three blows in all, her lifeless body began to move and the onlookers were terror-struck, until they saw her little dog emerge.

Throughout the court proceedings, Mary had attested her ignorance of any plot against Elizabeth, but her pleas were in vain. The flimsy case against her rested on certain incriminating letters, supposedly written to and from Babington, and on the strength of these Mary was strategically implicated. But it was to be another 250 years before a related collection of documents was discovered—Government papers which threw considerable new light on the conspiracy that set Mary Stuart's head to the axe.

In 1836 a lawyer named Robert Leigh, whose ancestor had represented the Elizabethan Court, found a small chest when clearing the archives of his family's Bardon House at Old Cleeve in Somerset—a chest whose contents were State papers relating to the incrimination and trial of Mary, Queen of Scots. These were submitted to the British Museum, where they were authenticated and are still held.

The *Bardon Papers* detailed the list of contrived complaints against Mary but, more importantly, they set out her repeated denials and the unpublished truth of her innocence. The various manuscripts disclosed the treacherous actions of Mary's persecutor, Francis Walsingham, and of his confederate High Treasurer, Lord William Cecil of Burghley. During the course of her trial, Mary had stated, "I am alone, without council or anyone to speak on my behalf. My papers and notes have been taken from me, so that I am destitute of all aid, taken at a disadvantage". With the discovery of the *Bardon Papers*, the true nature of Mary's disadvantage was revealed; the supposed correspondence between her and Babington (the very crux of her presumed guilt) was found to be counterfeit and concocted at Walsingham's own office. And so it became blatantly apparent to all that the incriminating letters were fabrications and Mary's signatures thereon had been forged—but it was 250 years too late!

15

Lorna Doone

House of the Grail

Of all the Grail dynasties that ever reigned, the most prominent and influential subsequent to the Merovingian Kings was Scotland's Royal House of Stewart (Stuart). For well over two centuries, the Plantagenet and Tudor houses of England endeavoured to overthrow the Kings of Scots, but to no avail. Each successive Stewart generation succeeded in retaining the nation's independence, though often at considerable cost, as battle after battle was fought to maintain an Albigensian culture north of the Anglo-Scottish border. The great irony of Mary Stuart's execution was that, following Elizabeth I's death in 1603, it was Mary's son James VI of Scots who was invited to become King James I of England, and it was this which ultimately led to the family's regnal demise.

Strictly speaking, although Mary was said to be Elizabeth's closest relative, her son James was not the rightful heir of England. The true successor should have been Edward Seymour, Lord Beauchamp, in descent from Henry VII's sister Mary Tudor. This points of course to a purposeful strategy by the Anglican Parliament to gain dominion over the ancient Scottish succession—a strategy which had been put into place some time prior to Elizabeth's death by her chief minister Robert Cecil, the son of William, Lord Burghley.[1]

Bringing King James to London was actually a politically conceived manoeuvre to sever the *Auld Alliance* between

Scotland and France, which had existed from the time of Charlemagne. It was designed to bring Scotland and England together under one monarch, and the fact that the sovereign position was reversed with a Scots king reigning overall was a mere technicality which could be rectified once the precedent had been established. In fact, this is precisely what happened two generations later when the Stuarts were deposed by the Westminster politicians.

When James arrived in England in 1603, he had no concept that he was to be a pawn in the one-time Tudor Secretary's plot to make the traditional Scottish monarchy subordinate to the English Parliament—but he was immediately confronted by two difficult problems, with the first related to matters of religion. Both Scotland and England were established as Protestant nations, but James had experienced a Presbyterian upbringing whereas England was positively Anglican. The second difficulty was that the Westminster administration was wholly English, and Scots born before James's accession were strictly debarred from any Government office. Hence, although many Scots had followed James down to London, not one of his colleagues was allowed to sit in his Parliament![2]

After many failed attempts to gain control of Scotland and dismantle its time-honoured Clan System, inherited from the *Tuadhe d'Anu*, the English politicians had finally discovered a strategic route to Scottish possession. Once James was settled on the united thrones, a solution to the long-standing ambition was in place: (a) future Kings of Britain would remain based in London, thereby restricting Scottish influence even in the affairs of Scotland; (b) Westminster could eventually dissolve the traditional Scottish *Three Estates* Parliament; (c) at an appropriate time, the Stuarts could be discredited and deposed, and (d) a puppet monarch of Westminster's own choosing could then replace the Scottish succession.

The perceived outcome of this strategy was a dismantling of the Grail heritage and Scotland's overall subjugation to English rule. This ambition had prevailed since the Plantagenet days of

King Edward I and finally came to pass in 1688 when King James VII (II) was usurped and sent into exile by Church and parliamentary conspirators.

Earlier, in 1560, the Presbyterian Kirk (regulated by elders rather than bishops) had become the National Church of Scotland. South of the Border the Anglican Church (*Anglicana Ecclesia*) had existed since Elizabeth I authorized the *Thirty-nine Articles* of the English doctrine in 1563. So when James succeeded as the overall monarch of Britain, he was obliged to uphold two major Churches, each without offence to the other. It was an impossible task—particularly since James was now supposed to be Head of the Church of England as laid down in the Elizabethan Acts of Supremacy and Uniformity. These afforded no toleration of any religion outside the Anglican Communion. Over and above that, there was another complication for, in addition to being King of Britain, James was also King of Ireland (the Irish Free State was not established until 1921) and accordingly had responsibilities towards the Irish people who were traditionally Catholic—responsibilities which were not upheld under customary English law.

In enforcing the Act of Uniformity in respect of the Anglican *Book of Common Prayer,* James upset the Catholics and prompted the unsuccessful Gunpowder Plot to blow him up in Parliament. Conversely, in introducing his Authorized Version of The Bible, he caused the Protestants to assert that he was siding with Rome. As for the Scottish National Kirk elders, they were more than displeased by James's concept of a new compromise in Scotland: a Scottish Episcopal Church that was neither Anglican, Presbyterian, nor Catholic. And, to cap it all, the Anglican Parliament grew particularly angry when James dared to suggest that there should be a liberal acceptance of Jews within the realm.

Elizabeth I had ruled without much parliamentary consultation and had put the crown into considerable debt. King James was thus obliged to implement higher taxation. However, in approving this measure, Parliament insisted that he could not rule in the autocratic Elizabethan style. The ministers put forward a series of restrictions which left James with hardly any individual powers at all. Having already been a successful King in Scotland for a number of years, James responded by declaring that, in the Scots tradition, he was not answerable to Parliament but to God and the Nation. It was his duty, he maintained, to uphold Scotland's Written Constitution (the 1320 *Declaration of Arbroath*) on behalf of the people, and to take constitutional stands against Parliament and the Church if and when the need arose. But unlike Scotland, England had no Written Constitution (as is still the case), and the people had nothing to protect their rights and liberties. All that existed was the *Magna Charta* and a feudal tradition which vested the power of the land in the wealthy upper classes.

Not only had the Stewarts been established as the overall guardians of the Scottish realm, but their family branches, emanating from the ancient House of Lorne, also held prestigious positions as Lords of Innermeath, Atholl, Lennox, Doune and Moray. In preparation for the final dismantling of Grail sovereignty, various hereditary lands and estates in Scotland were brought under English dominion by ousting the families who had long been the regional custodians. In respect of the Western Highlands of Dalriada (modern Argyll) these families, alike to the Pictish *Caille Daouine* forest people of Caledonia, were the Scots kin of the People of Loarn, who were called the *Loarna Daouine*. Loarn was one of the Milesian sons of King Erc of Irish Dal Ríata who, along with his brothers Fergus and Angus, settled the Western Highlands in the late 5th century (*see* chart: Meroveus and Mélusine). His part of Northern Argyll was called Loarna (now Lorne or Lorn), and it is the demolition of the Lorne heritage by the fire and sword tactics of the Anglican Parliament which forms the backdrop to one of the greatest Grail romances of all time—the classic tale of *Lorna Doone*.

This famous novel of love, revenge, treachery and intrigue, is one of the best loved literary works in the English language and a fitting tribute to all the stories of gallantry and lost brides which have gone before. It is the perfect fairy tale of a distressed maiden of high-born stock, discovered at the water's edge deep in the woods by a rural yeoman's son, who battles against all odds to secure her release and win his knighthood from King James II Stuart. But this tale (unlike many other knightly adventures) is no mere fiction, for in studying the chronicles which lie behind this story we discover an amazing web of political conspiracy which emerged after the execution of Mary Stuart. It therefore serves as an appropriate reminder that the jealousies which beset the 8th-century Merovingians were still operative in much more recent times. Here is an account which puts Mary, Queen of Scots', death into perspective as part of a far wider-reaching governmental plan to dismantle the last remnants of the old Ring Lord culture in favour of feudal land tenure backed by the Christian Church. All the details concerning the events which led to the predicament of the hostage heiress, Lorna Doone, are recorded in various State files, but they have been strategically obscured in the authorized books of establishment history. By virtue of this, the separated entries would probably never have seen the light of day as a cohesive sequence had they not been collated and preserved by the Oxford lawyer and Victorian author R. D. Blackmore (1825-1900).

The Waterslide

Generally, the fountains and springs of Grail romance are located deep within thicket woods or enchanted forests. This style of location creates a type of Netherworld environment, but still within the mortal plane, and the fountain-fey is usually first encountered beside the water. Like the tower damsels, these maidens (such as Mélusine) are often distressed, lost or somehow disinherited. Perhaps they are princesses or noblewomen who await the arrival of the prince or knight who will break some spell of circumstance to secure their release into the natural domain. On occasions the gallant hero will be a lowly fellow, akin to Perceval, who succeeds in his Grail quest where others of more apparent aptitude have failed. Thereby, the hero gains his knighthood and recognition, while often winning the lady as well. This type of story firmly expresses the Shakespearean sentiment that true nobility is a virtue of the soul, not an automatic birthright achieved by way of a family name.

In this context, the *Lorna Doone* narrative explains that, during the turbulent 17th century, young John Ridd of Exmoor in the South West of England wandered one St. Valentine's Day along the river which took him deep into Bagworthy Wood, where he came to the foot of a fast-running waterslide. On climbing to its top, he fell asleep at the water's edge, but was awakened by a lovely girl whose name, she said, was Lorna Doone. She explained that she lived in a nearby settlement with her grandfather Sir Ensor Doone, the captain of a notorious band of outlaws, but that she was confined to their valley and was not permitted to stray beyond the waterslide. John knew well of the outlaw Doones, for they were the very men who had killed his own father, and he promised that one day, when he came of age, he would return to rescue Lorna from her predicament.

In time, we rejoin John as he retraces his childhood footsteps into Glen Doone to meet once again by the rushing water with Lorna, who is now a beautiful young woman. She confides that she is betrothed against her will to the fearsome Carver Doone, who will succeed as captain of the clan when old Sir Ensor dies—which indeed he does soon afterwards. From that point, the tale moves to become one of romance and high adventure, with John, in the company of a local highwayman and a King's courier, taking on the might of forty outlaws in their bid to retrieve Lorna from the fortified Doone Valley.[3] They have learned that she is not Sir Ensor's granddaughter after all, but had been kidnapped by him in retribution against her father Lord Dugal, the outlaw's sworn and bitter enemy. Lorna, it transpires, is of high-born Scottish blood and her lineage is revealed by the crest on an ancient necklace she was wearing on the day of her abduction. On that account, it becomes necessary to retrieve the necklace as well as the maiden.

Eventually, after many battles and much intrigue, the mission is successful and Lorna Dugal is reinstated at the Stuart Court in London. John is duly knighted for his bravery by King James II and, eventually, Lady Lorna and Sir John return to Exmoor, where they are to be married at the little church of Oare. But then terror strikes once again as Carver Doone reappears at the moment of the blessing and, firing his carbine down the aisle, lays Lorna seemingly lifeless at John's feet upon the altar steps. The final battle then takes place between the two men and Carver meets his end in the deadly quagmire of the Wizard's Slough, whereupon Lorna, in the nature of all good nursery tales, recovers from her wound and the couple live happily ever after.

This then was the era which gave rise to the predicament of the Stewarts of Scotland – a time when, with their King on the throne in London, they were to discover that their Scottish lands now came under the authority of the English State. Their centuries of regional guardianship were duly challenged from South of the Border (or by other Scots families who were in league with the Anglican Parliament) and one of the Stewarts who suffered from the worst of this intrigue was the man who became known, in life and legend, as Sir Ensor Doone.

History of the Doones

Blackmore explains in *Lorna Doone* that Sir Ensor was a Scottish nobleman of very high birth and a cousin to the old Earl of Lorne. He became involved in a dispute over the old Earl's property, which was devolved in joint-tenancy, and he was married during this dispute to the old Earl's daughter.[4] In an attempt to divide the joint-tenancy arrangement, Sir Ensor became divided from it and lost his inheritance altogether, with the lost property being transferred through a female line. A woman's meddling was largely responsible for Sir Ensor Doone's downfall and, following the confiscation, he was outlawed from Scotland and left destitute.

According to the Exmoor Doone family annals,[5] including the journal of the 18th-century Rupert Doone and the Bible of his grandson Charles (which recorded the inscribed family lineage as was the custom), the Scottish exile of their noble Stewart ancestor took place in 1618 during the reign of King James VI (I). It is, therefore, easy enough to pin-point this man precisely, for the Stewart archives give a precise account of the very nobleman to whom all Blackmore's given details apply. He was Sir James Stewart of Lorne, 7th Earl of Atholl, 7th Lord of Innermeath.

The nature of how this man was expunged from history is immediately noticeable when consulting the 'Atholl' section in the establishment's own treasured 'bible' of nobility, *Burke's Peerage*. Here it is explained that, upon the death of John Stewart, 5th Earl of Atholl, without an heir in 1595, the Atholl title reverted to the Crown. Quite suddenly, the Atholl title reappears some years afterwards in the Murray family succession in 1629. The Murray inheritor's mother is said to have been Dorothea, the daughter of the 5th Earl, whom his father married sometime after 1662—impossibly more than three decades after their son supposedly gained the title!

In endeavouring to get to the root of the Register's missing thirty-four years from 1595 to 1629 (while ignoring the marriage date anomaly altogether), the 1908 Murray *Chronicles of Atholl and Tullibardine* certainly fill in some of the missing information, but still end up stating, 'It is somewhat difficult to understand what happened about the Earldom of Atholl '.[6]

In actual fact, there is nothing remotely difficult to understand here; one only has to consult the original Scottish MS Register[7] instead of the later English Register to see precisely what happened, and the story of those years between 1595 and 1629 is wholly in accord with Blackmore's account in Chapter 5 of *Lorna Doone*.

It tells that back in the early 1400s, two family strains emerged from the prevailing Stewart Lords of Lorne. From one of two brothers emerged the Earls of Atholl, while from the other sprang the Lords of Innermeath. The lines ran in parallel for five generations until John Stewart, the 5th Earl of Atholl (Blackmore's 'old Earl'), died without an heir in 1595. This is where *Burke's Peerage* elects to leave the story in order to pick it up again in another family line some years later, as applicable to the new Westminster ruling.

What happened was that upon the old Earl's death, his widow (Lady Mary Ruthven of Gowrie) married again in 1596 to her late husband's cousin, Sir James Stewart, the 6th Lord of Innermeath, who also became the 6th Earl of Atholl by grant of King James VI of Scots. But this Sir James Stewart already had a son by his previous wife—and this is the son we are looking for: Sir James Stewart of Lorne, 7th Earl of Atholl, 7th Lord of Innermeath (born 1583). He and his father have been completely ignored in the English records, but in understanding their story from the Scottish annals, the whole of R. D. Blackmore's *Lorna Doone* plot becomes clear.

In 1603 (the year of the union of Scotland and England's crowns) young James Stewart, the 7th Earl, married his cousin Mary—one of the old 5th Earl's three daughters—so that James's own step-mother also became his mother-in-law. This presented a terrible problem for Sir James since his step-mother and wife were the true heiresses of the Atholl estates which he, as the nominal Earl, was now supposed to manage. As Blackmore explains, the lands were held in joint-tenancy by the two women, along with his wife's other sisters—four women in all, who were at odds with each other as to how the estates should be run. Consequently, when the Privy Council in London reported to King James that chaos reigned in Atholl, it was the unfortunate Sir James who was reprimanded. And so (again as Blackmore explains) Sir James decided to divide the problematical joint-tenancy agreement, but he was now being closely watched because the parliamentary Privy Council wanted to remove the Stewart estates in total from the family, to pass them to another. It then transpired that, when a couple of sought-after villains were discovered hiding within the environs of Atholl, Sir James was immediately blamed for harbouring them and was flung into prison in Edinburgh castle!

From his dungeon, Sir James wrote a letter to King James in London—a letter which the King received, and to which he responded. The Privy Councillors dared not intercept their King's letter but, instead, they hastily released James under guard from the Castle so that he was not there to receive the royal communication. When King James heard what had transpired, he wrote a severe reprimand to the Privy Council on 27 June 1607, instructing them to have Sir James brought to him in London. On making his appearance, Sir James explained his untenable position and asked the King if he might sell his Atholl inheritance to relieve him of the responsibility—a request to which King James duly conceded. However, in drawing up the necessary document, the Privy Council referred to the deal as a 'transfer' instead of a 'sale'. At the same time, in their strategic relocation of regional boundaries in Scotland, the Council terminated for all time the Stewart heritage of Innermeath, which geographically ceased to exist. And so, when Sir James Stewart returned to Scotland, he had lost both his key titles, while his house, property and money had all been confiscated—in addition to which his wife and step-mother had abandoned him. He was absolutely penniless.

Ransom and Revenge

Once back in Edinburgh, Sir James was instructed to report to Lord Blantyre, the Government's Treasurer for Scotland, but having done this he learned that Blantyre was under orders to lock him away in Dumbarton Castle, and so before being transported from Edinburgh, Sir James escaped into the night. A woman called Margaret MacAllistair offered him shelter, and from her lodging he sent word to London asking for the money that was due from the sale of his Atholl title. Not only was there no money in response, but he was dared to try to collect it, while at the same time a Caution was placed upon him to the effect that if he strayed into England (which he would have to do in order to claim his sale proceeds), he would automatically be classified as an outlaw.

At that time, all adherents of the Clan of MacGregor, to which Margaret MacAllistair belonged, had been designated felon outlaws because of their feuding with another Clan who had more sway at Court. Most of them lived in the hills, in fear of their lives and, since they were forbidden under law to use the name MacGregor, they used Gaelic nicknames or the names of their ancestors—names such as *Aluin* (the Handsome), *Ruadh* (the Red) and *Eoin Dubg nan Luraig* (Black John of the coat of mail). Fearing that they would be seized in Edinburgh, Margaret and James eventually took to the MacGregor hills of Glenstrae in 1609, where they lived with Margaret's kinfolk. James, in the tradition of his own great ancestor, called himself Eoin of Lorne (John of Lorn), but the MacGregors, in the nature of their own more descriptive styling, dubbed him *Eoin Ciar Douine*—John the dusky man.

His chance for a royal audience came at last in 1617 when King James visited Falkland Palace in Scotland. But, on endeavouring to gain admittance, Sir James was immediately seized and flung into prison yet again. Once more, he escaped in the following year, knowing that regardless of the Caution he would have to see the King in London. Along with Margaret and a few retainers he duly crossed the Border into England, but his hopes were in vain and the Privy Council (though not imprisoning him for fear the King would find out) forbade him absolutely to return to Scotland, where he would be executed as a felon outlaw if discovered.

Sir James's days as a Scottish nobleman were over for ever and there was no hope of recouping any of his financial loss. He and his destitute group then set their feet westwards from London, following the setting sun until they reached Exmoor, where they took over a long abandoned medieval Knights Hospitallers' settlement in the Vale of Bagworthy. In the company of his MacGregor companions, James then forsook his family name altogether and the local inhabitants of Oare in

Somerset came to know him only by his Gaelic outlaw style: Sir Eoin Ciar Douine.[8]

After the statutory seven years from his apparent disappearance in 1618, James was recorded as being legally deceased in 1625 and his name, along with that of his father, was struck from the records. This left his Atholl title available to be passed to the family of Murray in due course, while the long established Stewart entitlement to Innermeath had become totally extinct.

While going through his problematical years with the Privy Council, Eoin Ciar's main rivals included the husbands of his wife's two sisters, but his main adversaries—the men who had fronted the Council's cause against him—were Marquis Gordon of Huntly and Baron Grant of Freuchie. These were the men against whom Eoin Ciar was ultimately bent on revenge—a revenge which eventually appeared possible in October 1644. In that month the offspring of his enemies were united when Lady Mary Grant of Freuchie was secretly married to Lewis Gordon of Huntly. Furthermore, a child was expected who would become the inheritor of the vast conjoined fortunes and estates. What a chance for a ransom!

The reason why this marriage was surprising to all and was held in secret, was partially because Mary was pregnant, but mainly because the Gordons were staunch Catholics, while the Grants were a Protestant family. The Scottish Register explains that, without any ceremony or warning, Mary and Lewis were married at a tiny presbytery near Elgin, in the dead of night and at gun-point.

By that time, Eoin Ciar Douine (locally pronounced, *Ensor Doone*) and Margaret MacGregor—as the Doone annals explain and as confirmed by Blackmore—had their own teenage sons and their Exmoor clan had grown in number by virtue of other outlawed MacGregors joining them. All they had to do was to wait for the birth of the Gordon-Grant child and then, at some convenient time afterwards, arrange the abduction.

Oddly, although the official Gordon family Register records the shotgun wedding, it makes no mention of the subsequent birth of a daughter, preferring to list the first child as a son, George, who was born a few years later (a son who appears in *Lorna Doone)*. Notwithstanding this, R. D. Blackmore was himself raised in foster care by the family of the Rev. Richard Gordon[9] and, accordingly, had access to more pertinent family archives. From these he constructed his story of the kidnapping of the young heiress, who was carried off to the Exmoor settlement and who, in recognition of her ancient ancestry, he called Lorna Doone (*Loarna Daouine*).[10] Clearly, the ransom was never paid—if it was ever requested—for as Blackmore explains, the bigger plan was for Eoin Ciar's son Charles (Carver Doone) to marry Lorna when she came of age, thereby enabling him to lay claim to her Scottish inheritance, with the proof of her identity being the all-important family necklace.

The relevance of all this to our current investigation is not so much that *Lorna Doone* is one of the most popular romantic tales of all time, but that its background history and the Stewart nobleman involved as a victim of the London plot were removed from all authorized historical record. With King James of Scots firmly established on the English throne, the one-time Tudor conspiracy to demolish the status of his House had begun. Sir James Stewart of Atholl and Innermeath was the first target in a series of strategically planned manoeuvres to remove the Stewarts from some of their traditional centres of Scottish operation. By 1629 the Stewart Earldom of Atholl was in the hands of the Murrays, while the Stewart title to Innermeath had been terminated altogether. As for the Stewart Lordship of Lorne, this had been transferred sometime earlier by virtue of a marriage arrangement and, when Queen Victoria's daughter Princess Louise married the Marquess of Lorne in 1871, the man she married was not a Stewart but a Campbell, whose family had been stalwart supporters of the Hanoverian Crown of England against the Stuarts and their fellow Scots in the 18th-century Jacobite Risings.

It was during the 17th century (between the years from James I's English accession in 1603 and 1688 when James II was deposed by the Anglican Parliament) that the last vestiges of the longest surviving Grail House were demolished—a demolition that had begun in 751 with the *Donation of Constantine*. Finally, after 937 years, the culture of the ancient Ring Lords (which made its last recognizable stand in the Scottish Clan System) was removed from the reckoning in terms of any national guardianship.

For a brief period after the Victorian marriage of Princess Louise, a flame of interest in the past history of the Doones was sparked by a perceptive journalist on London's *The Times* newspaper, who recognized the Stewart of Lorne connection. But Blackmore's hitherto foster father, Rev. Richard Gordon, was about to be canonized by the Church at that time, and so the author was reluctant to jeopardise this by revealing the family records from which he obtained his historical information. And so, when specifically questioned about the intrigue which provided the backbone for his classic novel, all Blackmore ever stated was, "Nothing will induce me to go into the genesis of *Lorna Doone*".[11]

16

Curse of the Werewolf

The Teeth of Beasts

When considering the various tribal cultures which existed in ancient Britain and Europe, we encountered the Wallan Wood Lords—the *Yulannu* of the BC years who introduced the winter solstice Yuletide festival. This high druidic caste from whose traditions much of the Dianic moon cult derived, were also called *Weres*. This is generally said to mean 'men'[1] but, strictly speaking, in the language of the Elder Faith (the 'elder' being a sacred tree of the Irish witches)[2] it related rather more to those regarded as 'god-men'. Their totem animal was the wolf—just as other tribes were represented by, say, a boar or a horse. These totems were really no more than the early precursors of heraldry, whereby families and clans became identified by the animals, plants, shells and other devices on their banners. It can be said, therefore, that their totem was the Were-wolf, but in the Church's denigration of all things connected with fairy lore, the term 'werewolf' has taken on a very sinister connotation: that of the man-wolf, who is particularly associated with the full moon.

Although the werewolf in its familiar Gothic guise is no more than an Inquisitional invention, the first apparent mention of men with the appearance of wolves comes from the Greek historian Herodotus in the 5th century BC. In his *Histories* he refers to an ancient Indo-European tribe called the Neurians, of whom he related:

Traditional portrayal of a werewolf

> The Greeks and Scythians who live in Scythia say that once a year every Neurian becomes a wolf for a few days and then reverts to his original state. Personally I do not believe this, but they make the claim despite its implausibility, and even swear that they are telling the truth.[3]

In practice, the Neurians did nothing more than to don wolf-skins at their sacred annual festivals, but the concept as seemingly portrayed by Herodotus was appealing enough to find its way into Greek and Roman mythology, with the most significant mention of the man-wolf phenomenon appearing in the *Metamorphoses* of Ovid (43 BC—AD 17). Here, in dealing with the *Creation and Ages of Mankind,* Ovid relates to Lycaon, King of Arcadia, who presented Jupiter (who did not eat meat) with a meal of flesh, thereby affronting the god who turned him into a wolf:

> With rabid mouth he turned his lust for slaughter
> Against the flocks, delighting still in blood.
> His clothes changed to coarse hair, his arms to legs.
> He was a wolf, yet kept some human trace,
> The same grey hair, the same fierce face.[4]

In the light of this Lycaon tale, the shapeshifting nature of the mythological werewolf was associated with a medical condition in which people suffered from the delusion that they were wolves, causing the medical establishment to classify that condition as Lycanthropy. The noted Victorian essayist Rev. Sabine Baring-Gould referred to this in 1865, stating that Lycanthropy "truly consists as a form of madness such as may be found in most asylums".[5]

The donning of wolf-skins appears quite often in old mythology, along with the premise that the wearer's nature can be transformed to become as wolf-like as his appearance. In the *Volsunga Saga* of the Ring Cycle, the characters Sigmund and Sinfjölti come upon the home of a sleeping skinner deep in the forest, whereupon each of them throws one of the man's wolf-skins onto his back. At this, the nature of the original animals becomes apparent and the companions howl like wolves, being quite unable to remove the skins. Once back in the forest they discover that they have acquired the strength of many men and begin to slaughter wayfarers with impunity, biting their throats.[6]

In Scandinavian lore the warrior Berserkers were seen to be diabolically possessed, working themselves into a fearful battle frenzy (hence, the phrase 'going berserk'). In this condition their demonic power gave them superhuman strength and they howled like hungry wolves. In accordance with all Church-promoted culture, however, the clergy decreed that even the awesome rage of the Berserkers could be extinguished by baptism!

By medieval times, when the Roman Church had become firmly established, the notion of werewolves had attracted the Christian imagination to some degree, especially since the wolf had been used as a predatory example in the Gospels, with Matthew 7:15 stating in the sayings of Jesus, 'beware of false prophets which come to you in sheep's clothing, but inwardly they are ravening wolves'. Also, in Matthew 10:16: 'Behold, I send you forth as sheep in the midst of wolves: be ye therefore as wise as serpents and harmless as doves'.

Although this Bible entry established the serpent firmly into position as a creature of wisdom rather than as something satanic, it also introduced a new adversary—the wolf. In practice, the wolf was only suggested figuratively here as being an enemy of sheep, but since the emergent Christians regarded themselves as sheep, the wolf became a symbolic enemy of Christianity—a concept further supported by another Jesus quotation in Luke 10:3: 'Go your ways; behold, I send you forth as lambs among wolves'.

Apart from this notional, but essentially unfounded, fear of wolves there was nothing which really associated them with anything devilish, and there was nothing in their nature or appearance which could be so ascribed. The wolf is actually a highly intelligent and social animal geared to a community environment, as are people. It is for this reason that uncommon individuals who separate themselves from conventional behaviour are referred to as 'lone wolves'. Even when the famous *Lay of the Werewolf* appeared in the 12th-century writings of Marie de France there was nothing unduly dark about the character. The story was simply of an unfortunate baron who, on being betrayed by his wife and her lover, was destined to live in the woods as a wolf called Bisclavaret. On being eventually befriended by a noble King and welcomed into his Court, the wolf-man was enabled to take his revenge on his wife and the dishonourable knight, as a result of which he regained his manhood.[7]

It was not for another three-hundred years that the subtle element of canine fear was linked with the legend of Lycaon, thereby providing enough ammunition for the Dominican Inquisitors, who were the true inventors of the werewolf of Gothic romance. Indeed, it was from the newly devised Inquisitional classifications associated with the Church's concept of Witchcraft that many creatures were dubbed with supernatural or anti-Christian significance. To support their claims in this regard, the Inquisitors moved beyond the New Testament Gospels, harking back to a pronouncement of the Old Testament book of Leviticus 26:22, which states in the apparent words of Jehovah when chastising the Israelites, 'I will also send wild beasts among you, which shall rob you of your children and destroy your cattle, and make you few in number'. Then again from Deuteronomy 32: 'I will also send the teeth of beasts upon them'.

Both of these biblical quotations are cited in the *Malleus Maleficarum* to establish the case against witches,[8] but it was in the latter of the two that the Church found its most strategic inspiration: 'the teeth of beasts'. For centuries, the bishops and friars had waged war upon the Albigensian tradition by miniaturising the significance of those of the Ring and Grail successions. They had been identified as sprites, elves and the like—even as malevolent, cannibalistic fairies—but in portraying them as being of small stature the required impetus of trepidation had itself become diminished. Something more fearsome and hideously supernatural was needed if the Church's strategy was to succeed—something which could be large in stature and more terrifying than man himself—something truly powerful; something with 'teeth', which are not regarded as a natural weapon of mortal man. One outcome of this thought process was the vampire, but the more immediately conceived enemy of the Christian flock was perceived as the werewolf.

Many wild animals, especially fanged creatures, are, by virtue of their strength, cunning ways and carnivorous habits, naturally avoided and treated with some reserve by humans, but that does not make them in any way sinister or devilish. However, a man or woman with the ability to transform into such a beast, with obvious harmful intent, becomes a very scary prospect, for this is the stuff of nightmares and the Church made very good use of this type of dream-state trepidation. Subsequently, in 1605, the official definition of a werewolf was laid down by the Catholic antiquarian and compiler of devotional books, Richard Verstegan, who wrote:

> The werewolves are certain sorcerers who, having anointed their bodies with an ointment which they make by instinct of the devil, and putting on a certain enchanted girdle, do not only into the view of others seem as wolves, but to their own thinking they have both the shape and nature of wolves'.[9]

Gypsy Rings

The Inquisition, although ostensibly set against heretics, managed to include all manner of groups and factions within this overall classification. A heretic was essentially anyone who disobeyed the rule of Rome and the word 'heresy' is defined as 'a belief or practice contrary to the orthodox doctrine'.[10] It actually derives from the Greek *hairesis*, meaning 'choice'. Thus, what was being denied by the Church was the right of any choice which did not conform with the dogmatic opinions of the bishops.

Once Witchcraft had been brought into the equation, the field was opened even wider so that just about anybody could be charged with heresy. In this regard, midwives were among those specifically targetted since the Church considered childbirth to be a defilement of both the mother and the child—with the Virgin

Mary conveniently escaping the doctrine since she had seemingly not committed the mortal sin which led to her divine conception. Consequently, women who died in childbirth were denied Church burial because they were unclean!

Midwives were clearly witches, it was decreed, because they were the upholders of the sinful act, in addition to which they used herbal potions for the relief of maternal pain and even had the audacity to defy the clergy by advising on matters of birth control. As for the new mothers, they had to undergo a humbling readmittance to the Church by way of 'churching', whereby they were not allowed into consecrated places until blessed by a priest and given permission. Meanwhile, the infants were separately cleansed by Church baptism, prior to which they existed only in sin!

Another of the unwitting groups dragged firmly into the Witchcraft net were the gypsies. Any person with no fixed place of residence was regarded with suspicion because an itinerant lifestyle was perceived as a means by which to evade Church authority.[11] Gypsies lived outside the towns and villages, and were deemed to be very mysterious. Many gained temporary employment as woodcutters or splitters (stave makers), as a product of which such trades, along with those of the pedlars, horse-dealers and animal trainers, were subjected to a blanket excommunication. At the same time, a Christian-inspired style of mythology was promoted in propagandist nursery tales which challenged the Grail stories of knightly quests and distressed damsels. These tales, such as inspired *Little Red Riding Hood* and *Hansel and Gretel*, were specifically designed to make children fearful of straying into the woods, where child-eating wolves and witches might lurk—a place which was the domain of the gypsies, where the Church was unable to wield any regulatory influence.

Other affronts said to be perpetrated against the Church by these wandering people were such things as palmistry and fortune-telling, which were reckoned to deny the unforeseen will of God. The most hideous outrage said to be committed by gypsies was the fact that they wore rings in their ears. This was clearly a mark of the Albigensian heresy, just as Joan of Arc was charged with having magical rings in her possession. They used Gypsy Rings, said the Inquisitors, as a means of storing spells, while even their homes were supported by spoked wheels, which plainly identified the defiant nature of the devil! Those skilled in the use of herbal remedies were denounced as the brewers of dark wizardry and witches' potions, while ventriloquists were undoubtedly in commune with satanic forces! In the 17th century, Henry Boguet, the notorious Witchfinder of Burgundy, wrote in his *Discourse des Sorciers*, 'It was good to hunt down our comedians and minstrels, considering that most of them are wizards and magicians'.[12]

The Boguet records make it quite plain that, when it came to werewolves, there was (within the hundreds that he tortured and executed) no distinction between men and women. They did not even have to commit a crime to encourage his vengeance. One poor girl was burnt alive at the stake by Boguet simply because she was accused of having been seen to turn into a wolf whilst hiding behind a bush! The common command which prevailed throughout the witch-hunting fraternity was the same as prevailed in the Albigensian Crusade: 'Kill them all; God will know his own'.

During the one-hundred years from 1525 there were no fewer than 30,000 werewolf trials in France, notwithstanding the rest of Europe, and in large measure these implicated either gypsies or poor people from the rural regions. It was actually reckoned that such folk of rude habits, who wandered in the woods and wild places, might naturally fall into evil ways. The main connection made by the Inquisitors between gypsies and werewolves was their association with the moon and in particular with the element of the moon: silver. This was said to be deadly to the werewolf who, while in the wolf state, could only be killed with a silver blade or bullet. Hence, to gain the trust and avoid the curse of a gypsy or potential werewolf, one was supposed to pass over one's silver as a mark of submission—'crossing the palm with silver', as it was called. For this, the gypsy—generally a female—would respond with her art of *dukkering*, a Romany word which actually means 'bewitching', but is a skill of fortune-telling through reading one's body signs. The art was said to have been a form of magic inherited from ancient Egypt, where the wolf was the god of Lycopolis.[13] By virtue of this (and irrespective of their true place of origin) they were always called Egyptians before this definition was abbreviated to Gypsies. It was for this reason that Mary Jacob, the Merri-maid, (Chapter 4) was alternatively styled Mary the Egyptian and Mary the Gypsy.

The moon is the realm of the Goddess, represented by those such as Kali and Diana, and is consequently anathema to the One-God Christian faith. And so the wolf, being essentially a nocturnal creature, is dubbed with its own lunar significance, while also being associated with the oak cult of the druids.[14] Apart from denoting time, periods and cycles, the waxing and waning of the moon (which governs magic in the Western tradition) causes the tides to flow. The wiccan peak or 'high-tide' of psychic energy is determined by the full moon, which is when werewolves are reckoned to take on their wolf form. The wolf's link with the night is also expressly significant since the night corresponds to the subconscious and the shadows. At night visibility is limited and even familiar objects become only vaguely defined, so there is uncertainty in the air. Resultantly, darkness has become associated with things that are hidden and are, therefore, *occult*—a word which means quite simply 'hidden'. In the Christian tradition, however, something hidden is regarded as something secret, while secrecy itself is considered to be sinister since it challenges Church supremacy. By virtue of this, darkness becomes sinister, leading to such expressions as 'the dark side' when referring to a negative or foreboding aspect.

Ultimately then, the werewolf was emblematic of the man who, according to Church doctrine, had strayed into the night having been overcome by dark forces. Through Inquisitional eyes, these dark forces were seen as being the evil magic of the witches and gypsies of the forest—people over whom the bishops had no enforceable jurisdiction and who, by virtue of this, they persecuted and murdered in their thousands.

Rise of the Revenant

Although the concept of bloodsucking demons appears to have been around for the longest time, dating back to ancient Sumer in the 3rd millennium BC, the first such creature of any literary significance appeared in Greek mythology. She was Lamia, a Queen of Libya and mistress of Zeus, who was punished by the goddess Hera and turned into a scaly four-footed creature with a woman's face and breasts. Subsequently, in Central and Eastern Europe, the idea became associated with an unholy cult of the living dead, but in Britain the tradition made a very slow start. It was not until the 12th century that the Augustinian chronicler William of Newburgh mentioned occasions when the dead were said to return to terrorise the living. He identified these apparent fiends as being *sanguisuga*—a Latin term for 'bloodsucking',[15] although relating rather more to ruthless extortion than sucking blood in the literal sense.

For many centuries (as was the case with werewolves) vampiric revenants were not featured in any way as a part of the Christian agenda, but they finally emerged as representatives of evil during the latter Inquisitional period. At that stage the concept of Satan had become established and he was said to have many heretical worshippers among the witches and gypsies.[16] However, just as Jesus had his perceived host of heavenly angels, Satan was also in need of some personal emissaries so that the divine war could be properly waged and preached with some gusto from the pulpits.

The main premise of Christianity was the promise of salvation as achieved through subservience to the bishops, aligned with the perpetuation of a serene afterlife in a heavenly environment. But how could the alternative notion of Hell be portrayed on Earth in a manner which would scare the life out of the tentative

1. *Shamash the Shining One.* Ancient Sumerian relief depicting the god Shamash with the Rod and Ring of divine justice

2. *Oberon and Titania* by Sir Joseph Noel Paton, 1849

3. *The Ring of Melusine* by Sir Peter Robson, depicting the Lily and Rose, with the Grail and the Vine

4. *Moses and the Serpent* by Sébastien Bourdon (1633-34)

5. *Lilith* by the Hon John Collier, 1887

6. *The Mermaid* by John William Waterhouse, c1901

7. *Scythian Warriors* by Angus McBride, 1983, depicting the Phrygian style headwear a
scale-like armour

Allegory of Chastity by Hans Memling (1435-94). Towers were always representative of feminine virtue

9. *Soul of the Forest* by Edgar Maxence, 1898. Allegory of the Star Fire

10. *Mary Magdalene* by Caravaggio, 1595, featuring the engrailed cup design on her skirt

11. *Hylas and the Nymphs* by John William Waterhouse, 1896

12. *The Portal of the Twilight World* by Sir Peter Robson

Important aspects of heritage are confined to a netherworld of fantasy to uphold an alternative vested interest

13. *The Death of Dagobert* by Sir Peter Robson. The Merovingian crown is usurped by th
Church

14. *Attainment of the Sangréal* by Dante Gabriel Rossetti (1828-82)

15. *La Belle Dame Sans Merci* by Arthur Hughes, 1863, from the poem by John Keats

16. *Diana the Huntress.* School of Fontainebleau, 16th century

17. *Ring Dance of Apollo and the Muses* by Baldassarre Peruzzi (1481-1536)

18. *The Birth of Venus* by William-Adolphe Bouguereau, 1879

19. *Marie of the Sea* by Sir Peter Robson. Allegory of *la Dompna del Aquae*

20. *The Lily Fairy* by Luis Ricardo Falero, 1888

21. *Robin Goodfellow (Puck)* by Johann Hienrich Füssli (1741-1825)

22. *The Pendragon Ring* by Sir Peter Robson, featuring the denounced *Donation of Constantine*

23. *Sleeping Beauty (The Rose Bower)* by Sir Edward Coley Burne-Jones, c1880

believers or reluctant worshippers? Somehow Hell had to be given an earthly form and what better than the concept of dead people who could not complete their dying because they were so hideously unclean—people who were, in fact, 'undead'. Such people, said the churchmen, had to roam the mortal world like lost souls with no dimension of life or death to call their own because they had attempted to die without the blessing or consent of God!

The concept was good enough in part, but it was really no more scary than the idea of ghosts with a physical form. Something else was needed; these beings had to become predators, like the werewolves, in order to make people fearful enough to lean wholly upon the Church for deliverance. So, what would all people, rich and poor alike, fear to lose the most if they were seeking salvation for their souls? The answer to this question was found (as it had to be if the plan were to succeed) in the Bible. To be precise, it was found in the Old Testament book of Leviticus (17:10-11), which states: 'It is the blood that maketh an atonement for the soul'. It was therefore decided that the 'undead' creatures would be said to prey upon people's blood, thereby divesting them of the route to atonement.

If there was a problem to be overcome in this regard it was the fact that this Leviticus statement was part of a very ancient Hebrew law and had little or nothing to do with Christianity. A way was soon found, though, to cope with this anomaly when the Church ruled that every good Christian who partook of the Communion wine was figuratively drinking the blood of Christ. This divine blood then became a part of his or her own body and any creature which then extracted blood from such a person was reckoned to be guilty of stealing the blood of Christ![17] In this regard, the demons could be portrayed as Antichrists endeavouring to devour the life-blood of the Christian Saviour.

17

Twilight of the Vampire

The Undead

But first on earth, as vampyre sent,
Thy corpse shall from its tomb be rent;
Then ghastly haunt thy native place,
And suck the blood of all thy race.
George Gordon, 6th Lord Byron – The Giaour

It was as late as 1645 when the first book concerning the bloodthirsty 'undead' was produced by the Greek Catholic clerk Leo Allatius. In his *De Graecorum hodie quorundam opinationibus* he told of the *vrykolakas*—a corpse taken over by a demon. This idea was something relatively new to western Christianity, but the vrykolakas had persisted for some time in Greek folklore and had already been recognized as a devil figure by the Eastern Orthodox Church. In 1657 the demonic revenant was mentioned again by the French Jesuit Fr. François Richard in his *Relation de ce qui s'est passe a Saint-Erini Isle de l'Archipel.*

In this context the Catholic and Protestant Churches found their greatest inspiration, for having brought this satanic creature into play they were then enabled to redesign and embellish the character of the vrykolakas for a market that had hitherto never heard of him. In doing this, it was perceived that such a devil could not possibly be seen to exist in the company of Christian artifacts—in consequence of which a whole new mythology was born in the latter 17th century. The creatures could be repelled, it was decreed, by such devices as consecrated holy water, the eucharistic wafer and the crucifix—or in the case of the Protestant Church (which did not generally use crucifixes) the open Latin cross without the Christ figure.

Dating from as far back as the 9th century was an old Romanian and Hungarian practice designed to prevent the dead from walking. In the minds of the pastoral folk, a person who died was seen as having been cut down from life, as might be a tree or a crop. In this regard it was customary to lay a sickle upon the buried body to serve as a reminder that it could no longer wander in the mortal world. This probably accounts for the fact that Death—the Grim Reaper—has long been portrayed as a partially clad skeletal figure carrying a sickle.

This burial practice was applied especially to those who had died before their allotted time—perhaps as the product of an accident, murder or disease—and might awaken without knowing they were supposed to be dead! Such people, it was thought, were the most likely candidates to become the walking 'undead', along with those who died from suicide, alcoholism or, as the clerics insisted, those who were illegitimately born. Just about anyone who might have been born or died without the consent of God's own timing was destined to become a revenant—as were those buried in unconsecrated ground. Very often people died of plague or communicable infection, following which they were interred in a hurry, with no ceremony, so as to confine their disease below ground. Such victims were expressly condemned by the Church, for to be interred without a priest in attendance was a certain route to a compact with the devil!

In some ways, the nominal definition of the vrykolakas was similar to that of the werewolf which, in the Slovakian and Bulgarian traditions, had been called the *verkolak*. The Byzantine Church Serbians were the first to link the two demonic types together, calling them jointly *vlkoslak*.[1] This was all very good news for the Church bishops because the shapeshifting werewolf had a limited trepidatory function, especially in places like England where wolves were generally unknown, although some existed then to the north in Scotland.

The work of the Catholic clerk Allatius was carefully devised so as to link the evolving vrykolakas with witches and gypsies, but subsequently a new strategy was implemented which drew a more forceful connection between the bloodsucking demons of the living dead and the Albigensian Ring Lord culture. This enabled the Church to add a truly fearsome creature to the realm of the fairies and elves, and before long the 'undead' were portrayed at their senior level as ungodly counts and barons. At the same time, for a reason that we shall soon discover, these noble revenants were strategically reclassified as vampires.

In the main, the vampire tradition emanated from the Carpathian regions of Europe and flourished within the Balkan and Germanic states. The direct connection between the vampire and witch cults appears to centre upon Romania, while the definition *strigoi* (female *strigoaica*), meaning 'witch', became a popularised description for a vampire in other regions. The word actually derived from *strix*, the Latin term for a screech-owl.[2] But what had a straightforward night-flying screech-owl to do with bloodsucking demons?

The answer to this question actually provides one of the most important of all links to the Church's denigration of the ancient Ring Lord heritage since it reverts immediately back to the biblical Lords of Edom, whom we encountered in our investigation of the Albigensian bloodline. These noble princes (the sons and descendants of Isaac's son Esau) were the very race from whom the *Tuadhe d'Anu* fairy kings emerged. They were those of whom the Old Testament book of Isaiah (35:1) says, 'The wilderness and the solitary place shall be glad for them, and the desert shall rejoice and blossom as the rose', while adding that 'the screech-owl shall also rest there, and find for herself a place of rest'.[3] However, in the Roman Church's Latin *Vulgate* Bible the 'screech-owl' definition is not used in its translation of this Isaiah verse, citing instead the name Lamia—the female bloodsucking demon of Greek mythology as mentioned at the outset of this chapter.[4] In the Hebrew tradition Lamia was associated with the Sumerian Lilith, who was said to fly like a night-owl[5] and who, in the esoteric Jewish tradition of medieval times rose to become God's own queenly consort.[6] Indeed, in his translation from the Hebrew text, the Semitic scholar Raphael Patai quotes the relevant screech-owl section of Isaiah 34:14 as: 'Yea, Lilith shall repose there, and find her a place of rest'.[7]

And so it was that Lilith, the great matriarch of the Ring Lords, went through the literary process of becoming a Lamia, a screech-owl (*strix*), a *strigoaica* witch and ultimately the mother of vampires. Thereby, the 17th-century Christian Church was enabled to directly attach the vampire mythology to her descendants of the fairy race. It was as a result of this very strategy that the term 'vampire' evolved from the ancient Scythian language of the *Tuadhe d'Anu*.

The Great Debate

Among the early vampiric creatures which followed the 17th-century vrykolakas of Leo Allatius, were the Slavonic-German demons known as the *nachtzehrers*, meaning 'night wasters'. They were said to be corpses who rose from their graves to feed upon other bodies, but had the rather odd habit of also chewing at their own extremities! When such presumed nachtzehrers were found during the obsessive grave huntings that went on in those times, it was customary to drive stakes through the creatures' mouths to pin their heads to the earth so they were prevented from their night wanderings.

In Prussia it was reported that some of these corpses showed signs of blood around their mouths, leading to their vampiric reputation. But this was actually a common symptom of death caused through pneumonic plague when blood was expelled from the victim's own lungs.[8] These said cowardly scavengers were also reported to have very white livers—hence the expression 'lily-livered coward', but this again was the result of blood disorders whereby the veins had become clogged in life, thereby severely restricting the circulation and causing death. It is actually a condition currently induced in geese for the production of liver *pâté de foie gras*. As for the supposed chewing of extremities, this was quite simply the work of underground predators.

Another said ghoul of the era was the Bavarian *blautsauger* (bloodsucker), who seemingly met his fate through not being baptised! The invention of this creature was one of the Church's best conceived strategies to ensure that infants were taken dutifully to the font. This fiendish night stalker, as against the generally red-faced nachtzehrer, was said to be very pale in colour and it was from the legends of blautsauger that the notion of garlic arose as a repellent, as so often used along with holy devices in modern film portrayals.[9] Garlic was smeared around door and window-frames to prevent demonic access but, more realistically, it was seen to be a protection against plague. The Church was keen enough to accept garlic as an anti-vampire measure alongside crucifixes and holy water because it was not regarded as an item of Witchcraft as were many other such plants, being widely used for culinary purposes in Rome. A wonderfully devised Catholic legend actually related that garlic had first been donated to the world by St. Andrew!

If a nachtzehrer or blautsauger did find its way into one's home, there were formally defined ways to check its authenticity—just in case a dirt-ridden half decomposed corpse was not enough for visual recognition! Firstly, it was reckoned that they cast no reflection in a mirror, since a mirror or water reflection was deemed to be the picture of one's soul. Therefore, given that revenants had no soul, it was impossible for them to have a reflection. It was customary to cover mirrors or turn them to the wall when in the presence of a corpse, for it was thought that the mirror might harness the spirit of death and cause another who looked in it to die.[10] The fact that mirrors were capable of capturing the reflected soul led to the superstition that to break a mirror resulted in seven years' bad luck since it would apparently take seven years for a person to regain his or her shattered spirit and would, meanwhile, be rendered soulless.

The second test of a revenant was to check for any bodily shadow, for they were said to have none—especially if their shadow had been stolen during their lifetime.[11] One method by which shadows could be stolen was if they had perhaps been nailed to a wall. Strange as it might seem, this actually was a practice on Romanian construction sites. By way of an old inexplicable superstition, it was thought that to have a man cast his shadow upon a newly erected building and then to drive a nail through the shadow's head would ensure the building's durability and longevity!

During the latter 1600s notable texts concerning the evil doings of the nachtzehrers were *De Masticatione Mortuorum* (by the German writer Philip Rohr) and *Die Miraculis Mortuorum* (by Christian Frederic Germann). Subsequently, in 1746, the French Benedictine abbot Dom Augustin Calmet published a treatise on Vampires, entitled *Dissertations sur les Apparitions des Anges des Démons et des Esprits et sur les revenants, et Oupires de Hingrie, de Boheme, de Moravic, et de Silésie*. He based his notes upon an Austrian military report concerning a series of murders in Serbia. The man blamed by the villagers for these killings was an ex-soldier called Arnold Paole, who was long dead and buried, having fallen from a hay-wagon and broken his neck. When his body was exhumed, however, it was said to carry an amount of what appeared to be fresh blood.

This story, as presented by the abbot, appears to suggest that the exhumation was carried out by the Austrian military team, but this was not the case for there was actually no corpse available when they arrived at the scene. Their extant report, entitled *Visum et Repertum (Seen and Discovered)*,[12] makes it quite clear that it is simply the account of a local story, and that Paole had been disinterred, staked and burned within six weeks of his death some five years earlier, immediately after the said murders had been committed. Having been published in Belgrade, various other journalists wrote about the field report, which was featured in England's *London Journal* in 1732, making use for the very first time in Britain of the word 'vampire', as extracted in translation from the Serbian press.

During the 17th and 18th centuries numerous so-called vampiric events were placed on record in Central and Eastern Europe. They all concerned folk who had died and been buried, but who then returned to torment the people of their regions. There are long-winded accounts of corpses who stole milk, clothes, poultry and even children. There are countless records of murders committed by the 'undead' and of their cattle rustling or, very commonly, rapings. The fact is, however, that in no instance is there anything which remotely resembles the type of vampiric regime which has become the stuff of popular legend. Indeed, there is nothing enchanting enough here to have prompted any long-standing mythology—simply some local superstitions which enabled the authorities to fasten blame upon the dead so as to avoid the bother of proper criminal investigation in the rural and poorer areas. All it took to satisfy the immediate residential requirement in each case was to unearth a body, stake it to the ground, sprinkle a few drops of holy water while uttering some suitably impressive Latin, and justice was seen to be done!

By the 1700s, in a climate of widespread plagues and Church propaganda, fear of the 'undead' had grown to such fanatical proportion that a reworked version of the Arnold Paole report became a bestseller at the Leipzig Book Fair. But then a great vampire debate ensued within the universities, initiated by the theologian Michael Ranft, whose 1728 work, *De Masticatione Mortuorum in Tumilis Liber*, launched a direct attack against the existence of vampires. This was followed in 1732 by John Christian Stock's *Dissertio de Cadauveribus Sanguiugis*,[13] as an outcome of which the scholarly debaters came to the conclusion that vampire revenants were a myth, created and upheld by Church-led superstition.

Outside the academies the story was very different and, after so many years of indoctrination, people (particularly the Serbians and others of the Slavonic regions) began to blame all sorts of deaths, ills and infirmities upon vampires, making them scapegoats for any number of evils and misfortunes. In consequence, it became common for graves to be raided and their occupants decapitated, with their hearts torn out and ritually burned. This caused such a problem within local communities (where the local people were distraught to see their deceased loved ones unearthed and desecrated) that in 1755 Empress Maria Theresa of Austria was obliged to enact laws to forbid the practice. Even as late as the middle 1800s special attractively boxed vampire killing sets were being sold, each containing a flask of holy water, a tin of eucharistic wafers, a small pistol with silver bullets, a crucifix and a mallet. Obviously, one was supposed to find the necessary impaling stake elsewhere!

Gothic Romance

In terms of entertaining literature, as against serious reports and theses, the very first vampire poem, *Der Vampir*, came from Heinrich August Ossenfelder of Germany in 1748. This was followed in 1797 by *Die Braut von Korinth* (*The Bride of Corinth*), a poem by the famed dramatist of *Faust*, Johann Wolfgang von Goethe. But it was in Britain that the literary tradition was largely progressed, although the word 'vampire' did not enter the English language until the middle 18th century. Hitherto, it did not feature in the most comprehensive and now famous *Bailey's Dictionary*, published in 1721. The related word 'vamp' is given in modern dictionaries as 'a woman who uses sexual attractions to exploit men', but in *Bailey's* this same word is given as 'a kind of short stocking'. Even the 1798 poem *Christabel* by Samuel Taylor Coleridge, although based upon a vampiric theme, did not actually use the word. In fact, the vampire terminology did not move into English literary usage until the 1800s. The first mention appears to have been in the poem *Thalaba* by Robert Southey, released in about 1800, but in the popular 1862 *Walker's Dictionary* the meaning of vampire is given simply as 'a demon', while that word is itself listed as 'an evil spirit or devil'. Although there is no reference anywhere to the bloodsucking aspect which has become so familiar, this does seem to have entered the arena somewhat earlier, as is apparent in George Gordon, Lord Byron's poem *The Giaour*, published in 1813.

The first work of fictional English prose on the subject came from a colleague of Lord Byron in 1819. This short story, *The Vampyre*, was written by John Polidori and told of the mysterious aristocrat Lord Ruthven (an actual Scottish family title in the 1500s)[14] who preyed upon the blood of innocent women. Another of the Byron-Polidori group was Mary Shelley (the wife of Percy Bysshe Shelley, the poet), whose own tale—created for her friends' amusement at a gathering near Geneva—emerged in print as the classic horror story *Frankenstein*: the first ever book of the science fiction genre. For some time after this, Lord Ruthven was taken up as a character by various magazine writers, with the concept of vampires being creatures of the moonlight introduced in the middle 1800s.

Next on the scene was James R. Planché, the heraldist, playwright and librettist for the opera *Oberon—The Elf King's Oath*, whom we met in connection with the Robin Hood legend. Planché was certainly not slow to recognize the vampiric potential on stage and, in 1820, his romantic Scottish drama *The Vampire—or The Bride of the Isles* opened in London. This was based upon a play, similarly entitled *The Vampyre*, which was staged the previous year in Paris by Charles Nodier, and which was itself inspired by Polidori's work. Similarly centred upon the same theme was Heinrich Marschner's German opera *Der Vampyre*, the first ever vampire opera, which was performed in Leipzig in 1829. Subsequently, in 1841, the Russian writer Alexei Tolstoy published his story *Upyr*, while ten years later in Paris was performed the last dramatic play by Alexandre Dumas (of *The Three Musketeers* fame), entitled *Le Vampire*.

One of the most popular British series of the era was *Varney the Vampire*, whose story appeared in weekly instalments in the 1840s editions of one of England's *Penny Dreadful* magazines. Subsequently published in book form, James Malcolm Rymer's tale was of Sir Francis Varney, a Royalist supporter in the 17th-century Civil War who was shot by Oliver Cromwell's soldiers but continued his cause as a rather agreeable vampire. It was Varney who cemented the literary turning point from the dusty, stenching zombie of old European lore to the seductively normal figure who moved in polite company. Prior to this, the typical vampire was a bloated and dishevelled Slavonic peasant with long fingernails, wrapped in a filthy linen shroud with his mouth and one eye open and his face hideously ruddy and swollen.[15] But quite suddenly in the 19th century emerged the new vampire of romantic literature—one who, far from being disgustingly obnoxious, now had elegance, flair and sex appeal!

Varney was also the character who introduced the ultimate mark of the modern vampire to the world stage, for he possessed what no previous 'undead' figure had ever displayed, and in his opening assault on young Flora Bannerworth it becomes apparent that Varney had bloodsucking fangs.

> With a plunge he seizes her neck in his fang-like teeth—a gush of blood and a hideous gushing noise follows .... [later] All saw on Flora's neck a small puncture wound, or rather two, for there was one a little distance from the other.

Also significant in Varney's tale was the emergent concept of the vampire's dislike of sunlight—although portrayed rather more in reverse with him gaining a particular resuscitation from moonbeams. Finally he cast himself into a volcano so that the moon could not reach him and he would truly die.

Progressing the fast developing mood in 1872, came the Irish lawyer J. Sheridan le Fanu with his short novel concerning the female vampire *Carmilla*—and this was another tale which introduced some of the brooding Gothic themes which have since become so familiar. Carmilla slept in a coffin, she had superhuman strength, she had become a vampire through being bitten by another, and she was finally killed by a stake driven through her heart. Subsequently, in 1897, Britain's poet laureate

Joseph Rudyard Kipling progressed the female vampire theme in his poem *The Vampire.*

The term 'Gothic', as applied to literature, was first introduced in 1764 by Horace Walpole (the son of Britain's prime minister Robert Walpole) in his novel *The Castle of Otranto – a Gothic Story.* In essence, Gothic writing centres upon a dark and sinister theme with a mysterious, perhaps supernatural, terror prevailing in a suspenseful environment. As such, Mary Shelley's *Frankenstein* might be considered Gothic, but so too can other books not necessarily associated with the horror genre as such—stories such as Jane Austen's *Northanger Abbey,* Emily Brontë's *Wuthering Heights,* Charlotte Brontë's *Jane Eyre* and Daphne du Maurier's *Rebecca*—interestingly, all works by English female authors.

Principal founding publications of the Gothic movement subsequent to Walpole's *Otranto* were the late 18th-century works *The Mysteries of Udolpho* and *The Italian* by Ann Radcliffe, *The Monk* by Matthew Lewis, and *Vathek* by William Beckford—again all from English authors. But then, a hundred years later in 1897, came the greatest Gothic romance of them all, Bram Stoker's ultimate story of the vampire, *Dracula.*

Stoker's account brought many of the previous themes together, while also initiating some new ones—in particular the shapeshifting connection with the vampire bat. The interesting thing here is that literary vampires were not named after the vampire bat as is often cited; in fact quite the reverse was the case. This particular bat was named by the French naturalist Comte George de Buffon, Keeper of the Jardin du Roi, author of the *Histoire naturelle* in 1765 and *Des époques de la nature* in 1778. Prior to these works there had never been any association in any culture between the vampire and bats, but since these particular South American nocturnal mammals fed upon the blood of sleeping animals, Buffon named them in accordance with the vampire myth[16] as had been presented in the *treatise* of Dom Augustin Calmet. Although Bram Stoker's *Dracula* was the first story to incorporate the bat imagery, there had been a bat illustration in the original edition of *Varney the Vampir*e and this might well have prompted Stoker's concept. Clearly, though, he cared little for the reality since his bloodlusting bat was large, whereas the vampire bat (which laps rather than sucks animal blood) is a relatively small creature. The key attraction of bats to demonology in general, however, relies not so much on the bloodthirsty aspect of a particular species, but that they are (like cats, wolves and owls) creatures of the night.

First Penny Dreadful *edition of the Varney series, c.1840*

In America and Canada, the vampire cult made its first obvious appearance in the late 19th century, although some of the earlier European settlers had taken their more traditional revenant beliefs with them. In the main, the culture was confined to the eastern seaboard and in particular the New England States, with the first documented report of 1888 concerning the Stukeley family of fourteen children who began to die one by one. When six had died the bodies were exhumed and all but one were found to have decomposed as expected. On that account, the better preserved daughter, Sarah, was blamed for the other deaths and the corpses were all dealt with according to custom, having their hearts cut out and burned. In real terms, this report was not vampiric in any way, but it brought the old lore of the dead affecting the living back into play, following which many similar events followed in places such as Connecticut, Vermont and Rhode Island.[17]

In 1927 *Dracula* was brought to the London stage by the actor and playwright Hamilton Deane, whose Irish mother had been acquainted with Bram Stoker, and this play was the first to introduce the Count's now almost prerequisite black opera cloak. Prior to that there had been a couple of vampire movies in Britain and Russia, but America was the first to bring the genre to the silver screen in any memorable fashion.The vampire in this regard was played by Lon Chaney in the 1927 film *London After Midnight*. In that same year the Hungarian exile Bela Lugosi introduced *Dracula* to the American stage with a forty-week Broadway production based upon Hamilton Deane's London play. Then, by special arrangement with Bram Stoker's widow, this was followed by Lugosi's screen role as the famous Count in 1931, from which point the movie, TV and video industries on both sides of the Atlantic Ocean have never looked back, harnessing for all time one of the most popular of all filmable Gothic themes.

18

The Portal of Dracula

Vision of a Vampire

> Never did I imagine such wrath and fury, even to the demons of the pit. His eyes were positively blazing. The red light in them was lurid, as if the flames of hell fire blazed behind them. His face was deathly pale, and the lines of it were hard like drawn wires. The thick eyebrows that met over the nose now seemed like a heaving bar of white-hot metal.
> *Bram Stoker – Dracula*

Bram Stoker (1847-1912) was born in Ireland and attended Trinity College, Dublin, where he became president of the Philosophical Society and auditor of the Historical Society. In 1870 he graduated with honours in science and, after some time as a journalist, became the manager of Sir Henry Irving's Lyceum Theatre, London, in 1878. This was primarily a Shakespearean establishment, but it was here that, in the days before Irving and Stoker, James R. Planché's *The Vampire* had been staged in 1820 – at which time the theatre was called The English Opera House. The influence of Shakespeare's plays is very apparent in Stoker's *Dracula* and immediately before its publication on 26 May 1897 the author led a four-hour dramatised reading from his book at the Lyceum. Unfortunately, fire swept though the theatre shortly afterwards, destroying all the *Dracula* costumes and props, and in 1902 the Lyceum was closed.

During the Irving-Stoker partnership, which persisted until Irving's death in 1905, Stoker had begun to write his watershed vampire novel in 1890, inspired particularly by J. Sheridan le Fanu's 1892 tale of *Carmilla*. Compiling his book after the style of *The Moonstone* by Wilkie Collins, Stoker elected to tell the story through the eyes of various people, settling upon an intriguing presentation by way of a series of letters, journal entries and newspaper extracts. His working papers are now held at the Rosenbach Museum in Philadelphia, and from these it is apparent that his originally intended vampire character was to be an Austrian by the name of Count Wampyr.[1] What happened was that while in England at the public library in Whitby, Yorkshire, he came upon an 1820 text concerning Romania, entitled *An Account of the Principalities of Wallachia and Moldavia*. It was written by William Wilkinson, a former British Consul in Bucharest, and it was from a reference in this work that Stoker's vision of a vampire was born. It referred to 'A voivode [prince] Dracula', who led his troops across the River Danube to do battle with the Turks.[2]

This was a major inspiration for Bram Stoker, who immediately transformed his Austrian Count Wampyr to the Transylvanian Count Dracula. He also used the Wilkinson text to good advantage, by ascribing its limited information to the words of his scholarly Dutch vampire hunter Dr. Abraham Van Helsing:

> He [Dracula] must indeed have been that voivode Dracula who won his name against the Turks, over the great rivers on the very frontier of Turkey-land. If that be so, then he was no common man; for in that time, and for centuries after, he was spoken of as the cleverest and most cunning, as well as the bravest of the sons of the 'land beyond the forest'. That mighty brain and that iron resolution went with him to the grave, and are even now arrayed against us.

What appealed to Stoker was not just the wonderful ring of the name Dracula, but a note in the Wilkinson text which suggested that the name (in Romanian) meant 'devil'. Hence, he deduced that Voivode Dracula meant 'Devil Prince', and this was perfect for his project. The fact was, however, that Dracula (more precisely *Draculea*) actually meant 'Son of Dracul',[3] while Dracul (from the Latin *Draco*) meant 'Dragon'. (The Romanian language actually evolved directly from 2nd-century Latin.)[4] Historically, it is apparent that these were the very styles used in 15th-century Romania by two Wallachian princes: Vlad II (*c.*1390-1447), who was called *Dracul*, and his son, the voivode Vlad III (*c.*1431-1476), known as *Dracula*. Wallachia was a Romanian province north of the River Danube and south of the Carpathian mountains. Bordering to its north were Transylvania (a Hungarian domain in those times) and Moldavia which lay to the east of the mountains, while to the east of Wallachia was the Black Sea, and to the south Bulgaria.

Although there is a nominal reference to Vlad in Francis Ford Coppola's 1992 film *Bram Stoker's Dracula*, the fact is that the name of this Romanian prince does not appear anywhere in Stoker's book. The extent of Stoker's knowledge of the historical Vlad III is, therefore, a matter of speculation. It is possible that he gleaned some information in this regard from the Hungarian professor Arminius Vambéry, whom he cites in his *Reminiscences of Henry Irving* as having met in 1890, but there is nothing in his *Dracula* notes to confirm that Vambéry was necessarily a *Dracula* source. Nevertheless, it is interesting to see that (again in the words of Van Helsing) Stoker does make use of this man's name in the story:

> I have asked my friend Arminius, of Buda-Pesth University, to make his record; and, from all the means that are, he tells me of what he [Dracula] has been. He must, indeed, have been that voivode Dracula who won his name against the Turks.

There is actually a good deal of evidence that Vlad III used the sobriquet 'Dracula', since it features in several 15th and 16th century sources and in his own signatures.[5] But there is no reference to the fact that he was ever considered to be a bloodsucking demon, whether in a literal or extortionary context. In practice, quite the reverse was the case and, to the Romanian people, Vlad was a great national hero with a fine statue at Tirgoviste and another by his castle ruin at Capîtîneni on the River Arges. Even though *Dracula* was published in 1897, it was to be nearly a century before the Romanians became significantly aware of the connection between the fictional Count and their own noble Prince. This awareness only became significantly apparent after the 1989 fall of Communism, when Western literature found its way into the previously forbidden countries. This has now led to the legendary Dracula becoming a central feature of the expanding Romanian tourist industry. In real terms, Vlad is seen to have been a noted supporter of the peasant classes against the unscrupulous aristocrats; an upholder of law and order in turbulent times and a vigilant defender of his Wallachian principality against the might of the threatening Ottoman Empire of the Turks.[6] He is often cited in modern reference books as having been a brutal tyrant responsible for many atrocities and he certainly was harsh and ruthless to the extreme, but no such reference comes from his own nation, only from the Turks and Germanic Saxons who had infiltrated the Romanian regions.

Another intriguing reference in Stoker's text, relating to information received from Arminius of Budapest, states with regard to Dracula:

> He was in life a most wonderful man: soldier, statesman, and alchemist. Which latter was the highest development of the science knowledge of his time. He had a mighty brain, a learning beyond compare, and a heart that knew no fear and no remorse. He dared even to attend the

> Scholomance, and there was no branch of knowledge of his time that he did not essay.

The Scholomance (or School of Solomon), located in the mountains near Hermannstadt in Austria, was referred to in *The Land Beyond the Forest* (1888) by the Romanian folklore specialist Emily de Laszowska Gérard. Bram Stoker was acquainted with her work, being a fellow correspondent for *The Nineteenth Century* journal, and learned from her various useful items concerning the vampire cult in Europe. Regarding the Scholomance, Gérard wrote that this was considered to be a 'devil's school', where 'the secrets of nature, the language of animals and all magic spells are taught'.[7] But what appealed particularly to Stoker was the fact that Prince Vlad had attended this alchemical mystery school. Also important in relation to the work of Emily Gérard (who referred to Romanian vampires as *nosferatu*) was her 1885 essay *Transylvanian Superstitions* which prompted Stoker to locate his Count Dracula in Transylvania, whereas the historical Vlad, although having his castle near the Transylvanian border, was actually a reigning dynast of neighbouring Wallachia. Gérard additionally confirmed the tradition that the nosferatu were capable of creating other vampires by extracting their blood, and that the creatures could be exorcised by way of stakes driven through their corpses—aspects that were well used by Bram Stoker in his novel.[8]

Society of the Dragon

In 1431, at the fortress of Sighisoara in Romania, Vlad III was born into the Wallachian princely House of Barsarab the Great (1310-52). Vlad's father, Prince Vlad II of Wallachia, was the appointed military governor of Transylvania and on 8 February (in the year of his son's birth) he was inducted into the Society of the Dragon by Zsigmond von Luxembourg, King of Hungary. This installation was directly responsible for Vlad II's style of

Lord Draconis, from which derived his sobriquet 'Dracul' (the Dragon), with his son Vlad III (who inherited the Dragon office at his father's pledge) becoming 'Dracula' (son of the Dragon).

The original fraternity that was resurrected to become the Hungarian Society of the Dragon can first be identified as the Dragon Court of ancient Egypt under the patronage of the priest-prince Ankhfn-khonsu in about 2170 BC. It was later established more formally as a pharaonic institution by the 12th-dynasty Queen Sobeknefru (*c*.1785-82 BC) and its operation was much like that of a present day royal academy, being a unique assembly of science and scholarship.

The Court provided a foundation for priestly pursuits associated with the teachings of Thoth, which had prevailed from the time of King Raneb, a pharaoh of the 2nd dynasty and grandson of the biblical Nimrod (Genesis 10:8-10). Raneb reigned *c*.2852-13 BC, about three centuries before the Gizeh pyramids are reckoned to have been built. In those far-off times, the priests and temples were not associated with religion as were their later successors in other lands, but rather more with the duties of preserving and teaching the old wisdom. The temples were, therefore, places of 'work-ship', rather than of worship in the modern sense, and they incorporated the *al-khame* (alchemical) workshops of the Master Craftsmen.[9] It was the obligation of these Masters and the temple priests to maintain the spiritual welfare of the pharaohs, while ensuring the purity of a continuing royal bloodline which progressed through the Dragon Queens of the matrilinear Grail succession. Unfortunately, however, much of the old wisdom was lost as the great empires of Persia, Macedonia and Rome took their successive holds in the Mediterranean world. Around a million valuable documents were destroyed by fire when Julius Caesar invaded Egypt in 48 BC, and many more hundreds of thousands were lost in AD 391 when the Christians destroyed the great Library of Alexandria.

Long afterwards, on 13 December 1408 (when Britain was in her late Plantagenet era), the fraternal aspect of the Dragon Court was formally reconstituted by King Zsigmond of Hungary at a

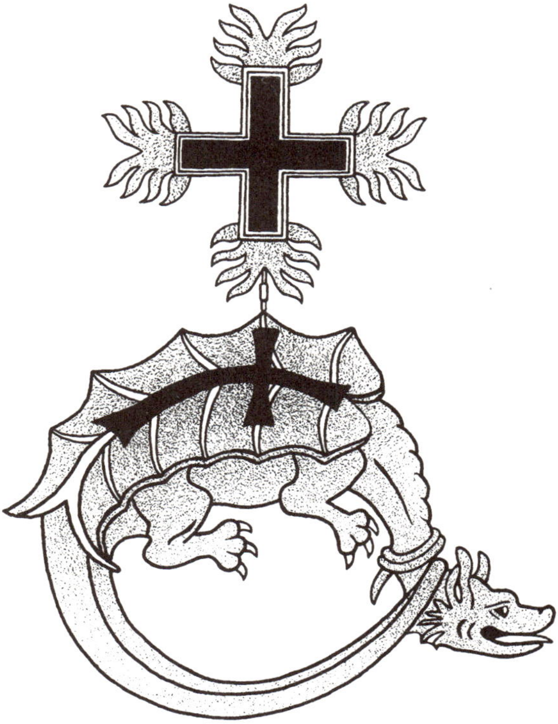

15th-century Insignia of the Hungarian Societas Draconis
The official device of the Imperial and Royal Dragon Court and Order, Sárkány Rend 1408

time of wars and general political turmoil. Having inherited the ancient legacy in 1397, he drew up a pact with twenty-three royals and nobles who swore to observe 'true and pure fraternity' within the *Societas Draconis* (Society of the Dragon)[10]—a style which later became *Ordo Draconis* (Hungarian: *Sárkány Rend*—Order of the Dragon), although the Court was by no means a conventional Order in the recognized chivalric sense.

Along with Zsigmond, other officers of the Court were his second wife Barbara Cilli (daughter of Duke Hermann II of Styria) and their daughter Elizabeth, thereby achieving the traditional overall standard of twenty-six members (two covens of thirteen). Others prominent in the *Societas Draconis* were King Vladislav Jagello of Poland, King Alfonse V of Aragon, Grand Prince Vitovd of Lithuania, and Duke Ernst of Austria, along with Christopher III, Duke of Bavaria and King of Denmark, Sweden and Norway. Later, in 1439, Thomas de Mowbray, England's Duke of Norfolk, was admitted to the Order. The founding document of *Zsigmondus dei rex Hungaraie* confirmed that members of the Court might wear the insignia of a dragon incurved into a circle, with a red cross[11]—based upon the original emblem of the *Rosi-crucis* which, in its various forms, had identified the Grail succession from the 4th millennium BC.

Shortly after this foundation, Zsigmond was crowned Holy Roman Emperor in 1411 and, although the Court's ancient origins were steeped in pre-Christian lore, Pope Gregory XII was obliged to approve his Emperor's non-Catholic establishment—for the nature of the Dragon is such that its princely tradition surmounts the mundane constraints of denominational dispute. After all, King David, Solomon and even Jesus were all pre-Christian dynasts of the Albigensian line and, in any event (for the time being at least), the main concern of the Order was to help protect regional Europe against the invading sultans of the expanding Turkish Empire, so there were more important things than religion to consider. Modern historical writers are often inclined to perceive the Ottoman invasions as being a matter of Muslims against Christians, but that was not the crux of the matter. The reality was quite simply that the Turks, like others before and after them, were building an empire and their greatest obstacle was the long-existing Byzantine Empire established by Rome, to which much of the Balkan region had been in some way affiliated. The religious differences were of secondary consequence and, in any event, Christianity was by no means supreme in countries like Hungary and Romania, which supported a strong pagan contingent.

Today the Hungarian Order of the Dragon is registered at the High Court of Budapest as The Imperial and Royal Dragon Court and Order (Ordo Draconis)—Sarkany Rend, 1408. The Grand

Chancellor is Chev. Dr. Gyorgy von varhegyi Lehr, Count of Oberberg, with Inner Court members including HRH Prince Michael of Albany, Head of the Royal House of Stewart, Grand Duke Peter Galicin of Carpathia and Baron Wodiank Zoltan Nemessary. Bishop Bela Csernak is the Grand Prior in Transylvania and Chev. Baron Andreas G. von Lehr the Grand Prior in Germany. Other notable members are Count Monsignor Laszlo Esterházy, Chev. Count Dr Janos szeki Teleki and Chev. Monsignor Laszlo von galantal Esterházy, Papal Chaplain, Provost Parochus of the Mariaremete Cathedral in Budapest. In Britain the Order resides within the Protectorate of the Royal House of Stewart, with the Grand Prior being Dr. Andrew von Zsigmond, Baron de Lemhény, of the Hungarian Consulate.

On 21 March 2000, Patrick O'Kelly de Conejera, Baron of Coul Finne and Past Vice President of the International Commission for Orders of Chivalry, was invested with the Order at the Mansion House, York, in the company of the Lord Mayor and Lady Mayoress representing the host City, and the Sheriff of York representing Her Majesty the Queen. At this ceremonial function, both Chev. Dr. Gyorgy von varhegyi Lehr, Count of Oberberg, Chancellor of the Imperial and Royal Dragon Court and Order, and Chev. Baron Andreas G. von Lehr, Grand Prior in Germany, were invested with the Household Order of the Royal House of Stewart as Knights of The Noble Order of the Guard of Saint Germain by HRH Prince Michael of Albany, Grand Protector of the Order of the Dragon for Great Britain and the English speaking world, Grand Master of the Order of Knights Templars of Saint Anthony and President of the European Council of Princes (for photographs and further details, *see* also Internet <http://www.mediaquest.co.uk/RDCsite/RDChome.html>).

Guardian of the Sidhé

Succeeding his father in 1448, Vlad Dracula was responsible for building the fortified Wallachian citadel of Bucharest, now the capital city of Romania. His founding document is dated 20 September 1459. Prior to that, his principal Court was at Tirgoviste. Castle Dracula, now only a shell (but well decked, with good stairways for visitors), stands high on a mountain peak near Curtea-de-Arges by the Transylvanian border and the Borgo Pass (as featured in *Dracula*). On the other side of the Fagaras range is the Teutonic Castle Bran, whose interior design was used in part for some of Bram Stoker's residential descriptions, though it was never occupied by Vlad Dracula himself.

Vlad Dracula
From a 16th-century woodcut

Vlad the Impaler
From a German propagandist pamphlet–Nuremberg 1499

As well as being called *Dracula,* Prince Vlad was also styled *Tepes,* and since this word pertains to wooden poles it is generally said to relate to the fact that his favoured punishment for enemies of the State was to impale them upon wooden stakes. On that account, he is often referred to these days as Vlad the Impaler. The 15th century was an era when tortures and executional punishments by the Church and governments alike were hideous and brutal spectacles, designed to provoke their own controls upon the people at large. Therefore, atrocious as Vlad's method appears in hindsight, it was in line with other terrible punishments of the day such as boiling victims in oil, burning them at the stake or roasting them alive over slow fires.

Even so, we must remember that Vlad Dracula was a somewhat unique individual in that, although not considered in any way to be a vampire in the sense of being a bloodsucking revenant, he was certainly an Overlord of the old tradition, even having the reddish hair and green eyes of his Scythian ancestors. He had attended the Austrian School of Solomon[12] and had graduated with honours in a ritual known as Riding the Dragon. This mystery-school establishment was a centre of scientific and alchemical learning, from where he emerged with a keen understanding of the glandular bodily effects of those endocrinal secretions which enhance longevity and increase consciousness. Clearly, Vlad was a high melatonin producer—possibly even an adept of the old-time Star Fire culture—and such people are adversely affected by sunlight, for they are night-operatives (*melos tosos*).

The Overlord's realm was centred upon the royal seat of the Rath—a portal to the Netherworld constructed upon a framework of wooden poles and referred to as *tepes* in the ancient style of the Cassi Wood Lords. Hence, whatever connotation Vlad's Turkish and Germanic-Saxon enemies might have attributed to the name Vlad Tepes, it actually referred to the fact that he was a designated Portal Guardian of the transcendent *Sidhé*. In the event, he is remembered as a tenacious champion of his people, especially of the peasant classes, while his severities were directed towards the corrupt aristocracy and certain hostile invaders.

Reign of the Voivode

Vlad Dracula became the seventeen year-old Voivode (Prince) of Wallachia after his father's murder by the henchmen of the treacherous Transylvanian governor János Hunyadi. This man had usurped the princely title in 1447, while also killing Dracula's elder brother Mircea. Prior to that, Vlad Dracula and his younger brother Radu had, from the ages of thirteen and nine respectively, been held captive by the Ottoman Turks at the fortress of Egrigöz in Anatolia.[13] Under the circumstances, Vlad Dracula was released to inherit the throne of Wallachia, which was subject to an overall Turkish control, but Radu remained in custody until he succeeded his brother.

On taking up his princely office, Dracula's immediate reign lasted for only two months until he was ousted by a remote kinsman and confederate of Hunyadi, called Vladislav II. Eventually, however, Vladislav was killed in battle and Dracula regained his throne on 6 September 1456 to reign in Wallachia and the Transylvanian duchies of Amlas and Fagaras. But, three years earlier the Turks had made their most significant conquest, having overrun Constantinople—the Byzantine (East Roman) capital which had survived for more than a thousand years since the fall of the Western Empire—duly renaming it Istanbul.

From the very outset, Dracula was determined to wreak his revenge upon the aristocratic *boyars* who were responsible for slaying his father and burying his brother Mircea alive—and this led to an act of retribution that was to cement his unrelenting image for all time. The boyars were the landowning class in Romania. They possessed vast domains including many towns, villages and conveniently tax-exempt monasteries, being the local aristocrats even if not of noble birth. Originally the peasants had lived in predetermined 'free land' communities, but the boyars had introduced a tithe-paying serfdom similar to the feudal regimes of other European countries, and they were ruthless in their exploitation of the people.

János Hunyadi was dead when Dracula returned to his throne (as was Vladislav II), but Dracula knew the identities of their murderous henchmen and their boyar families. The time had come, Dracula decided, for a show of strength that would purge the land of these troublesome self-seeking aristocrats. At the height of the Easter festivities in 1459 his Palace Guard entered the courtyard and feasting-hall in Tirgoviste, where they seized five-hundred boyars in readiness for either execution or hard labour as the extent of their crimes determined. Of the latter, the Romanian press reported:

> He had found that the boyars of Tirgoviste had buried one of his brothers alive. In order to know the truth he searched for his brother

> in the grave and found him lying face downward. So when the day of Easter came, while all the citizens were feasting and the younger ones were dancing, he surrounded them ... led them ... to Poenari, where they were put to work until their clothes were torn and they were left naked.[14]

The work to which they were sentenced (as a working chain from the Poenari quarry to the precipice above the River Arges) was the building of Castle Dracula. Meanwhile the treacherous boyar elders had been even less fortunate; they were conducted to a place outside the city wall, where they were individually impaled upon upright wooden stakes—a fearsome practice which Dracula had learned from the Turks while he was in their captivity. Subsequently, he established his own new style of nobility, replacing the old-time boyars with appointees from the free peasant class, particularly those who had shown their bravery on the battlefields. He protected his citizens totally from the rigours of Germanic and Turkish exploitation, refusing to acknowledge their tithe levies, while even granting his own tax immunity to certain of the poorer villages and settlements under an egalitarian policy whereby the better-off were expected to help support those less fortunate.

Dracula also managed, where others had failed, to bring even the Church to submission within his realm, where he was considered to be as equally empowered as the Pope. If any monk or cleric dared to protest, he was simply shown the rotten corpses and skeletons of the boyars, which hung upon their stakes for years, and a change of heart was soon engendered. Stakes were also strategically placed in readiness, and very often used, in the Tirgoviste Palace yard and other public places, so that none could forget that law and order was a primary requirement of the Overlord's regime. Consequently, Dracula's position in history presents its own paradox which depends wholly upon the perspective of the beholder. To many he is seen as a heartless and ruthless despot akin to Ivan the Terrible, while to others he appears like a welcome and popular benefactor in the manner of Robin Hood.

According to the Romanian archives, such things as crime, immorality, unemployment and homelessness were quite unknown in Dracula's Wallachia. So revered and feared was he that a solid gold cup which he placed by the fountain of Tirgoviste for the benefit of thirsty travellers, remained quite unmolested throughout the whole of his reign.[15]

Early in 1462 Dracula battled against the powerful Turkish forces of Sultan Mehmed the Conqueror, who occupied regions along the River Danube. He gained many victories, but Mehmed responded with a mighty invasion of Wallachia, leading an army of three-times the size of Dracula's own, with intent to take control of the region once and for all. This forced the Prince into a hurried retreat to Tirgoviste where, to the Sultan's horror on his subsequent arrival, he was confronted by some 20,000 of his own men suspended upon stakes. Historically, this became known as the Forest of the Impaled, and it was too much even for the Sultan to bear. Upon witnessing such a devastating and strategically organized defeat, he surrendered his arms and led his men away in their own retreat from the city.

At that stage it became apparent that Dracula's younger brother Radu (by then in league with the Turks) had been willing the Sultan's success, for he was now making his own bid for the crown of Wallachia. He, therefore, wasted no time in taking up Mehmed's abandoned cause, leading his own troops into Tirgoviste and pursuing his brother overland to Castle Dracula. From the heights of nearby Poenari, an arrow flew into a window of Dracula's quarters. The note tied to its shaft was retrieved and read by Dracula's wife who, recognizing that capture and torture were imminent, threw herself from the battlements into the river below. That part of the water is still known as *Rîul Doamnei* (Princess River).[16] Dracula managed his escape across the four-thousand-foot mountains into Transylvania, where he sought refuge with Matthias Corvinus, the new King of Hungary. But instead of helping, he had Dracula seized, chained and thrown into a dungeon. Not only is this episode somewhat reminiscent of the later tragedy which befell Mary, Queen of Scots, but it too relied for its outcome on a series of forged letters which had been received by King Matthias. These letters, which had been fabricated by Germanic-Saxons of the boyar fraternity, convinced Matthias that Dracula was actually in league with the Ottoman Turks! (*see* Appendix VIII concerning the Magyar inheritance of Hungary).

And so in 1462, for the second time in his career, Dracula lost his crown and, much to the surprise and dismay of King Matthias, Radu took the throne of Wallachia in the name of the Turks. It was to be twelve years before the return of Dracula, during which period (in 1466) he was married to his second wife, a Hungarian cousin of King Matthias, and they took up residence in Pest (when Buda and Pest—now Budapest—were separate). In 1474 Dracula led a Hungarian contingent against the Turks, after which a formal compact was signed between him and Matthias, with an eventual and successful offensive launched against Radu shortly afterwards.

In November 1476 King Matthias advised other Courts that Dracula was restored to his throne—but it was not to be for long. The great bloodbath was yet to come and Dracula was obliged to confront the Turks and boyar forces near Bucharest just a few weeks later. His newly mustered army was out-classed and outnumbered, as a result of which Dracula lost the day and was killed in the battle. Any slim chance for a regained independent Wallachia was lost on that day in December 1476 and, to prove to the world that the Overlord had truly departed, his decapitated head was sent to Istanbul for all to see on public display. Dracula did, however, have a son by his Transylvanian wife, who reigned as the voivode Mihnea for a while after the death of Radu, to be followed by his descendants. Dracula had other sons by his Hungarian wife. His second younger brother Vlad the Monk, who reigned 1482-95, also had offspring and the descendants of Vlad Dracul survive to this day. But that is another story.

19

Beyond the Forest

Web of the Wise

As we approach the end of our investigation, it is the vampire who begins to draw many other related aspects of the story together—a story which began with the cultures of ancient Sumer and the mighty Ring Lords of Greater Scythia.

To recap: about 3800 years ago the original Wallans (the *Yulannu* Wood Lords) were apparent in Mesopotamia, where they reigned from the 18th century BC. They had originated long before in Greater Scythia, bringing their writing and culture to Sumer and Akkad in the earliest days of civilization. Until about 1550 BC, they were the governors of all Babylonia and subsequently emerged as the Carpathian princes of the *Sidhé*, being of the *Tuadhe d'Anu* fairy strain.

Stemming from this race were the Caledonian warlords of the *Pict Sidhé*, the priestly caste of the *Fir Bolg* and the kurgan mound-building caste of the *Cassi* kings. They were the Overlords of the Fairy Rings and some of their great *Yulannu* shrines, erected on truly ancient and previously established megalithic sites, exist today in the Boyne Valley of Ireland, north of Dublin. Now known as Newgrange, Dowth and Knowth, these constructions were centred upon the *Raths*—the primary royal seats, which were turf-covered dwellings constructed upon a framework of poles and located upon the great barrows. In later times the Raths were called *Tepes* and they were reckoned to be Portals to the Netherworld—the sacred domain of ancestral souls which lay beneath. It was from this time-honoured Rath-dwelling practice that the tribal name of the Cassi kings evolved—for a *cassi* was a 'place of wood'. They were, therefore, the high seats of the Portal Guardians—the ultimate Ring Lords of the transcendent *Sidhé*—the Web of the Wise.

These royal Guardians were known in the Central European tradition as the *Oupires,* a term which derived from one of the most important Scythian words of the *Tuadhe d'Anu*—the word *uper,* which meant 'over' or 'above'. We still use this word in today's English-language definitions such as 'upper' (topmost), 'umpire' (no equal) and 'super' (over or above), leading to the descriptive terms 'supervisor' and 'superintendent'. In titular form, a Scythian *Uper* was an overseer or, more importantly, an Overlord—the equivalent of a Pendragon. Later, in the Hungarian and Romanian regions, the word gained the variant form of *Oupire,* and this was the word used by Dom Augustin Calmet in his 18th-century work, translated to become *A Treatise on Vampires.*

Until the medieval intrigue of the Christian Church and its emergent Inquisition, there was nothing remotely sinister or supernatural about the definition Oupire, but this was destined to change when the witch-hunts began since it was conveniently similar to the Byzantine word *uber,* meaning 'witch'. By virtue of this the priest-kingly Oupires were seen, in the eyes of Rome, to be the equivalent of magian druids. Accordingly, they were designated witches and the *Sidhé* definition, Web of the Wise, became clerically mocked as being the 'web of the weird'.

In the main, outside the Gaelic regions of Britain, the traditional Oupires had been apparent in the Balkan and Carpathian regions of Europe—having prevailed from Transylvania to the Black Sea in ancient times. For this reason, they were not only associated with witches by the Inquisitors, but with the transient gypsies. The Christian bishops and friars suspected them of being the ultimate rulers of the Land of Elphame: the twilight realm of fairy gold, magic springs and the abiding lore of the Greenwood, all of which were anathema to the

Church. They were said to be wandering people of the night, who consorted with evil spirits, and at that stage the word 'vampire' was born into the language of Christian Europe—being a straightforward corruption of Oupire or (alternatively, *Upire*).[1] It occurred in the same way that *Wicking* became Viking, because there was no 'w' or 'u' in the Latin alphabet, only a 'v'. It then progressed via the Slavonic intermediate words *vapir* and *vbpir*,[2] with the additional 'm' of vampire appearing by way of a Gaelic consonantal group which allied the letter with 'b' and 'p'.[3] (Wicking stemmed from *wicce*, to bend or rove, whence *wick* = twist. The inherent 'Wi' syllable also meant contentious or warlike. Thus, the Vikings were *Wi-kings* = roving warlike kings.)[4]

Quite suddenly, along with the werewolves and a variety of other demonic inventions, there appeared to be no end to the fantastic creatures who were reckoned to stalk the streets and forests in search of unsuspecting victims. This had the desired effect of making people lean more heavily upon the Church, which was the only perceived route to salvation. The vampires, it was said, could not be killed by conventional means; only the power of Jesus the Saviour could defeat these diabolical beings. They were portrayed as fiendish demons and emissaries of the devil, who had to be exorcised and destroyed by the monks and clerics. And so the Church was in business with a whole new genre of scary folklore to counter the Grail and Ring traditions—giving rise to the genre which has become known as Gothic Romance. The premise behind these tales was not so much about saving victims, but rather more about destroying the enemies of contrived 'churchianity', with crucifixes galore and gallons of holy water being the essential weapons in the dreaded undertaking against the sinister 'evil ones'.

On the one hand there were the Albigensian tales of Swan princes, Grail queens and Elf-maidens—comprising the lore of the forgotten Bloodline and the Lost Bride—wherein knights and chivalric champions battled against all odds to preserve the sacred heritage of the Holy Grail. In these stories there were wizards of the druidic school and wise hermits to guide the knights upon their journeys and missions. But nowhere in these tales of enchantment did a gallant priest or bishop ever ride to the aid of a damsel in distress—for the Church was, in practice, the adversary.

At the 1545 Council of Trento, in Northern Italy, the bishops formally blacklisted and outlawed the *Prophecies of Merlin*, withdrawing all related material from the public domain. Within the Britannic Church of the Dark Ages—subsequently referred to as the Celtic Church—there had been (along with Taliesin and the Merlin seers to the kings) some very prominent adepts of the old wisdom: abbots and culdees such as St. David, St. Patrick and St. Columba—all of whom were denounced in their day by the Roman Church for their so-called wizardry and pagan beliefs. Even the later papal establishment regarded them as necromancers and sorcerers—but this is not the way things are currently portrayed. Although the Merlin prophecies were expressly banned, the teachings of David, Patrick and Columba were so firmly cemented in society that the Church was obliged to pursue a very different strategy of incorporation.

A thousand years after the lifetimes of these druidic magi, the Vatican officials elected to bring them posthumously into the orthodox saintly fold so that the real truth of their pagan environment would be lost to history. Then, only a few years ago, the British Post Office and the Anglican Church joined forces to promote the gentle St. Columba of the *Pict-Sidhé* alongside his bitter Catholic rival St. Augustine of Rome, who came to England with an express papal brief to destroy the Columban movement immediately after Columba's death in 597. Disregarding this historical fact, the 1400th anniversary postage stamps and substantially hyped propagandist material of 1997 portrayed these two arch-enemies as if they had been blood-brothers in a common cause—proving beyond doubt that new myths of 'churchianity' are still being created to this day.

Since the Church's original strategy of intimidation did not work sufficiently on its own, as was the case in the Renaissance

Columban Cross at the Glencolumcille Heritage Centre

era (a period of a more general awareness and enlightenment), a second stage of the plan was then brought into operation. This was more specifically targeted at the key members of the Messianic strain—the ultimate Elf succession of the *Albi-gens*: the dynastic kings and queens of the *Sangréal* and their senior Oupires. These people were real, and everyone knew that—so they could not be confined to the superficial realm of fairy fantasy. They could, however, be portrayed as if they were of a weird, half-human strain, beyond the Christian pale. At the least they were perhaps mermaids, and at worst they were said to be werewolves or vampires but, either way, they were proclaimed to all and sundry as the evil shapeshifting disciples of Satan!

The Overlords

Notwithstanding all the European folklore and traditions concerning the vrykolaka, nachtzehrer, blautsauger and various other revenants, there would be no mainstream interest in vampires today were it not for the 19th-century switch of emphasis from the gruesome to the romantic. This change of direction occurred solely by virtue of the fact that the grubby zombie was forsaken and literally replaced by figures who represented the Overlord culture of the Oupires. Historically, there had never been any real or perceived connection between the lordly Oupires and the rustic revenants, but it is significant that certain notable writers sought to overthrow the old European superstitions in favour of something with a more appropriate allegory. Unfortunately, in recent decades, there have been any number of non-classical, so-called 'vampire' films which have brought back the gruesome aspect by portraying characters who are not vampires in the strict historical sense, but are rather more 'undead' hooligans. Far from perpetuating the mystery of the vampire, such films actually destroy the cultural heritage by linking the tradition with a type of morbid science fiction which is not Gothic, nor even ghostly, but ghastly.

To understand the historical vampire one first needs to separate the *oupire* from the revenant—for the Oupire was real while the revenant was a morbid fantasy. Having made that mental separation, it is then necessary to consider what aspects of the individual traditions bear some similarity—enough similarity for the Abbé Calmet to have recognized the points of comparison and to use the word Oupire in 1732, when actually he was not discussing vampires but mythical zombies.

Was there something in the Oupire tradition which linked them with death? Was there something which suggested that they had extraordinary aptitudes and powers? Was there something which linked them specifically with the Carpathian regions of Europe—especially with such places as Transylvania? The single answer to these questions, and to many others which could be similarly asked, is 'Yes'—for the historical Oupire, even if not fulfilling these requirements in as late a period as the 18th century, certainly did so in more ancient times.

In the days long before any bloodlusting vrykolaka superstition took hold in Christian Europe—and long before there was any Christian Church—the Oupires were the *Upers* or Overlords of the old Scythian race of the Ring Lords. They were of the highest-bred priestly caste of these legendary warriors, being Portal Guardians of the Raths and masters of the transcendent *Sidhé*. These were the people whose tribes made their homes in wood-framed Cassi dwellings and whose culture was centred upon their kurgan burial mounds, within one of which were found the tall chieftains' bodies, tattooed with ring-tailed lemurs. They were notable travellers who set their sights eastwards across the European mainland, through the Black Sea and Caspian Sea regions as far as Mongolia and Tibet, while also later travelling westwards to Ireland. But, for all that, the Oupire's place of origin was the land of the Carpathian mountains where, in 1968, their pre-Sumerian writings were discovered at Tartaria in Transylvania (the aptly named Land Beyond the Forest), which is still the recognized homeland of the vampire.

Earlier, we looked at the ancient Star Fire customs of Mesopotamia and Indo-Europe, wherein the *Amrita* and menstrual *Rasa* of the Goddess were jointly considered to be the Vehicle of Light, the Gold of the Gods and the nectar of supreme excellence. Subsequent to Anunnaki times, however (from around 1960 BC), the culture centred upon specially bred virgin priestesses of the Orders of those such as Kali, Vesta and Diana of Ephesus. These red-robed fire maidens became known as the sacred *hierodulai* or beloved Scarlet Women, whose essences were prized in the time-honoured tradition of the *Rosi-crucis*—the Dew-cup of the *Sangréal*.

In communities whose calendars and customs were lunar based, these female extracts (romantically defined in the *Song of Solomon* as the Lily and the Rose) were used as supplemental foods for the royal bloodline. Star Fire was related to the *ritu* (the redness or truth) and, since menstruum contains valuable endocrinal secretions (secrets), the recipients' own hormonal levels were thereby increased, leading to greater powers of awareness, perception and general intuition in a process referred to in fairy lore as the Quickening.

We now know that certain attributes of ancient Mesopotamia, such as scriptural writing, were not uniquely devised in regional Akkad and Sumer, but had been taken there by the earlier Scythians of the Carpathian culture—as had the godly traditions of those such as Anu, Enki and Lilith, regardless of where these deiform figures might themselves have come from. It seems apparent, therefore, that the art of Tantra, which is generally considered to have been Asian in origin, was also a part of the Oupire legacy since it too had its Star Fire element.

Among the body's endocrinal secretions, the melatonin hormone (a product of the pineal gland) has only been isolated by medical scientists in very recent times, receiving its name as late as 1968. It was so called because people with a high melatonin output react strongly against sunlight which affects their mental capability. By virtue of this, they are inclined to be night operatives, and melatonin is called the 'hormone of darkness', being produced only at night or away from ultraviolet influence.[5] Exposure to an excess of natural light makes the pineal gland smaller and lessens spiritual awareness, whereas darkness and high pineal activity enhance the keen intuitive knowledge of the subtle mind, while reducing the stress factor. Consequently, melatonin is itself a 'night-worker', and that is precisely what its name means—from the Greek *melos* = black, and *tosos* = labour.

Prince of Darkness

On entering the world of ritualistically enhanced melatonin production, we have entered the true realm of the original vampire—the realm of the night operative (the Oupire prince of darkness), whose powers were enhanced by the nectar of the Star Fire virgins—the *Elixir Rubeus*.[6] It was considered that the foremost aspect of life was active blood, since without it one was simply a shade—a ghost of oneself. This relates to the vampire's association with the mirror, as previously discussed. The mirror, by virtue of its reflective quality, produces a duplicate image—a shade—but an image which is devoid of life because it has no blood. Even the Old Testament book of Genesis (9:4) qualifies the belief in this regard, stating that blood is representative of life. Hence, bloodless, soulless reflections were seen to be representative of death. Indeed, the old Egyptian word for a 'shade' was *khaibit*, which perpetuates in the English language as 'habit'—meaning something repeated.[7] It can thus be seen that the superstition whereby a vampire was said to have no reflection (as used to good effect in Chapter 2 of Bram Stoker's *Dracula*) was a subtle bending of the truth. More relevant to the point was the fact that a vampire would have avoided mirrors at all costs—a matter which is identified by Stoker when his story's central character, Jonathan Harker, is introduced to his room in Count Dracula's castle:

> The curtains and upholstery of the chairs and sofas and the hangings of my bed are of the costliest and most beautiful fabrics, and must have been of fabulous value when they were made, for they are centuries old, though in excellent order. I saw something like them in Hampton Court, but they were worn and frayed and moth-eaten. But still in none of the rooms is there a mirror. There is not even a toilet glass on

> my table, and I had to get the little shaving glass from my bag before I could either shave or brush my hair.

Melatonin is manufactured by the pineal gland through an activated chemical messenger called Serotonin, a product of the pituitary gland. This transmits nerve impulses across chromosome pairs at a moment (called *meiosis*) when the cell nuclei are divided and the chromosomes are halved to be combined with other half-sets upon fertilization.[8] Melatonin enhances and boosts the body's immune system, and those with high pineal secretion are less likely to develop cancerous diseases. High melatonin production increases energy, stamina and physical tolerance levels, and is directly related to sleep patterns, keeping the body temperately regulated with properties that operate through the cardiovascular system. It is the body's most potent and effective antioxidant, and it has positive mental and physical anti-ageing properties.[9]

The pineal gland is impregnated by eternal ideas and gives us the possibility of formulating our own images.[10] It is an organ of thought by means of which we acquire inner perception and can thereby change eternal ideas into earthly conceptions. Yoga masters associate the pineal gland with the *Ajna Chakra* (Sanskrit: *ajna* = command; *chakra* = wheel). Chakras are energy centres corresponding to each of the glands of the endocrine system and it is believed that the pineal is a receiver and sender of subtle vibrations which carry thoughts and psychic phenomena. (Endocrine glands, named from the Greek verb 'to arouse', are ductless bodies which secrete directly into the bloodstream.) The pineal is also known as the Eye of Wisdom: the chakra of the mind, of heightened self-awareness and inner vision,[11] representing the ability to see things clearly with intuitive knowledge.

Shaped like a pine-cone and about the size of a grain of corn, the pineal is centrally situated within the brain, although outside the ventricles and not forming a part of the brain-matter as such. It was thought by the French philosopher and optical scientist René Descartes (1596-1650) to be the 'seat of the soul',[12] the point at which the mind and body are conjoined. The ancient Greeks considered likewise, and in the 4th century BC, Herophilus described the pineal as an organ which regulated the flow of thought. The onset of puberty is directly controlled by the pineal gland and melatonin secretion is at its highest during childhood and the teenage years. It is apparent that above average melatonin production in childhood, although heightening the extent of young intellect, can also be an inhibitor of sexual development,[13] since the two aspects are in physical conflict during the growing years.

In symbolic form, the dynastic blood of the *Rosi-crucis* has long been represented by red wine, as in the Christian Eucharist (Communion) sacrament—and was introduced as a figurative relic of the old Star Fire custom. In this ritual, extracts from the bodily essence of the Goddess were ingested—although the wine is now said to represent the blood of Christ. In practice, this Christian custom is the longest-standing remnant of what might be defined as the original vampiric blood rite. However, the truly physical ritual began to diminish in history from about 1960 BC during the time of Abraham, when a special form of bread took over as the instrument of heightened melatonin production. This too has been perpetuated in Christian lore, having now become symbolized by the eucharistic wafer.

At the northern doorway of Chartres Cathedral in France (the Gate of the Initiates) is a statue of Melchizedek, the priest-king of Salem—a statue designed by the Knights Templars after their initial return from Jerusalem in 1128. In accordance with the Old Testament entry in Genesis 14:18, Melchizedek is portrayed with the bread and wine which he evidently offered to Abraham, but his chalice does not contain the wine; it actually contains the bread. In this respect, it identifies the time (*c*.1960 BC) when the fully-fledged Star Fire customs of the Anunnaki gave way to a new method of supplementally feeding the kingly bloodline.

The particular bread in question (known as *shewbread* in the old Hebrew tradition and called *shem-an-na* by the

Mesopotamians) was made of the white powder of gold (as confirmed in the Exodus story of the goldsmith Bezaleel).[14] This was gold in its superconductive, monatomic state—a subject due for considerably more explanation in the next book of this Grail cycle, *Destiny of the House of Gold*. For our present purposes, it is sufficient to recognize that this emergent gold culture was at the root of the Barat An-na (Britannia) Goddess tradition brought to Britain by the ancient *Yulannu* Wood Lords. As cited earlier, Barat An-na was the great Mother of the Fire-stone, whose shield banner was the Rosi-crucis Grail emblem. The significance here is that *shem-an-na* (in translation from the Akkadian) means 'highward fire-stone'. Why 'highward'? Because its effect on the pineal gland (as now proven by modern scientific research) is to stimulate melatonin production and thereby enhance individual powers and personal attributes so that the regular recipient attains a heightened state of being.

It is, therefore, apparent that the most ancient customs of the Oupires were identical to those of the Grail Kings, and this is hardly surprising since they were of precisely the same root culture from the biblical Lords of Edom. This pharaonic and Mesopotamian kingly line, by way of certain strategic marriages into the patriarchal line of the Old Testament, led ultimately to King David of Israel and onwards to the Albigensian (Elven) dynasty of Jesus. Resultantly, no matter how dramatically the vampires were romanticised in the 19th-century Gothic writings, the inherent Church hatred and pursuance of this high-bred caste was, in essence, an allegory of the factual truth. This was not because the vampires were bloodsucking Antichrists, but because they were historically representative of the Albigensian heritage against which the whole Inquisition was set. The fangs, neck-bitings and 'undead' characteristics were all part of a literary fiction born from the superstition cult of the revenants, while the fact that the Church always won the day by defeating the said 'evil ones' was firmly dictated by the prevailing propagandist message of these Christianized tales. Had this not been the case, then the stories would not have survived in the staunchly Church-influenced environment of Victorian times, since the vampire challenged all the strait-laced and restrictive values by which society was controlled.

20

Realm of the Ring Lords

Cups and Rings

In concluding our story of the associated Grail and Ring quests, it is relevant to mention that the two related emblems have been symbolically portrayed together for the longest time. Indeed, Scotland, Ireland and parts of Northern England[1] are well known for their ancient 'Cup and Ring' rock carvings, with primary examples located at Achnabrech in the Kilmartin Valley, Argyll, dating back to around 2000 BC.[2] The precise original purpose of these circular hollows (cups) and their surrounding single or multiple rings has not yet been ascertained, but they are generally located near to stone-circled fairy rings, or are incorporated into the early Rath sites—the barrow-mounds and royal seats of the *Pict-sidhé*. These are especially apparent in the Irish barrows of Newgrange, Knowth and Dowth—also in the Crieff, Loch Earn and Loch Tay areas of Scotland. However, the noted dowser David R. Cowan has discovered some intriguing earth energies emanating from cup-marked stones[3]—reminiscent of the statement accredited to Merlin in Geoffrey of Monmouth's *Historia*: 'Laugh not so lightly O King, for in these stones is a mystery and a healing virtue'.

Sometimes petroglyphs of this Cup and Ring style can be found on monuments to which further embellishments have been made through the ages. In this regard, *Rosi-crucis* carvings have been popularly attached (being the time-honoured Grail emblem which evolved into what is today called the Celtic

Cross), along with various other devices, so that many of these stones have become very ornate.[4] A good example of this ongoing process is the *Guinevere Stone*, now held at the Meigle Museum in Angus, near to where Arthur's Queen Guinevere was said to have been buried.

The Grail Code

Having journeyed through a vast expanse of time, from a starting point many millennia ago, we have witnessed an exciting but often tragic course of events which began in the mists of antiquity and culminated in the horrendous Church Inquisitions against the said heretics and 'evil ones'. In the course of our journey we have met with fairies, elves, goblins, pixies, sprites, gnomes, satyrs, nymphs, mermaids and vampires, only to discover that, in the face of what we were always told, the foundation for these supposedly mythical characters was very real. (Even some characters of the most basic children's nursery rhymes have a factual historical origin—*see* Appendix IX.)

During the course of our research into fable and folklore we have encountered a number of characters, such as Mélusine, Robin Hood, Morganna, King Arthur, Lorna Doone and Count Dracula, each of whose stories hold their separate mysteries and fascinations. We have discovered, however, that these are not mere tales of mythology, but literary records based upon historical fact and concerning figures whose positions in history were, in one way or another, quite special. They were, nevertheless, figures whose stories have been subjected to substantial manipulation by those who sought to suppress the truth—or subjected to substantial veiling by those who fought to preserve history in the face of that suppression.

In these modern times of an ever-increasing desire to learn the truths which have been lost or purposely obscured, it is apparent that preserved within the Land of Elphame is a magical domain of pure enlightenment whose allegorical cycle is so vividly portrayed in Sir Peter Robson's painting *The Portal of the Twilight World*. Here, beyond the slumber of our hitherto complacency, is a wealth of knowledge and enchantment from which we have been strategically separated by those with otherwise vested interests—those who have presented themselves as our guardians, but have in fact been our mind-bending manipulators. They have confined many of the most intriguing aspects of our heritage to a netherworld of supposed illusion and fantasy, while following a course of calculated, and generally fabricated, indoctrination for the purposes of maintaining a self-serving control.

In covering the ground which has been the subject matter of these pages, it is apparent that we have really only scratched the surface of what can, at its least, be classified as a duplicitous reign of concealment. This has been perpetuated for centuries to the extent that many of us have perhaps truly believed the contrived propaganda. In reality there is more truth within the fairy tales than exists within much of the establishment history with which we have become so familiar. But, however subtly embellished and however deftly embroidered, the webs which surround the popular legends can be disentangled once the nature of the weave is known. The first rule to recognize is that few stories which have been captured and preserved in such a way were unworthy of the preservation. Similarly, those which were purposely concealed within the wrap of dishonesty in order to hide the truth were also important enough to have been deemed in some way threatening to those in power.

From the time of the Anunnaki overlords of the Scythian and Sumerian cultures, the lore of the eternal Ring of wholeness and justice prevailed within the culture of the Dragon Queens and Grail Kings of the Messianic *Albi-gens*: the Elven bloodline. This lore was surmounted by a Code of leadership and kingly practice—a Code of mutual Service, as personified by Jesus himself when he washed the feet of his own Apostles at the Last Supper. But this was a Code which the emergent Church could not abide for it relied upon a fraternal relationship between leaders and followers alike. In order for the Church to maintain its regime of power, the Code and its supporters had to be destroyed—a destruction largely facilitated by the fraudulent *Donation of Constantine,* which established a Church prerogative that has survived the centuries to the present day.

During the medieval era of the Church's torments and persecutions, which persisted through the Middle Ages and beyond, all manner of Grail-related subject matter fell prey to the wrath of the bishops and friars. Unsuspecting victims were accused of satanic Witchcraft and all manner of unsavoury practices, while any association with the Ring culture was proscribed, as in the lamentable case of Joan of Arc.

One way or another, the fairy tales and nursery stories which emanated from the Albigensian supporters—those said heretics who formed their own 'underground stream'—were tales of lost brides and usurped kingship. They were fashioned by the absolute and heinous subjugation of the Grail bloodline by the Church of Rome and in later times by the sectarian Puritans of the Protestant movement who based their allied cause upon the common command: 'Kill them all; God will know his own'.

The fairy tale concept was essentially geared to stories relating to these persecutions. They were allegorical accounts of the predicament of the true royal family—the Ring Lords of the *Sangréal,* whose fairies and elves (having been manoeuvred from the mortal plane of orthodoxy and *status quo*) were confined to a seemingly Otherworld existence. They were the Shining Ones, whose story began with the *Uper-ad* culture of the Royal Scyths—the original Oupires from whom evolved the *Tuadhe d'Anu* priest-kings, the Wood Lords of the *Yulannu,* the forest people of the *Caille Daouine* and the princely race of the *Pict-sidhé.*

These ancient guardians have never been positively featured in our academic teachings for the very reason that they were the real progenitors of our spiritual heritage. Instead, their reality was quashed from the earliest days of Roman suppression as the literal diminution of their figures caused a parallel diminishing of their history. Notwithstanding this, the fact is that for all we have been told about our cultural identity being from the classical scholarship of Greece or from the imperial majesty of Rome, these things are entirely untrue. Such establishments appeared very late in the day. The true sovereign heritage of Western culture—the culture from which derived all the so-called myth and legend which sits so comfortably within our collective memory comes from one place alone. It comes from a place and time which, to use J. R. R. Tolkien's definition, might just as well be called 'Middle-earth' as by any other name. It comes from the long distant Realm of the Ring Lords.

NOTES AND REFERENCES

1: THE RING AND THE GRAIL

1. From *The Fellowship of the Ring*, ch. 2, 'The Shadow of the Past'.

2. *The Lord of the Rings* trilogy, first published in 1954-55, consists of *The Fellowship of the Ring*, *The Two Towers* and *The Return of the King*.

3. Day, David, *Tolkien's Ring*, Harper Collins, London, 1994, ch. 6, p. 63.

4. Graves, Robert, with Patai, Raphael, *Hebrew Myths – The Book of Genesis*, Cassell, London, 1964, ch. 16, p. 97.

5. Genesis 1:2 (*King James Authorized Bible*).

6. In Ring Lore, the One Ring was called the Draupnir – which means 'dripper'. Hence it had the power to 'drip' other rings where sub-kingdoms were established. In Volsunga lore the Saxon god Odin held the One Ring of the Kingdom of the Nine Worlds – as did Anu, god of old Sumer.

He who held the Ninth Ring: the One Ring, was the Lord of the Rings. In ancient times, the One Ring was representative of the overlordship of the Sun, with the other key Eight Rings representing the planetary kingdoms of Earth, Venus, Mars, Jupiter, Saturn, Uranus, Neptune and Mercury. However, within the environment of the Earth Ring, the Draupnir was said to 'drip' other Rings to accommodate the individual kingdoms of the Pendragons and Oupire Earth Lords.

7. Plate 1 – Lilith – in Gardner, Laurence, *Bloodline of the Holy Grail*, Element Books, Shaftesbury, 1996. Also Plate 8 – Lilith – in Gardner, Laurence, *Genesis of the Grail Kings*, Bantam Press, London, 1999, and Element Books, Boston, 2000.

8. *See* figure depiction of Marduk.

9. Day, David, *Tolkien's Ring*, ch.1, pp. 13-14.

10. *Ibid*, ch. 3, p. 31.

11. *See* various related genealogical charts in Gardner, Laurence, *Bloodline of the Holy Grail*.

12. Ravenscroft, Trevor, *The Spear of Destiny*, Samuel Weiser, York Beach, ME, 1982, Epilogue, p. 342

13. Stein, Walter Johannes, *The Ninth Century*, Temple Lodge, London, 1991, ch. 5, pp. 138-42.

14. *Ibid*, ch. 5, pp. 323-24, note 45.

15. The Pentacle is correctly a flat disc with a pentagram (5-point) star engraved upon it. *See* also Chapter 11, under 'The Horned One'.

16. Jewish holy writings include the Mishnah and the Talmud. The Mishnah (Repetition) is an early codification of Jewish law, based upon ancient compilations and edited in Palestine by the Ethnarch (Governor) Judah I in the early 3rd century AD. It consists of traditional law (Halakah) on a wide range of subjects, derived partly from old custom and partly from Biblical law (Tannaim) as interpreted by the rabbis (teachers).

The Talmud is essentially a commentary on the Mishnah, compiled originally in Hebrew and Aramaic. It derives from two independently important streams of Jewish tradition: the Babylonian and the Palestinian.

17. The esoteric tradition of Solomon spanned the centuries to the era of Gnostic Christianity which preceded the Merovingian age. The Gnostics, whose texts referred to the *Book of Solomon*, were the inheritors of the early Jewish sects of Babylonia. Their form of Christianity was closely allied to the metaphysical doctrines of Plato and Pythagoras, with their creeds being largely founded upon astrology and cosmic awareness. In addition they claimed a particular insight (*gnosis*: 'knowledge') into Jesus's teaching that was unknown to the Church of Rome.

2: LEGACY OF THE DAMNED

1. It was customary for priest-kings to be known as 'fishers' or 'king-fishermen' as in the 13th-century *High History of the Holy Grail* (the *Perlesvaus*). The 1st-century relationship between priests and fishers is discussed in Thiering, Barbara *Jesus the Man*, Doubleday, London, 1992, Appendix II, pp. 325-30.

2. *See* Chapter 3 under 'Dragons and Merlins' and Chapter 10. Also *see* sub-section 'Star Fire' in Gardner, Laurence, *Genesis of the Grail Kings*, ch. 13, pp. 125-131.

3. In the time of King Herod the Great documents of genealogical record relating to the family of Jesus (the *Desposyni)* were officially burned at the King's instruction. Eusebius, *The History of the Church from Christ to Constantine*, Penguin, Harmondsworth, 1989, Book 1:7, p. 22. Also *see* Schonfield, Hugh J., *The Passover Plot*, Element Books, Shaftesbury, 1985, ch. 5, p. 245-46.

Regarding subsequent burning of records by the Romans in their AD 70 sacking of Jerusalem under General Titus, in Baigent, Michael, with Leigh, Richard and Lincoln, Henry, *The Messianic Legacy*, Jonathan Cape, London, 1986, ch. 7, p. 89.

The 2nd-century Palestinian historian Hegesippus reported in his *Hypomnenata* (Memoirs) that, during the reign of the Roman Emperor Domitian (AD 81-96), the execution of all *desposynic* inheritors of the Davidic succession was ordered by Imperial decree. However, although many were seized, including known descendants of Jesus's brother Jude, some were released and 'On their release they became leaders of the churches, both because they had borne testimony and because they were of the Lord's family'. This is also confirmed by Eusebius (c.AD 260-340), Bishop of Caesarea in Eusebius, *The History of the Church from Christ to Constantine*, Penguin, Harmondsworth, 1989, Book 3:17, pp. 80-82.

The historian Julius Africanus of Edessa in Anatolia (as against Edessa in Greece), who lived AD 160-240, wrote that following the 1st-century burning of the genealogical registers of Jesus's family, 'A few careful people had private records of their own, having either remembered the names or recovered them from copies, and took pride in preserving the memory of their aristocratic origin. These included the people ... known as the *Desposyni* because of their relationship to the Saviour's family'. *Ibid*, Book 1:7, p. 22.

Julius Africanus made his reputation by translating into Latin a series of works written by the 1st-century disciple Abdias, Nazarene Bishop of Babylon. The *Books of Abdias* amounted to ten volumes of first-hand Apostolic history. However, like so many other important eyewitness accounts of the era, they were rejected outright for 4th-century inclusion in the eventual New Testament. (Abdias is recorded as one of the 70 disciples of Jesus—as per Luke 10. He was the first Bishop of Babylon, consecrated by Simon and Jude, the brothers of Jesus.)

Only those in the bloodline of Jesus through his mother qualified as *Desposyni* (meaning 'Belonging to [or heirs of] the Lord'). They and their supporters were hunted down by Imperial Roman decree and put to the sword. However, in AD 318 (as confirmed by Fr. Malachi Martin, a Jesuit professor who served in Rome with Cardinal Augustine Bea and Pope John XXIII), a *Desposyni* delegation journeyed to Rome, where, at the newly commissioned Lateran Palace, the men were given audience by Bishop Silvester. Through their chief spokesman Joses (a descendant of Jesus's brother Jude), the delegates argued that the Church should rightfully be centred in Jerusalem, not in Rome. They claimed that the Bishop of Jerusalem should be a true hereditary *Desposynos*, while the bishops of other major centres—such as Alexandria, Antioch and Ephesus—should be related. Not surprisingly, their demands were in vain, for Silvester was hardly in a position to countermand the decrees of the Emperor. The teachings of Jesus had been superseded by a doctrine more amenable to Imperial requirement and, in no uncertain terms, Silvester informed the men that the power of salvation rested no longer in Jesus, but in Emperor Constantine! *See* Martin, Malachi, *The Decline and Fall of the Roman Church*, Secker & Warburg, London, 1982, pp. 42-44.

4. In practice, wars, plagues, famines and other causes of early death would play a significant part in preventing such a perfect continuation through 2000 years, while many in the descent would produce no offspring at all. On the other hand, there would be those producing more than two offspring.

5. Albany, HRH Prince Michael Stewart of, *The Forgotten Monarchy of Scotland*, Element Books, Shaftesbury, 1998, ch. 5, p. 59.

6. In the 4th century (from AD 382), St. Jerome made a Latin translation of the Bible from the earlier Hebrew and Greek texts for subsequent Christian usage. It was called the *Vulgate* because of its 'vulgar' (general) application – from *vulgata editio* (common edition). Emperor Constantine died before this in AD 337.

7. A translated transcript of the *Donation of Constantine* is given in Henderson, Ernest F. (Trans.), *Select Historical Documents of the Middle Ages*, G. Bell, London, 1925, pp. 319-29.

8. In the late 5th century, the Romans' Western Empire collapsed – demolished by the Visigoths and Vandals. The last Emperor, Romulus Augustulus, was deposed by the German chieftain Odoacer, who became King of Italy in AD 476. In the absence of an Emperor, the prevailing High Bishop, Leo I gained the title of Pontifex Maximus (Chief pontiff or bridge-builder). In the East, however, the story was different and the Byzantine Empire was destined to flourish for another thousand years.

9. Martin, Malachi, *The Decline and Fall of the Roman Church*, pp. 56-57.

10. Gregory of Tours, *A History of the Franks* (trans. Lewis Thorpe), Penguin, Harmondsworth, 1964, Book 2:30-31, pp. 143-44.

11. Initially, Clovis succeeded his father in the region of Tournai at the age of fifteen, but during the next five years he led his armies southwards from the Ardennes, pushing out the Gallo-Romans, so that by AD 486 his realm included such centres as Reims and Troyes. The Romans managed to retain a kingdom at Soissons, but Clovis defeated the forces of their ruler, Syagrius, who fled to the Visigoth court of King Alaric II. At this, Clovis threatened war against Alaric and the fugitive was handed over for execution. By his early twenties (with both the Romans and the Visigoths at his feet) King Clovis was destined to become the most influential figure in the West.

Following a succession of military conquests, King Clovis died in Paris at the age of forty-five. He was succeeded by his sons Theuderic, Chlodomir, Childebert and Lothar. At that time, in 511, the Merovingian domain was divided into separate kingdoms. Theuderic succeeded in Austrasia (from Cologne to Basle), based at Metz. From Orléans in Burgundy, Chlodomir supervised the Loire Valley and the west of Aquitaine around Toulouse and Bordeaux. Childebert governed the region from the Seine across Neustria to Armorica (Brittany), with his capital at Paris, and Lothar inherited the kingdom between the Scheldt and the Somme, with his centre at Soissons. Their decades of combined Frankish lordship were tempestuous; conflicts continued against the Gothic tribes and eventually afforded Merovingian penetration into Eastern Aquitaine, with Burgundy being fully absorbed into the realm.

Lothar was the last of the four to die in 561, having previously become overall king. His sons Sigebert and Chilperic succeeded, with the line from Chilperic settling four generations later on Dagobert II, who became King of Austrasia in 674. By then a council of leading bishops had extended the authority and immunities of the Church, while also reducing the powers of taxation and general administration by the royal house.

The relationship between Clovis and the Vatican is covered in Baigent, Michael, with Leigh, Richard and Lincoln, Henry, *The Holy Blood and the Holy Grail,* Jonathan Cape, London, 1982, ch. 9, p. 209 and *passim.*

12. Nazarites were ascetic individuals bound by strict vows through predetermined periods, as related in the law of the Nazarites, as given in Numbers 6:2-21 (*King James Authorized Bible*).

13. After their defeat by Charles Martel in the 730s, the Moors retreated to the city of Narbonne in the south of France, which became their base for further military resistance. This posed a difficult and prolonged problem for Pepin the Short, who duly sought assistance from the Jews who lived in Narbonne. He finally gained their support, but at a price. The Jews agreed to deal with the problem if Pepin guaranteed the setting up of a Jewish kingdom of Septimania within the territory of Burgundy: a kingdom that would have at its head a recognized descendant of the Royal House of David. For detailed information, *see* Zuckerman, Arthur J., *A Jewish Princedom in Feudal France,* Columbia University Press, New York, NY, 1972.

14. The earliest known manuscript of the *Donation* is in the Codex Parisiensis Lat. 2778 in the *Collectio Sancti Dionysii,* found in the monastery of St. Denis in France. *See* also Coleman, Christopher B., *The Treatise of Lorenzo Valla on the Donation of Constantine,* University of Toronto Press, Toronto, 1993, p. 6.

15. Nicholas of Cusa (Nicholas Cusanus) published his critical appraisal of the *Donation* in his *De Concordantia Catholica. Ibid,* p. 3.

16. *Ibid,* p. 20, ff. presents the *Treatise of Lorenzo Valla* (Laurentii Vallensis) as a translated discourse.

17. *Ibid,* p. 25.

18. An account of Henry Edward Manning's life and Catholic conversion is given in Newsome, David, *The Convert Cardinals,* John Murray, London, 1993, *passim.*

19. At the time of Christopher B. Coleman's publication, he was Professor of History at Allegheny College, Meadville, Pennsylvania, compiling his work with assistance from that College and from Columbia University, New York.

3: THE SHINING ONES

1. This Albigensian Crusade receives good coverage in Baigent, Leigh and Lincoln, *The Holy Blood and the Holy Grail,* ch. 2, pp. 19-34.

Further reading on the subject may be found in Oldenbourg, Zoé, *Massacre at Montségur,* (trans. Peter Green), Pantheon, New York, NY, 1961.

2. Stoyanov, Yuri, *The Hidden Tradition in Europe*, Arkana-Penguin, Harmondsworth, 1994, ch. 4, p. 159.

3. O'Brien, Christian and Barbara Joy, *The Shining Ones*, Dianthus, Cirencester, 1997, and *The Genius of the Few*, Dianthus, Cirencester, 1999.

4. O'Brien, Christian and Barbara Joy, *The Genius of the Few*, ch. 2, p.27. Also *see* Gardner, Laurence, *Genesis of the Grail Kings*, ch. 3, p. 24.

5. Of particular relevance in this regard is Sitchin, Zecharia, *The 12th Planet*, Avon Books, New York, NY, 1978.

6. In reference to Adam and Eve, a direct translation from the Hebrew, by the Semitic linguist E. A. Speiser, renders their description as the *Adâma* to mean Earthlings—as in Genesis 5:2 (King James edition): 'Male and female created he them; and blessed them, and called their name Adam [*Adâma*], in the day when they were created'.

See Speiser, E. A., *The Anchor Bible* (*Genesis*), Doubleday, Garden City, New York, 1964, p. 16.

7. Sitchin, Zecharia, *The 12th Planet*, ch. 13, p. 371.

8. Genesis 3:4 (*King James Authorized Bible).*

9. From the earliest times the serpent was identified with wisdom and healing. It was a sacred emblem of the Egyptian pharaohs, a symbol of the Essene Therapeutate (the ascetic healing community) of Qumrân, and has become identified with today's medical institutions. The serpent has never had any dark or sinister connotation except for that imposed on the Genesis text by latter-day Church doctrines.

A serpent depiction from old Mesopotamia is wholly indicative of the emblems of the American and British Medical Associations, where in each case a single serpent is coiled around the Tree (plant/staff) of Knowledge and Wisdom. *See* depiction in Gardner, Laurence, *Genesis of the Grail Kings*, ch. 10, p. 93.

As reported in the *Journal of the American Medical Association*, Vol. 270, no. 18, 10 November 1993, professional medical institutions generally use the single-serpent and staff emblem, whereas (from the 19th century) commercial medical associations (such as the Association of American Medical Colleges) generally use the winged caduceus of Hermes (Mercury) with its two spiralling serpents. *See* depiction in Gardner, Laurence, *Genesis of the Grail Kings*, ch. 13, p. 127.

In the ancient Greek tradition, the great Father of Medicine was Asklepios of Thessaly (*c*.1200 BC), whom the Romans called Aesculapius. His statue (*c*.200 BC) at the Capodimonte Museum, Rome, also portrays the staff and coiled serpent. The eighteenth lineal descendant from Asklepios was the medical teacher Hippocrates, whose Hippocratic Oath is sworn by physicians to this day.

10. *Compact Oxford English Dictionary*, under 'Lac'.

11. *See* Chapter 10. Also, sub-section 'Star Fire' in Gardner, Laurence, *Genesis of the Grail Kings*, ch. 13, pp. 125-131.

12. Song of Solomon 2:1 (*King James Authorized Bible*).

13. Graves, Robert, *The White Goddess*, Faber & Faber, London, 1961, ch. 4, p. 64.

14. Keating, Geoffrey, *The History of Ireland*, (trans. David Comyn and Rev. P. S. Dinneen), 1640, reprinted Irish Texts Society, London, 1902-14, Vol. IV, Index p.466—under 'Tuatha De Danann'.

15. Carpenter, Clive, *The Guinness Book of Kings, Rulers and Statesmen*, Guinness Superlatives, Enfield, 1978, p. 68.

16. *See* genealogical chart 'Rulers of Scots Dalriada' in Gardner, Laurence *Bloodline of the Holy Grail*, p. 194.

17. *See* above under Chapter 1, Note 5, concerning the *Desposyni* inheritors and their persecution by the Church.

18. *See* also Gardner, Laurence, *Bloodline of the Holy Grail*, ch. 9, pp. 122-26.

19. Voragine, Jacobus de, *The Golden Legend*, (trans. William Caxton. ed. George V. O'Neill), Cambridge University Press, Cambridge, 1972.

La Légende de Sainte Marie Madeleine forms part of ***The Golden Legend***—one of the earliest books printed at Westminster, London, by William Caxton in 1483. Previously published in French and Latin, Caxton was persuaded by William, Earl of Arundel, to produce an English version from the European manuscripts. It is a collection of ecclesiastical chronicles detailing the lives of selected saintly figures. Highly venerated, the work was given public readings on a regular basis in medieval monasteries and churches.

20. Starbird, Margaret, *The Woman With the Alabaster Jar*, Bear, Santa Fe, NM, 1993, ch. 3, p. 50.

21. *See* Plate 10 in Gardner, Laurence *Bloodline of the Holy Grail*.

4: THE RING CYCLE

1. Day, David, *Tolkien's Ring*, ch. 5, p. 45.

2. A recommended current translation of the *Volsunga Saga* is Byock, Jesse (ed.), *The Saga of the Volsungs*, Penguin, Harmondsworth, 1999.

3. Carpenter, Humphrey, *J. R. R. Tolkien*, Harper Collins, London, 1987, ch. 6, p. 77.

4. The *Briar Rose* paintings series by Sir Edward Coley Burne-Jones is held on display by the Faringdon Collection of the National Trust at Buscot Park, Faringdon, Oxfordshire.

5. Morris, William, *Sigurd the Volsung*, Thoemmes Press, Bristol, 1994.
Prior to compiling this work William Morris and Eirikr Magnusson had made the first complete English translation of the *Volsunga Saga* in 1970—a work which Morris proclaimed to be the *Illiad* of Northern Europe.

6. Day, David, *Tolkien's Ring*, ch. 15, p. 162.

7. This textual and audio essay, along with interviews and illustrated Grail Cycle talks by the author, is to be found on the CD-ROM *Realm of the Holy Grail*, Volume I from MediaQuest Multimedia <http://www.mediaquest.co.uk/RlmCDR1.html>.

8. Day, David, *Tolkien's Ring*, ch. 7, p. 72.

9. Stein, Walter Johannes, *The Ninth Century*, ch. 7, p. 282.
Roman Christianity was allied with the progressive powers of State politics, whereas Grail Christianity was concerned with human development.

10. Castries, Duc de, *The Lives of the Kings and Queens of France* (trans. Anne Dobell for Académie Francaise), Weidenfeld & Nicolson, London, 1979, Part 2, p. 41.

11. Day, David, *Tolkien's Ring*, ch. 7, p. 73.

12. *See* Chapter 3, Note 19.

13. From the *Dictionnaire étymologique des noms de lieux en France*.

14. Porter, J. R., *The Illustrated Guide to the Bible*, Duncan Baird, London, 1995, Intro, p. 20.

15. Robinson, James M. (ed.), *The Nag Hammadi Library*, Coptic Gnostic Library: Institute for Antiquity and Christianity, E. J. Brill, Leiden, 1977, *The Origen*: Codex II-5.

16. *Hebrew Myths – The Book of Genesis*, Cassell, London, 1964, p. 31.

17. Sir Peter Robson's Internet Home site is at Entropic Fine Art <http://www.entropic-art.com/>.

18. Taylor, J. W., *The Coming of the Saints*, Covenant Books, London, 1969, ch. 6, p. 105.

19. In medieval Britain, mermaids were called merrimaids, while in Ireland they were merrows.

20. Graves, Robert, *The White Goddess*, ch. 22, p. 395.

21. *Ibid*, ch. 22, p. 395.

22. Ames, Delano (trans.), *Greek Mythology*, [from *Mythologie Générale Larousse*], Paul Hamlyn, London, 1963, p. 102.

23. Cavendish, Richard, *The Black Arts*, Perigee, New York, NY, 1983, Appendix 2, p. 314.

24. Ames, Delano (trans.), *Greek Mythology*, p. 100.

5: DAWN OF THE DRAGON QUEENS

1. *See* also Gardner, Laurence, *Genesis of the Grail Kings*, ch. 16, p. 165.

2. Jones, Steve, *In the Blood – God, Genes and Destiny*, Harper Collins, 1996, ch. 2, p. 93.

3. In the Sumerian language, a lush pastureland between irrigated areas (a steppe or grassy plain) was called an 'eden' (the Akkadian variant was 'edin'). *See* also Speiser, E. A., *The Anchor Bible* (*Genesis*), p.16.

The most notable eden of ancient times – the biblical garden – was at Eridu (modern Abu Sharain), about 16 miles (c.26km) south-west of Ur in the Euphrates delta. Eridu was a most sacred city of ancient Mesopotamia and was the very first seat of Sumerian kingship before the Flood. *See* Roux, Georges, *Ancient Iraq*, George Allen & Unwin, London, 1964, p. 68.

4. A recommended translation of the *Enûma elish* is in Heidel, Alexander, *The Babylonian Genesis*, University of Chicago Press, Chicago, IL, 1942.

5. It was with Tiâmat that the dynasty of the Dragon Queens was said to have begun. However, as previously mentioned (Chapter 2, Note 3), it is important to recognize the potential enormity of descendant numbers when calculated down to date.

There are some today who claim (whether positively or negatively) that they, or certain others, are of a particular blood strain from these early queens of wisdom, whom the Sumerians referred to as Serpent Ladies. To make such claims, however, is quite ludicrous since everyone on Earth could, in theory, make the same presumption. As detailed in Chapter 4, a couple living in the 1st century of the Christian Era could be responsible, through two millennia, for some 1,208,925,819,574,363,856,306,176 births in the year 2000.

If this same basis of calculation were projected from a starting-point not 2000 years ago, but 6000 years ago in 4000 BC (at around the time of Adam, Eve and Dragon Queen Lilith), then it is not difficult to imagine this present year's potential birth figure from any individual living that long ago. In comparison to the above 25-digit number, it calculates to an astonishing 66-digit number – way beyond any comprehension. Hence, as previously stated, the apparent 'bloodline' significance of early times has no relevance whatever in today's environment since it was overridden long ago in all branches by inter-marital dilution. It was, nevertheless, extremely important to the ancient dynasties, and it is from their days of yore that the relevance of the Grail families of the *Rosi-crucis* emerged.

6. O'Brien, Christian and Barbara Joy, *The Genius of the Few*, ch. 6, pp. 134-35.

7. Jacobsen, Thorkild, *The Sumerian King List*, (Assyrialogical Studies No.11), University of Chicago Press, Chicago, 1939, pp. 129-31.

Between 1906 and 1923, a number of eminent Sumerologists translated and published the contents of ancient texts and fragments concerning the early kings of Sumer. In the later 1920s and the 1930s a good deal of further information was unearthed in this regard, and in 1939 Professor Thorkild Jacobsen of the Oriental Institute collated the various texts for publication by the University of Chicago. In his introduction to the work, Jacobsen made the point that, since the information recorded by the ancient Sumerians did not conform with the ideals of some of his fellow academics, it was treated with an amount of scepticism by them.

Despite the considerable efforts of high-ranking scholars to translate and compile the *Sumerian King List*, it was largely ignored by traditional historians and theologians because it was not in line with biblical scripture, and it was not in keeping with the books that others had previously written. In his attempt to break through the dogmatic barriers of the Western teaching establishments, Jacobsen stated, 'In late years, the *King List* has come almost to a standstill, and its evidence is hardly ever used for purposes of chronology .... It is our hope that this essay will contribute to bringing the study of the *King List* out of the dead water in which it now lies'.

8. King, John, *The Modern Numerology*, Blandford / Cassell, London, 1996, ch. 3, pp. 73-76 and Appendix 3, p. 206.

9. *See* Chapter 10, under 'Grail of the World'.

10. Waddell, L. A., *The Phoenician Origin of the Britons, Scots and Anglo-Saxons*, Luzac, London, 1931, ch. 7, pp. 52-55.

11. O'Brien, Christian and Barbara Joy, *The Genius of the Few*, ch. 3, pp. 33-37.

12. *See* Plate 4 in Gardner, Laurence *Genesis of the Grail Kings*.

13. *Ibid*, Plates 8 and 10.

14. Gimbutas, Marija, *The Gods and Goddesses of Old Europe*, Thames & Hudson, London, 1974, ch. 4, pp. 57-66.

15. O'Brien, Christian and Barbara Joy, *The Genius of the Few*, ch. 10, p. 260.

16. 1 Enoch, LXIX:12—Charles, R. H. (trans.), *The Book of Enoch* (Revised from Dillmann's edition of the Ethiopic text, 1893), Oxford University Press, Oxford, 1906 and 1912.

17. O'Brien, Christian and Barbara Joy, *The Genius of the Few*, ch. 5, p. 98.

18. Yatri, *Unknown Man*, Sidgwick & Jackson, London, 1988, p. 86.

19. Hall, Manly P., *The Secret Teachings of all Ages*, The Philosophical Research Society, Los Angeles, 1989, pp. XXXII and LXXXIX. (The Swan is the symbol of the initiates of the ancient mysteries, and of incarnate wisdom.)

See also Yatri, *Unknown Man*, p. 86.

20. Wood, Michael, Legacy—*A Search for the Origins of Civilization*, BBC Network Books, London, 1992, ch. 1, p. 34.

21. Clayton, Peter A., *Chronicle of the Pharaohs*, Thames & Hudson, London, 1994, p. 140.

22. Keating, Geoffrey, *The History of Ireland*, Vol. I, p. 233.

23. Osman, Ahmed, *Out of Egypt*, Century, London, 1998, Prologue, p. xi.

24. Fideler, David (ed.), *Alexandria No.2*, Phanes Press, Grand Rapids, MI, 1993, p. 57

25. Osen, Lynn M., *Women in Mathematics*, Massachusetts Institute of Technology, Cambridge, MA, 1997, p. 28.

26. Wallace-Hadrill, J. M., *The Long Haired Kings*, Methuen, London, 1962, ch. 7, pp. 205-6.

27. For Bible references, *see* Chapter 10 under 'Grail of the World'.

28. Hocart, A. M., *Kingship*, Oxford University Press, Oxford, 1927, ch. 8, p. 102.

29. *Ibid*, ch. 8, p. 103.

30. Woolley, Sir C. Leonard, *Coronation Rites*, Cambridge University Press, Cambridge, 1915, ch. 2, p. 22, and ch. 6, p. 94.

6: WARLORDS OF THE PICT- SIDHÉ

1. 1-Chronicles 1 (*King James Authorized Bible*).

Also *see* Alter, Robert (trans.), *Genesis*, W. W. Norton, New York, 1996, ch. 36, p. 204.

2. *Ibid*, ch. 36, p. 204.

3. Roux, Georges, *Ancient Iraq*, ch. 15. p. 202.

4. Woolley, Sir C. Leonard, *The Sumerians*, W. W. Norton, London, 1965, p.20.

5. The Vinca culture was named after a major Neolithic settlement in Yugoslavia, some 120 miles south-west of Tartaria.

6. M. S. F. Hood in the *Scientific American*, May 1968, p. 265.

7. An example of the cuneiform text of the *Enûma elish* is shown in Gardner, Laurence, *Genesis of the Grail Kings*, ch. 4, p. 38.

8. A full report of the discovery and unearthing of the royal graves of Ur is given in Woolley, Sir C. Leonard, *Ur of the Chaldees*, Ernest Benn, London, 1929.

9. Roux, Georges, *Ancient Iraq*, ch. 5, p. 75. The name Sumer derived from Sumerian speaking people, not the other way about.

10. Piggott, Stuart, *Ancient Europe*, Edinburgh University Press, Edinburgh, 1965, ch. 4, pp. 129-30.

11. M. I. Artamonov in the *Scientific American*, May 1965.

12. The mummification process is well described in Brier, Bob, *The Murder of Tutankhamen*, Berkley books, New York, NY, 1998, ch. 1, pp. 5-6.

13. Barber, Elizabeth Wayland, *The Mummies of Urümchi*, Macmillan, London, 1999, ch. 9, p. 181.

14. *Ibid*, ch. 1, pp. 18-19.

15. *Ibid*, ch. 2, p. 34.
The Phrygian cap (ostensibly red) is depicted on Rude's sculpture of *la Marseillaise* on the Arc de Triomphe, Paris.

16. Waddell, L. A., *The British Edda*, Chapman & Hall, London, 1930, Scene 5, p. 53.

17. Keating, Geoffrey, *The History of Ireland*, Vol. I, p. 213.

18. Sutherland, Elizabeth, *In Search of the Picts*, Constable, London, 1994, Part 2, p. 43.

19. Albany, HRH Prince Michael Stewart of, *The Forgotten Monarchy of Scotland*, ch. 2, p. 15.

20. Keating, Geoffrey, *The History of Ireland*, Vol. IV, Index p. 347.

NOTES AND REFERENCES

7: THE FOUNT OF MÉLUSINE

1. Moncreiffe, Sir Iain of that Ilk, Bt., *Royal Highness Ancestry of the Royal Child*, Hamish Hamilton, London, 1982, p. 62.

2. Harvey, John, *The Plantagenets*, B. T. Batsford, London, 1948, Intro, p. 30.

3. Baring-Gould, Sabine, *Myths of the Middle Ages*, (ed. John Matthews), Blandford. London, 1996, ch. 8, pp. 76-77.

4. *See* Chapter 4 under 'Sirens and Water Nymphs'.

5. In 1478 the *Hystoire de Lusignan* was lodged with the Geneva Reserve of Rare and Precious Books.

6. Baring-Gould, Sabine, *Myths of the Middle Ages*, ch. 8, p. 82.

7. *Ibid*, ch. 8, p. 82.

8. Tudor-Craig, Sir Algernon, *Melusine and the Lukin Family*, Century House, London, 1932.

9. Even today, in the region around Poitiers, gingerbread cakes in the serpent-tailed image of Mélusine are baked for the Maytime festivals.

See also Ashley, Leonard R. N., *The Complete Book of Devils and Demons*, Robson Books, London, 1997, ch. 6, p. 129.

10. *See* Chapters 3 and 10.

11. Watson, W. J., *The History of the Celtic Place Names of Scotland*, William Blackwood, Edinburgh, 1926, ch. 3, p. 97.

12. Sutherland, Elizabeth, *In Search of the Picts*, Part 2, p. 56.

13. Skene, William Forbes (ed.), *Chronicles of the Picts and Scots*, HM General Register, Edinburgh, 1867, Preface pp. cxxi, cxix. Also pp. 72, 351, 402.

14. The Antonine Wall extended between the Firth of Forth and the Clyde estuary. Hadrian's Wall traversed the lower land between the Solway Firth and Tynemouth.

15. Stein, Walter Johannes, *The Ninth Century*, Temple Lodge, London, 1991, ch. 5, p. 191.

16. *Ibid*, ch. 5, p. 259.

17. During the 1400s when Rosslyn Chapel was being built, René d'Anjou (a scion of Godefroi de Bouillon's House of Lorraine) was Helmsman of the Prieuré de Sion. In this capacity he was succeeded by his daughter Yolande,

whose successors included Botticelli and Leonardo da Vinci. René's other daughter, Margaret, married King Henry VI of England. Among René's most prized possessions was a magnificent Egyptian cup of red crystal, which he obtained in Marseilles. It was said to relate to the betrothal of Jesus and Mary Magdalene at Cana, and it bore the inscription (translated), 'He who drinks well will see God. He who quaffs at a single draught will see God and the Magdalene'. *See* Baigent, Leigh and Lincoln, *The Holy Blood and the Holy Grail,* ch. 6, p. 108.

The leather-bound oak cover of René's *Battles and the Order of Knighthood, and the Government of Princes* (in the library of Lord William Sinclair) bears the names 'Jhesus-Maria-Johannes' (Jesus-Mary-John). Similarly, a mason's inscription at Melrose Abbey reads, 'Jhesus-Mari-Sweet Sanct John', while René's Rosslyn manuscript symbolizes St. John by way of a Gnostic serpent and a Grail emblem.

18. Tolstoy, Count Nikolai, *The Quest for Merlin,* Hamish Hamilton, London, 1985, ch. 5, p. 65.

19. *See* also Gardner, Laurence, *Bloodline of the Holy Grail, c.*12, p. 191.

20. Chadwick, Nora K., *Early Brittany,* University of Wales Press, Cardiff, 1969, ch. 8, pp. 299-311.

8: THE ROUND TABLE

1. Herodotus, *The Histories,* (trans. Robin Waterfield), Oxford University Press, Oxford, 1998, Book 4, Items 21, 57, 117.

2. Newark, Tim, and McBride, Angus, *Barbarians,* Concord Publications, Hong Kong, 1998, p. 24.

3. Coghlan, Ronan, *The Illustrated Encyclopaedia of Arthurian Legends,* Element Books, Shaftesbury, 1993, p. 221.

4. Dixon, Karen R., and Southern, Pat, *The Roman Cavalry,* Routledge, London, 1997, ch. 3, p. 61.

5. Turner, P. F. J., *The Real King Arthur,* SKS Publishing, Ankhorage, Alaska, 1993, ch.18, p. 162.

6. *See* also Gardner, Laurence, *Bloodline of the Holy Grail,* ch. 12, pp. 187-88.

7. *Ibid,* ch. 12, pp. 192-202.

8. Barber, Richard, *The Figure of Arthur,* Longman, London, 1972, ch. 3, pp. 34-38.

9. Stokes, Whitley (ed.), *Félire Óengusso Céli Dé,* (*The Martyrology of Oengus the Culdee*) Dublin Institute for Advanced Studies, Dublin, 1984, Item: January, note 27, p. 53

10. 'Tract on the Tributes Paid to Baedàn, King of Ulster' in Skene, William Forbes (ed.), *Chronicles of the Picts and Scots.*

The Battle of Badon Hill (Dún Baedan) was fought at the hill-fort of Baedan against King Baedan McCairill of Antrim in 575. *See* Gardner, Laurence, *Bloodline of the Holy Grail*, ch. 12, pp. 196-200.

11. See genealogical chart 'Arthur and the House of Avallon del Acqs' in *Ibid*, ch. 12, p. 199

12. The *Mostyn Manuscripts* are held at the National Library of Wales (Bangor section).

13. Harry, Rev. George Owen, *The Genealogy of the High and Mighty Monarch, James*, Simon Stafford, London, 1604.

14. Wood, Michael, *In Search of the Dark Ages*, BBC Books, London, 1981, ch. 2, p. 50.

15. *See* genealogical chart 'Arthurian Descent' in Gardner, Laurence, *Bloodline of the Holy Grail*, p. 197

16. *See* genealogical chart 'Descent to the Rulers of Wales and Brittany' in *Ibid*, pp. 184-86

17. It was Chrétien de Troyes who transformed the name of Arthur's queen from the Celtic Gwynefer to the more romantically poetic Guinevere. *See* Chrétien de Troyes, *le Conte del Graal*, (trans. Ruth Harwood Cline), University of Georgia Press, 1985.

18. This subject is covered at some length in Day, David, *Tolkien's Ring*, ch. 6, pp. 62-69.

9: THE LAND OF ELPHAME

1. Holt, J. C., Robin Hood, Thames & Hudson, London, 1982, ch. 3, p. 56.

Also *see* listed under 'Hood' in the *Dictionary of National Biography*.

2. Scholem, Gershom G., *On the Kabbalah and its Symbolism*, Schocken Books, New York, NY, 1965, ch. 5, p. 192.

See also Grant, Kenneth, *Nightside of Eden*, Skoob Books, London, 1994, ch. 1, p. 8.

3. Grant, Kenneth, *The Magical Revival*, Skoob Books, London, 1991, ch. 2, p. 28.

4. Michelet, Jules, *Satanism and Witchcraft*, Citadel Press, New York , 1992, ch. 3. p. 24.

5. Oberon, King of the Fairies in Shakespeare's *A Midsummer Night's Dream,* was synonymous with Alberic, Dwarf Lord of *The Nibelungenlied,* and with Aubrey, the historical 12th-century Elf King. Prior to the time of Shakespeare, he appeared as Dwarf King Oberon in the French tale of Huon de Bordeaux (*see Encyclopedia Britannica,* under 'Oberon'), to be revived by Joseph Rudyard Kipling in his 1910 story *Rewards and Fairies,* which states, 'Sir Huon of Bordeaux; he succeeded King Oberon. He had been a bold knight once, but he was lost on the road to Babylon a long while back'.

Similarly, the name of Oberon's queen, Titania, was invented by the great Bard. She was extracted from Ovid's *Metamorphoses,* written by the Roman poet some 1600 years before. In this work, which deals with the birth of the world from formless chaos, Diana the Huntress (in the Book III tale of *Diana and Actaeon*) is dubbed with the name Titania because she was a daughter of the Titans. Consequently, it is not surprising that Shakespeare's Titania is reminiscent of the Dianic *Caille Daouine* forest people of the Ring Lord fairy strain.

Shortly before Shakespeare made use of the name, Oberon was also mentioned in *The Scottish History of James the Fourth* by his competitor playwright Robert Greene who, in 1592, actually accused Shakespeare of being an unoriginal writer. Titania and Oberon are now the well-known given names of the two largest moons of the planet Uranus.

An interesting connection between these characters of William Shakespeare's play and the figure of Robin Hood was made by the later historian, playwright and heraldist James Robinson Planché (1796-1880), who wrote the libretto for Carl von Weber's opera *Oberon – The Elf King's Oath.*

6. These chronicles, compiled from 12th-14th century annals, include the 1164-73 writings of Jean de Marmoutier, historian of Anjou, Thomas de Loches, chaplain to Count Foulques V in 1130, and Gerald of Wales, archdeacon of Brecon who, in reference to the family of Mélusine recorded that the Angevin dynasty was descended from devils.

See also Hallam, Elizabeth (ed.), *The Plantagenet Chronicles,* Guild Publishing, London, 1986, p. 22.

7. *Ex Libris Comites Oxensis* in *The Itinerary of John Leyland, c.*1540 (at the British Library), Appendix Ia, p. 145.

See also *The Itinerary of John Leland in or about the Years 1535-1543,* (5 vols., ed. L. Toulmin Smith), London, 1906-10.

8. Castries, Duc de, *The Lives of the Kings and Queens of France,* (trans. Anne Dobell for Académie Francaise), Weidenfeld & Nicolson, London, 1979, Part 2, p. 39.

9. *Ibid,* Part 3, p. 55.

10. Potter, Jeremy, *Good King Richard,* Constable, London, 1983, ch. 14, pp. 140-41.

11. *Compact Oxford English Dictionary,* under 'Celt'

12. Gregor, Walter, *Notes on the Folk-lore of the North East of Scotland,* Folk-lore Society, London, 1881, pp. 8-9.

13. *See* Chapter 12 under 'The Holly and the Ivy'.

14. Other natural hallucinogens are Mescaline, from the Peyote cactus (*Lopophore*) and Psilocybin, from the Psylocybe (pixie-cap) mushroom varieties, Coprophilia, Montana and Panaeohisfoeniscii. Details concerning the effects of Mescaline are given in Huxley, Aldous, *The Doors of Perception: Heaven and Hell,* Flamingo, London, 1994.

15. Murray, Margaret A., *The God of the Witches,* Oxford University Press, Oxford, 1970, ch. 3, pp. 75-77.

10: THE LILY AND THE ROSE

1. Song of Solomon 2:1 (*King James Authorized Bible*).

2. Hastings, James, *Dictionary of the Bible,* T. & T. Clark, Edinburgh, 1909 (under 'Rose of Sharon'), confirms that 'all authorities are agreed that the 'rose' translation is incorrect'.

3. Porter, J. R., *The Illustrated Guide to the Bible,* ch. 8, p. 131.

4. Song of Solomon 2:16 and 4:15 (*King James Authorized Bible*).

5. *See* also Gardner, Laurence, *Genesis of the Grail Kings,* ch. 14, p. 138.

6. *See* Chapter 4 under 'Sirens and Water Nymphs'.

7. Grant, Kenneth, *The Magical Revival,* ch. 7, p. 119.

8. *Ibid,* ch. 7. p. 120.

9. Shu'al, Katan, *Sexual Magick,* Mandrake, Oxford, 1995, ch. 1, pp. 10-12.

10. *Ibid,* ch. 1, p. 10-12.

11. Grant, Kenneth, *The Magical Revival,* ch. 7, p. 119.

12. *Ibid,* ch. 7, p. 120.

13. *Ibid,* ch. 2, p. 44 and ch. 7, pp. 121-24.

14. *Ibid,* ch. 2, p.35

15. Lewis, H. Spencer, *The Mystical Life of Jesus,* Ancient and Mystical Order Rosae Crucis, San Jose, CA, 1982, ch. 4, p. 82.

16. *See* Plate 21 in Gardner, Laurence, *Genesis of the Grail Kings*.

17. Hastings, James, *Dictionary of the Bible*, T. & T. Clark, Edinburgh, 1909 (under 'Shulamite').

18. For a succinct study of female fluids, *see* Sevely, Josephine Lowndes, *Eve's Secret*, Bloomsbury, London, 1987. ch. 3, pp. 49-98.

19. Grant, Kenneth, *The Magical Revival*, ch. 8, p. 146.

20. *Ibid*, ch. 8, p. 148.

21. *Ibid*, ch. 7, p. 120.

22. Ladas, Alice Kahn, with Whipple, Beverly, and Perry, John D., *The G Spot*, Dell Publishing, New York, NY, 1993, ch. 1, p. 27.

23. *Ibid*, ch. 3, p. 59.

24. Grant, Kenneth, *The Magical Revival*, ch 8, p. 148.

25. Grant, Kenneth, *Outside the Circles of Time*, Frederick Muller, London, 1980, ch 10, pp. 113-14.

26. Ladas, Whipple and Perry, *The G Spot*, ch. 2, pp. 56-57.

27. As discovered in 1981 by Dr. Beverly Whipple, Dr. Frank Addiego and others, a most surprising feature of the female Skene's fluid is that it reveals certain male characteristics. A tabular analysis published that year in the *Journal of Sex Research* (Vol. 17, No. 1) indicates a measurable quantity of Prostatic Acid Phosphatase (PAP). Subsequently in 1997, Dr. F. Cabello Santamaria reported that Prostate Specific Antigens (PSA) had been isolated, while in the August 1997 issue of *Acta Histochem*, Dr. Milan Zaviaccic reported the discovery of Protein-1 of PSA within the epithelial Skene's lining. In fact, as pointed out by Dr. Gary Schubach, studies from the 1980s have concluded that the Skene's glands are 'a small functional organ that produces female prostatic secretion and possesses cells with neuroendocrine function comparable to the male prostate'.

Dr. Beverly Whipple is a Professor of Nursing at Rutgers University, New Jersey, and a Fellow of the American Academy of Nursing. A certified sexologist and educator, she is a winner of the Hugo G. Beigel Research Award, the New Jersey State Nurses' Association Award, and the Distinguished Scientific Achievement Award for sexuality research, being also the current President of the American Association of Sex educators, Counsellors and Therapists.

Dr. Gary Schubach is a Doctor of Education and Associate Professor of the Institute for Advanced Study of Human Sexuality, San Francisco. Certified by the American College of Sexologists, he is a guest lecturer at California State University.

28. A recommended book on the subject of PSA is Brawer, Michael K., and Kirby, Roger, *Fast Facts: Prostate Specific Antigen*, Health Press, Abingdon, 1997.

29. 'Fountain of Youth – Telomerase' in *Science*, Vol. 279, 23 January 1998, p. 472. Published by the American Association for the Advancement of Science.

30. *Ibid*, Vol. 279, 16 January 1998, pp. 349-352.

31. An excellent work in this regard is Brenner, Sydney (ed.), *Telomeres and Telomerase*, Ciba Foundation and John Wiley, New York, NY, 1997. For specific details concerning Telomerase and reproductive cells, *see* p. 133 by Calvin B. Harley of the Geron Corporation.

32. *Ibid*, p. 188 for Robert Newbold gene isolation.

33. Diploid status relates to two chromosome sets per cell.

34. Bodnar, Andrea G., Quellette, Michel, Frolkis, Maria, Holt, Shawn E., Chiu, Choy-Pik, Morton, Gregg B., Harley, Calvin B., Shay, Jerry W., Lichtsteiner, Serge, and Wright, Woodring E. in *Science*, Vol. 279, 16 January 1998, pp. 349-52.

35. *See* also Gardner, Laurence, *Genesis of the Grail Kings*, ch. 19.

36. Jennings, Hargrave, *The Rosicrucians – Their Rites and Mysteries*, Routledge, London, 1887, ch. 9, pp. 65-67.

37. *See* also Gardner, Laurence *Bloodline of the Holy Grail*, ch. 9.

38. Taylor, Gladys, *Our Neglected Heritage*, Covenant Books, London, 1969-74, Vol. 1, p. 17.

39. This subject is sensitively portrayed from the female perspective in Starbird, Margaret, *The Woman With the Alabaster Jar*, Bear, Santa Fe, NM, 1993, chs. 1 and 2, pp. 23-47.

11: ROBIN OF THE GREENWOOD

1. Mistress Page in Act 4, Scene 4 of William Shakespeare's *The Merry Wives of Windsor*.

2. Graves, Robert, *The White Goddess*, Faber & Faber, London, 1961, ch. 9, p. 151.

3. Hellequin constitutes the original model for the brightly-clad Harlequin character in the Italian *Commedia dell'arte*. Hellequin was the leader of a ghostly troop of horsemen who rode across the sky at night and could well be based upon King Herla (in Old English *Herla cyning*), who has been identified with the Anglo-Saxon god Woden (Wotan/Odin).

4. Cavendish, Richard, *The Black Arts*, ch. 7, p. 304.

5. Murray, Margaret A., *The Witch Cult in Western Europe*, Oxford University Press, Oxford, 1971, ch. 4, p. 102.

6. *Ibid*, ch. 5, p. 133.

7. Graves, Robert, *The White Goddess*, ch. 10, p. 166, note 1.

8. Walker, Barbara G., *The Women's Encyclopedia of Myths and Secrets*, Harper & Row, New York, 1983, p. 234.

9. *Compact Oxford English Dictionary*, under 'Nightmare'.

10. Cavendish, Richard, *The Black Arts*, ch. 7, p. 316.

11. Clayton, Peter A. *Chronicle of the Pharaohs*, p. 26.

12. Hall, Manly P. *The Secret Teachings of all Ages*, The Philosophical Research Society, Los Angeles, 1989, p. CIV.
See also Wood, David, *Genisis – The First Book of Revelations*, Baton Press, Tunbridge Wells, 1985, p. 158.

13. Holt, J. C., *Robin Hood*, ch. 2, p. 15, and note 2, p. 191.

14. *Ibid*, ch. 7, p. 161.

15. Graves, Robert, *The White Goddess*, ch. 18, p. 318.

16. The Abbots Bromley Horn Dance was an autumn harvesting and winter Yuletide or Twelfth Night dance based upon an old fire ritual. The team consisted of six antlered men, two of whom would enact a combat. It was as a result of this dance that Archbishop Theodore of Canterbury imposed a three year penance for devilish behaviour (*see* Chapter 13, under 'Horns and Hooves').

17. Graves, Robert, *The White Goddess*, ch. 22, pp. 396-98.

18. Frazer, Sir James George, *The Golden Bough*, Papermac, London, 1987, ch. 12, pp. 138-40.

19. The ten volumes of John Major's 1521 publication, *A History of Greater Britain as well as England and Scotland*, were translated by Archibald Constable for the Scottish History Society in 1892.

20. Holt, J. C., *Robin Hood*, ch. 7, p. 162.

21. *Ibid*, ch. 3, p. 45.

22. On one occasion in 1572, for the entertainment of Queen Elizabeth I, a lusty mock battle was conducted in this regard between the earls of Warwick and Oxford. A canvas fort was erected and the battle fought with fireworks. Unfortunately, though, a misdirected squib set fire to a nearby house and the proceedings of the pretended border dispute were brought to an early close as everyone rushed to the aid of the sleeping residents.

See Anderson, Verily, *The De Veres of Castle Hedingham*, Terence Dalton, Lavenham, 1993, ch. 13, pp. 185-86.

23. *Ibid*, ch. 3, p. 38.

24. *Ibid*, ch. 1, pp. 6-7.

25. *Ibid*, ch. 3, p. 40.

26. *Ibid*, ch. 3, p. 38.

27. *Cockayne's Complete Peerage*, under 'Oxford'.

12: THE WITCHES' RING

1. The most notable work in this regard is Gardner, Gerald B., *Witchcraft Today*, I-H-O Books, Thame, 1954.

2. Williamson, John, *The Oak King, the Holly King and the Unicorn*, Harper & Row, New York, 1986, ch. 5, pp. 58-78.

3. Murray, Margaret A., *The Witch Cult in Western Europe*, Intro, p. 12.

4. Leviticus 23:4-6 (*King James Authorized Bible*).

Nisan is the first month (i.e. the Spring month) of the Jewish calendar. The Passover celebrates the Israelites' exodus from Egypt, and is followed from the 15th Nisan by the seven days of unleavened bread.

5. Patai, Raphael, *The Hebrew Goddess*, Wayne State University Press, Detroit, 1967, ch. 11, p. 255.

6. Apart from the 8 Sabbats, there are other festivals, usually held at each full moon, called Esbats.

7. Cavendish, Richard, *The Black Arts*, ch. 7, p. 306.

8. Williamson, John, *The Oak King, the Holly King and the Unicorn*, ch. 5, p. 67.

9. The Oxford *Dictionary of Saints* states that, if not mythical, the 4th-century Catherine of Alexandria is only semi-historical and there was no mention of her cult until the 9th century. Apparently, she protested against the persecution of

Christians by Emperor Maxentius, who sentenced her to be broken upon a wheel, but the machine collapsed and she was beheaded instead. *See* Farmer, David, *Dictionary of Saints*, Oxford University Press, Oxford, 1997.

10. Murray, Margaret A., *The God of the Witches*, ch. 4, pp. 111-12.

11. *See* also Gardner, Laurence, *Genesis of the Grail Kings*, ch. 13, p. 127.

12. Murray, Margaret A., *The God of the Witches*, ch. 4, pp. 111.

13. James, Montague R. (ed.) , *The Apocryphal New Testament*, Clarendon Press, Oxford, 1924, Acts of John 94-95, p. 253.

14. *See* also Gardner, Laurence, *Bloodline of the Holy Grail*, ch. 6, pp. 76-77.

15. Tacitus, *The Annals of Imperial Rome*, (trans. Michael Grant), Cassell, London, 1963, XIV, ref. AD 64.

16. Scot, Reginald, *The Discoverie of Witchcraft*, London, 1584 and 1665, p. 246.

17. Graves, Robert, *The White Goddess*, ch. 4, p. 70 and ch. 23, p. 410.

18. Murray, Margaret A., *The Witch Cult in Western Europe*, ch. 5, p. 130.

19. More, Dr. Henry, *Antidote Against Atheism*, London, 1653.

20. Miriam's story, from the Book of Jasher and other non-biblical accounts, is featured at length in Gardner, Laurence, *Genesis of the Grail Kings*, ch. 19, pp. 207-11.

13: SATAN AND THE YULETIDE ELF

1. Pagels, Elaine, *The Origin of Satan*, Random House, New York, 1995, ch. 2, p. 39.

2. Stoyanov, Yuri, *The Hidden Tradition in Europe*, Arkana-Penguin, Harmondsworth, 1994, *passim* on Dualism.

3. Pagels, Elaine, *The Origin of Satan*, ch. 2, p. 48.

4. Malan, Rev. S. C. (trans.), *The Book of Adam and Eve* (from the Ethiopic text), Williams & Norgate, London, 1882.

5. Budge, Sir Ernest A. Wallis (trans.), *The Book of the Cave of Treasures*, The Religious Tract Society, London, 1927.

6. Budge, Sir Ernest A. Wallis (trans.), *The Book of the Bee* (from the Syriac text), Clarendon Press, Oxford, 1886.

7. The Bull of Pope Innocent VIII is given in full in Kramer, Heinrich, and Sprenger, James, *The Malleus Maleficarum,* (trans. Rev. Montague Summers), Dover Publications, NY, 1971, p. xliii.

8. Michelet, Jules, *Satanism and Witchcraft,* ch. 4, p. 32.

9. Siefker, Phyllis, *Santa Claus, Last of the Wild Men,* MacFarland, Jefferson, NC, 1997, ch. 4, pp. 65-66.

10. Murray, Margaret A., *The God of the Witches,* ch. 1, p. 23.

11. A good overview of the Pagan year is given in Pennick, Nigel, *The Pagan Book of Days,* Destiny Books, Rochester, Vermont, 1992, Intro, p. 1.

12. Siefker, Phyllis, *Santa Claus, Last of the Wild Men,* ch. 4, p.66.

13. *Hutchinson's Encyclopedia,* under 'Inquisition'.

14. Kramer, Heinrich, and Sprenger, James, *The Malleus Maleficarum,* Part III, Question 14.

Individual translations from the original Dominican Latin vary to some extent in terms of the precise words used, but the essential elements of all translations remain consistent.

15. Felix, Marcus Minucius, *The Octavius of Marcus Minucius Felix,* Paulist Press, New York, 1974, Item 9.

The Paulists are Roman Catholic missionary priests operative in North America and Canada.

By virtue of the difficulties associated with translating ancient Latin of the Felix style, there are some variations in individual translations of this work. For example in Clarke, G. W. (trans.), *The Octavius of Marcus Minucius Felix,* Newman Press, New York, 1974.

Although also a Paulist translation, here the word 'flour' is used instead of 'meal'; the word 'pontiff' instead of 'priest', etc. Essentially, however, the content is the same, as is the case in the further translation, Freese, J. H.(trans.), *The Octavius of Marcus Minucius Felix,* Macmillan, New York, 1919.

16. Justin Martyr also wrote in the 2nd century about Christians partaking of human flesh. Clement of Alexandria (writing in the 3rd century) made reference to debauchery at Christian love-feasts. And Epiphanius of Cyprus similarly wrote of a Christian group eating babies in representation of the Body of Christ.

See also Wilken, Robert L., *The Christians as the Romans Saw Them,* Yale University Press, New Haven, Conn., 1984, ch. 1, pp. 19-20.

17. By the time of Emperor Decius (AD 249), the Christians had become so rebellious that they were proclaimed criminals and their mass persecution began on an official basis. This continued into the reign of Diocletian, who

became Emperor in AD 284. He dispensed with all advisory procedure and instituted an absolute monarchy. Christians were required to offer sacrifices to the divine Emperor and they suffered the harshest punishments for disobedience.

It was ruled that all Christian meeting-houses be demolished and disciples who convened alternative assemblies were put to death. All Church property was confiscated by the magistrates, while all books, testaments and written doctrines of the faith were publicly burned. Christians of any prominent or worthy birthright were barred from public office and Christian slaves were denied any hope of freedom. The protection of Roman law was withdrawn and those who argued with the edicts were roasted alive over slow fires or eaten by animals in the public arena.

18. *See* also Gardner, Laurence, *Bloodline of the Holy Grail*, ch. 15, pp. 270-72

19. Farmer, David, *Dictionary of Saints*, under 'Nicholas', p. 364.

20. *The Times* newspaper reported on 21 December 1996 that 'Belgian children are more confused than ever this Christmas by the duelling Santas. Like their cousins in The Netherlands, they know that St. Nicholas is an austere, thin, white-bearded old man in a bishop's mitre who turns up with presents on a boat from Spain on 5 December .... He is, however, increasingly rivalled by the jolly, fat, red-clad man who flies in three weeks later'. [The concept of Nicholas coming from Spain doubtless arose because Holland was ruled from Spain in the 16th century.]

In Denmark St. Nicholas is called Sinterklaas, which is said to derive from his name, but is actually a corruption of Santa Claus, which has a quite different origin. In practice, the bishop had long been called Sint Nicolaas in Denmark—the 'N' of his name (which does not feature in Sinterklaas) being an all-important factor.

21. In the middle 1600s, the future King James II Stuart of Britain (James VII of Scots) was Duke of York and Lord High Admiral, while his elder brother, King Charles II, reigned from the 1660 Restoration. During the previous Cromwellian Protectorate, however, the nation's shipping and foreign interests had collapsed, as a result of which the Dutch had established settlements in the English colonies of North America. A key centre in this regard was New Amsterdam, but in 1665 James of York's Fleet was victorious over the Dutch and New Amsterdam was subsequently renamed New York.

22. Phyllis Siefker's *Santa Claus, Last of the Wild Men* (*see* Note 9, above) constitutes the most thoroughly researched work ever published in this regard, and is recommended reading.

23. Good reading on Pelznichol (or Belsnickle) may be found in Shoemaker, Alfred L., *Christmas in Pennsylvania*, Stackpole Books, Mechanicsburg, PA, 1999, pp. 75-90.

24. Heidel, Alexander, *The Gilgamesh Epic and Old Testament Parallels*, University

of Chicago Press. Chicago, IL, 1949.

25. Siefker, Phyllis, *Santa Claus, Last of the Wild Men*, ch. 2, pp. 33-34.

26. Shoemaker, Alfred L., *Christmas in Pennsylvania*, pp. 33-36 and Notes p. 152.

27. *Waes Haile* was the Middle English for 'Be in Health'. The Wassail was a hot punch made from ale, spices and apples.

28. In referencing Old Nick, Dr. Margaret Murray relates the Pelznichol character to Curnunnos (*see* Chapter 11, under 'The Horned One'), maintaining that, because of people's affection for the character, the Church was forced to accept him, and he was canonized as St. Nicholas.

See also Murray, Margaret A., *The God of the Witches*, ch. 1, p. 38.

29. Carus, Dr. Paul, *The History of the Devil and the Idea of Evil*, Gramercy Books, New York, 1996, p. 288.

30. Grimm, Jacob, *Teutonic Mythology*, Routledge—Thoemmes Press, London, 1999, ch.17, pp. 105, 115.

14: THE FAERIE QUEEN

1. Spenser, Edmund, *The Fairy Queen*, Everyman—J. M. Dent, London, 1996, Appendix, pp. 583-86.

2. Deacon, Richard, *A History of the British Secret Service*, Grafton Books, London, 1982, ch, 1, pp. 23-24.

3. *Ibid*, ch. 2, p. 34.

4. *Ibid*, ch. 2, p. 40.

5. Brumby, Robin, *Doctor John Dee – The Original 007*, Academic Board of Dacorum College, Hemel Hempstead, 1977, ch. 1, p. 1.

6. Deacon, Richard, *A History of the British Secret Service*, ch. 2, p. 43.

7. Yates, Frances A., *The Rosicrucian Enlightenment*, Routledge & Kegan Paul, London, 1972, pp. 109-110.

8. Anderson, Verily, *The De Veres of Castle Hedingham*, ch. 14, p. 203.

9. Deacon, Richard, *A History of the British Secret Service*, ch. 2, pp. 47-48.

10. *Ibid*, ch. 2, pp. 51-52.

11. The Marlowe Society <http://www.marlowe-society.org/05death.htm>.

In practice, the Elizabethan Star Chamber was virtually an executionary court in which trials were for show since the outcomes had already been decided.

12. Phillips, Graham and Keatman, Martin, *The Shakespeare Conspiracy*, Century, London, 1994, chs. 5-7, pp. 50-89.

13. *The Oxford de Vere Files* <http://www.geocities.com/Athens/Delphi/9744/index.html>.

14. *See* also Gardner, Laurence, *Bloodline of the Holy Grail*, ch. 16, pp. 273-86, and ch. 19, pp. 315-34.

15. The Mary, Queen of Scots, story is told in greater detail in Albany, HRH Prince Michael Stewart of, *The Forgotten Monarchy of Scotland*, ch. 7, pp. 105-14.

15: LORNA DOONE

1. Albany, HRH Prince Michael Stewart of, *The Forgotten Monarchy of Scotland*, ch. 7, p. 114.

2. *Ibid*, ch. 8, pp. 128-29.

3. For a romantic picture guide to the Land of Lorna Doone, *see* Gardner, Barry, *Lorna Doone's Exmoor*, Exmoor Press, Dulverton, 1990.

Today, Lorna Doone's exquisite bronze statue by George Stephenson graces the frontage of the Exmoor National Park headquarters in Dulverton, while on the northern moor, Oare Church, the Waterslide and the famous Doone Valley are among England's foremost West Country tourist attractions. In the 1920s the American Nabisco Corporation introduced the still popular *Lorna Doone* shortbread cookie to commemorate the first silent film of the story, subsequent to which further cinema films have been made, along with television and radio productions and a stage musical. Also, Exmoor's famous Lorna Doone stagecoach has been restored and is now operative once again.

4. The background story is told in separated extracts throughout *Lorna Doone*, but has its fullest explanations in chapters 5 and 66. *See* Blackmore, R. D., *Lorna Doone*, Sampson, Low, Marston, London, 1869.

5. Details of the Doone family Annals were privately published in 1901 by Audrie Doon (Ida Marie Brown), entitled *A Short History of the Original Doones of Exmoor*, now held at the British Library. Extracts were published on 12 October 1901 in the *West Somerset Free Press* and, subsequently, in *The King Magazine of World News*.

6. Murray John (7th Duke of Atholl), *Chronicles of Atholl and Tullibardine Families*, Ballantyne, London, 1908, p. 91.

7. Douglas, Sir Robert of Glenbervie, *The Peerage of Scotland*, MS, 1764.

8. *See* genealogical chart 'Stewart Kings and Noble Houses' in Albany, HRH

Prince Michael Stewart of, *The Forgotten Monarchy of Scotland*, p. 93.

9. Dunn, Waldo Hilary, *R. D. Blackmore – a Biography*, Robert Hale, London, 1956, ch. 3, p. 25.

10. Prior to the publication of Blackmore's classic novel in 1869, Lorna was never used as a female name, although it became very popular afterwards, especially from 1871 when Queen Victoria's daughter Louise married the prevailing Marquess of Lorne. The name of Blackmore's heroine, Lorna Doone, was actually contrived to represent the *Loarna Daouine* tradition of the early regional Ring Lords.

11. Dunn, Waldo Hilary, *R. D. Blackmore – a Biography*, ch. 17, p. 126.

16: CURSE OF THE WEREWOLF

1. Were (or *wér*) meant 'men' in Anglo-Saxon. Other equivalents were the Gothic *vair*, Latin vir, Icelandic verr and old Sanskrit *vîra*.
See also Baring-Gould, Sabine, *The Book of Werewolves*, Senate, London, 1995, ch. 8, p. 102.

2. Graves, Robert, *The White Goddess*, ch. 10, p. 185.

3. Herodotus, *The Histories*, Book 4, Item 105, p. 270.

4. Ovid, *Metamorphoses*, (trans. A. D. Melville), Oxford University Press, Oxford, 1986, Book I, p. 8.

5. Baring-Gould, Sabine, *The Book of Werewolves*, ch. 2, p. 8.

6. Byock, Jesse (ed.), *The Saga of the Volsungs*, ch. 8, pp. 44-45.
Also *see* Baring-Gould, Sabine, *The Book of Werewolves*, ch. 3, pp. 18-19.

7. Marie de France, *Lays*, (trans. Eugene Mason), J. M. Dent, London, 1954, ch. 8, pp. 83-90.

8. Kramer, Heinrich, and Sprenger, James, *The Malleus Maleficarum*, Part I, Question 10, p. 65.

9. *Oxford Compact English Dictionary*, under 'Werewolf'.

10. *Oxford Concise English Dictionary*, under 'Heresy'.

11. Clébert, Jean-Paul, *The Gypsies*, (trans. Charles Duff), Visita Books, London, 1963, pp. 50-51.

12. *Ibid*, p. 52.

13. Frazer, Sir James George, *The Golden Bough*, ch. 52, p. 494.

14. Graves, Robert, *The White Goddess*, ch. 7, p. 282.

15. Melton, J. Gordon, *The Vampire Book*, Visible Ink Press, Farmington Hills, MI, 1999, Foreword, p. x.

16. Carus, Dr. Paul, *The History of the Devil and the Idea of Evil*, p. 307.

17. Melton, J. Gordon, *The Vampire Book*, pp. 55-56.

17: TWILIGHT OF THE VAMPIRE

1. Baring-Gould, Sabine, *The Book of Werewolves*, ch. 8, p. 115.

2. Melton, J. Gordon, *The Vampire Book*, p. 627.

3. Isaiah 34:14 (*King James Authorized Bible*).

4. Summers, Montague, *The Vampire*, Dorset Press, New York, 1996, pp. 226-28.

5. Unterman, Alan, *Dictionary of Jewish Lore and Legend*, Thames & Hudson, London, 1991, under 'Lilith', p. 120.
See also *Encyclopaedia Judaica Decannial*, Keter Publishing, London, 1997, under 'Lilith', pp. 246-48.

6. Patai, Raphael, *The Hebrew Goddess*, ch. 10, p. 221.
Also *see* Lilith as the consort of Enki-Samael in Gardner, Laurence, *Genesis of the Grail Kings*, ch. 11, p. 106.

7. Patai, Raphael, *The Hebrew Goddess*, ch. 10, pp. 222-23.

8. Barber, Paul, *Vampires, Burial and Death*, Yale University Press, New Haven, 1988, ch. 6, p. 42.
See also Barber, Elizabeth Wayland, *The Mummies of Urümchi*, ch. 2, p. 30.

9. Melton, J. Gordon, *The Vampire Book*, pp. 283-84 and 288.

10. Barber, Paul, *Vampires, Burial and Death*, ch. 5, p. 33.

11. Melton, J. Gordon, *The Vampire Book*, p. 467.

12. This report is fully transcribed in Barber, Paul, *Vampires, Burial and Death*, pp. 16-17.

13. Melton, J. Gordon, *The Vampire Book*, p. 288.

14. In Chapter 15 Lady Mary Ruthven is cited as the mother-in-law of Sir James Stewart of Innermeath (Sir Ensor Doone).

15. Barber, Paul, *Vampires, Burial and Death*, Intro, p. 2.

16. Melton, J. Gordon, *The Vampire Book*, Foreword, p. xi.

17. *Ibid*, p. 11.

18: THE PORTAL OF DRACULA

1. Miller, Elizabeth, *Dracula: Sense and Nonsense*, Desert Island Books, Westcliff-on-Sea, 2000, ch. 2, p. 72.

Elizabeth Miller, Professor of English at the Memorial University of Newfoundland, is the founder of the Canadian Chapter of the Transylvanian Society of Dracula.

2. *Ibid*, ch. 5, pp. 187-88.

3. Melton, J. Gordon, *The Vampire Book*, pp. 758-59.

4. *Ibid*, p. 573.

5. Florescu, Radu, and McNally, Raymond, *Dracula*, Robert Hale, London, 1973, Intro, pp. 9-10

6. Succeeding the empire of the Seljuk Turks, the Ottoman Empire was founded *c*.1300. In 1452 the Ottoman Turks recovered Constantinople, which had long been the citadel of the East Roman Byzantine Empire. By the late 16th century the Ottoman domain extended from Hungary to Egypt and parts of Persia. Then a gradual decline followed until the establishment of the Republic of Turkey saw the end of imperialism in 1920.

7. Florescu, Radu, and McNally, Raymond, *Dracula*, ch. 7, p. 151.

8. Melton, J. Gordon, *The Vampire Book*, p. 573.

9. The word 'alchemy' comes from the Arabic *al* (the) and the Egyptian *khame* (blackness). *Al-khame* is defined as the science which overcomes the blackness, or that which enlightens through intuitive perception.

10. Some published information concerning the Societas Draconis is in Boulton, D'Arcy Jonathan Dacre, *The Knights of the Crown*, Boydell Press, London, 1987, ch. 12, pp. 348-55.

11. *Ibid*, p. 350.

An example of this variable device is held at Bayeriches National Museum, Society of the Dragon in Munich, Inventory No. T3792.

12. Florescu, Radu, and McNally, Raymond, *Dracula*, ch. 7, p. 152.

13. *Ibid*, ch. 1, p. 23.

14. *Ibid*, ch. 3, p. 60.

15. *Ibid*, ch. 3, p. 67.

16. *Ibid*, ch. 4, p. 107.

19: BEYOND THE FOREST

1. *Oxford Compact English Dictionary*, under 'Vampire'.

2. Melton, J. Gordon, *The Vampire Book*, p. 626.

3. Examples of this type of alphabetical difference can be found in the old Welsh (Brythonic-Cymric) language as against Irish Scots (Goidelic-Scotic) wherein the words for 'son' were *map* and *mac* respectively. There was also a sub-variant which enabled 'p' and 'b' to be interchangeable, as in the words relating to a hill or peak, which were *pen* (Welsh) and *ben* (Scots). The Cymric language of Wales stemmed originally from the Cimmerian tongue of Northern Scythia, whereas Scotic was a Southern Scythian dialect.

4. *Oxford Compact English Dictionary*, under 'Vikings' and 'Wi'.

5. Utiger, Robert D. on 'Melatonin, the Hormone of Darkness', in the *New England Journal of Medicine*, Vol. 327, no. 19, November 1992.

6. Grant, Kenneth, *The Magical Revival*, ch. 8, pp. 141-42.

7. *Ibid*, ch. 8, p. 139.

8. Becker, Robert O., and Selden, Gary, *The Body Electric*, William Morrow, New York, 1985, pp. 42-43.

9. Hardland, R., Reiter, R. J., Poeggeler, B., and Dan, D. X. on 'The Significance of the Metabolism of the Neurohormone Melatonin: Antioxidative Protection of Bioactive Substances', in *Neuroscience and Biobehavioural Review*, Vol. 17, 1993, pp. 347-57.

Recommended reading with regard to the nature and effects of melatonin is Reiter, Russel J., and Robinson, Jo, *Melatonin*, Bantam Books, New York, 1996.

10. Walji, Hasnain, *Melatonin*, Thorsons, London, 1995, Epilogue, pp. 59-61

11. Shapiro, Debbie, *The Body Mind Workbook*, Element Books, Shaftesbury, 1990, p. 49.

12. Roney-Dougal, Serena, *Where Science and Magic Meet,* Element Books, Shaftesbury, 1993, ch. 4, p. 91.

13. *Ibid,* ch. 4, p. 106.

14. Full details of this sequence are given in Gardner, Laurence, *Genesis of the Grail Kings,* pp. 236-49.

20: REALM OF THE RING LORDS

1. Albany, HRH Prince Michael Stewart of, *The Forgotten Monarchy of Scotland,* ch. 2, p. 19.

During the reign of Malcolm I of Scots (942-954), King Edmund of England conceded the Northern English regions of Cumberland, Northumberland and Westmoreland to the Scottish crown. As a result, the overall Scottish domain was about one-third larger than it is today. These regions were passed back to English ownership two centuries later by Malcolm IV (1153-1165).

2. Although some of these ancient rock carvings have been moved into museums, while others remain preserved *in situ,* there are those which have been thoroughly ignored and even treated with some irreverence. An example of particularly inconsiderate treatment in this locational regard can be found in the Ratho environs of the Platt Hills, near Edinburgh. In this picturesque area is the old Ratho quarry, where the Society of Antiquaries of Scotland recorded the discovery of an ancient double burial chamber containing Cup markings in November 1897, with another kist chamber discovered close by in 1993. Near to Ratho (a place distinguished by the very antiquity of its name) there are also significant Cup and Ring carvings at Tormain Hill, about 500 yards (c.457 metres) from the quarry where there was once a tall standing-stone called the Witches' Stane. This ancient monument was demolished by quarry workers some years ago—an action which should have been warning enough that the regional authorities were not in the least concerned with preserving local heritage when faced with the alternative of some commercially viable enterprise.

The Ratho situation has now worsened since the old quarry was sold to facilitate another financial venture in recent times. Now, as part of a general destruction of the surrounding landscape and vegetation, the adjacent hillside has been unthinkingly destroyed without any systematic site search for further Cup and Ring markings which might well exist upon rocks within the topsoil. All is now obscured by many thousands of tons of rubble and waste in the process of constructing a rock-climbing centre and it is seemingly intended to re-profile this land! When questioned about this disgraceful matter by the Lord Provost of Edinburgh in August 1999, the City Development Planning Authority replied that they were 'unable to exercise any control under the planning legislation with regard to these operations'. Plainly, the Town and Country Planning (Scotland) Act 1997 is completely ineffectual when commercial projects are weighed against national heritage. In this context, it is perfectly clear that—as with just about all we have seen in our investigation—politics, religion and monetary interests govern the extent to which our history is preserved and portrayed, whether in books, art or on the ground. Further information in this regard may be obtained from Jim Naples <naples@mew.uk.com>.

3. Cowan, David R., and Silk, Ann, *Ancient Energy of the Earth*, Thorsons, London, 1999, ch. 2, pp. 9-13.

4. Gerber, Pat, *Stone of Destiny*, Cannongate, Edinburgh, 1997, ch. 21, p. 179.

APPENDIX I

PENDRAGONS OF THE BRITANNIC ISLE

Pen Dracos Insularis

Cymbeline (Cunobelinus)
King in the South East (d. *c.*AD 17) – Court at Colchester (Camu-lot)
Great-grandson of Beli Mawr, Lord of the Britons

Caractacus
Regulus of the Britons (d. *c.*AD 54) (Son of Cymbeline)
= *Eurgain*

Arviragus
King of Siluria [South Wales and Mid West] (d. AD 54) – Brother of Caractacus
= *Genuissa,* dau. of Emperor Claudius

Marius
High King of the South (d. 125) – Son of Arviragus
= *Penardun,* dau. of Bran Vendigaid, Archdruid of Siluria

Llieffer Mawr (Lucius)
King of the South and Siluria *c.*AD 180 – Grandson of Marius
= *Gladys,* g-granddaughter of Arviragus

Cadwan
Prince of Cambria – Son-in-law of Lleiffer Mawr
= *Gladys*

Coel II
King of Colchester and South East (d. AD 262) – Son of Cadwan
Father of *St. Helena,* wife of Emperor Constantius Chlorus

Confer
Prince of Strathclyde – Grandson of Coel II

Caradawc Vreichvras (Caradog)
Welsh Regulus of Gwent & Archenfield – Cousin of Confer in Lucius descent

Eudes (Eudaf)
King of Breton Dumnonia (Dux of the Gewissi) – Son of Caradawc Vreichvras
= *Daughter* of Carausius II of the Saxon Shore

Coel Hen Godebog
King of Carlisle, Rheged and Gwyr-y-Gogledd (b. *c.*AD 380) – Tanist of Eudes
= *Ystrafael*

Vortigern (Foirtchernn)
Regulus of Powys (Wales) and Sovereign Guletic (d.AD 464)
Son-in-law of Magnus Maximus, Imperial Guletic, and Elen, dau. of Eudes
= *Gladys* (*Severa*)

Cunedda Wledig
Prince of Manau Guotodin (North) and Gwynedd (Wales) – Son-in-law of Coel Hen
= *Gwawl*

Brychan I
Regulus of Welsh Breichniog (Brecknock) – Son-in-law of Vortigern
= *Ribrwast*

Dyfnwal Hen
Regulus of Strathclyde – Cousin of Brychan in descent from Confer

Brychan II
Prince of Manau Guotodin – Son of Brychan I and son-in-law of Dyfnwal Hen
= *Ingenach*

Maelgwyn Gwynedd
Prince of Gwynedd (d. 548) – Great-grandson of Cunedda Wledig

Aedàn Mac Gabràn
King of Scots Dalriada (d. 608) in descent from Dyfnwal Hen
Grandson of Brychan II and Ingenach
= *Ygerna del Acqs*

Cadfan
Prince of Gwynedd (d. 625) in descent from Maelgwyn Gwynedd
= *Acha,* dau. of Anglo-Saxon King Aelle of Deira

Cadwallon II
Prince of Gwynedd (d. 634) – Son of Cadfan
= *Helen,* dau. of Wibba the Angle

Cadwaladr (the Blessed)
Prince of Gwynedd (d. 664) [The Last Pendragon]
= *Widow* of Alain II of the Bretons

APPENDIX II

THE DONATION OF CONSTANTINE

From *Die Constantinische Schenkungsurkunde,* Brunner-Zeumer Edition, Berlin, 1888

In the name of the holy and indivisible Trinity, the Father, namely, and the Son and the Holy Spirit. The emperor Caesar Flavius Constantine in Christ Jesus, the Lord God our Saviour, one of that same holy Trinity—faithful merciful, supreme, beneficent, Alamannic, Gothic, Sarmatic, Germanic, Britannic, Hunic, pious, fortunate, victor and triumpher, always august: to the most holy and blessed father of fathers Sylvester, bishop of the city of Rome and pope and to all his successors the pontiffs who are about to sit upon the chair of St. Peter until the end of time—also to all the most reverend and of God beloved catholic bishops, subjected by this our imperial decree throughout the whole world to this same holy, Roman church, who have been established now and in all previous times—grace, peace, charity, rejoicing, long-suffering, mercy, be with you all from God the Father almighty and from Jesus Christ his Son and from the Holy Ghost. Our most gracious serenity desires, in clear discourse, through the page of this our imperial decree, to bring to the knowledge of all the people in the whole world what things our Saviour and Redeemer the Lord Jesus Christ, the Son of the most High Father, has most wonderfully seen fit to bring about by the intervention of our father Sylvester, the highest pontiff and the universal pope. First, indeed, putting forth, with the inmost confession of our heart, for the purpose of instructing the mind of all of you, our creed which we have learned from the aforesaid most blessed father and our confessor, Sylvester the universal pontiff; and then at length announcing the mercy of God which has been poured upon us.

For we wish you to know, as we have signified through our former imperial decree, that we have gone away from the worship of idols, from mute and deaf images made by hand, from devilish contrivances and from all the pomps of Satan; and have arrived at the pure faith of the Christians, which is the true light and everlasting life. Believing, according to what he—that same one, our revered supreme father and teacher, the pontiff Sylvester—has taught us, in God the Father, the almighty maker of Heaven and earth, of all things visible and invisible; and in Jesus Christ, his only Son, our Lord God, through whom all things are created; and in the Holy Spirit, the Lord and vivifier of the whole creature. We confess these, the Father and the Son and the Holy Spirit, in such way that, in the perfect Trinity, there shall also be a fullness of divinity and a unity of power. The Father is God, the Son is God, and the Holy Spirit is God; and these three are one in Jesus Christ.

There are therefore three forms but one power. For God, wise in all previous time, gave forth from himself the word through which all future ages were to be born; and when, by that sole word of His wisdom, He formed the whole creation from nothing, He was with it, arranging all things in His mysterious secret place.

Therefore, the virtues of the Heavens and all the material part of the earth having been perfected, by the wise nod of His wisdom first creating man of the clay of the earth in His own image and likeness, He places him in a paradise of delight. Him the ancient serpent and envious enemy, the devil, through the most bitter taste of the forbidden tree, made an exile from these joys; and, he being expelled, did not cease in many ways to cast his poisonous darts; in order that, turning the human race from the way of truth to the worship of idols, he might persuade it, namely, to worship the creature and not the creator; so that, through them (the idols), he might cause those whom he might be able to entrap in his snares to be burned with him in eternal punishment. But our Lord, pitying His creature, sending ahead His holy prophets, announcing through them the light of the future life—the coming, that is, of His Son our Lord and Saviour Jesus Christ—sent that same only begotten Son and Word of wisdom: He descending from Heaven on account of our salvation, being born of the Holy Spirit and of the Virgin Mary—the word was made flesh and dwelt among us. He did not cease to be what He had been, but began to be what He had not been, perfect God and perfect man: as God, performing miracles; as man, sustaining human sufferings. We so learned Him to be very man and very God by the preaching of our father Sylvester, the supreme pontiff, that we can in no wise doubt that He was very God and very man. And, having chosen twelve apostles, He shone with miracles before them and an innumerable multitude of people. We confess that this same Lord Jesus Christ fulfilled the law and the prophets; that He suffered, was crucified, on the third day arose from the dead according to the Scriptures; was received into Heaven, and sitteth on the right hand of the Father. Whence He shall come to judge the quick and the dead, whose kingdom shall have no end. For this is our orthodox creed, placed before us by our most blessed father Sylvester, the supreme pontiff.

We exhort, therefore, all people, and all the different nations, to hold, cherish and preach this faith; and, in the name of the Holy Trinity, to obtain the grace of baptism; and, with devout heart, to adore the Lord Jesus Christ our Saviour, who, with the Father and the Holy Spirit, lives and reigns through infinite ages; whom Sylvester our father, the universal pontiff, preaches. For He himself, our Lord God, having pity on me a sinner, sent His holy apostles to visit us, and caused the light of His splendour to shine upon us. And do ye rejoice that I, having been withdrawn from the shadow, have come to the true light and to the knowledge of truth. For, at a time when a mighty and filthy leprosy had invaded all the flesh of my, body, and the care was administered of many physicians who came together, nor by that of any one of them did I achieve health: there came hither the priests of the Capitol, saving to me that a font should be made on the Capitol, and that I should fill this with the blood of innocent infants; and that, if I bathed in it while it was warm, I might be cleansed. And very many innocent infants having been brought together according to their words, when the sacrilegious priests of the pagans wished them to be slaughtered and the font to be filled with their blood: our serenity perceiving the tears of the mothers, I straightway abhorred the deed. And, pitying them, I ordered their own sons to be restored to them; and, giving them vehicles and gifts, sent them off rejoicing to their own. That day having passed therefore—the silence of night having come upon us—when the time of sleep had arrived, the apostles St. Peter and Paul appear, saying to me: 'Since thou hast placed a term to thy vices, and hast abhorred the pouring forth of innocent blood, we are sent by Christ the Lord our God, to give to thee a plan for recovering thy health.

Hear, therefore, our warning, and do what we indicate to thee. Sylvester—the bishop of the city of Rome—on Mount Serapte, fleeing thy persecutions, cherishes the darkness with his clergy in the caverns of the rocks. This one, when thou shalt have led him to thyself, will himself show thee a pool of piety; in which, when he shall have dipped thee for the third time, all that strength of the leprosy will desert thee. And, when this shall have been done, make this return to thy Saviour, that by thy order through the whole world the churches may be restored. Purify thyself, moreover, in this way, that, leaving all the superstition of idols, thou do adore and cherish the living and true God—who is alone and true—and that thou attain to the doing of His will'.

Rising, therefore, from sleep, straightway I did according to that which I had been advised to do by the holy apostles; and, having summoned that excellent and benignant father and our enlightener—Sylvester the universal pope—I told him all the words that had been taught me by the holy apostles; and asked him who were those gods Peter and Paul. But he said that they where not really called gods, but apostles of our Saviour the Lord God Jesus Christ. And again we began to ask that same most blessed pope whether he had some express image of those apostles; so that, from their likeness, we might learn that they were those whom revelation had shown to us. Then that same venerable father ordered the images of those same apostles to be shown by his deacon. And, when I had looked at them, and recognized, represented in those images, the countenances of those whom I had seen in my dream: with a great noise, before all my satraps, I confessed that they were those whom I had seen in my dream.

Hereupon that same most blessed Sylvester our father, bishop of the city of Rome, imposed upon us a time of penance—within our Lateran palace, in the chapel, in a hair garment—so that I might obtain pardon from our Lord God Jesus Christ our Saviour by vigils, fasts, and tears and prayers, for all things that had been impiously done and unjustly ordered by me. Then through the imposition of the hands of the clergy, I came to the bishop himself; and there, renouncing the pomps of Satan and his works, and all idols made by hands, of my own will before all the people I confessed: that I believed in God the Father almighty, maker of Heaven and earth, and of all things visible and invisible; and in Jesus Christ, His only Son our Lord, who was born of the Holy Spirit and of the virgin Mary. And, the font having been blessed, the wave of salvation purified me there with a triple immersion. For there I, being placed at the bottom of the font, saw with my own eyes a hand from Heaven touching me; whence rising, clean, know that I was cleansed from all the squalor of leprosy. And, I being raised from the venerable font—putting on white raiment, he administered to me the sign of the seven-fold holy Spirit, the unction of the holy oil; and he traced the sign of the holy cross on my brow, saying: God seals thee with the seal of His faith in the name of the Father and the Son and the Holy Spirit, to signalize thy faith. All the clergy replied: 'Amen'. The bishop added 'peace be with thee'.

And so, on the first day after receiving the mystery of the holy baptism, and after the cure of my body from the squalor of the leprosy, I recognized that there was no other God save the Father and the Son and the Holy Spirit; whom the most blessed Sylvester the pope doth preach; a trinity in one, a unity in three. For all the gods of the nations, whom I have worshipped up to this time, are proved to be demons; works made by the hand of men; inasmuch as that same venerable father told to us most clearly how much power in Heaven and on earth He, our Saviour, conferred on his apostle St. Peter, when finding him faithful after questioning him He said: 'Thou art Peter, and upon this rock (petram) shall I build My Church, and the gates of hell shall not prevail against it'. Give heed ye powerful, and incline the ear of your hearts to that which the good Lord and Master added to His disciple, saying: 'and I will give thee the keys of the kingdom of Heaven; and whatever thou shalt bind on earth shall be bound also in Heaven, and whatever thou shalt loose on earth shall be loosed also in Heaven'. This is very wonderful and glorious, to bind and loose on earth and to have it bound and loosed in Heaven.

And when, the blessed Sylvester preaching them, I perceived these things and learned that by the kindness of St. Peter himself I had been entirely restored to health: I—together with all our satraps and the whole senate and the nobles and all the Roman people, who are subject to the glory of our rule—considered it advisable that, as on earth he (Peter) is seen to have been constituted vicar of the Son of God, so the pontiffs, who are the representatives of that same chief of the apostles, should obtain from us and our empire the power of a supremacy greater than the earthly clemency of our imperial serenity is seen to have had conceded to it—we choosing that same prince of the apostles, or his vicars, to be our constant intercessors with God. And, to the extent of our earthly imperial power, we decree that his holy Roman church shall be honoured with veneration; and that, more than our empire and earthly throne, the most sacred seat of St. Peter shall be gloriously exalted; we giving to it the imperial power, and dignity of glory, and vigour and honour.

And we ordain and decree that he shall have the supremacy as well over the four chief seats Antioch, Alexandria, Constantinople and Jerusalem, as also over all the churches of God in the whole world. And he who for the time being shall be pontiff of that holy Roman church shall be more exalted than, and chief over, all the priests of the whole world; and, according to his judgment, everything which is to be provided for the service of God or the stability of the faith of the Christians is to be administered. It is indeed just, that there the holy law should have the seat of its rule where the founder of holy laws, our Saviour, told St. Peter to take the chair of the apostleship; where also, sustaining the cross, he blissfully took the cup of death and appeared as imitator of his Lord and Master; and that there the people should bend their necks at the confession of Christ's name, where their teacher, St. Paul the apostle, extending his neck for Christ, was crowned with martyrdom. There, until the end, let them seek a teacher, where the holy body of the teacher lies; and there, prone and humiliated, let them perform the service of the heavenly king, God our Saviour Jesus Christ, where the proud were accustomed to serve under the rule of an earthly king.

Meanwhile we wish all the people, of all the races and nations throughout the whole world, to know: that we have constructed within our Lateran palace, to the same Saviour our Lord God Jesus Christ, a church with a baptistery from the foundations. And know that we have carried on our own shoulders, from its foundations, twelve baskets weighted with earth, according to the number of the holy apostles. Which holy church we command to be spoken of, cherished, venerated and preached of, as the head and summit of all the churches in the whole world—as we have commanded through our other imperial decrees. We have also constructed the churches of St. Peter and St. Paul, chiefs of the apostles, which we have enriched with gold and silver; where also, placing their most sacred bodies with great honour, we have constructed their caskets of electrum, against which no force of the elements prevails. And we have placed a cross of purest gold on each of their caskets, and fastened them with golden keys. And on these churches, for the providing of the lights, we have conferred estates, and have enriched them with different objects; and, through our sacred imperial decrees, we have granted them our gift of land in the east as well as in the west; and even on the northern and southern coast—namely in Judaea, Greece, Asia, Thrace, Africa and Italy and the various islands: under this condition indeed, that all shall be administered by the hand of our most blessed father the pontiff Sylvester and his successors.

For let all the people and the nations of the races in the whole world rejoice with us; we exhorting all of you to give unbounded thanks, together with us, to our Lord and Saviour Jesus Christ. For He is God in Heaven above and on earth below, who, visiting us through His holy apostles, made us worthy to receive the holy sacrament of baptism and health of body. In return for which, to those same holy apostles, my masters, St. Peter and St. Paul; and, through them, also to St. Sylvester, our father—the chief pontiff and universal pope of the city of Rome—and to all the pontiffs his successors, who until the end of the world shall be about to sit in the seat of St. Peter: we concede and, by this present, do confer, our imperial Lateran palace, which is preferred to, and ranks above, all the palaces in the whole world; then a diadem, that is, the crown of our head, and at the same time the tiara; and, also, the shoulder band—that is, the collar that usually surrounds our imperial neck; and also the purple mantle, and crimson tunic, and all the imperial raiment; and the same rank as those presiding over the imperial cavalry; conferring also the imperial sceptres, and, at the same time, the spears and standards; also the banners and different imperial ornaments, and all the advantage of our high imperial position, and the glory of our power.

And we decree, as to those most reverend men, the clergy who serve, in different orders, that same holy Roman church, that they shall have the same advantage, distinction, power and excellence by the glory of which our most illustrious senate is adorned; that is, that they shall be made patricians and consuls—we commanding that they shall also be decorated with the other imperial dignities. And even as the imperial soldiery, so, we decree, shall the clergy of the holy Roman church be adorned. And even as the imperial power is adorned by different offices—by the distinction, that is, of chamberlains, and door keepers, and all the guards—so we wish the holy Roman church to be adorned. And, in order that the pontifical glory may shine forth more fully, we decree this also: that the clergy of this same holy Roman church may use saddle cloths of linen of the whitest colour; namely that their horses may be adorned and so be ridden, and that, as our senate uses shoes with goats' hair, so they may be distinguished by gleaming linen; in order that, as the celestial beings, so the terrestrial may be adorned to the glory of God. Above all things, moreover, we give permission to that same most holy one our father Sylvester, bishop of the city of Rome and pope, and to all the most blessed pontiffs who shall come after him and succeed him in all future times—for the honour and glory of Jesus Christ our Lord—to receive into that great Catholic and apostolic church of

God, even into the number of the monastic clergy, any one from the whole assembly of our nobles, who, in free choice, of his own accord, may wish to become a clerk; no one at all presuming thereby to act in a haughty manner.

We also decreed this, that this same venerable one our father Sylvester, the supreme pontiff, and all the pontiffs his successors, might use and bear upon their heads – to the Praise of God and for the honour of St. Peter – the diadem; that is, the crown which we have granted him from our own head, of purest gold and precious gems. But he, the most holy pope, did not at all allow that crown of gold to be used over the clerical crown which he wears to the glory of St. Peter; but we placed upon his most holy head, with our own hands, a tiara of gleaming splendour representing the glorious resurrection of our Lord. And, holding the bridle of his horse, out of reverence for St. Peter we performed for him the duty of groom; decreeing that all the pontiffs his successors, and they alone, may use that tiara in processions.

In imitation of our own power, in order that for that cause the supreme pontificate may not deteriorate, but may rather be adorned with power and glory even more than is the dignity of an earthly rule: behold we – giving over to the oft-mentioned most blessed pontiff, our father Sylvester the universal pope, as well our palace, as has been said, as also the city of Rome and all the provinces, districts and cities of Italy or of the western regions; and relinquishing them, by our inviolable gift, to the power and sway of himself or the pontiffs his successors – do decree, by this our godlike charter and imperial constitution, that it shall be (so) arranged; and do concede that they (the palaces, provinces etc.) shall lawfully remain with the holy Roman church.

Wherefore we have perceived it to be fitting that our empire and the power of our kingdom should be transferred and changed to the regions of the East; and that, in the province of Byzantium, in a most fitting place, a city should be built in our name; and that our empire should there be established. For, where the supremacy of priests and the head of the Christian religion has been established by a heavenly Ruler, it is not just that there an earthly ruler should have jurisdiction.

We decree, moreover, that all these things which, through this our imperial charter and through other godlike commands, we have established and confirmed, shall remain uninjured and unshaken until the end of the world. Wherefore, before the living God, who commanded us to reign, and in the face of his terrible judgment, we conjure, through this our imperial decree, all the emperors our successors, and all our nobles, the satraps also and the most glorious senate, and all the people in the whole world now and in all times previously subject to our rule: that no one of them, in any way allow himself to oppose or disregard, or in any way seize, these things which, by our imperial sanction, have been conceded to the holy Roman church and to all its pontiffs. If anyone, moreover – which we do not believe – prove a scorner or despiser in this matter, he shall be subject and bound over to eternal damnation; and shall feel that the holy chiefs of the apostles of God, Peter and Paul, will be opposed to him in the present and in the future life. And, being burned in the nethermost hell, he shall perish with the devil and all the impious.

The page, moreover, of this our imperial decree, we, confirming it with our own hands, did place above the venerable body of St. Peter chief of the apostles; and there, promising to that same apostle of God that we would preserve inviolably all its provisions, and would leave in our commands to all the emperors our successors to preserve them, we did hand it over, to be enduringly and happily possessed, to our most blessed father Sylvester the supreme pontiff and universal pope, and, through him, to all the pontiffs his successors—God our Lord and our Saviour Jesus Christ consenting.

And the imperial subscription: May the Divinity preserve you for many years, oh most holy and blessed fathers.

Given at Rome on the third day before the Kalends of April, our master the august Flavius Constantine, for the fourth time, and Galligano, most illustrious men, being consuls.

APPENDIX III

TOLKIEN'S TIMELESS LEGACY

When considering the *Volsunga Saga*, the *Nibelungenlied* and even the tale of Charlemagne's Ring, it is clear that these old stories all have common roots which date back to the Ring cultures of Scythian and Mesopotamian times when Anu held the Ring of Power and Divine Justice. It is equally apparent that various aspects of this ancient lore found their way into the individual Arthurian tales of medieval times, only to come together as a recognizable whole in Sir Thomas Malory's *Morte d'Arthur*. Then, many hundreds of years later, came the operatic composer Richard Wagner to resurrect the legacy of *Der Ring des Nibelungen*, while the poet and translator William Morris did likewise with *Sigurd the Volsung*. Shortly after that, the young John R. R. Tolkien received from his mother a copy of Andrew Lang's *The Red Fairy Book*, within which was 'the best story he had ever read'—the tale of *Sigurd the Volsung* (*see* Carpenter, Humphrey, *J. R. R. Tolkien*, ch. 2, p. 30). "I desired dragons with a profound desire", he stated long afterwards.

Subsequently, in his school studies of Middle English vocabulary, Tolkien's attention was drawn to the Arthurian tale of *Sir Gawain and the Green Knight*, along with other related legends. Then, at the age of twenty-two, he purchased copies of the *Volsunga* epic and *The House of the Wolfings*, subsequently gaining an Oxford professorship in Anglo-Saxon language.

In the wake of all this research, linguistic study and general enthusiasm for all things related to the Ring and Arthurian lore, it therefore comes as no surprise that Tolkien eventually produced his 1950s trilogy *The Lord of the Rings*. Neither is it surprising that this compelling work became so popular as to outsell all other books worldwide in the 20th century, rivalling even the Bible. What is wholly surprising, in the light of Tolkien's own records and confirmation from his College and his friends of his compulsive interest in all matters concerning the Ring Cycle, is that ill-informed or jealous commentators still have the effrontery to state that J. R. R. Tolkien simply composed a lengthy fairy tale with no particular knowledge of any background subject matter. In truth, few could have been more fervently enlightened, and fewer still, even if empowered by the knowledge of such judicious study, could possibly have constructed a work of such might and magnitude.

What is equally surprising, if not discourteous, is the fact that one so often finds copies of Tolkien's works on bookshop shelves containing childish pulp fiction. In reality, however, *The Lord of the Rings* constitutes a modern rendering of the world's greatest mythological tradition and should rightly be placed with the classics of the genre, from Homer to Malory. The fact that the late J. R. R. Tolkien was a writer of our modern time does not detract from the issue that classic mythology is, in any event, timeless. The fact that his work is far from wholly unique does not detract from its value. To the contrary, it has an enhanced value because it is based upon qualified lore of the most ancient kind—preserving it for future generations within a modern market arena which has, for the most part, forsaken the more archaic root material because it is not necessarily conducive to everyday reading.

During the past forty or so years, over fifty million people have purchased Tolkien's *The Lord of the Rings*, while William Morris's epic translation of *Sigurd the Volsung* is still in print after more than 120 years, and large audiences continue to attend performances of Richard Wagner's *Der Ring des Nibelungen*. It is because of the concerted efforts of these latter-day writers that the inherent wisdom and morals of old lore survive, and it would be a sad day indeed if these were ever lost.

APPENDIX IV

JOAN OF ARC

Of all the historical characters who fell to the fate of the Burning Times, perhaps the most popularly known is Jeanne d'Arc (Joan of Arc), the famous Maid of Orléans. Born in 1412, Joan was the daughter of a Domrémy farmer in the French Duchy of Bar. In the following year Henry V (one of the most power-crazed of all English monarchs) became King of England. He was described by his own nobles as "a cold, heartless warmonger", even though historical propaganda has since conferred upon him the mantle of a patriotic hero. At the time of his accession, the Plantagenet war which had been waged for some years against France had subsided, but Henry decided to lay claim to the kingdom of France. This he did on the basis that his great-grandfather Edward III's mother of a whole century before was the daughter of King Philippe IV of France.

King Henry, with 2000 men-at-arms and 6000 archers, swept through Normandy and Rouen, defeating the French at Agincourt in 1415. He was subsequently proclaimed Regent of France at the Treaty of Troyes. Then, with the aid of the faithless French Queen Isabau, he married the French King's daughter, Katherine de Valois, and set a course towards overthrowing her brother, the Dauphin, who was married to King René d'Anjou's sister Mary. It transpired, however, that Henry V died two years later, as did King Charles VI of France. In England the heir to the throne was Henry's infant son, whose uncles—the Dukes of Bedford and Gloucester—became Overlords of France. The French people were somewhat concerned about their future prospects, but all was not lost for along came the inspired Joan of Arc. In 1429 she appeared at the fortress of Vaucouleurs, near Domrémy, announcing that she had been commanded by the saints to besiege the English at Orléans.

At the age of seventeen, Joan departed for the Royal Court at Chinon, along with the Dauphin's brother-in-law, René d'Anjou. Once at Chinon on the Loire, she proclaimed her divine mission to save France from the invaders. At first the Court resisted Joan's military ambitions, but she gained the support of Yolande d'Aragon, who was the Dauphin's mother-in-law and the mother of René d'Anjou, author of *le Livre du Cueur d'Amours Espris*. Joan was then entrusted with the command of more than 7000 men, including the prestigious Scots Royal Guard of the *Gendarmes Ecossais* and the most prominent captains of the day. With René at her side, Joan's troops destroyed the blockade at Orléans and overthrew the English garrison. Within a few weeks the Loire Valley was again in French hands and, on 17 July 1429, Charles the Dauphin was crowned at Reims Cathedral by Archbishop Regnault of Chartres.

Less than a year after her success, the Maid of Orléans was captured while besieging Paris, and the Duke of Bedford arranged for her trial by Pierre Cauchon, Bishop of Beauvais, who condemned her to life imprisonment on bread and water. When Joan refused to submit to rape by her captors, the Bishop pronounced her an ungrateful sorceress and, without further trial, she was burned alive as a witch in the Old Market Square of Rouen on 30 May 1431.

APPENDIX V

THE EARLDOM OF HUNTINGDON

Originally, the Earldom of Huntingdon was a Saxon foundation and the first Earl was Harold Godwinsson of Wessex. He later became King Harold II of England and was killed at the Battle of Hastings against William the Conqueror in 1066. Prior to his becoming king, however, Harold's brother-in-law and predecessor, King Edward the Confessor, had transferred the Earldom in 1050 from Harold to Siward Digara, Earl of Northumbria. This was because Harold and his brother Swein had unlawfully killed Siward's father, Bjorn of Mercia.

Siward died in 1055, but his son Waltheof was under age and so King Edward then passed both Huntingdon and Northumbria to Tostig—another Godwinsson brother of Harold and Swein. Tostig was charged to hold the two earldoms in trust until Waltheof came of age. This happened in 1065, at which time Waltheof duly regained his titles and then married Judith, the Flemish daughter of Lambert of Lens, son of Count Eustace I of Boulogne.

They had no son—only a daughter, Maud, who married Simon de Senlis of the House of Vermandois. In 1090 Simon was made Earl of Huntingdon, with the succession settled upon his and Maud's heirs—but then the intrigue began. Simon died in 1111, at which time his son (Simon II de Senlis) was under age—so his mother, Maud, held the reins, in trust, on his behalf. Then, in 1114, Maud was remarried to King David I of Scots, whom she nominated as her joint trustee of Huntingdon. However, after the birth of their son Henry, King David pursued his own course in this regard. Instead of transferring Huntingdon back to Simon II de Senlis when he came of age, David retained the title for Henry. And so Henry, Prince of Scots, became Earl of Huntingdon—much to the displeasure of the Flemish houses of Lens, Vermandois and Senlis.

In 1152 Prince Henry died, whereupon Huntingdon was transferred to his son David and, subsequently, to David's son John, who died without an heir. Hence, the title expired in the Scottish line in 1219. Ten years prior to Henry's 1152 death, however, Empress Matilda (the wife of Geoffrey Plantagenet of Anjou) offered the Cambridgeshire earldom to Aubrey de Vere (as detailed in Chapter 11 under 'The Historical Robin'). Since the minor-shire earldom of Huntingdon was within the greater-shire of Cambridge, this was clearly meant as a challenge to King David and his son Henry. Empress Matilda (previously married to Henrich V of Germany) was the daughter of Henry I of England, heiress of England and mother of the future Henry II. But in 1142 (when she made the offer to Aubrey) she was battling with Stephen de Blois, who had seized the English crown at her father's death in 1135. Stephen's wife was the daughter of Eustace III of Boulogne, whose own wife was King David of Scots' sister Mary.

Plainly, Empress Matilda was wanting to confront both the Boulogne and Scots houses who were supporting Stephen the usurper. In the context of this, she would have thought it strategically appropriate to give away lands and titles held by the Scots with the approval of Stephen and the house of Boulogne—and at the top of the list was the prized Earldom of Huntingdon.

Aubrey, who declined the Cambridge earldom, would have done so because he knew that it embraced Huntingdon, which rightfully belonged not to him or to the Prince of Scots, but to Simon II de Senlis. And so he opted for the Oxford earldom instead. Nevertheless, his son Robert and his supporters would have recognized the real implication of Matilda's cleverly worded Cambridgeshire offer, which stated, 'unless that county were held by the King of Scots'—which, of course, it was not. King David did not hold Cambridgeshire since the earldom did not exist; he held only Huntingdon (in trust), and had transferred this title to his son Henry, notwithstanding the heritable right of the Senlis branch of Vermandois.

In retrospect, Aubrey's son, Robert de Vere, could justifiably have presumed an entitlement to Huntingdon, just as the Robin Hood stories convey. His family certainly had the best moral pretension—especially from 1219 when the Scots Huntingdon line expired, by which time the Senlis male line was also extinct. Following the demise of the Scots line, however, there was no further Earl of Huntingdon officially appointed until George, Lord Hastings, was granted the title by Henry VIII in 1529.

APPENDIX VI

WEARING OF THE GREEN

Factors which do not become immediately apparent in Chapter 11, concerning Robin Hood, are his popularly supposed wearing of Lincoln green, along with his formal outlawry and traditional involvement with archers. However, these matters are all explained by the fact that the famous *Geste of Robyn Hode* was not published until about 1500. This work, a combination of at least two distinct tales, was the first to establish Robin in these particular respects. It states that the outlawed Robin Hood sought to undermine the formal government and that every yeoman of his company wore a livery of scarlet and striped cloth. On one occasion, however, they entered Nottingham in the customary Lincoln green livery of royal service, which spread panic through the town.

From the 12th century, Lincoln was a major centre of England's wool industry and was especially famed for its unique red and green dyes, which were used in the best military and ceremonial apparel. Green was especially the colour of the royal ambassadors and was particularly associated with Fenian Ireland, where the 'wearing of the green' was symbolic of the shamrock and of the ancient fairy culture. It was also the paramount colour of the elves and of the Green Stag of the *Caille Daouine*.

The Vere heritage was indeed that of the Green Stag and of Aubrey (Oberon) the Elf King, but the family also had an Irish connection and, in particular, a royal service connection, as made apparent by the specifically identified Lincoln green of Robin's liveried yeomanry.

The explanations in these respects do not in fact come from Robert, 3rd Earl of Oxford in the 11th century, but relate to his descendant—another Robert, 9th Earl of Oxford in the 14th century. Hence, the introduction of some new narrative features in the *Geste* begins to make sense. Something else which also becomes apparent is the reason for the legendary Robin's seeming loyalty to King Richard (as against King John) when in practice Robert, 3rd Earl of Oxford, did not support the crusading Richard I at all. What we are looking at, with regard to these aspects of the story, is the subsequent loyalty of Robert, 9th Earl, to King Richard II during the lengthy build-up towards the Wars of the Roses (1455-85) between the Plantagenet Houses of Lancaster and York.

Richard II (the son of Edward, the Black Prince) came to the English throne in 1377, succeeding his grandfather Edward III, in descent from King John. On 10 January 1382 (a specially chosen date midway between their two January birthdays) Richard appointed Robert of Oxford as his Royal Chamberlain and, subsequently, as a Privy Councillor and Knight of the Garter. In 1385 Robert also became Commander of the Kings division of two-hundred archers *(see* Anderson, Verily, *The De Veres of Castle Hedingham*, ch. 6, p.78).

In the autumn of that year Richard II and Robert received an envoy from Ireland, who said the Irish were being badly treated by the Norman barons and, therefore, requested the King's intervention. Consequently, Robert became Duke of Ireland, as well as becoming Chief Justice of Chester and North Wales. Intrigue was brewing at home, however, and a significant faction of nobles (led by the Duke of Gloucester and the Earls of Arundel and Warwick), with

Parliament in their control, were unhappy about their colleagues in Ireland having a new overlord. In retaliation, they accused Robert of siding with King Richard who, they maintained, interfered with the Law of Statutes and made decisions without the parliamentary sanction of the Church and barons in accordance with the terms of the *Magna Charta*. In fact, the Earl of Warwick formally charged Robert (Robin II) with treason against the London Parliament and had him proclaimed an 'outlaw' in 1388.

As a result, Robert, Duke of Ireland—the official wearer of the Royal Green—was sentenced to be hung and drawn, but King Richard disguised him as an archer and secreted him to the comparative safety of Chester in the Welsh border country. There Robert raised a force of fighting men with whom to pursue his cause against his persecutors but, meanwhile, the Earldom of Huntingdon (by then extinct in the Scottish line) was removed from Robert's legacy and granted by Parliament to the King's half-brother John de Holland.

Once again (with the King unable to do anything about it), the Oxford titles and family estates became forfeit. Robert became a fugitive felon for the rest of his life—an outlaw whose most loyal friend and supporter through it all was King Richard II of England, who finally managed to secure a posthumous Pardon for Robert after he was killed by a wild boar some years later.

And so it was that, by virtue of the *Geste of Robyn Hode* and the resultantly expanded accounts, the two Roberts of history became conjoined as the one Robin of legend. In some ways, their stories were very similar and, if anything, their historic reality was probably rather more fraught and adventurous than the resultant mythical romance. In these two characters of the same de Vere family (both Earls of Oxford and Royal Chamberlains) we have the heritage of the Elf Kings, the tradition of the Stag and stewardship of the Royal Forest. We also have the legacy of Fitzooth, along with the ramifications of confiscated estates, excommunication and formal outlawry. We have seen how both King John and King Richard fit into the picture, and have established how the yeomen of the Lincoln green took up arms against the tyrannical Norman barons. Running throughout, we have witnessed the family's disputed claim to the Earldom of Huntingdon—all just as portrayed in the familiar tales of Robin Hood.

APPENDIX VII

EXCOMMUNICATION OF ELIZABETH I

Pope Pius V's 1570 Bull Against Queen Elizabeth

Pius Bishop, servant of the servants of God, in lasting memory of the matter.

He that reigneth on high, to whom is given all power in heaven and earth, has committed one Holy Catholic and Apostolic Church, outside of which there is no salvation, to one alone upon earth, namely to Peter, the first of the Apostles, and to Peter's successor, the Pope of Rome, to be by him governed in fullness of power. Him alone He has made ruler over all peoples and kingdoms, to pull up, destroy, scatter, disperse, plant and build, so that He may preserve His faithful people (knit together with the girdle of charity) in the unity of the Spirit and present them safe and spotless to their Saviour.

In obedience to which duty, we (who by God's goodness are called to the aforesaid government of the Church) spare no pains and labour with all our might that unity and the Catholic religion—which their Author, for the trial of His children's faith and our correction, has suffered to be afflicted with such great troubles—may be preserved entire. But the number of the ungodly has so much grown in power that there is no place left in the world which they have not tried to corrupt with their most wicked doctrines; and among others, Elizabeth, the pretended Queen of England and the servant of crime, has assisted in this, with whom as in a sanctuary the most pernicious of all have found refuge. This very woman, having seized the Crown and monstrously usurped the place of supreme Head of the Church in all England together with the chief authority and jurisdiction belonging to it, has once again reduced this same kingdom—which had already been restored to the Catholic faith and to good fruits—to a miserable ruin.

Prohibiting with a strong hand the use of the true religion, which after its earlier overthrow by Henry VIII (a deserter therefrom) Mary, the lawful Queen of famous memory, had with the help of this See restored, she has followed and embraced the errors of the heretics. She has removed the Royal Council, composed of the nobility of England, and has filled it with obscure men, being heretics; oppressed the followers of the Catholic faith; instituted false preachers and ministers of impiety; abolished the sacrifice of the Mass, prayers, fasts, choice of meats, celibacy, and Catholic ceremonies; and has ordered that books of manifestly heretical content be propounded to the whole realm and that impious rites and institutions after the rule of Calvin, entertained and observed by herself, be also observed by her subjects. She has dared to eject bishops, rectors of churches and other Catholic priests from their churches and benefices, to bestow these and other things ecclesiastical upon heretics, and to determine spiritual causes; has forbidden the prelates, clergy and people to acknowledge the Church of Rome or obey its precepts and canonical sanctions; has forced most of them to come to terms with her wicked laws, to abjure the authority and obedience of the Pope of Rome, and to accept her, on oath, as their only lady in matters temporal and spiritual; has imposed penalties and punishments on those who would not agree to this and has exacted then of those who persevered in the unity of the faith and the aforesaid obedience; has thrown the

Catholic prelates and parsons into prison where many, worn out by long languishing and sorrow, have miserably ended their lives. All these matter and manifest and notorious among all the nations; they are so well proven by the weighty witness of many men that there remains no place for excuse, defence or evasion.

We, seeing impieties and crimes multiplied one upon another the persecution of the faithful and afflictions of religion daily growing more severe under the guidance and by the activity of the said Elizabeth; and recognising that her mind is so fixed and set that she has not only despised the pious prayers and admonitions with which Catholic princes have tried to cure and convert her, but has not even permitted the nuncios sent to her in this matter by this See to cross into England, are compelled by necessity to take up against her the weapons of justice, though we cannot forbear to regret that we should be forced to turn, upon one whose ancestors have so well deserved of the Christian community. Therefore, resting upon the authority of Him whose pleasure it was to place us (though unequal to such a burden) upon this supreme justice seat, we do out of the fullness of our Apostolic power declare the foresaid Elizabeth to be a heretic and favourer of heretics, and her adherents in the matters aforesaid to have incurred the sentence of Excommunication and to be cut off from the unity of the body of Christ. And moreover (we declare) her to be deprived of her pretended title to the aforesaid Crown and of all lordship, dignity and privilege whatsoever.

And also the nobles, subjects and people of the said realm and all others who have in any way sworn oaths to her, to be forever absolved from such an oath and from any duty arising from lordship, fealty and obedience; and we do, by authority of these presents, so absolve them and so deprive the same Elizabeth of her pretended title to the crown and all other of the above said matters. We charge and command all and singular the nobles, subjects, peoples and others aforesaid that they do not dare obey her orders, mandates and laws. Those who shall act to the contrary we include in the like sentence of Excommunication.

Because in truth it may prove too difficult to take these presents wheresoever it shall be necessary, we will that copies made under the hand of a notary public and sealed with the seal of a prelate of the Church or of his court shall have such force and trust in and out of judicial proceedings, in all places among the nations, as these presents would themselves have if they were exhibited or shown.

Given at St. Peter's, Rome on 27 April 1570 of the Incarnation; in the fifth year of our pontificate.

APPENDIX VIII

THE MAGYAR INHERITANCE OF HUNGARY

The *Rosi-crucis* tradition is very apparent when considering the history of the Hungarian State, where the legacy of the Dragon was inherited by King Zsigmond in the 15th century. The name Hungary comes originally from the nomadic *Hun* tribe, while the Hungarian nation was founded by the Magyar dynasty of King Arpád in the 9th century. His house expired in 1301, by which time the Magyar culture was well established in the Carpathian basin. By way of the most ancient Ouroboros imagery of the eternal cycle of the years, the Magyar symbol was a circular device within which the four seasons were segmented by way of an inner Cross in accordance with the Grail emblem of the various tribes which had emanated from the original caste of the Royal Scythian Ring Lords.

The most famous chieftain of the Hunnic Empire was the legendary Attila who, in AD 452, met with Pope Leo I and an unarmed body of monks by the River Po in northern Italy. At that time, Attila's domain stretched from the Rhine across into Central Asia and his well-equipped hordes were ready with chariots, ladders, catapults and every martial device to sweep on towards Rome. The conversation lasted no more than a few minutes, but the outcome was that Attila ordered his men to vacate their encampments and retreat northwards. What actually transpired between the men was never revealed, but afterwards Pope Leo the Great was destined to wield supreme power in the West.

Some time earlier, in AD 434, an envoy sent by the Byzantine Emperor Theodosius II had met with Attila in very similar circumstances by the Morava River, south of modern Belgrade. He had given Attila the contemporary equivalent of millions of dollars as a price for the Church's unmolested supremacy in the East. Pope Leo's arrangement was probably much the same (Martin, Malachi, *The Decline and Fall of the Roman Church*, pp. 64-67). Thus, it can be seen that, in circumstances when the power of the Roman Church was threatened by some outside agency, it was certainly not beyond paying out fortunes to maintain its own *status quo*. In this regard it is no secret that the Vatican's monetary power-base is equally significant today when it comes to bringing governments and corporate establishments into line by directing or withholding organized funding as the occasion determines.

Immediately prior to their Carpathian settlement, the Magyar (Magiar) tribes prevailed in the Caucasus regions of the Black Sea steppe lands (Stoyanov, Yuri, *The Hidden Tradition in Europe*, ch. 3, p. 125). As explained by the Magyar writer Támás Zoltán Forray (*The Cross of the Magiar*—privately published in Peterborough, Ontario, 1995), they are more correctly defined as the *Magi-ar*, being the people of the Magi whose belief system was largely that of the Persian Zoroastrians. Recognized for this Eastern influence, they were sometimes reckoned to be 'of the East', for which the Magyar word was *keleti*—another root source (along with *keltoi* = strangers) for that race of people who eventually became known as the Celts. They were also connected to the Wood Lord culture of the *Yulannu*, with that definition surviving today in the female name Jolán.

Hungary is also called *Magyar Ország*, with the second word stemming from Körszak—the Magyar equivalent of the segmented Witches' Ring of the seasonal Sabbats. This relates directly to the old Sumerian word *Khursag*, denoting the 'lofty enclosure' of the gods (O'Brien, Christian and Barbara Joy, *The Genius of the Few*, ch. 3, p. 37).

APPENDIX IX

RHYME AND REASON

It has been the case that the individual histories studied within this work are in some way related to Grail or Ring lore, but before leaving the world of supposed fantasy, it is fair to say that not all popular lore emanates from these particular bases. It is of interest to recognize, however, that most of this culture is historically founded, and this is especially the case with those little songs and poems which, among the best loved of our traditions, we refer to as nursery rhymes.

Rhymes such as *Ride a Cock Horse* and *Here we go 'round the Mulberry Bush* have their origins in the pagan Witchcraft of medieval times. Also, it is perhaps well enough known that the *Ring-a-Ring o'Roses* rhyme centres upon a particular Ring Dance that was designed to ward off the 14th-century bubonic plague of the Black Death. The early tell-tale skin symptoms of this disease were rose-coloured blistery rings, while posies of supposed remedial flowers were carried as a safeguard. These were often tagged with personal names written within circles as an added protection and, for this reason even today, finger-rings engraved with goodwill messages are called 'posy rings'.

But what about those rhymes which identify specific characters such as *Old King Cole, The Grand Old Duke of York, Georgy Porgy* and *Lucy Locket*? Were these real people? They certainly were, as were many others likewise named in the rhymes. Old King Cole was the wise King Coel Hen (meaning Cole the Old) of Rheged in the North of Britain. He reigned in the early 5th century (*see* genealogical chart 'Rulers of Scots Dalriada' in Gardner, Laurence, *Bloodline of the Holy Grail*, ch. 12, p. 201), governing the Men-of-the-North tribes of the Gwyr-y-Gogledd.

The Grand Old Duke of York was James Stuart, Duke of York (James VII of Scots), who became King James II of Britain. New York was named in his honour, having previously been the Dutch settlement of New Amsterdam. In 1688 England was invaded by the Dutch Prince William of Orange (subsequently Britain's King William III) and it was King James's first inclination to meet the invader upon the battlefield. He therefore took his army to the height of Salisbury Plain, but soon discovered that there were many treacherous defectors in his own camp, including certain prominent nobles. Hence, James was well advised to vacate Salisbury Hill before the battle and he marched his army down again.

As for Georgy Porgy, he was the Hanoverian Prince Regent who became King George IV of Britain (1820-30)—a fat and faithless glutton, who was criticised by his Court and subjects alike for his despicable treatment of his numerous mistresses.

Lucy Locket was an illegitimate daughter of Charles Edward Stuart (*Bonnie Prince Charlie*), with the 'Locket' name being contrived for rhyming purposes. Born in 1751 of a Welsh mother, Lucy was raised by way of an arrangement with Charles Edward's colleague Frederick, Prince of Wales, who died the year after Lucy's birth. (Despite being the son and heir of King George II at the time of the Jacobite Rebellion, Frederick was actually a Stuart sympathizer against his own family.) By the age of sixteen, Lucy had become the mistress of Frederick's son Edward Augustus, Duke of York—much to the dismay of Edward's most renowned mistress, the notorious Kitty Fisher.

Kitty was the leading courtesan of her day and she used to charge Prince Edward one-hundred guineas a night for her services—chasing him from the room on one occasion when he offered her only fifty guineas. Being so coveted in high society, Kitty Fisher simply could not understand Edward's preoccupation with Lucy and she presumed, in her arrogance, that Lucy must be charging a good deal less—failing to recognize that there was rather more to the relationship than a paying agreement. So one night Kitty arranged for Lucy's purse to be secreted from the royal bedroom in order to check the amount of money within—but there was none:

> Lucy Locket lost her pocket; Kitty Fisher found it
> Not a penny was there in it—but a ribbon 'round it.

Another well-known, though seemingly obscure, tale which makes it apparent that even the oddest of such rhymes are founded upon historical events, concerns the English Civil War of 1642-49. In this protracted affair, the Royalist Cavaliers of King Charles I Stuart were challenged by the Parliamentary Roundheads of the politician Oliver Cromwell. The two sides held various bastions in different parts of the country, with each endeavouring to win these strategically placed strongholds from the other.

One such fortified centre was the ancient city of Colchester, where the tower of St. Mary's Wall Church was a well positioned look-out post. Colchester was a Cromwellian stronghold, but for a number of weeks in 1648 it was captured and held by the Royalist forces. King Charles's army had a wonderfully bulbous and powerful cannon which was placed on top of St. Mary's tower in readiness to greet the attacking enemy. But a well-aimed shot from Cromwell's men hit the height of the wall and the great gun crashed to the ground, breaking into pieces. The King's men did their best to effect a repair, but it was no use and, try as they might, they could not fix the cannon, which they had named, by virtue of its appearance, *Humpty Dumpty*.

APPENDIX X

Genealogical Charts

ANUNNAKI AND THE DRAGON QUEENS

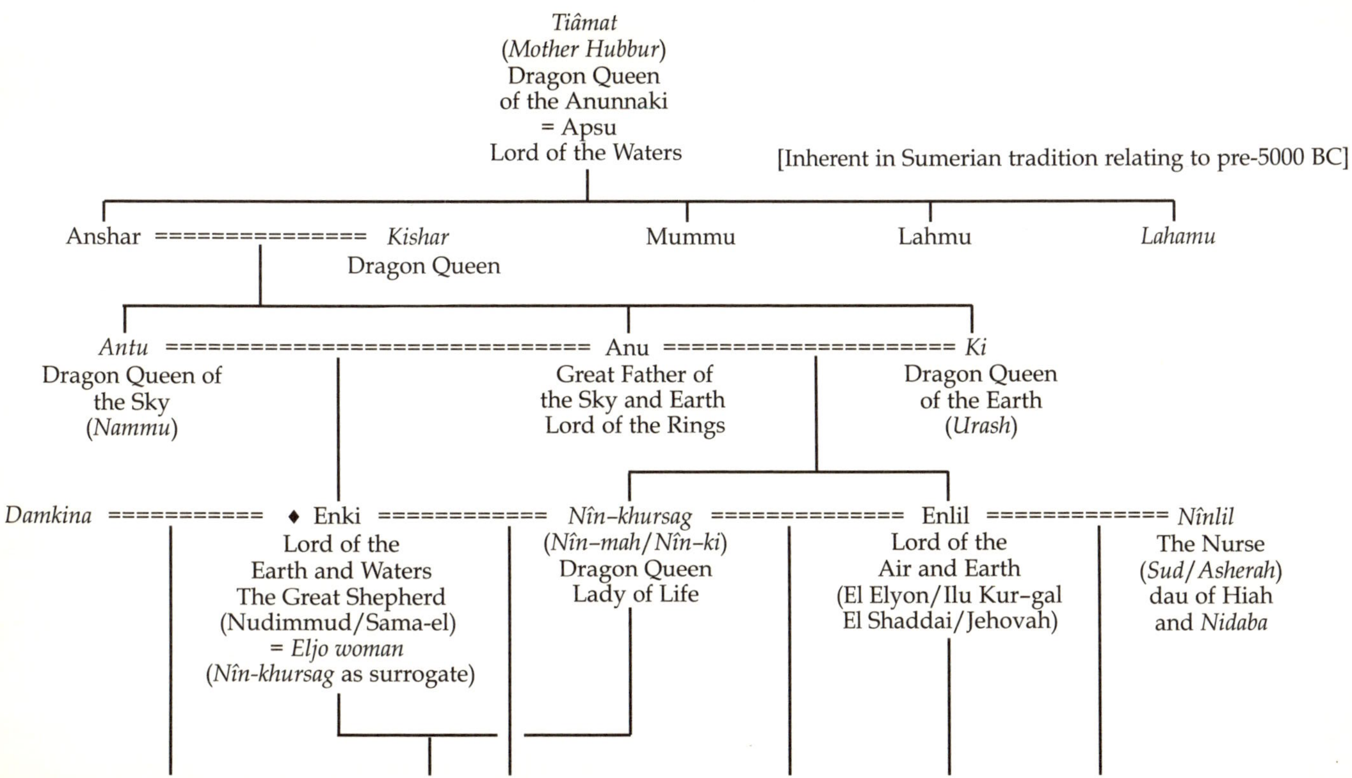

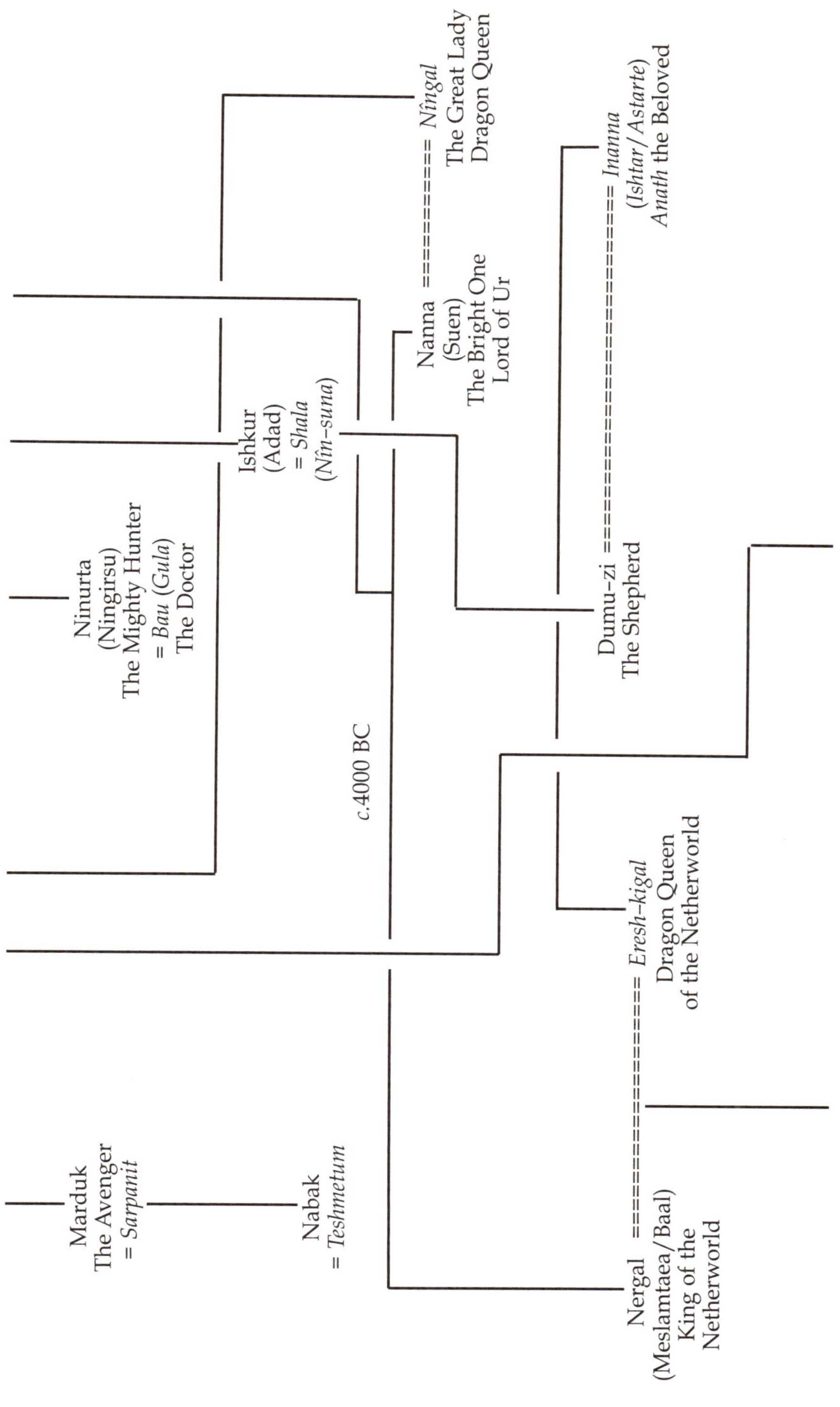
Nîngal
The Great Lady
Dragon Queen
Inanna
(Ishtar/Astarte)
Anath the Beloved
Nanna
(Suen)
The Bright One
Lord of Ur
Ishkur
(Adad)
= Shala
(Nîn-suna)
Ninurta
(Ningirsu)
The Mighty Hunter
= Bau (Gula)
The Doctor
Dumu-zi
The Shepherd
c.4000 BC
Eresh-kigal
Dragon Queen
of the Netherworld
Marduk
The Avenger
= Sarpanit
Nabak
= Teshmetum
Nergal
(Meslamtaea/Baal)
King of the
Netherworld

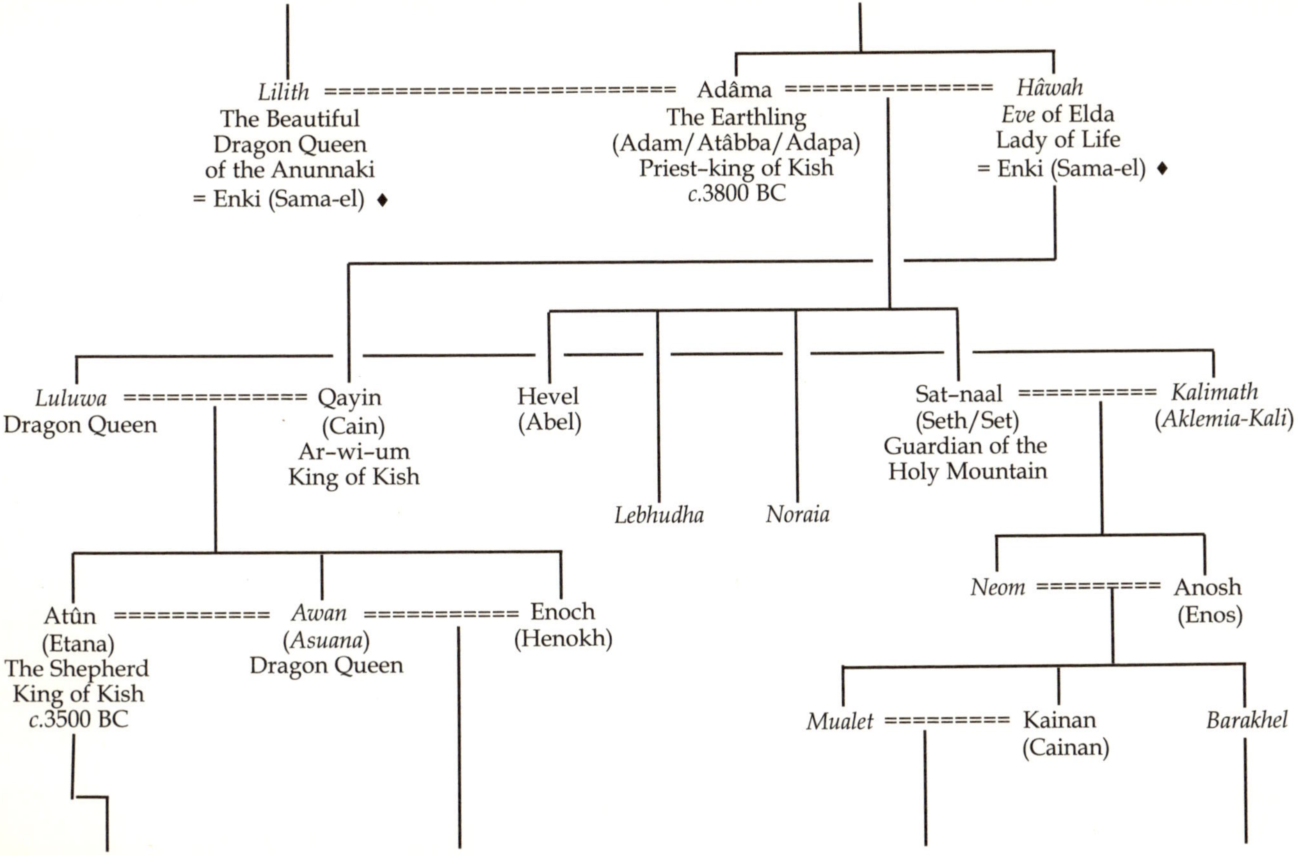
Lilith ======================== Adâma ================ *Hâwah*
The Beautiful
Dragon Queen
of the Anunnaki
= Enki (Sama-el) ♦
The Earthling
(Adam/Atâbba/Adapa)
Priest–king of Kish
*c.*3800 BC
Eve of Elda
Lady of Life
= Enki (Sama-el) ♦
Luluwa ============= Qayin
Dragon Queen
(Cain)
Ar–wi–um
King of Kish
Hevel
(Abel)
Lebhudha
Noraia
Sat–naal ========== *Kalimath*
(Seth/Set)
Guardian of the
Holy Mountain
(*Aklemia-Kali*)
Atûn =========== *Awan* =========== Enoch
(Etana)
The Shepherd
King of Kish
*c.*3500 BC
(*Asuana*)
Dragon Queen
(Henokh)
Neom ========= Anosh
(Enos)
Mualet ========= Kainan
(Cainan)
Barakhel

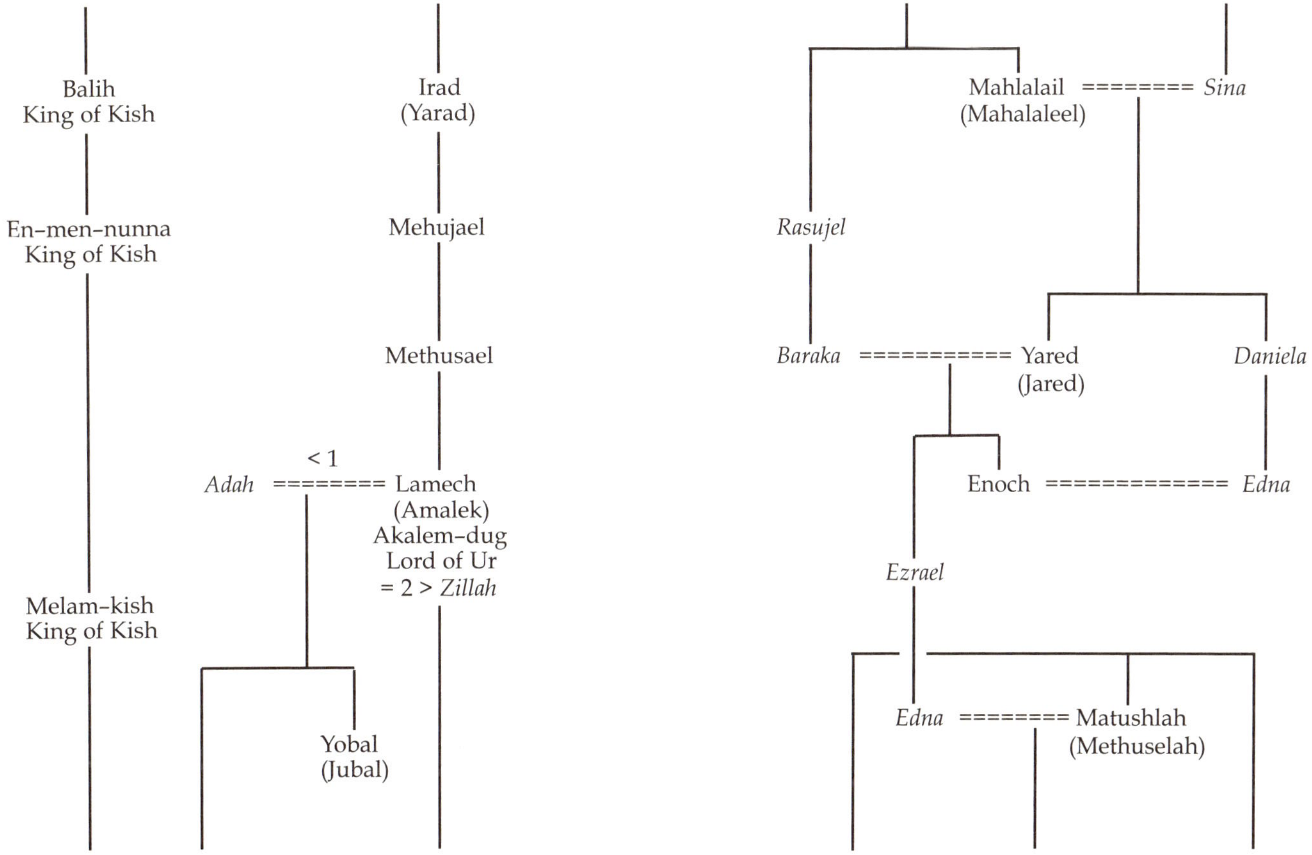
Balih
King of Kish
En-men-nunna
King of Kish
Melam-kish
King of Kish
Irad
(Yarad)
Mehujael
Methusael
< 1
Adah ======== Lamech
(Amalek)
Akalem-dug
Lord of Ur
= 2 > Zillah
Yobal
(Jubal)
Mahlalail ======== Sina
(Mahalaleel)
Rasujel
Baraka =========== Yared
(Jared)
Daniela
Enoch ============= Edna
Ezrael
Edna ======== Matushlah
(Methuselah)

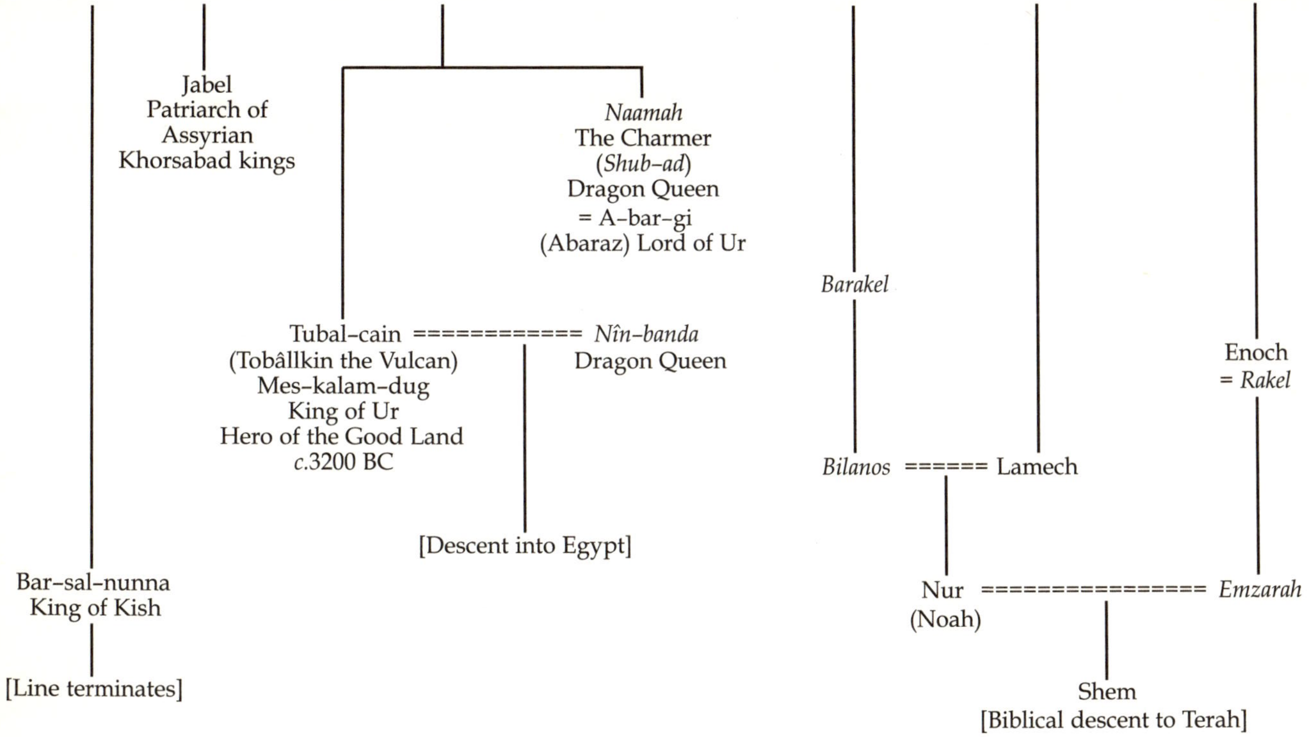
Jabel
Patriarch of
Assyrian
Khorsabad kings
Naamah
The Charmer
(Shub-ad)
Dragon Queen
= A-bar-gi
(Abaraz) Lord of Ur
Barakel
Enoch
= Rakel
Tubal-cain ============ Nîn-banda
(Tobâllkin the Vulcan)
Mes-kalam-dug
King of Ur
Hero of the Good Land
c.3200 BC
Dragon Queen
Bilanos ====== Lamech
[Descent into Egypt]
Bar-sal-nunna
King of Kish
Nur ================ Emzarah
(Noah)
[Line terminates]
Shem
[Biblical descent to Terah]

MATRILINEAR DESCENT IN EGYPT

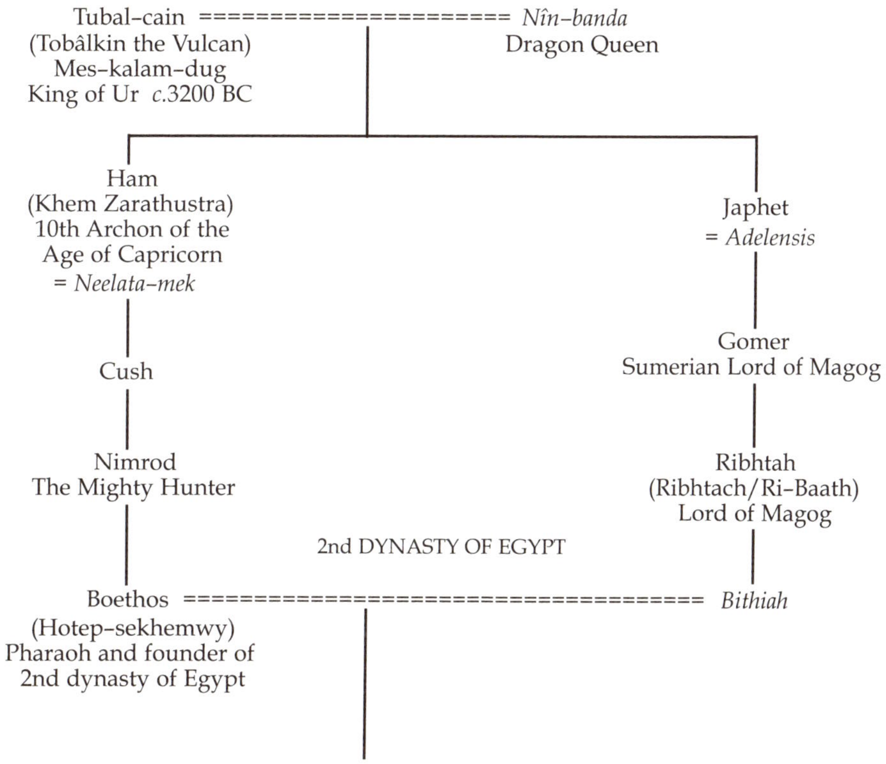

Raneb
(Kaienhkos)
Pharaoh of Egypt *c.*2800 BC
[Introduced culture of Khem of Capricorn at Mendes]

Nynetjer
Pharaoh of Egypt
[Decreed that dynastic queens could reign in their own right]

Sekhemib
(Seth–Peribsen)
Pharaoh of Egypt

Khasekhemwy ==================== *Nemathap*
Pharaoh of Egypt
d *c.*2686 BC

3rd DYNASTY OF EGYPT

(*daughter*) =========== Sanakhte
Pharaoh *c.*2686–68 BC
[Mount Horeb Temple in Sinai]

Djoser
Pharaoh *c.*2668–49 BC
[Step Pyramid at Saqqara]

4th DYNASTY OF EGYPT

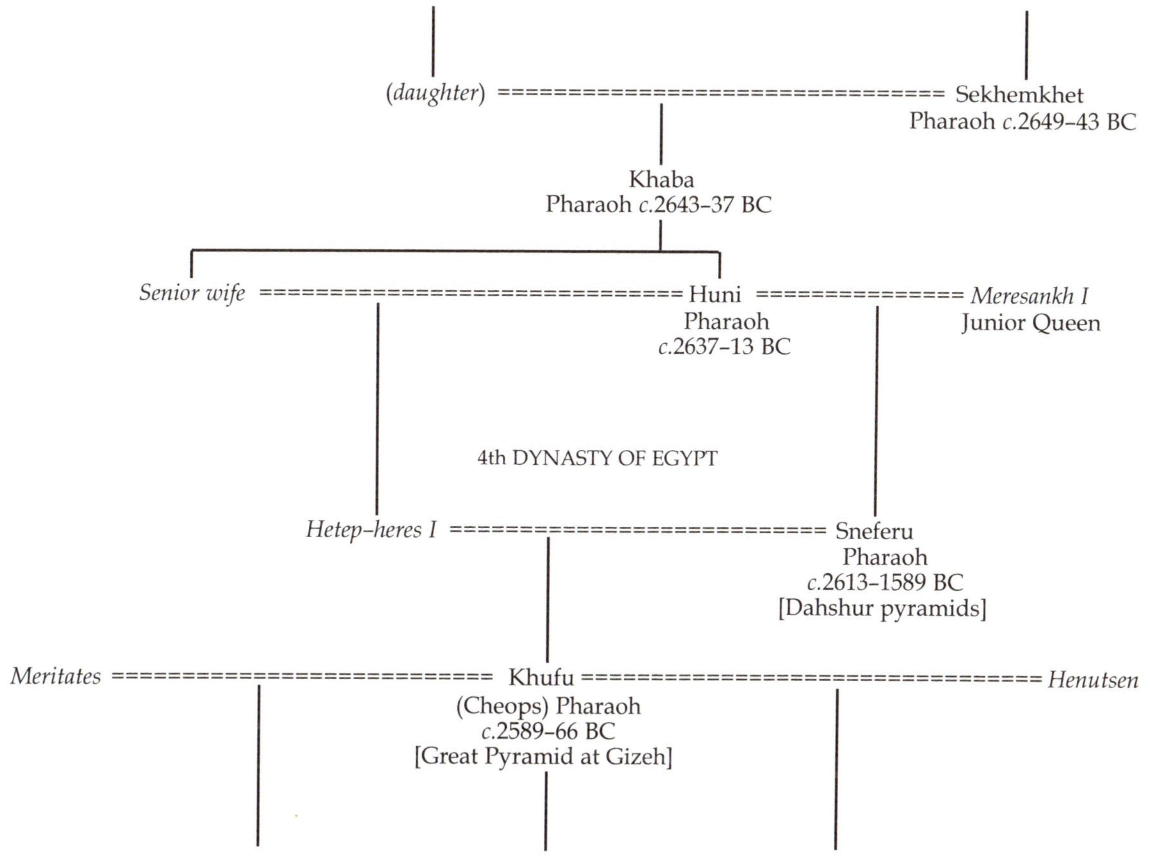

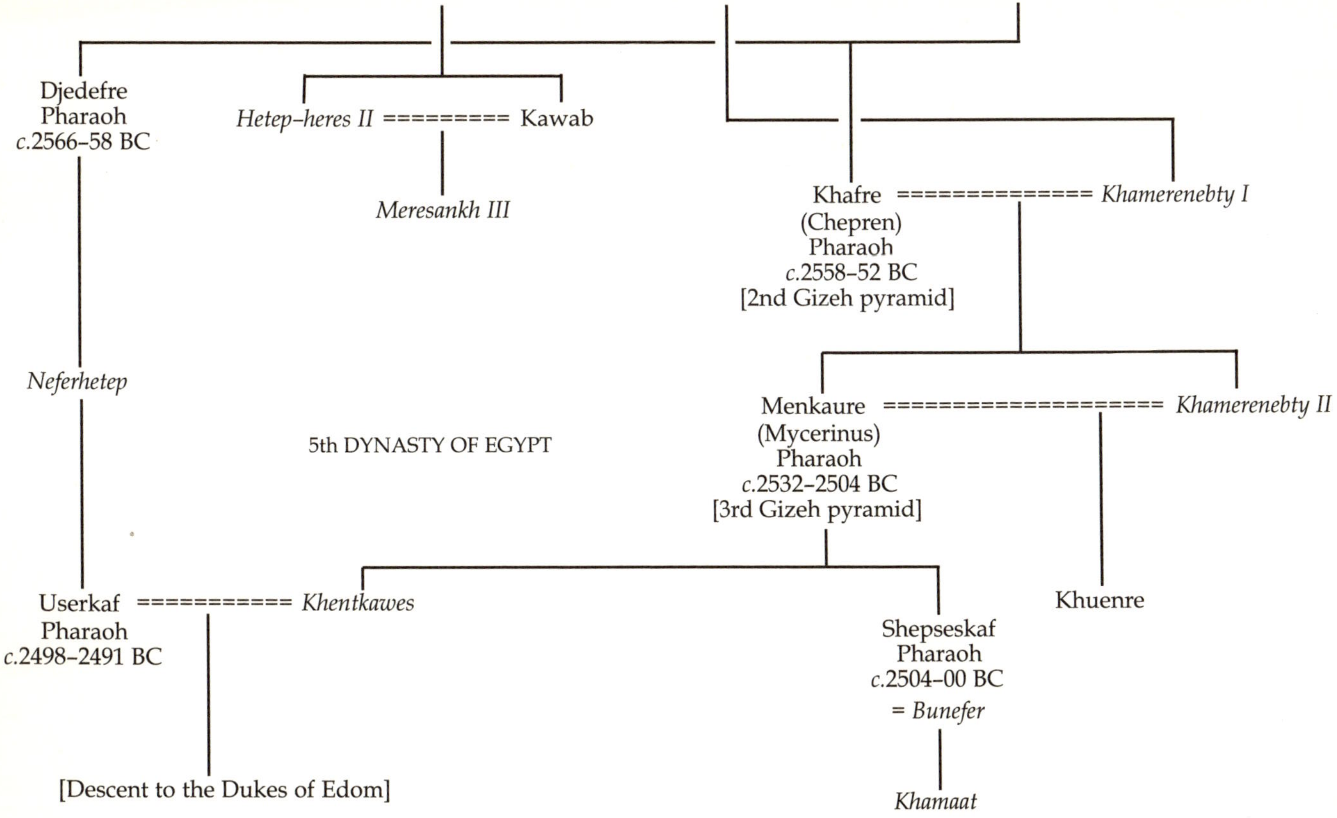
Djedefre
Pharaoh
c.2566–58 BC
Hetep-heres II ========= Kawab
Meresankh III
Khafre ============== Khamerenebty I
(Chepren)
Pharaoh
c.2558–52 BC
[2nd Gizeh pyramid]
Neferhetep
5th DYNASTY OF EGYPT
Menkaure ==================== Khamerenebty II
(Mycerinus)
Pharaoh
c.2532–2504 BC
[3rd Gizeh pyramid]
Userkaf =========== Khentkawes
Pharaoh
c.2498–2491 BC
Khuenre
Shepseskaf
Pharaoh
c.2504–00 BC
= Bunefer
[Descent to the Dukes of Edom]
Khamaat

PHARAOHS AND THE LORDS OF EDOM

Userkaf ============================ *Khentkawes*
Pharaoh
*c.*2498–2491 BC

Sahure
Pharaoh
*c.*2491–77 BC

Neferirkare
Pharaoh *c.*2477–67 BC

Shepseskare
Pharaoh *c.*2467–60 BC

Neferefre
Pharaoh *c.*2460–53 BC

Niuserre
Pharaoh *c.*2453–22 BC

Menkauhor
Pharaoh *c.*2422–14 BC

Djedkare
Pharaoh *c.*2414–2375 BC

6th DYNASTY OF EGYPT

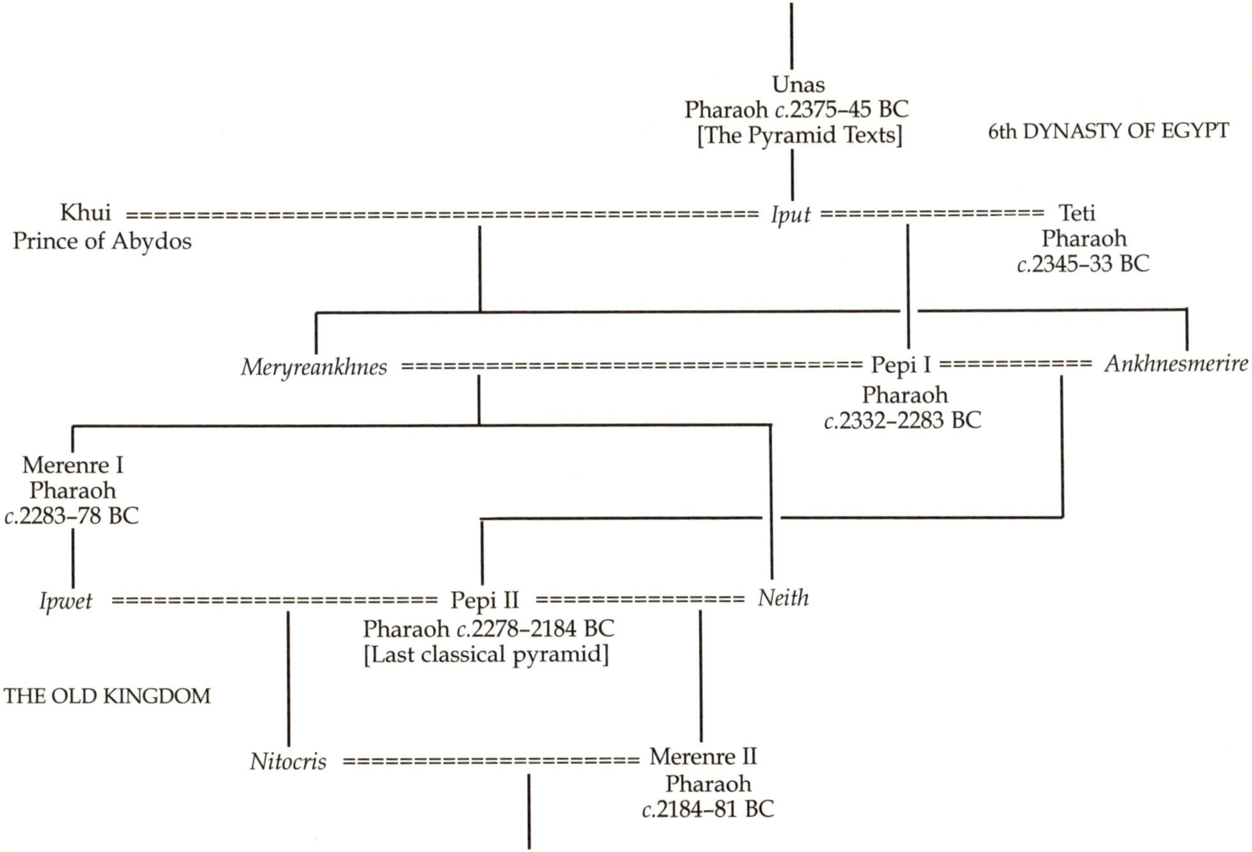

END OF THE OLD KINGDOM

FIRST INTERMEDIATE PERIOD
Civil war and usurpation under
coextensive Dynasties 7–10

Ankhfn-khonsu
Hereditary Prince of Egypt
[King *de jure*]
Founder of the Dragon Court

Intef I (The Great)
Hereditary Prince of Egypt
Governor of Thebes *c.*2134–17 BC
[King *de jure*]

Intef II
Governor of Thebes *c.*2117–2069 BC
[King *de jure*]

THE MIDDLE KINGDOM

Intef III
Governor of Thebes *c.*2069–60 BC
[King *de jure*]

11th DYNASTY OF EGYPT

Nefru ======================== Mentuhotep I ===================== *Tem*

Pharaoh of Egypt *c.*2060–10 BC
(Reunifier of Egyptian kingdoms)
[The Coffin Texts]

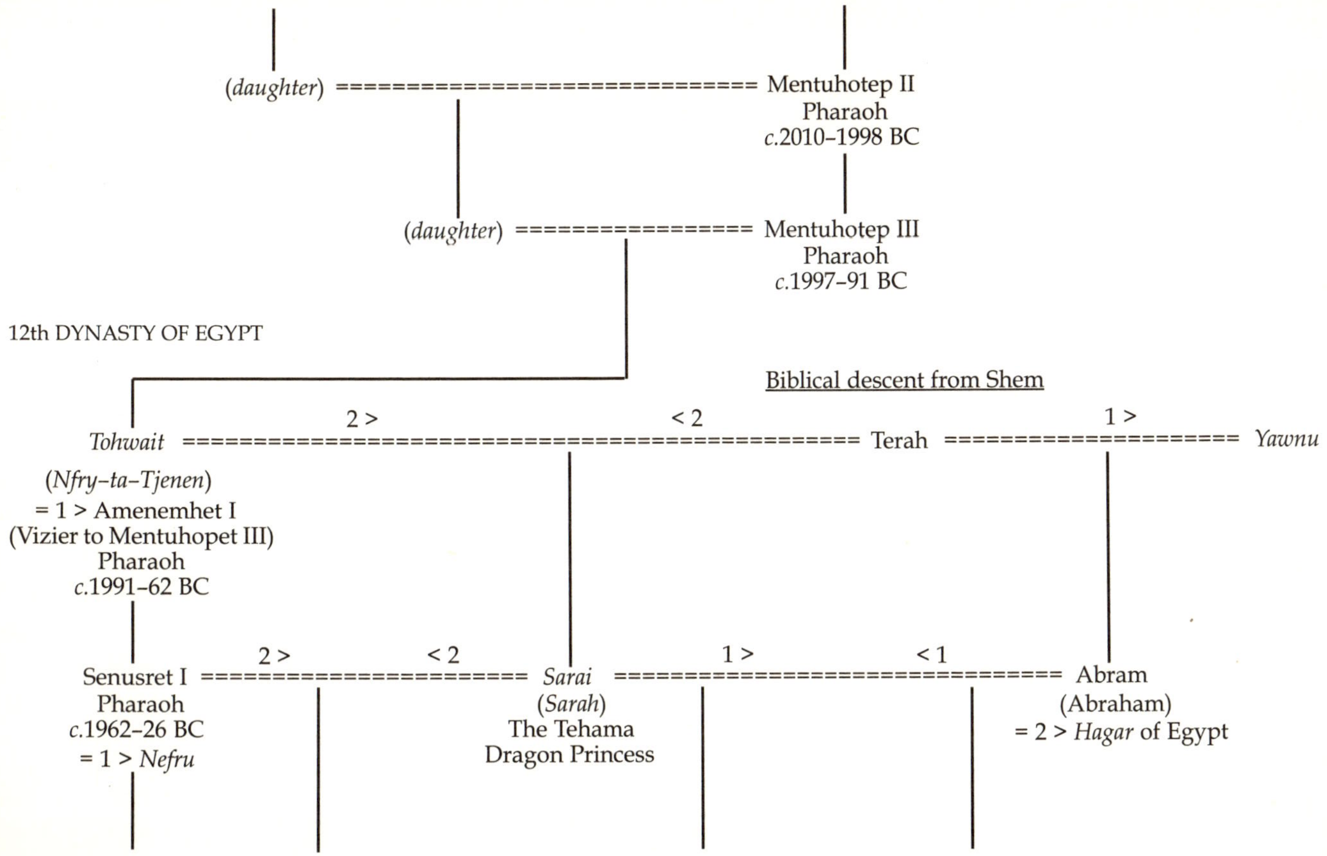
(daughter) ============================== Mentuhotep II
Pharaoh
c.2010–1998 BC
(daughter) ================ Mentuhotep III
Pharaoh
c.1997–91 BC
12th DYNASTY OF EGYPT
Biblical descent from Shem
2 >
< 2
1 >
Tohwait == Terah ===================== Yawnu
(Nfry–ta–Tjenen)
= 1 > Amenemhet I
(Vizier to Mentuhopet III)
Pharaoh
c.1991–62 BC
2 >
< 2
1 >
< 1
Senusret I ======================== Sarai ================================= Abram
Pharaoh
c.1962–26 BC
= 1 > Nefru
(Sarah)
The Tehama
Dragon Princess
(Abraham)
= 2 > Hagar of Egypt

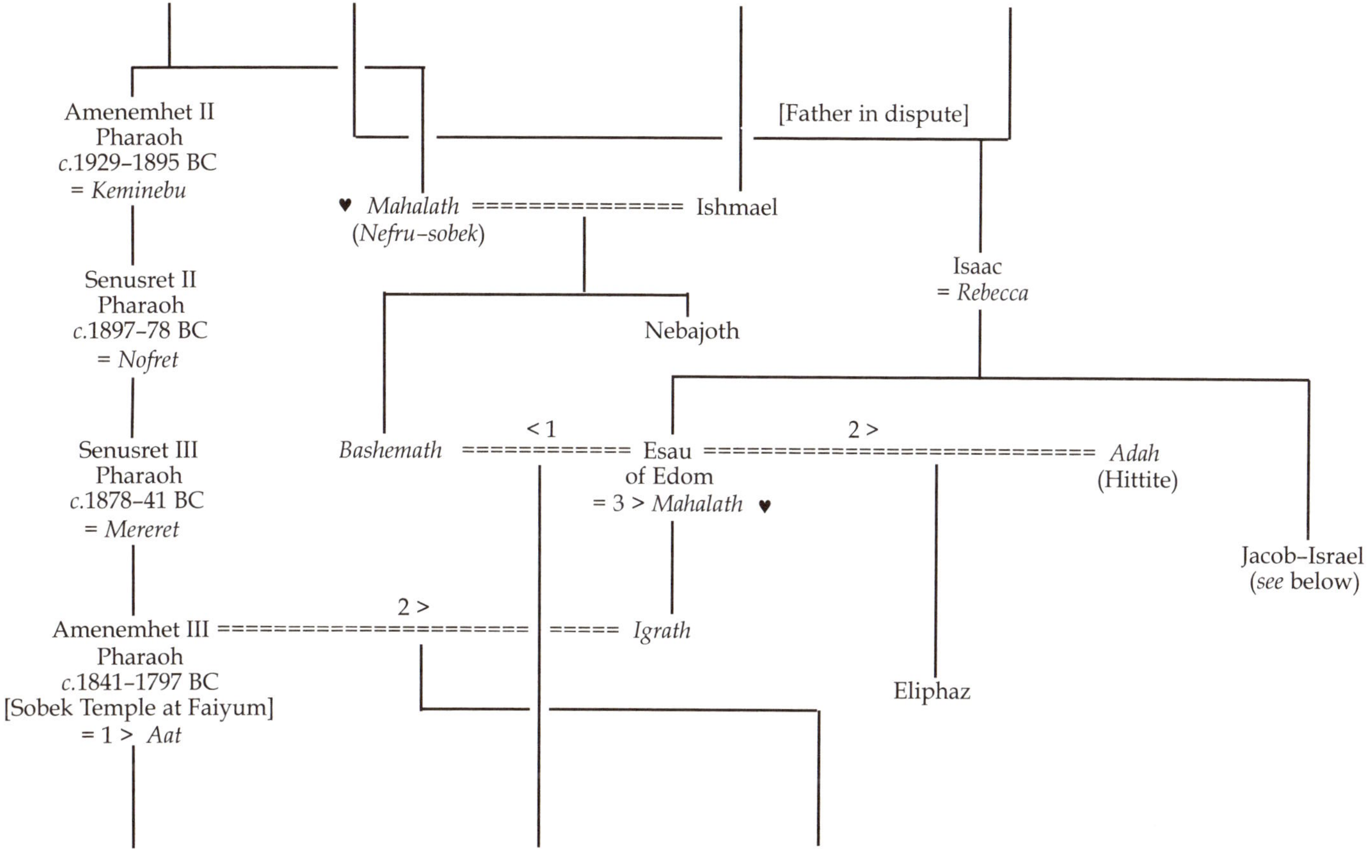

Amenemhet II
Pharaoh
c.1929–1895 BC
= Keminebu
♥ Mahalath ============== Ishmael
(Nefru-sobek)
[Father in dispute]
Isaac
= Rebecca
Nebajoth
Senusret II
Pharaoh
c.1897–78 BC
= Nofret
Senusret III
Pharaoh
c.1878–41 BC
= Mereret
Bashemath
< 1
Esau
of Edom
= 3 > Mahalath ♥
2 >
Adah
(Hittite)
Jacob–Israel
(see below)
Amenemhet III
Pharaoh
c.1841–1797 BC
[Sobek Temple at Faiyum]
= 1 > Aat
2 >
Igrath
Eliphaz

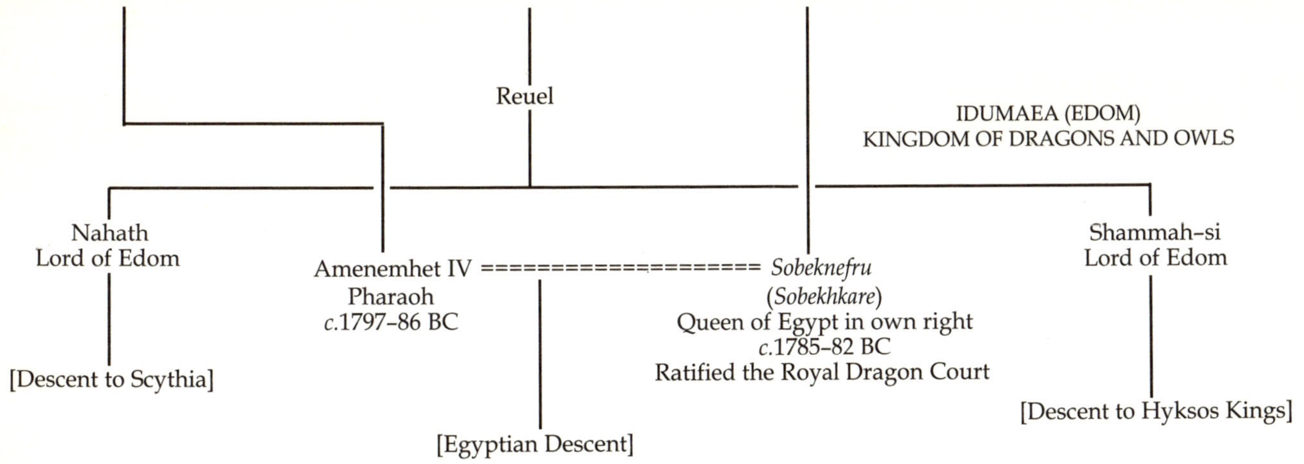
Reuel
IDUMAEA (EDOM)
KINGDOM OF DRAGONS AND OWLS
Nahath
Lord of Edom
[Descent to Scythia]
Amenemhet IV ==================== *Sobeknefru*
Pharaoh
*c.*1797–86 BC
(*Sobekhkare*)
Queen of Egypt in own right
*c.*1785–82 BC
Ratified the Royal Dragon Court
[Egyptian Descent]
Shammah-si
Lord of Edom
[Descent to Hyksos Kings]

HERITAGE OF THE WOOD LORDS

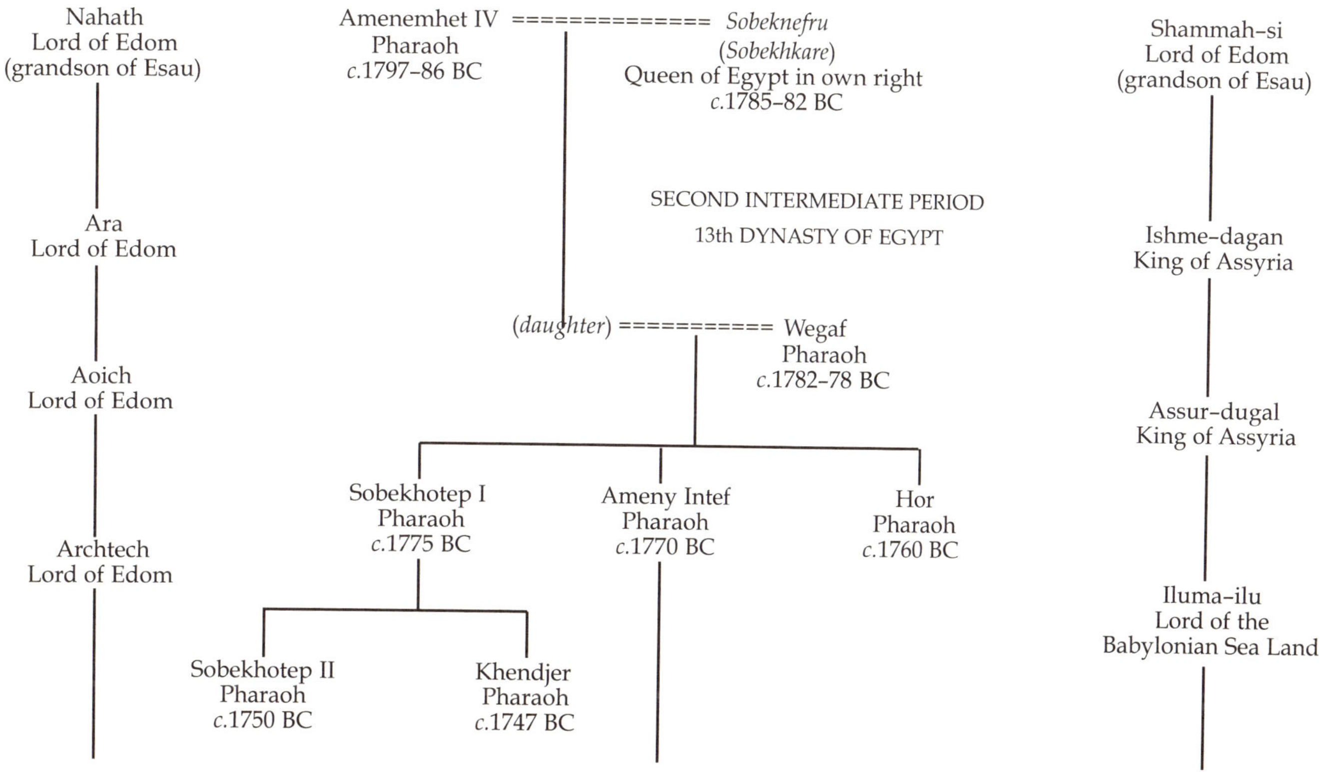

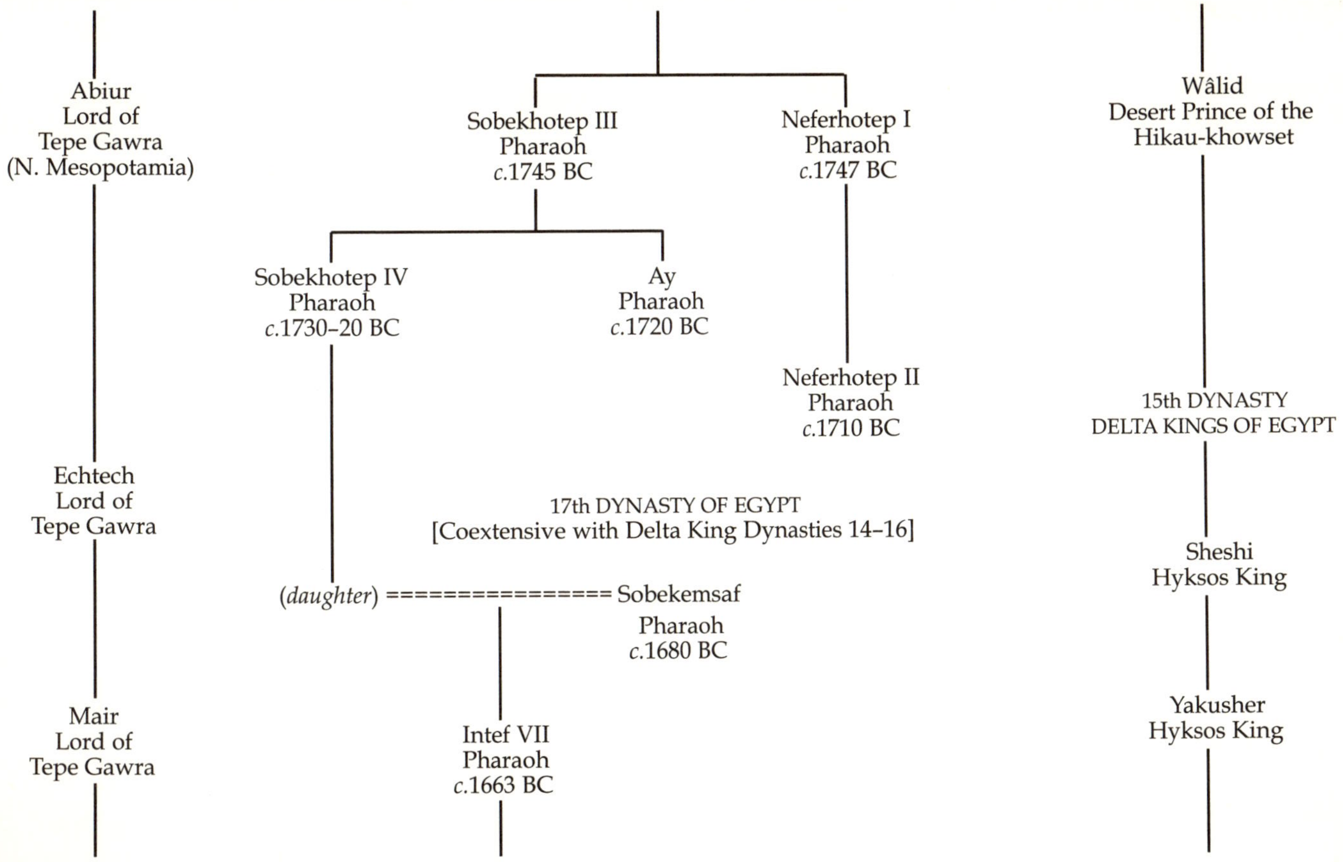
Abiur
Lord of
Tepe Gawra
(N. Mesopotamia)
Echtech
Lord of
Tepe Gawra
Mair
Lord of
Tepe Gawra
Sobekhotep III
Pharaoh
c.1745 BC
Neferhotep I
Pharaoh
c.1747 BC
Sobekhotep IV
Pharaoh
c.1730–20 BC
Ay
Pharaoh
c.1720 BC
Neferhotep II
Pharaoh
c.1710 BC
17th DYNASTY OF EGYPT
[Coextensive with Delta King Dynasties 14–16]
(daughter) ================ Sobekemsaf
Pharaoh
c.1680 BC
Intef VII
Pharaoh
c.1663 BC
Wâlid
Desert Prince of the
Hikau-khowset
15th DYNASTY
DELTA KINGS OF EGYPT
Sheshi
Hyksos King
Yakusher
Hyksos King

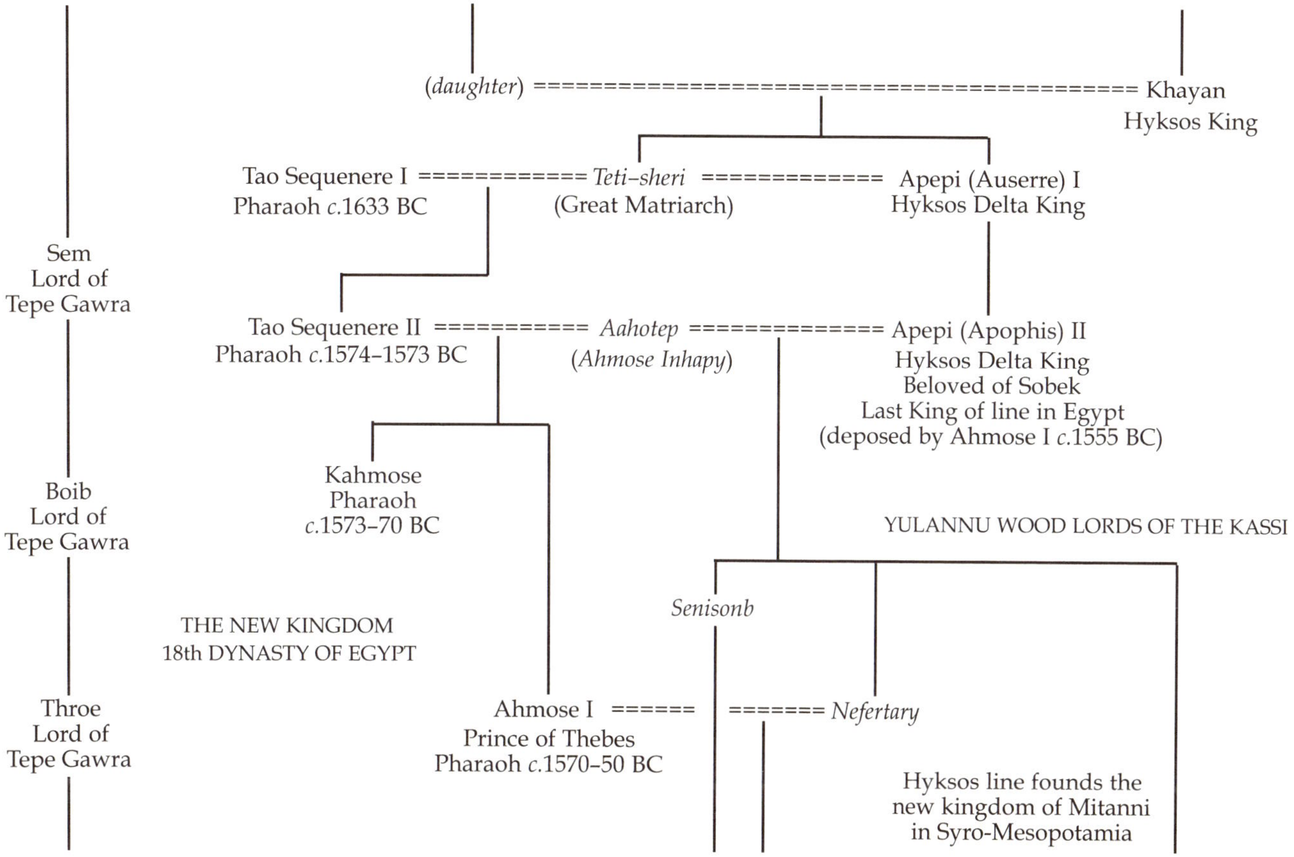

(daughter) ============ Khayan
Hyksos King
Tao Sequenere I
Pharaoh c.1633 BC
Teti–sheri
(Great Matriarch)
Apepi (Auserre) I
Hyksos Delta King
Sem
Lord of
Tepe Gawra
Tao Sequenere II
Pharaoh c.1574–1573 BC
Aahotep
(Ahmose Inhapy)
Apepi (Apophis) II
Hyksos Delta King
Beloved of Sobek
Last King of line in Egypt
(deposed by Ahmose I c.1555 BC)
Kahmose
Pharaoh
c.1573–70 BC
Boib
Lord of
Tepe Gawra
YULANNU WOOD LORDS OF THE KASSI
Senisonb
THE NEW KINGDOM
18th DYNASTY OF EGYPT
Ahmose I
Prince of Thebes
Pharaoh c.1570–50 BC
Nefertary
Throe
Lord of
Tepe Gawra
Hyksos line founds the
new kingdom of Mitanni
in Syro-Mesopotamia

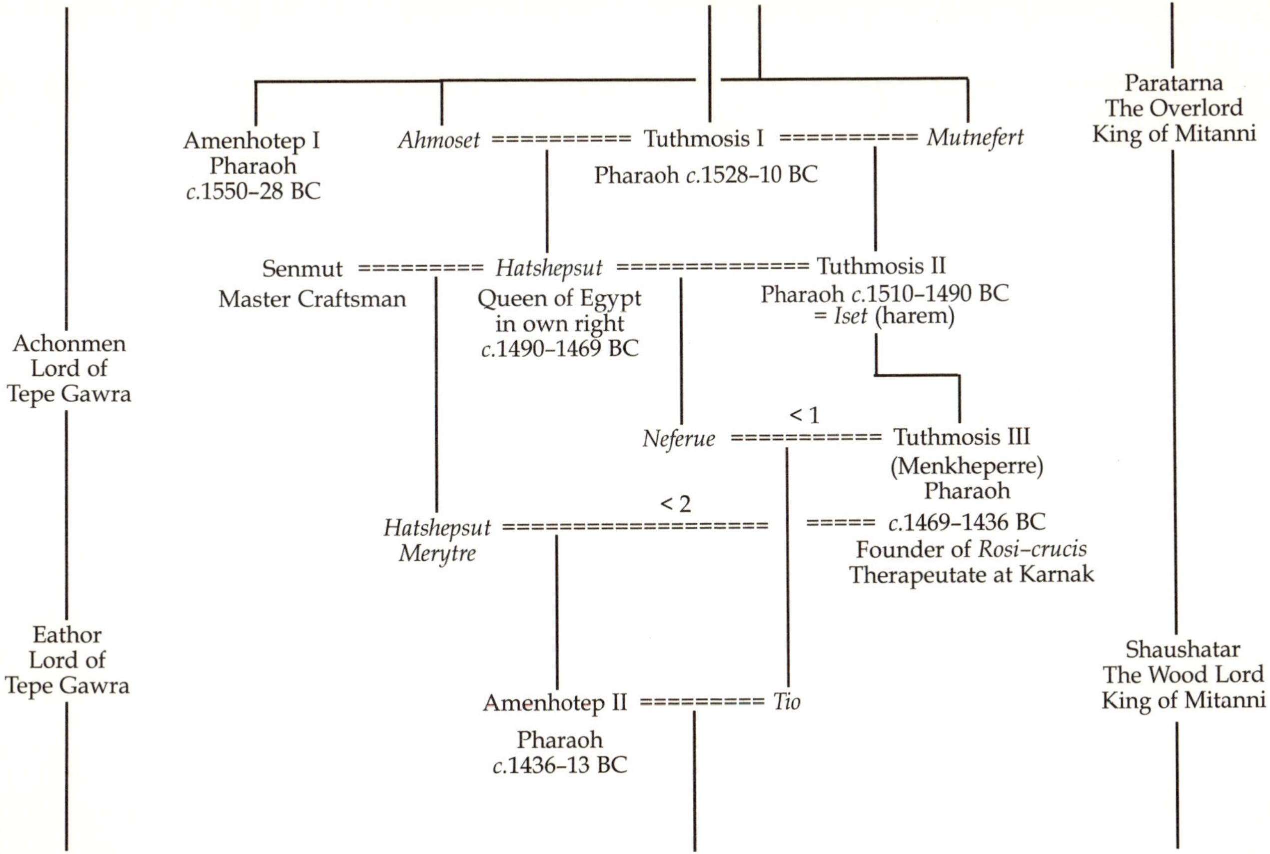

Paratarna
The Overlord
King of Mitanni
Amenhotep I
Pharaoh
c.1550–28 BC
Ahmoset ========== Tuthmosis I ========== Mutnefert
Pharaoh c.1528–10 BC
Senmut
Master Craftsman
Hatshepsut
Queen of Egypt
in own right
c.1490–1469 BC
Tuthmosis II
Pharaoh c.1510–1490 BC
= Iset (harem)
Achonmen
Lord of
Tepe Gawra
< 1
Neferue
Tuthmosis III
(Menkheperre)
Pharaoh
c.1469–1436 BC
Founder of Rosi-crucis
Therapeutate at Karnak
< 2
Hatshepsut
Merytre
Eathor
Lord of
Tepe Gawra
Shaushatar
The Wood Lord
King of Mitanni
Amenhotep II ========= Tio
Pharaoh
c.1436–13 BC

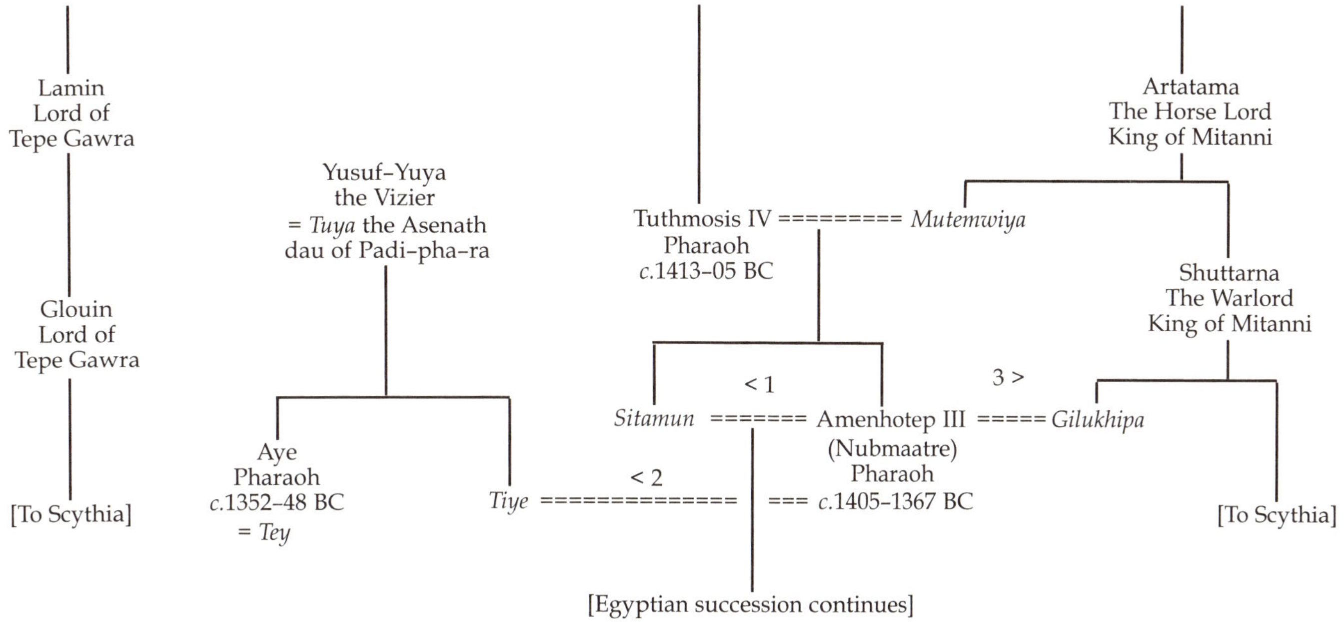
Lamin
Lord of
Tepe Gawra
Glouin
Lord of
Tepe Gawra
[To Scythia]
Yusuf-Yuya
the Vizier
= *Tuya* the Asenath
dau of Padi-pha-ra
Aye
Pharaoh
*c.*1352–48 BC
= *Tey*
Tiye
Tuthmosis IV ========= *Mutemwiya*
Pharaoh
*c.*1413–05 BC
Artatama
The Horse Lord
King of Mitanni
Shuttarna
The Warlord
King of Mitanni
< 1
3 >
Sitamun ======= Amenhotep III ===== *Gilukhipa*
(Nubmaatre)
Pharaoh
< 2
Tiye ============== === *c.*1405–1367 BC
[To Scythia]
[Egyptian succession continues]

SCYTHIA AND THE TUADHE D'ANU

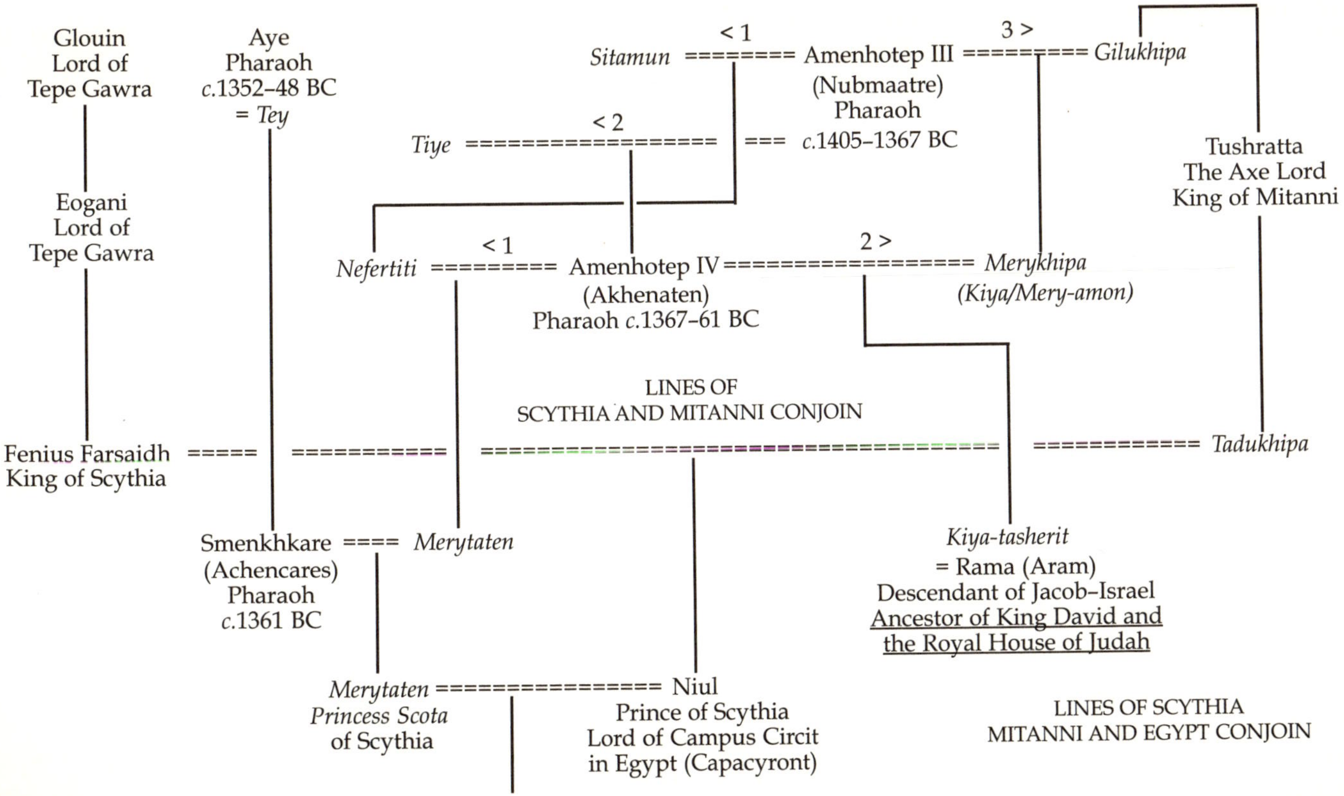

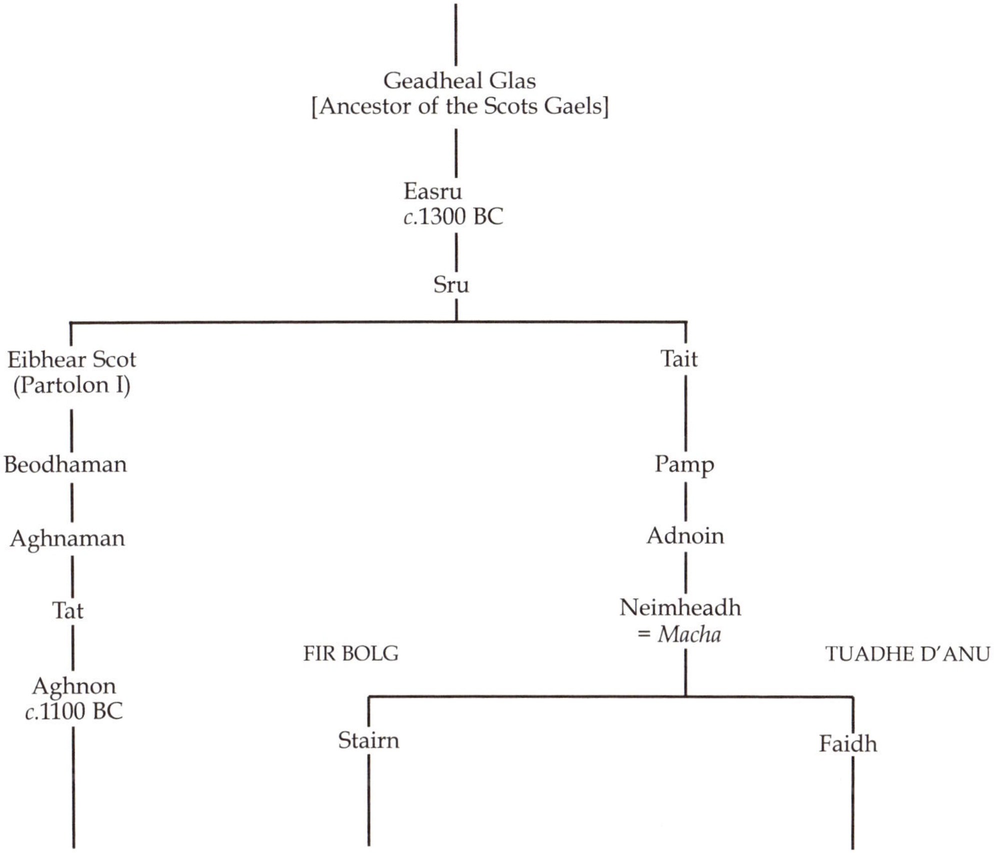

Geadheal Glas
[Ancestor of the Scots Gaels]
Easru
c.1300 BC
Sru
Eibhear Scot
(Partolon I)
Beodhaman
Aghnaman
Tat
Aghnon
c.1100 BC
Tait
Pamp
Adnoin
Neimheadh
= Macha
FIR BOLG
TUADHE D'ANU
Stairn
Faidh

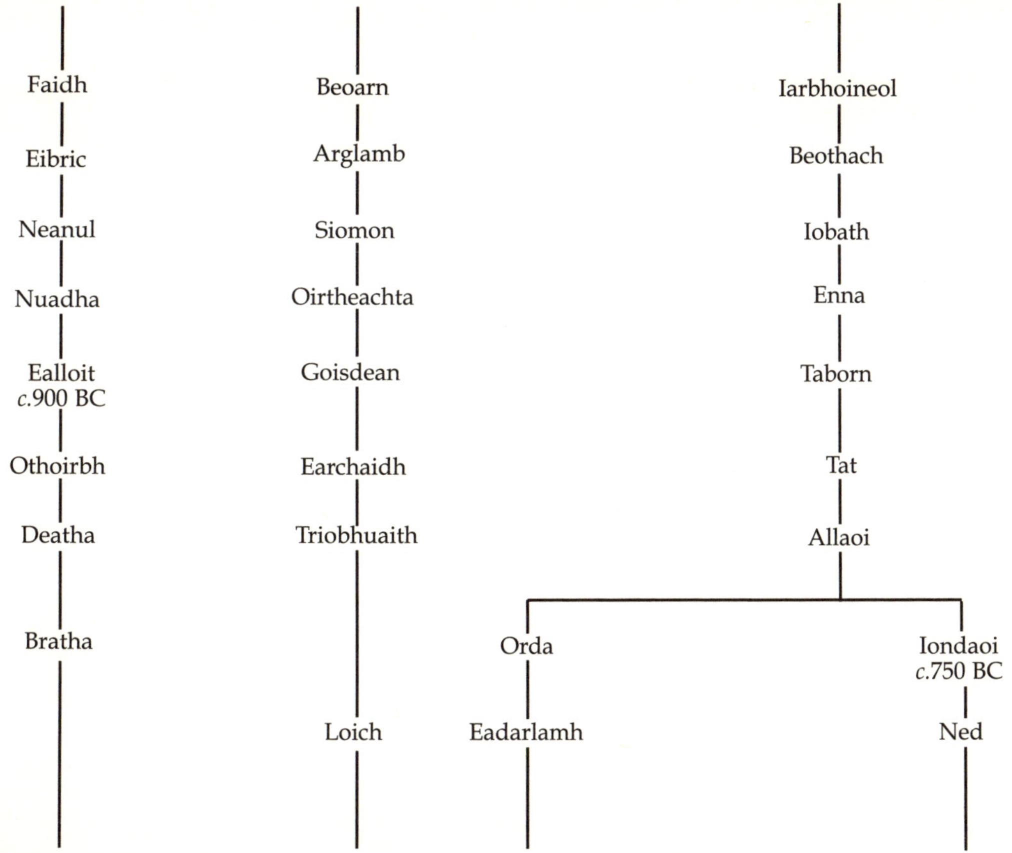
Faidh
Eibric
Neanul
Nuadha
Ealloit
c.900 BC
Othoirbh
Deatha
Bratha
Beoarn
Arglamb
Siomon
Oirtheachta
Goisdean
Earchaidh
Triobhuaith
Loich
Iarbhoineol
Beothach
Iobath
Enna
Taborn
Tat
Allaoi
Orda
Eadarlamh
Iondaoi
c.750 BC
Ned

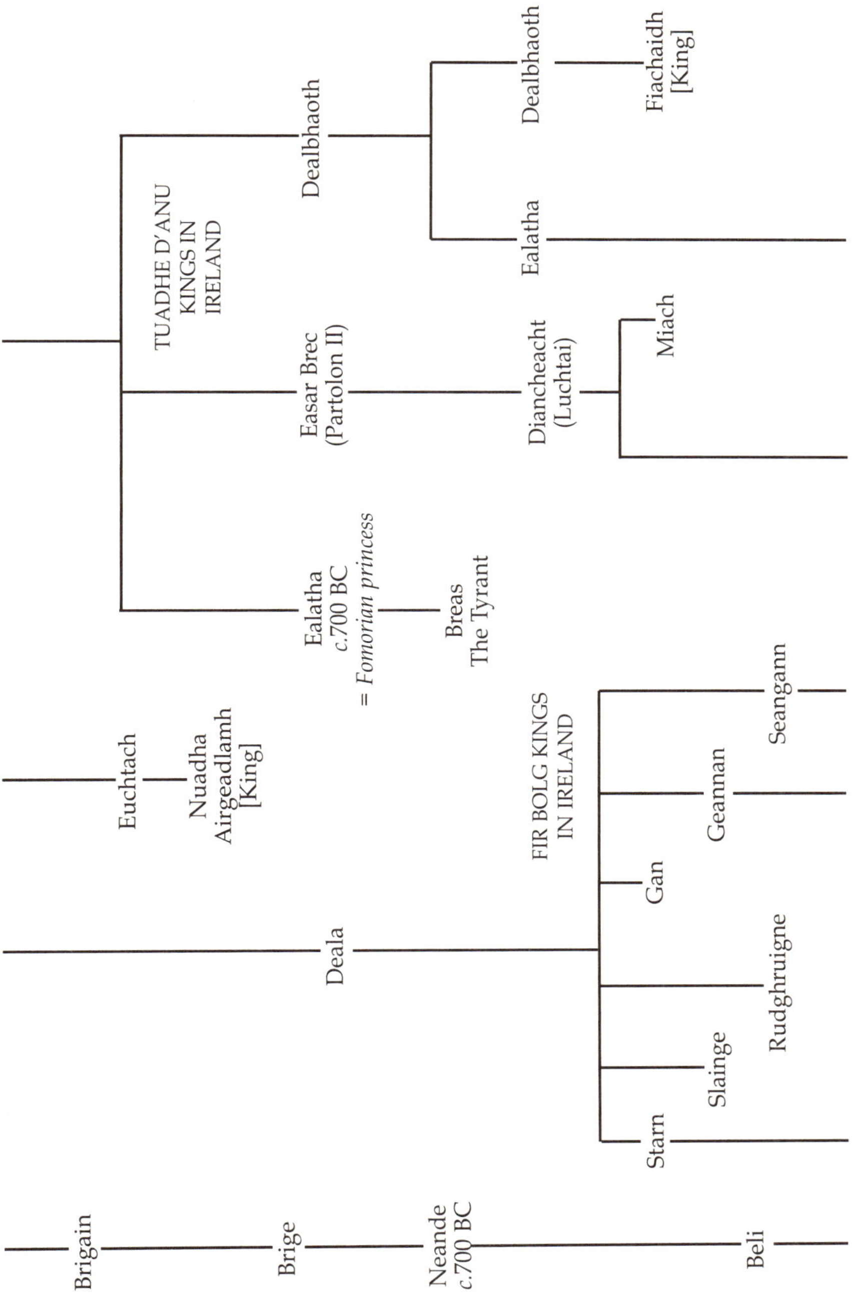

TUADHE D'ANU KINGS IN IRELAND
Dealbhaoth
Dealbhaoth
Fiachaidh [King]
Ealatha
Easar Brec (Partolon II)
Diancheacht (Luchtai)
Miach
Ealatha c.700 BC = Fomorian princess
Breas The Tyrant
Euchtach
Nuadha Airgeadlamh [King]
FIR BOLG KINGS IN IRELAND
Deala
Seangann
Geannan
Gan
Rudghruigne
Slainge
Starn
Brigain
Brige
Neande c.700 BC
Beli

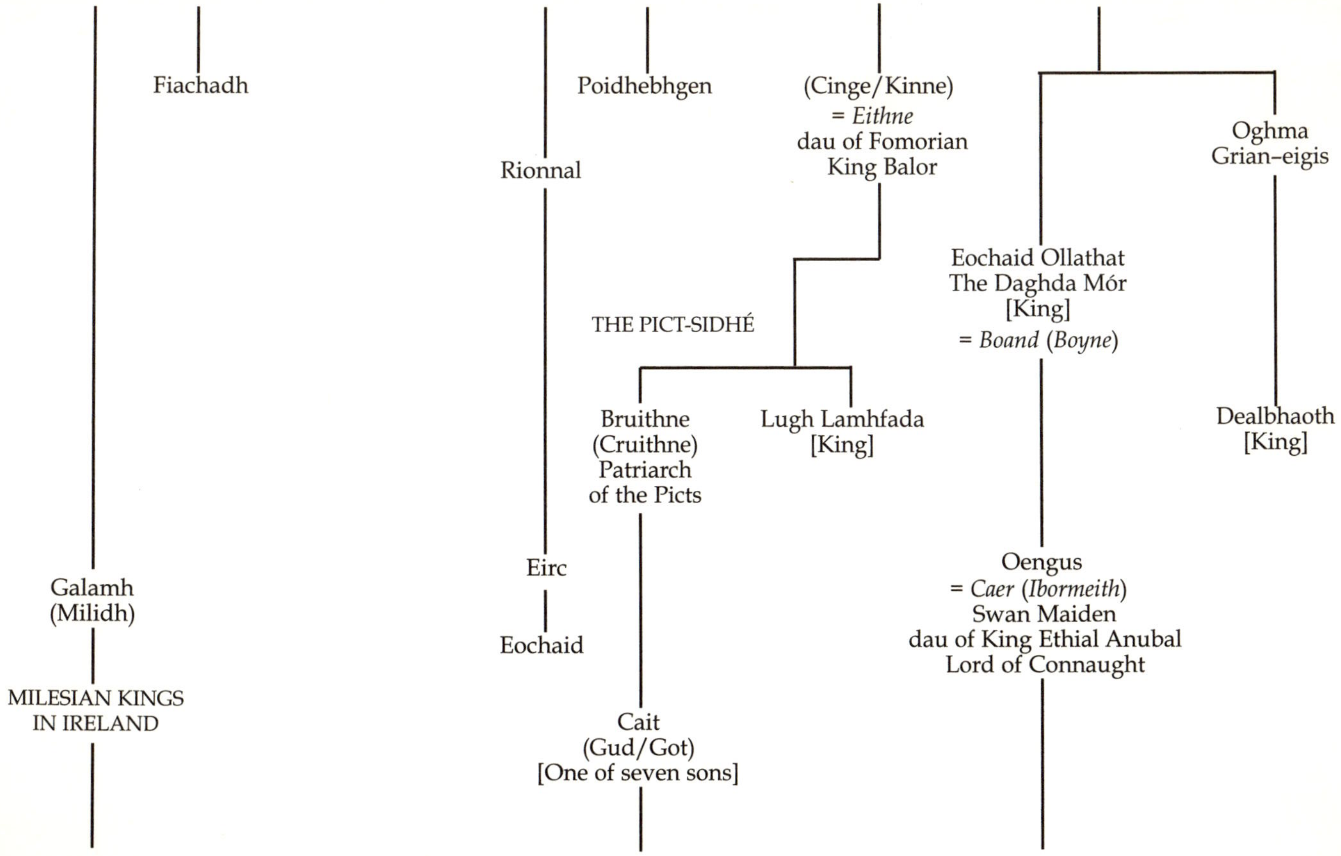
Fiachadh
Galamh
(Milidh)
MILESIAN KINGS
IN IRELAND
Rionnal
Eirc
Eochaid
Poidhebhgen
THE PICT-SIDHÉ
(Cinge/Kinne)
= *Eithne*
dau of Fomorian
King Balor
Bruithne
(Cruithne)
Patriarch
of the Picts
Lugh Lamhfada
[King]
Cait
(Gud/Got)
[One of seven sons]
Eochaid Ollathat
The Daghda Mór
[King]
= *Boand* (*Boyne*)
Oengus
= *Caer* (*Ibormeith*)
Swan Maiden
dau of King Ethial Anubal
Lord of Connaught
Oghma
Grian-eigis
Dealbhaoth
[King]

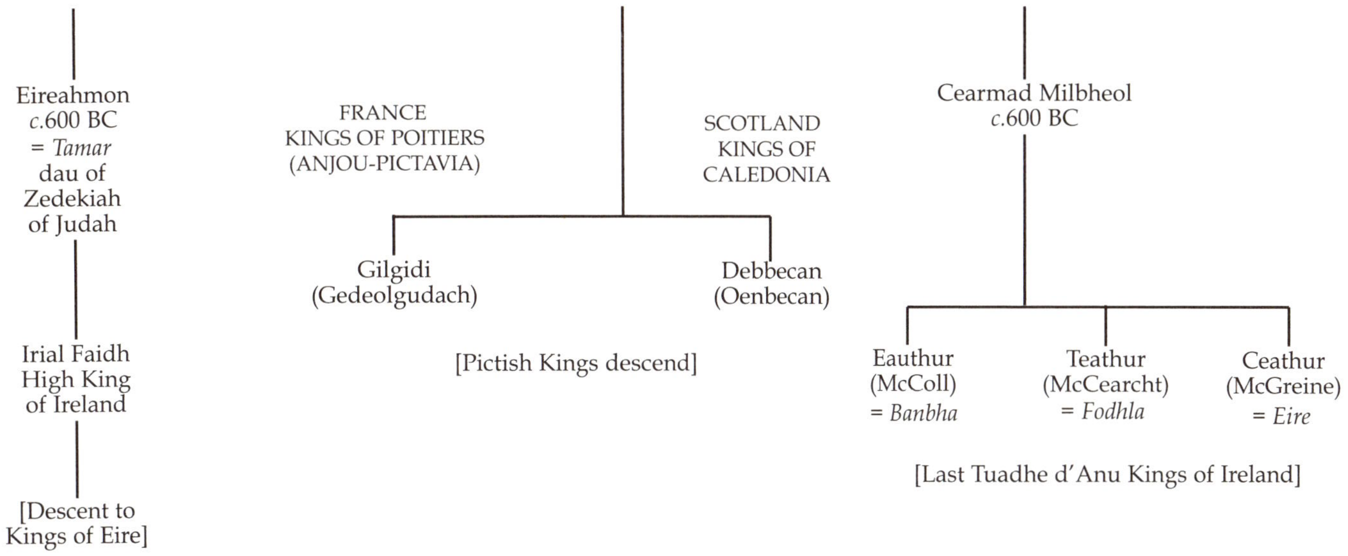
Eireahmon
c.600 BC
= Tamar
dau of
Zedekiah
of Judah
Irial Faidh
High King
of Ireland
[Descent to
Kings of Eire]
FRANCE
KINGS OF POITIERS
(ANJOU-PICTAVIA)
SCOTLAND
KINGS OF
CALEDONIA
Gilgidi
(Gedeolgudach)
Debbecan
(Oenbecan)
[Pictish Kings descend]
Cearmad Milbheol
c.600 BC
Eauthur
(McColl)
= Banbha
Teathur
(McCearcht)
= Fodhla
Ceathur
(McGreine)
= Eire
[Last Tuadhe d'Anu Kings of Ireland]

PICTS AND THE FISHER KINGS

IRELAND

Irial Faidh
High King
of Ireland
|
Eithriall
|
Tighernmas
|
Fiacha
Labrhuine
|
Aonghus
Oilbhuagh
|
Siorna
Saoghalach
|

ANJOU PICTAVIA

Gilgidi
(Gedeolgudach)
|
Tarain
(Tharan)
|
- Morleo (Morleg)
- Artcois
  |
  Cinioid
  |

CALEDONIA

Debbecan
(Oenbecan)
|
Olfinecta
(Finnechta)
|
Guididgaedercach
(Guidd gaed-brechach)
|
Feth
|
Gestgurtich
(Gest-guridh)
c.400 BC
|

JUDAEA

<u>Descent from Biblical Line of King Solomon</u>

Zerubbabel
Prince of Jerusalem
Dynastic heir of the
Davidic Royal House of Judah
c.536 BC
= *Maukab*
|
- Rhesa
  = *Zakhyath*
  |
  Johannan
  |
- Abiud
  = *Tsamita*
  |

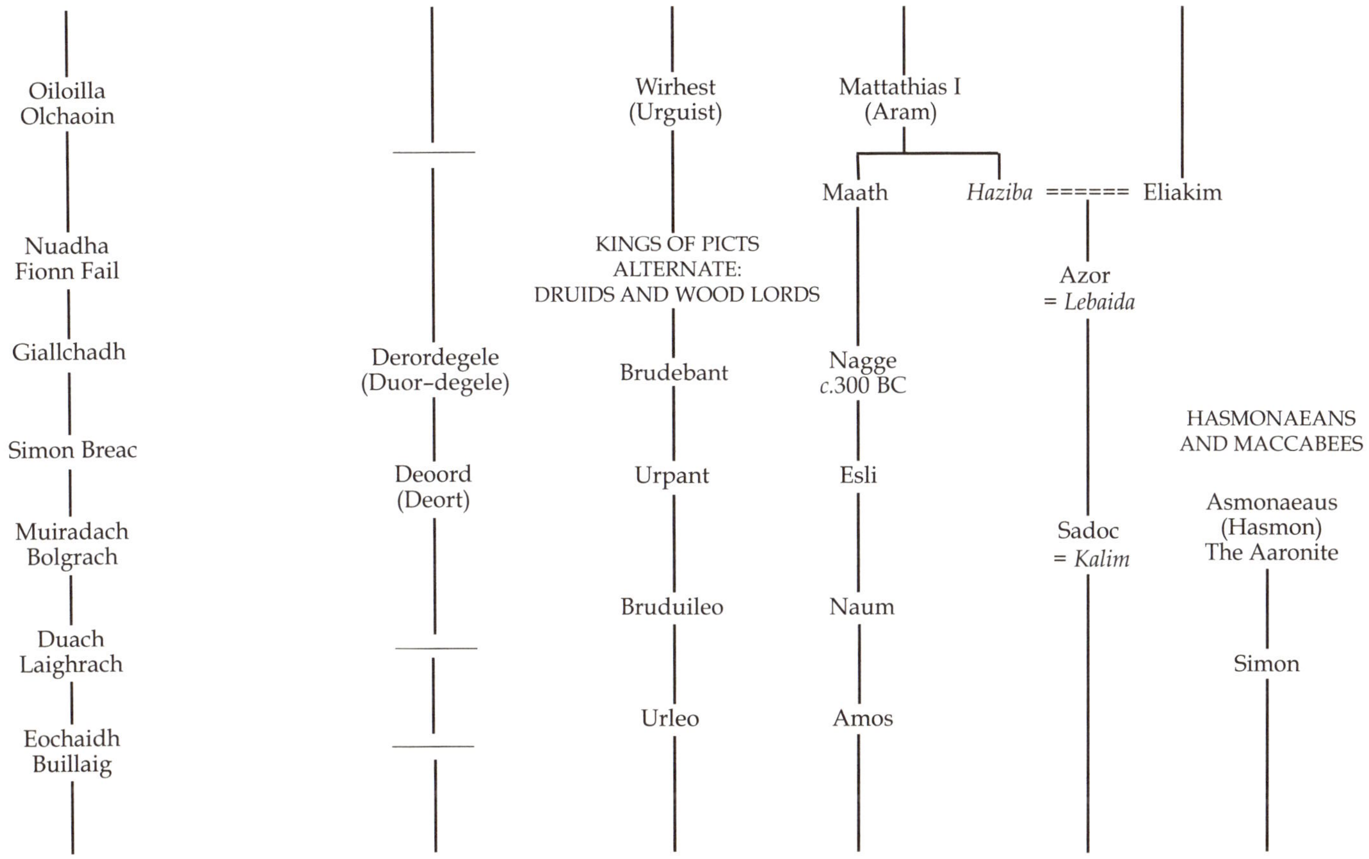
Oiloilla Olchaoin
Nuadha Fionn Fail
Giallchadh
Simon Breac
Muiradach Bolgrach
Duach Laighrach
Eochaidh Buillaig
Derordegele (Duor-degele)
Deoord (Deort)
Wirhest (Urguist)
KINGS OF PICTS ALTERNATE: DRUIDS AND WOOD LORDS
Brudebant
Urpant
Bruduileo
Urleo
Mattathias I (Aram)
Maath
Nagge c.300 BC
Esli
Naum
Amos
Haziba ====== Eliakim
Azor = Lebaida
Sadoc = Kalim
HASMONAEANS AND MACCABEES
Asmonaeaus (Hasmon) The Aaronite
Simon

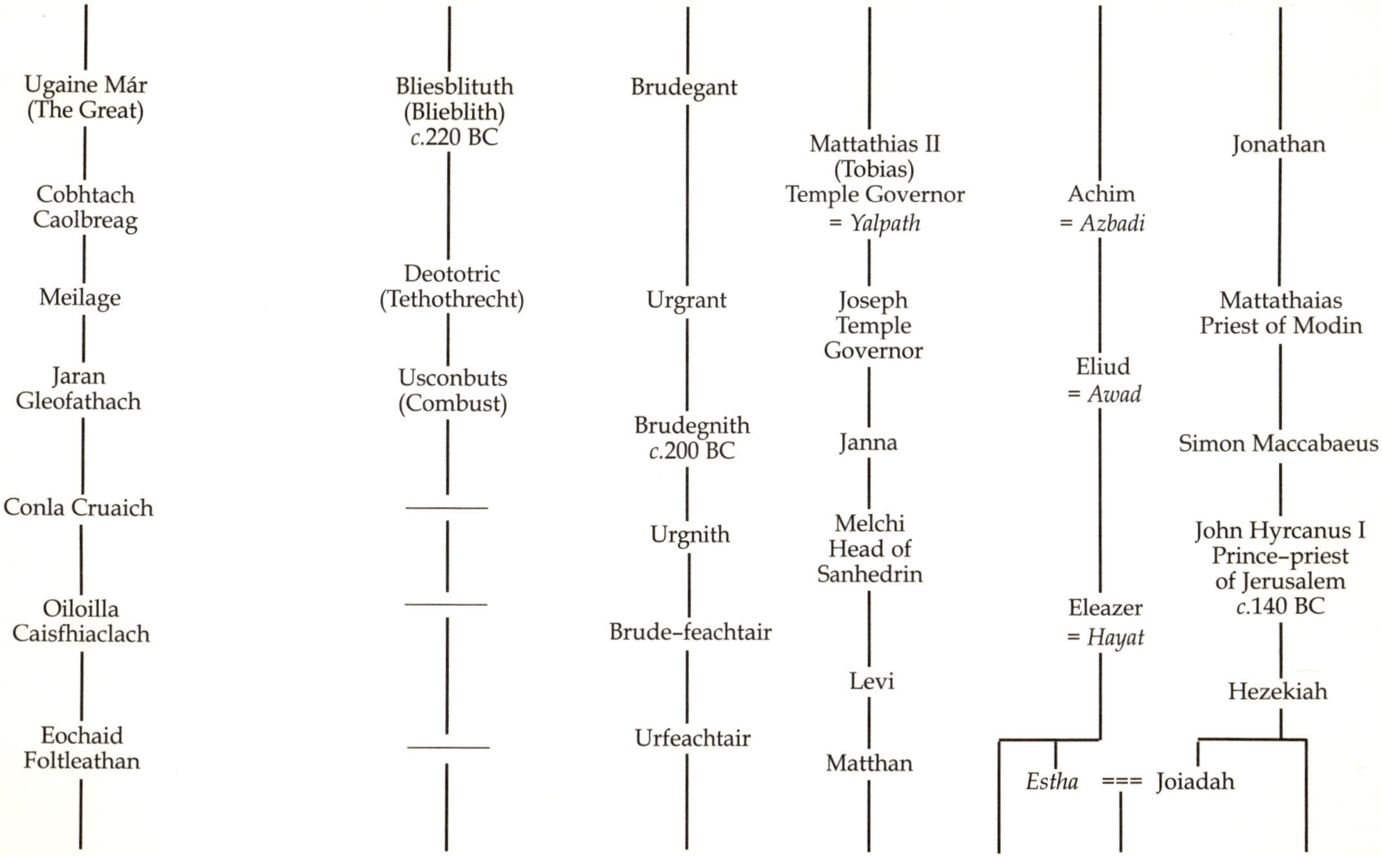
Ugaine Már
(The Great)
Cobhtach
Caolbreag
Meilage
Jaran
Gleofathach
Conla Cruaich
Oiloilla
Caisfhiaclach
Eochaid
Foltleathan
Bliesblituth
(Blieblith)
*c.*220 BC
Deototric
(Tethothrecht)
Usconbuts
(Combust)
Brudegant
Urgrant
Brudegnith
*c.*200 BC
Urgnith
Brude-feachtair
Urfeachtair
Mattathias II
(Tobias)
Temple Governor
= *Yalpath*
Joseph
Temple
Governor
Janna
Melchi
Head of
Sanhedrin
Levi
Matthan
Achim
= *Azbadi*
Eliud
= *Awad*
Eleazer
= *Hayat*
Estha === Joiadah
Jonathan
Mattathaias
Priest of Modin
Simon Maccabaeus
John Hyrcanus I
Prince-priest
of Jerusalem
*c.*140 BC
Hezekiah

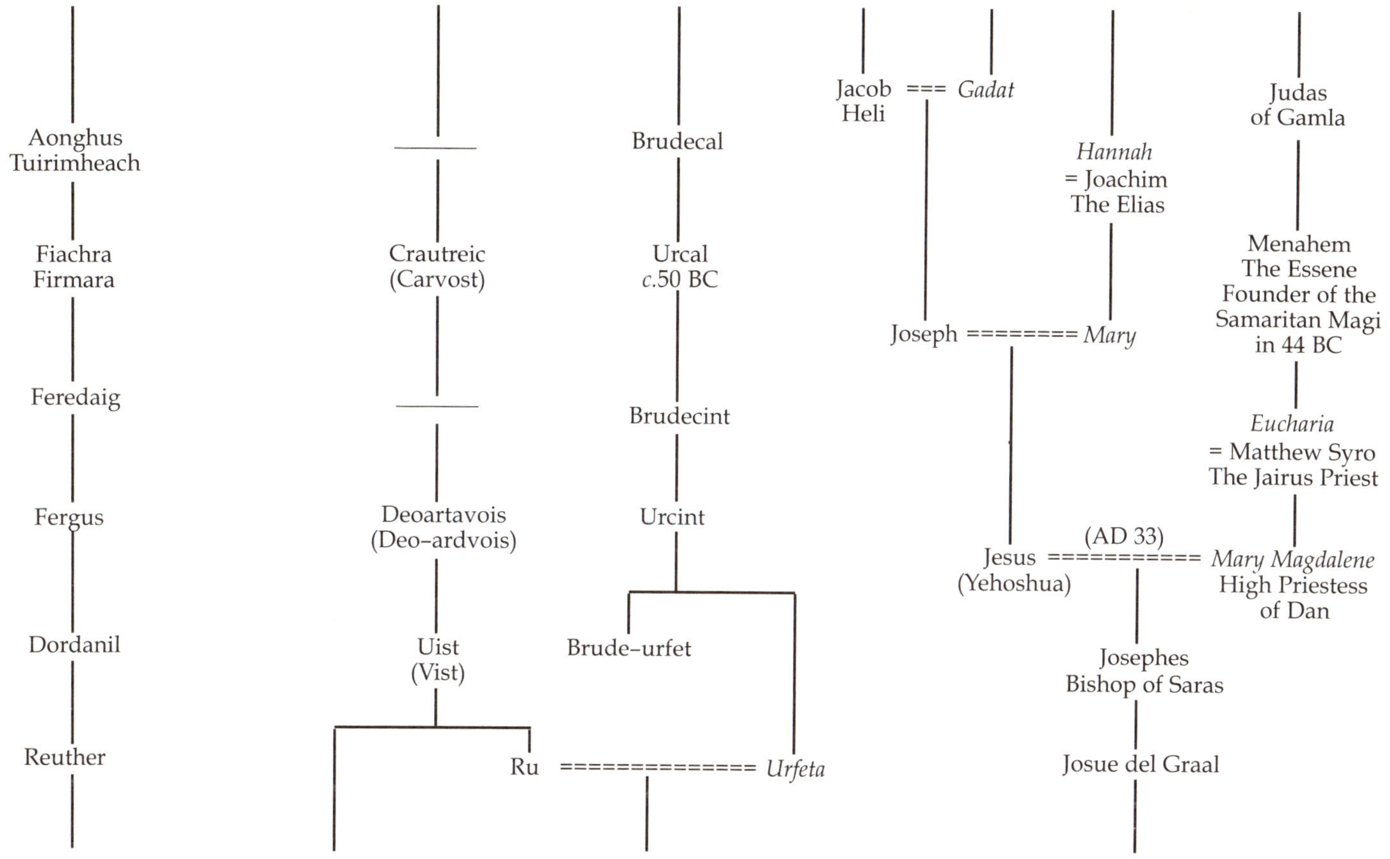
Aonghus Tuirimheach
Fiachra Firmara
Feredaig
Fergus
Dordanil
Reuther
Crautreic (Carvost)
Deoartavois (Deo-ardvois)
Uist (Vist)
Ru
Brudecal
Urcal c.50 BC
Brudecint
Urcint
Brude-urfet
============== *Urfeta*
Jacob Heli
=== *Gadat*
Hannah
= Joachim The Elias
Joseph ======== *Mary*
Jesus (Yehoshua)
(AD 33)
=========== *Mary Magdalene* High Priestess of Dan
Josephes Bishop of Saras
Josue del Graal
Judas of Gamla
Menahem The Essene Founder of the Samaritan Magi in 44 BC
Eucharia
= Matthew Syro The Jairus Priest

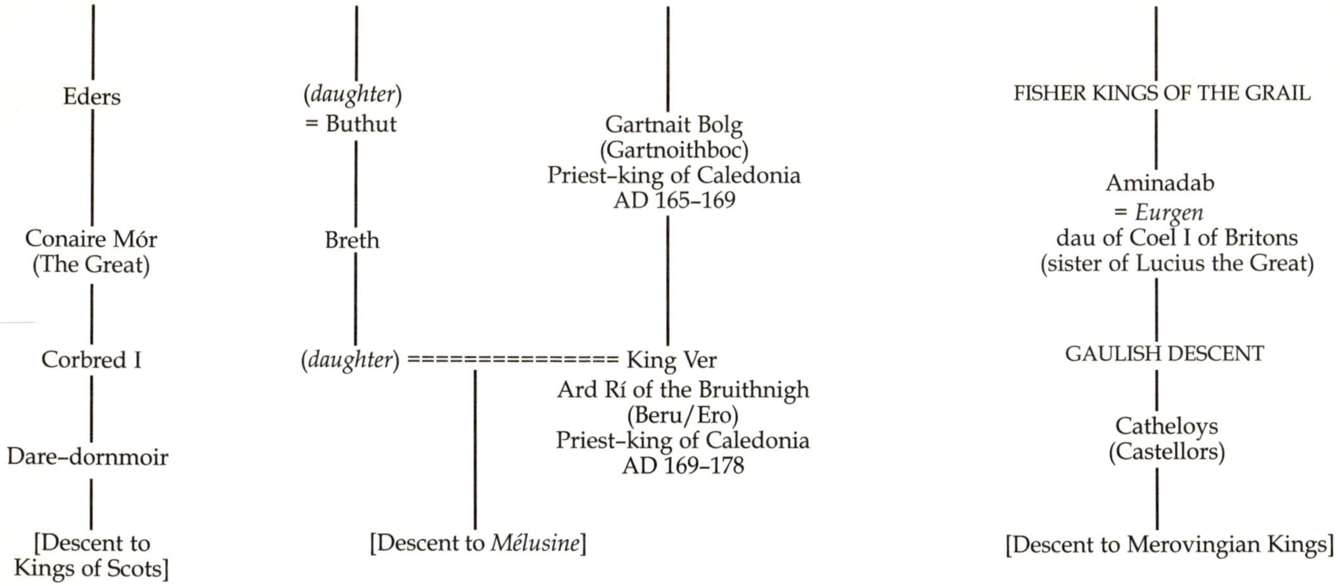
Eders
Conaire Mór
(The Great)
Corbred I
Dare-dornmoir
[Descent to
Kings of Scots]
(daughter)
= Buthut
Breth
(daughter) =============== King Ver
Ard Rí of the Bruithnigh
(Beru/Ero)
Priest-king of Caledonia
AD 169–178
[Descent to Mélusine]
Gartnait Bolg
(Gartnoithboc)
Priest-king of Caledonia
AD 165–169
FISHER KINGS OF THE GRAIL
Aminadab
= Eurgen
dau of Coel I of Britons
(sister of Lucius the Great)
GAULISH DESCENT
Catheloys
(Castellors)
[Descent to Merovingian Kings]

MEROVEUS AND MÉLUSINE

IRISH KINGS

- Dare-dornmoir
- Corbred II
- Lughaidh Allathaim
- Modha Lamha
- Conaire II
- Corbred
King of Antrim

PICTISH KINGS OF CALEDONIA

- King Ver
Ard Righ of the Bruithnigh
(Beru/Ero)
Priest-king of Caledonia
AD 169–178
- Vipiog
(Vipoguenech)
- Fiacha Albus
- Canutumel
(Canutulachama)
- Dovernach Vetalec
(Donarmahl-netalec)
- Verdaich Vetla
(Feradach Finlegh)

FISHER KINGS IN GAUL

- Catheloys
(Castellors)
- Manael
- Titurel
- Boaz
(Anfortas)
- Frotmund
(Frimutel)

Findacher

Aonghus

Eochaid

Erc
of the
Royal House
of Dal Ríata

SCOTS
DALRIADA

Gartnait Diuperr
(Garnard-dives)
High King *c.*AD 355

Achivir
(Keother)
[Various descendent branches from his sons Aniel and Erp reigned in Tanist alternation with marriages to princesses in the parallel regnal lines]

Aniel

Giron

Mailcon

Faramumd
*c.*AD 420
(Sire of the French monarchy)
= *Argotta* – dau of Genebaud
of the Sicambrian Franks

Clodion of Tournai
d AD 446
= *Queen Basina* of Thuringia

MEROVINGIANS KINGS IN GAUL

Meroveus
Founder of the
Merovingian Dynasty
d AD 456

Childeric
King of the Franks
d AD 481
= *Basina II of Thuringia*

Sigimer
= *Daughter* of Roman
Senator Ferreolus

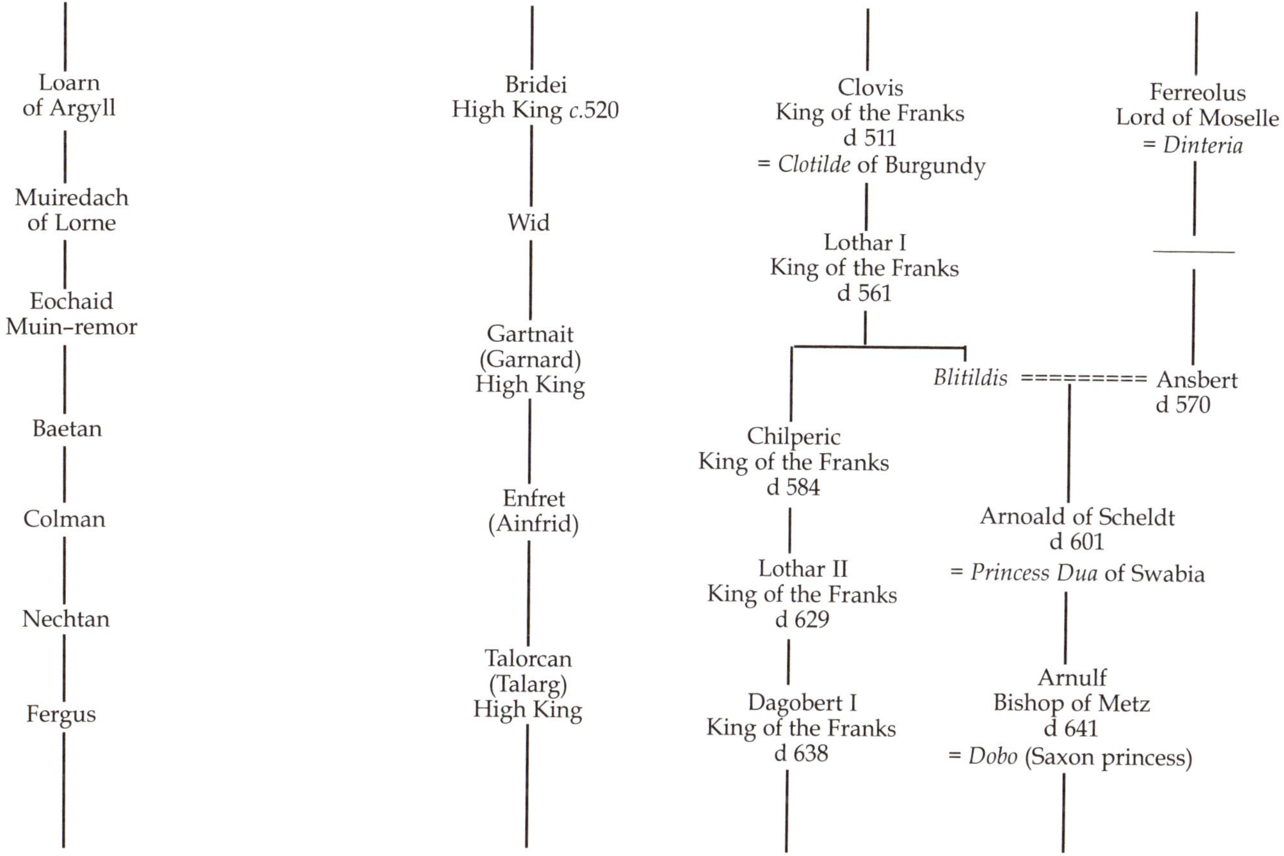

Loarn
of Argyll
Muiredach
of Lorne
Eochaid
Muin-remor
Baetan
Colman
Nechtan
Fergus
Bridei
High King *c.*520
Wid
Gartnait
(Garnard)
High King
Enfret
(Ainfrid)
Talorcan
(Talarg)
High King
Clovis
King of the Franks
d 511
= *Clotilde* of Burgundy
Lothar I
King of the Franks
d 561
Chilperic
King of the Franks
d 584
Lothar II
King of the Franks
d 629
Dagobert I
King of the Franks
d 638
Ferreolus
Lord of Moselle
= *Dinteria*
Blitildis ========= Ansbert
d 570
Arnoald of Scheldt
d 601
= *Princess Dua* of Swabia
Arnulf
Bishop of Metz
d 641
= *Dobo* (Saxon princess)

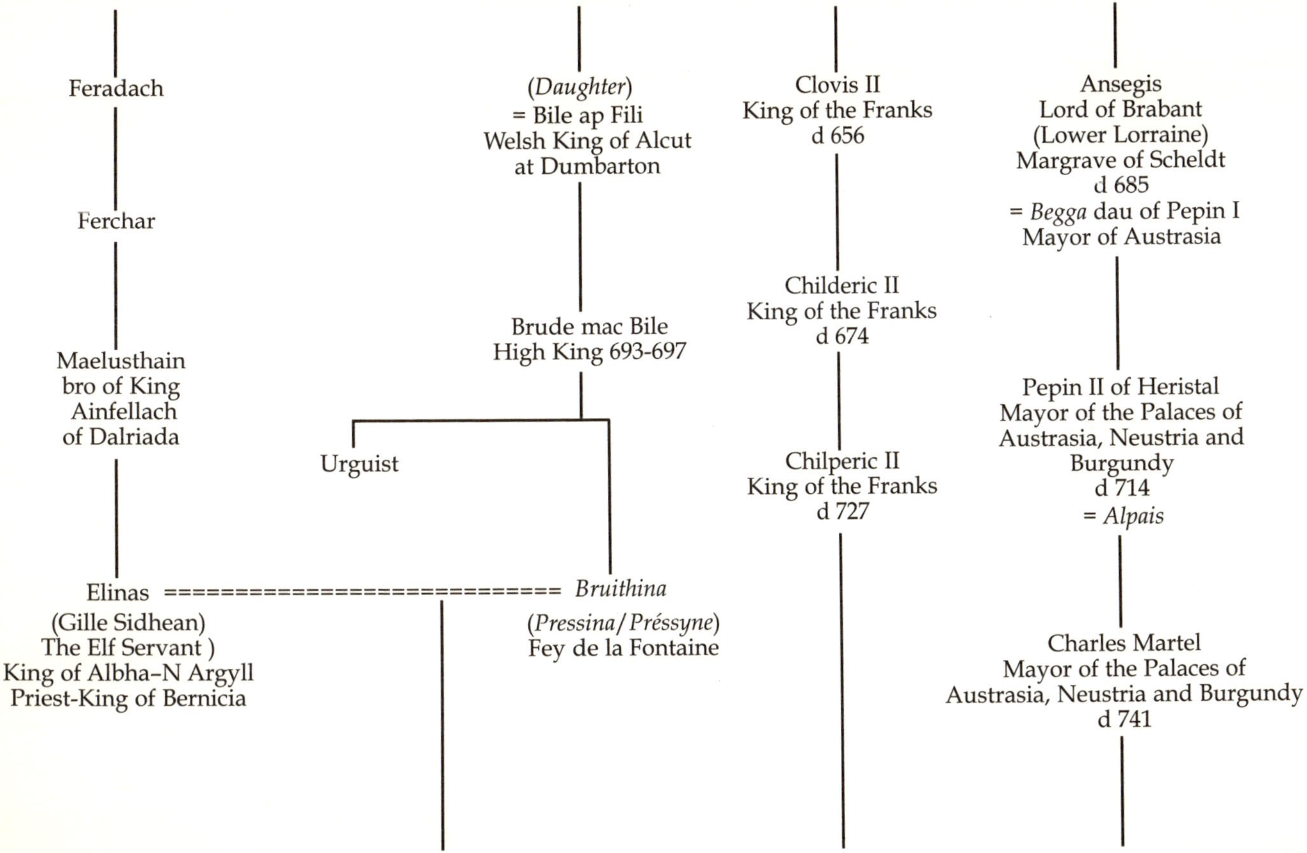
Feradach
Ferchar
Maelusthain
bro of King
Ainfellach
of Dalriada
Elinas ============================ *Bruithina*
(Gille Sidhean)
The Elf Servant)
King of Albha-N Argyll
Priest-King of Bernicia
(*Daughter*)
= Bile ap Fili
Welsh King of Alcut
at Dumbarton
Brude mac Bile
High King 693-697
Urguist
(*Pressina/Préssyne*)
Fey de la Fontaine
Clovis II
King of the Franks
d 656
Childeric II
King of the Franks
d 674
Chilperic II
King of the Franks
d 727
Ansegis
Lord of Brabant
(Lower Lorraine)
Margrave of Scheldt
d 685
= *Begga* dau of Pepin I
Mayor of Austrasia
Pepin II of Heristal
Mayor of the Palaces of
Austrasia, Neustria and
Burgundy
d 714
= *Alpais*
Charles Martel
Mayor of the Palaces of
Austrasia, Neustria and Burgundy
d 741

Aymeri de Poitiers
Prince Comte de Forez

Rainfroy ============ (733) ============ *Princess Maelasanu*
de Verrières en Forez, Languedoc (Raymond)
1st Comte d'Anjou

Princess Maelasanu Mélusine de Lusina
(*Milouziena* des Scythe)
Fey de la Fontaine
de Soif de Lusignan

[Descent to the Elf Kings]

Childeric III
King of the Franks
Deposed by papal decree 751
(Unlawfully deposed by forged
Donation of Constantine)

Leuthergis ================ < 1 ================ Pepin III (Brevis)
Duc de Brabant
Mayor of Neustria
King of the Franks 751 – 768
= 2 > *Bertha* – dau of King Flora of
Hungary and Princess Blanche Fleur
dau of Merovingian Dagobert III

[Carolingian Descent]

DESCENT OF THE ELF KING

Rainfroi
de Verrières en
Forez, Languedoc
(Raymond)
1st Comte d'Anjou

(733) = *Princess Maelasanu*
Mélusine de Lusina
(*Milouziena* des Scythe)
Fey de la Fontaine
de Soif de Lusignan

Leuthergis
dau of
Childeric III

< 1 = Pepin III Brevis
Duc de Brabant
Mayor of Neustria
King of the Franks 751–768
= 2 > *Bertha* – dau of King Flora of
Hungary and Princess Blanche Fleur
dau of Merovingian Dagobert III

Maelo I de Verrières = *Bertha*
(Maelus) Duc d Angiers, Comte d'Anjou
Commander-in-Chief of 2nd Imperial Army

Bertha
(*Berthelde*)

Maelo II de Verrières
Comte de Guisnes d'Anjou
by Grant of Charlemagne
= *Avelina* de Nantes

Roland de Verrières
Comte Palatine & Mainz
Keeper of the Sword of Durandel
dsp at Roncesvalles 778

Charlemagne the Great
King of France 771–814
Emperor Charles I 800–814
= 4 > *Hildegarde*

Louis I
King of France and
Emperor 814-840
= 2 > *Judith* of Bavaria

Nicholas de Verrières
Comte de Guisnes d'Anjou
= *Agatha* de Champagne

Otho de Verrières
Comte de Guisnes d'Anjou
= *Constance* de Chartres

Descent from Charlemagne's
daughter *Bertha* and
Angilibert de Ponthieu

Ernicule I
Comte de Ponthieu 965
= *Adeline* de Boulogne

Amelius de Verrières ========= 1 > *Maud* (*Mahaut*) de Ponthieu
Comte de Guisnes d'Anjou
= 2 > *Helen* de Blois

Charles II
Western Emperor from 840
King of France from 843
Emperor 867-877

Louis II
King of France 877–879

Charles III
King of France 893 - dep 922
[succeeded elder brothers]
= *Eadgifu*

Louis IV
King of France 936–954
[succeeded Dukes of France]

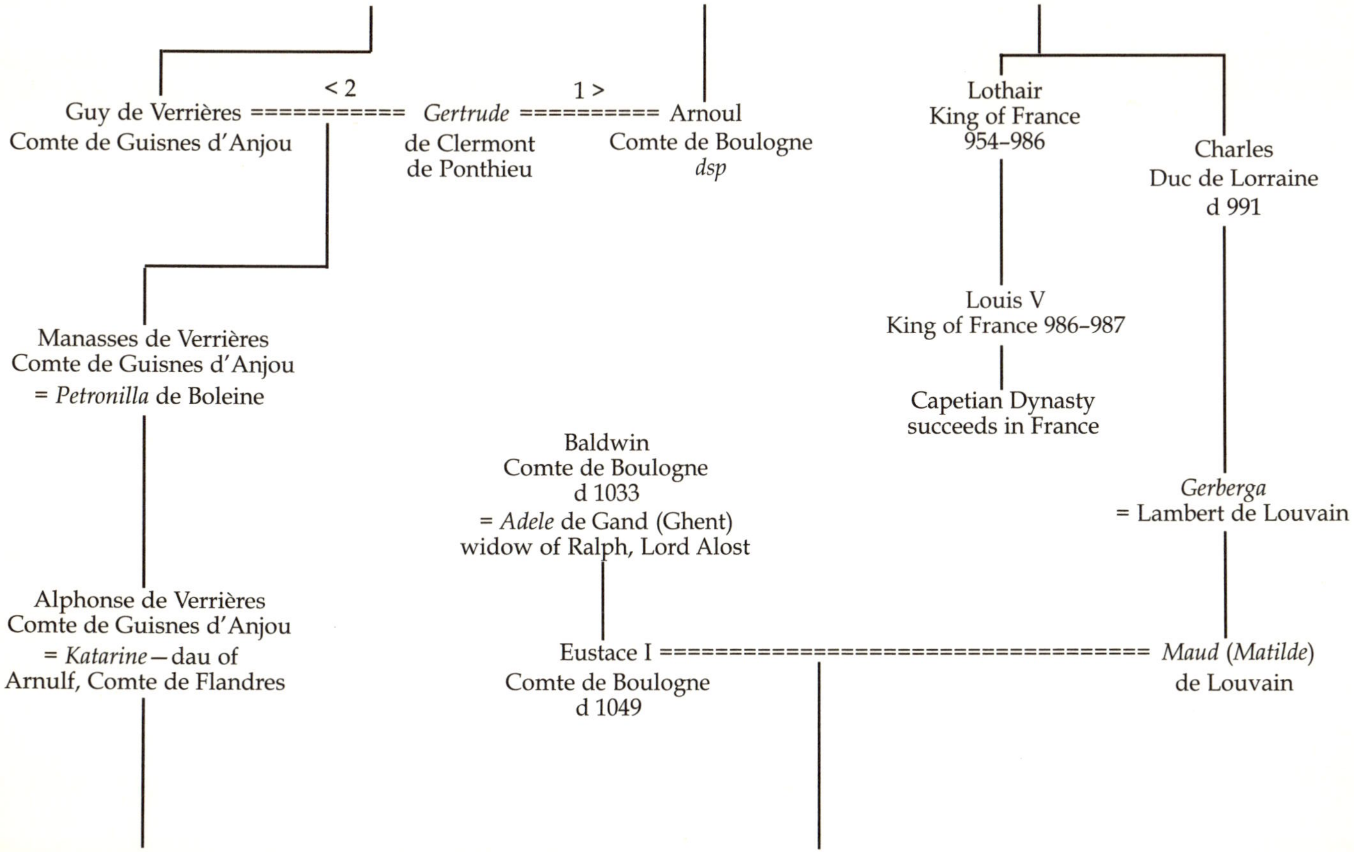
Guy de Verrières
Comte de Guisnes d'Anjou
< 2
Gertrude
de Clermont
de Ponthieu
1 >
Arnoul
Comte de Boulogne
dsp
Lothair
King of France
954–986
Charles
Duc de Lorraine
d 991
Manasses de Verrières
Comte de Guisnes d'Anjou
= Petronilla de Boleine
Louis V
King of France 986–987
Capetian Dynasty
succeeds in France
Baldwin
Comte de Boulogne
d 1033
= Adele de Gand (Ghent)
widow of Ralph, Lord Alost
Gerberga
= Lambert de Louvain
Alphonse de Verrières
Comte de Guisnes d'Anjou
= Katarine—dau of
Arnulf, Comte de Flandres
Eustace I
Comte de Boulogne
d 1049
Maud (Matilde)
de Louvain

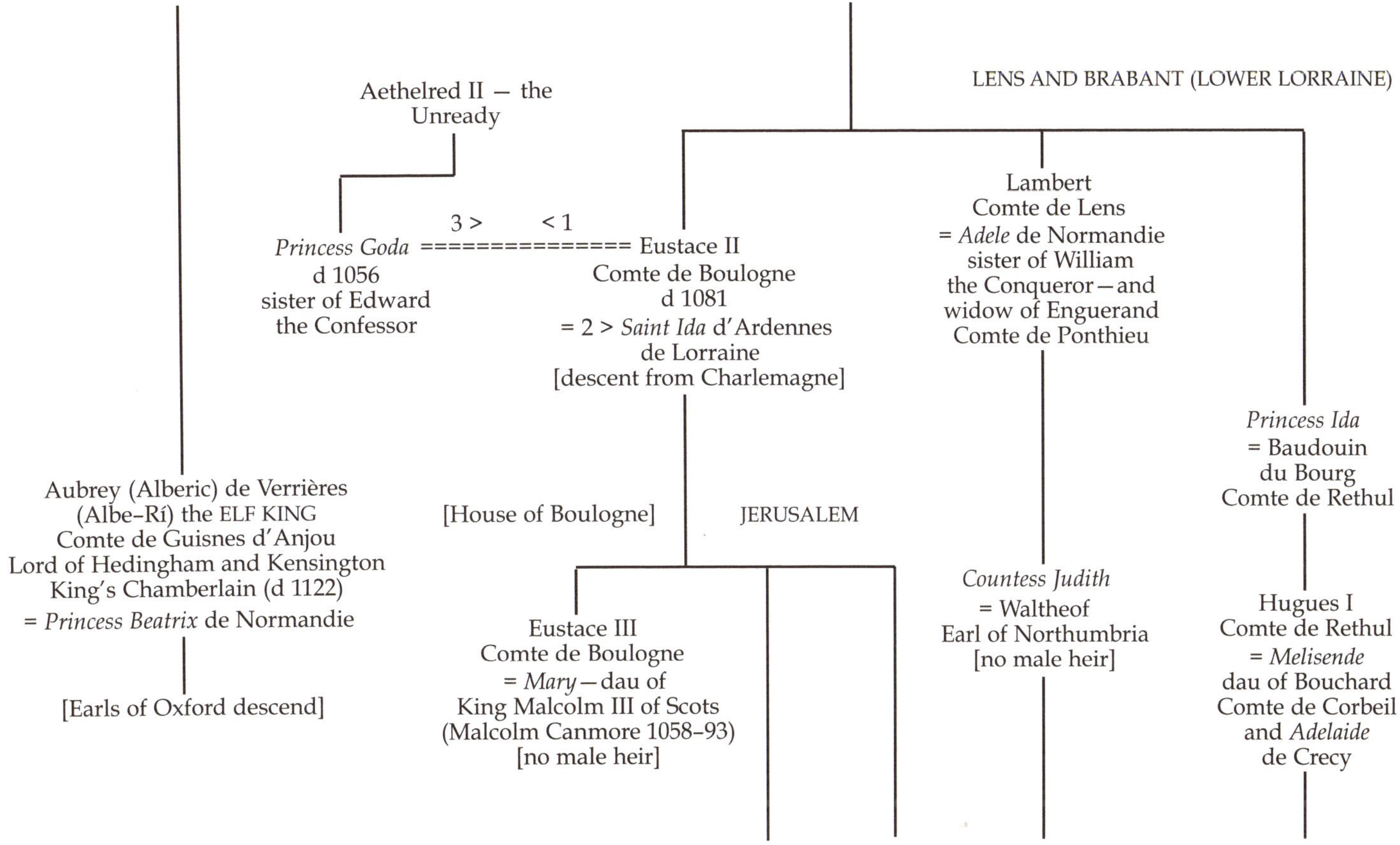
LENS AND BRABANT (LOWER LORRAINE)
Aethelred II — the Unready
Princess Goda d 1056 sister of Edward the Confessor
3 > ================ < 1
Eustace II Comte de Boulogne d 1081
= 2 > Saint Ida d'Ardennes de Lorraine [descent from Charlemagne]
Lambert Comte de Lens = Adele de Normandie sister of William the Conqueror—and widow of Enguerand Comte de Ponthieu
Princess Ida = Baudouin du Bourg Comte de Rethul
Aubrey (Alberic) de Verrières (Albe-Rí) the ELF KING Comte de Guisnes d'Anjou Lord of Hedingham and Kensington King's Chamberlain (d 1122)
= Princess Beatrix de Normandie
[Earls of Oxford descend]
[House of Boulogne]
JERUSALEM
Eustace III Comte de Boulogne = Mary—dau of King Malcolm III of Scots (Malcolm Canmore 1058–93) [no male heir]
Countess Judith = Waltheof Earl of Northumbria [no male heir]
Hugues I Comte de Rethul = Melisende dau of Bouchard Comte de Corbeil and Adelaide de Crecy

Godefroi de Bouillon
de Bouillon
Duke of Lower Lorraine
King of Jerusalem 1099–1100
dsp

Baudouin I
King of Jerusalem
1100–1118
dsp

Maud de Lens
= 2 > King David I of Scots
(1124–1153)
son of Malcolm III

[Kings of Scots]

Baudouin II
du Bourg
King of Jerusalem
1118–1131
= *Morfia* of Armenia
[no male heir]

[Jerusalem Kings]

ROBIN AND THE CHAMBERLAINS

Eustace III
Comte de Boulogne
= *Mary* – dau of
King Malcolm III of Scots
(Malcolm Canmore 1058–93)
[no male heir]

Godefroi de Bouillon
de Bouillon
Duke of Lower Lorraine
King of Jerusalem 1099–1100
dsp

Boudoin I
King of Jerusalem
1100–1118
dsp

Baudoin II du Bourg
King of Jerusalem
1118–1131
= *Morfia* of Armenia
[no male heir]

Aubrey de Verrières
THE ELF KING
Comte de Guisnes d'Anjou
King's Chamberlain (d 1122)
= *Beatrix* de Normandie

Aubrey II de Verrières
d'Anjou de Lorraine Comte de Guisnes
Great Chamberlain of England for Henry I
Sheriff of Cambridge and Essex
d 1140
= *Adeliza* – dau of Gilbert FitzRichard
Lord of Clare and Tunbridge

Mathilde
Stephen de Blois
King of England
g.son of William
the Conqueror
1135–1154

Maud de Lens
= King David I of Scots
(1124–1153)
son of Malcolm III

Henry
Earl of Huntingdon
= *Ada* – dau of William de
Warenne, Earl of Surrey

[Kings of Scots descend]

Melisende
Queen of Jerusalem
(1131–1152)
= Foulques V d'Anjou

[Lusignan Kings]

Eustace
Comte de Boulogne
d 1153
= *Constance* — dau of
Louis VI of France

William
Comte de Mortain
= *Isabel* — dau of
William of Warenne

Aubrey (Alberic) III de Vere
Comte de Guisnes d'Anjou
1st Earl of Oxford 1142
Great Chamberlain of England
by Grant of Empress Matilda
d 1194
= 3 > *Agnes* — dau of Henry of Essex

Aubrey de Vere
2nd Earl of Oxford
Great Chamberlain of England
Sheriff of Essex and Hereford
dsp 1214

Robert de Vere
3rd Earl of Oxford
Great Chamberlain of England
Justice of the King s Bench
Steward of the Royal Forest of Essex
Heritor of Fitzoath
Pretender to the Earldom of Huntingdon
[ROBIN HOOD Model-1]
d 1221
= *Isabel* — dau of Hugh de Bolebec

Hugh de Vere
Knight of Henry III
4th Earl of Oxford
Great Chamberlain of England
d 1263
= *Hawise* – dau of Sayer de Quincy,
Earl of Winchester

Robert de Vere
5th Earl of Oxford
d 1296
= *Alice* – dau of Gilbert de Saundford

Robert de Vere
6th Earl of Oxford
dsp 1331
= *Margaret* – dau of Roger
Mortimer, Earl of March

Sir Alphonsus de Vere
= *Jane* – dau of Sir Richard Foliot

John de Vere
7th Earl of Oxford
Great Chamberlain of England
Commander for Edward III at Cressy
and Poitiers (d 1360)
= *Maud* – dau of Bartholomew,
Lord Badlesmere

Sir Thomas de Vere
8th Earl of Oxford
Great Chamberlain of England
d 1371
= *Maud* — dau of Sir Ralph de Ufford
Chief Justice of Ireland

Aubrey de Vere
10th Earl of Oxford
d 1400
= *Alice* — dau of John,
Lord Fitzwalter

Sir Robert de Vere KG
9th Earl of Oxford
Great Chamberlain of England
Duke of Ireland 1386
Marquess of Dublin 1387 by Grant
of King Richard II
Proclaimed a outlaw by Parliament
in 1388 [ROBIN HOOD Model-2]
dsp 1392

Sir Richard de Vere KG
11th Earl of Oxford
Knight of the Garter by Henry IV
d 1417
= 2 > *Alice* — dau of Sir
Richard Serjeaux of Cornwall

John de Vere
12th Earl of Oxford
Lancastrian supporter of
Henry VI. Beheaded 1461
by Edward IV of York
= *Elizabeth* — dau of Sir John
Howard of Norfolk

Robert de Vere
= *Jeane Courtenay*

Sir George de Vere
d 1503
= *Margaret*—dau of
Sir William Stafford

John de Vere
14th Earl of Oxford
dsp 1526

Sir John de Vere KG
13th Earl of Oxford
Lord High Admiral
Great Chamberlain of England
dsp 1513

John de Vere
= *Alice Kilrington*

Sir John de Vere KG
15th Earl of Oxford
Great Chamberlain and
Privy Councillor to
Henry VIII. (d 1539)

= 2 > *Elizabeth Trussel*

John de Vere
16th Earl of Oxford
Great Chamberlain
d 1562
= 2 > *Marjorie Golding*
of Halstead

Edward de Vere
17th Earl of Oxford
Lord Great Chamberlain
Student of John Dee
d 1604
= 2 > *Elizabeth Trentham*
of Rowcaster Priory

Aubrey de Vere
= *Margaret Spring*

[Male Oxford line expires in 1702 with Aubrey, 20th Earl]

THE HOUSE OF VLAD DRACULA

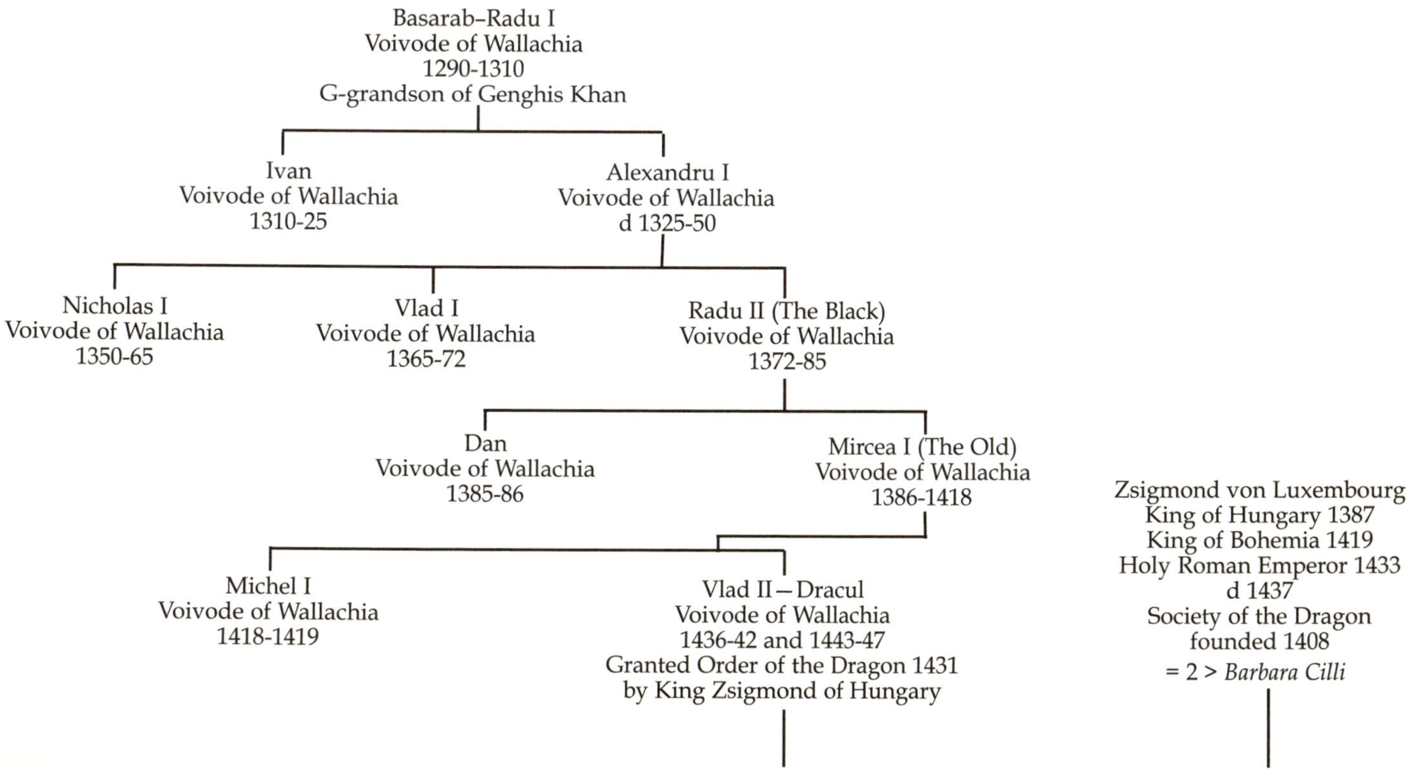

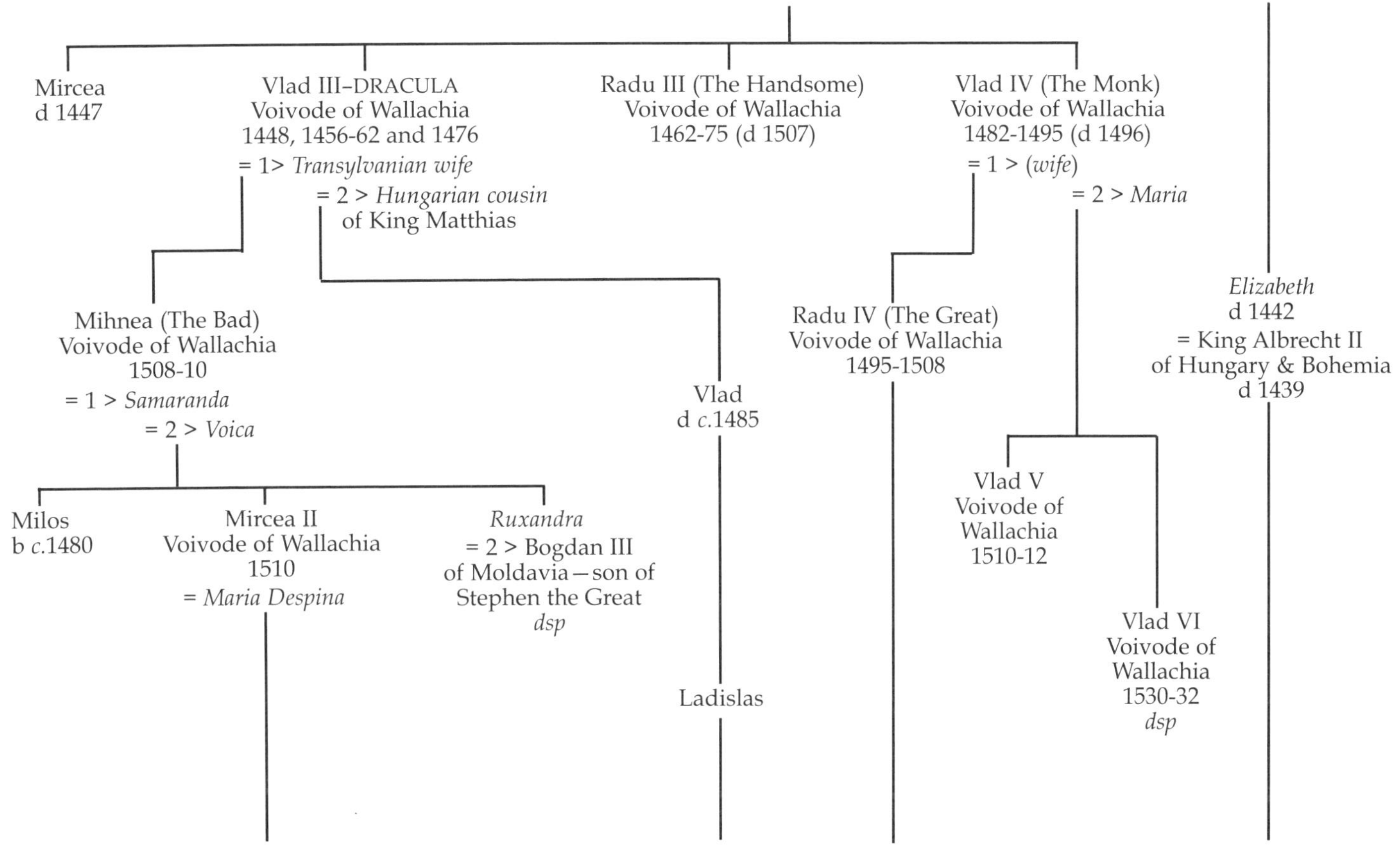
Mircea
d 1447
Vlad III–DRACULA
Voivode of Wallachia
1448, 1456-62 and 1476
= 1> *Transylvanian wife*
= 2 > *Hungarian cousin*
of King Matthias
Radu III (The Handsome)
Voivode of Wallachia
1462-75 (d 1507)
Vlad IV (The Monk)
Voivode of Wallachia
1482-1495 (d 1496)
= 1 > (*wife*)
= 2 > *Maria*
Mihnea (The Bad)
Voivode of Wallachia
1508-10
= 1 > *Samaranda*
= 2 > *Voica*
Vlad
d *c*.1485
Radu IV (The Great)
Voivode of Wallachia
1495-1508
Elizabeth
d 1442
= King Albrecht II
of Hungary & Bohemia
d 1439
Milos
b *c*.1480
Mircea II
Voivode of Wallachia
1510
= *Maria Despina*
Ruxandra
= 2 > Bogdan III
of Moldavia – son of
Stephen the Great
dsp
Ladislas
Vlad V
Voivode of
Wallachia
1510-12
Vlad VI
Voivode of
Wallachia
1530-32
dsp

Alexandru II
Voivode of Wallachia
1574-77
= *Catherine Salvarezi*

Mihnea II (The Islamized)
Voivode of Wallachia
1577-1583 (d 1601)
= 1 > *Neasca* of Cislau
= 2 > *Visa*

Radu Mihnea
Voivode of Wallachia
Moldavia and Transylvania
1601-23 (intermittently)
= *Arghira Bartolomeo Minetti*

Alexandru III (Coconul)
Voivode of Wallachia 1623-27
& Moldavia 1629-30 (d 1632)
= *Ruxandra Scarlat Regilitzi*
dsp

Peter (The Lame)
Prince of Moldavia
1574-77 (d 1594)
= 2 > *Irina Botezata*

Stefinata
dsp 1603

Ladislas

John
de Band
= *Anna*

John

George

Mircea III (The Shepherd)
Voivode of Wallachia
d 1560
= *Chuina* of Moldavia

Stanca Basarab
= John Norocza
of Pitesti
d 1599

Zamphira
d 1602
= Peter Raez de Galco

Adam Raez de Galco

Peter Raez de Galco

Elizabeth
d 1505
= King Casimir IV
of Poland

King Vladislav II
of Hungary & Bohemia
d 1516
= *Anne* of Foix-Cundale

Anne of Hungary
d 1547
= King Ferdinand I
of Hungary & Bohemia

Joanna of Austria
d 1578
= Francis de Medici
Grand Duke of Tuscany
d 1587

(Daughter)
= into Getzi
family

[Line descends]

Ilona
= Jan Danilowicz

Theophile
= Jacob Sobieski
Castellan of Cracow

Jan Sobieski
King Jan III of Poland
1674-1696
= *Mary Casimira* – dau of
Henry de la Grange d'Arquien

Prince James Louis Sobieski
d 1737
= *Hedwig* of Palatine

Maria de Medici
d 1642
= Henri III de Bourbon
King of Navarre
King Henri IV of France

Henriette Maria
= Charles I Stuart
King of Britain
1625-1649

King James VII of Scots
(James II of England)
1685-1688
d 1701
= *Maria Beatrix de Este*
de Modena
d 1718

Maria Clementina Sobieska ============ James Francis Edward Stuart
d 1735

James Francis Edward Stuart
King *de jure*
James VIII of Scots
d 1766

Charles Edward Stuart
(Bonnie Prince Charlie)
1st Count of Albany
King Charles III *de jure* of Britain
d 1788

[For descent from Charles Edward Stuart down to date see chart: Counts of Albany in *Bloodline of the Holy Grail*. Also in *The Forgotten Monarchy of Scotland*]

BIBLIOGRAPHY

Albany, HRH Prince Michael Stewart of, *The Forgotten Monarchy of Scotland*, Element Books, Shaftesbury, 1998.

Alexander, David and Pat (eds.), *Handbook to the Bible*, Lion Publishing, Oxford, 1983.

Alter, Robert (trans.), *Genesis*, W. W. Norton, New York, 1996.

with Kermode, Frank, *The Literary Guide to the Bible*, Fontana, London, 1989.

Alviella, Count Goblet, *Migration of Symbols* (1892–facsimile), Aquarian Press, Wellingborough, 1979.

Ames, Delano (trans.), *Greek Mythology*, [from *Mythologie Générale Larousse*], Paul Hamlyn, London, 1963.

Anderson, Alan Orr, *Early Sources of Scottish History*, (ed. Marjorie Anderson), Paul Watkins, London, 1990.

Anderson, Verily, *The De Veres of Castle Hedingham*, Terence Dalton, Lavenham, 1993.

Apocrypha, The Old Testament, Oxford University Press, Oxford, 1998.

Ashley, Leonard R. N., *The Complete Book of Devils and Demons*, Robson Books, London, 1997.

Baigent, Michael, with Leigh, Richard and Lincoln, Henry, *The Holy Blood and the Holy Grail*, Jonathan Cape, London, 1982.

The Messianic Legacy, Jonathan Cape, London, 1986.

Bailey, James, *The God-Kings and the Titans*, Hodder & Stoughton, London, 1973.

Barber, Elizabeth Wayland, *The Mummies of Urümchi*, Macmillan, London, 1999.

Barber, Paul, *Vampires, Burial and Death*, Yale University Press, New Haven, 1988.

Barber, Richard, *The Figure of Arthur*, Longman, London, 1972.

Baring-Gould, Sabine, *The Book of Werewolves*, Senate, London, 1995.

Myths of the Middle Ages, (ed. John Matthews), Blandford/Cassell, London, 1996.

Barnstone, Willis (ed.), *The Other Bible*, HarperSanFrancisco, San Fransisco, CA, 1984.

Becker, Robert O., and Selden, Gary, *The Body Electric*, William Morrow, New York, 1985.

Becker, Udo, *The Element Encyclopedia of Symbols*, Element Books, Shaftesbury, 1996.

Blackmore, R. D., *Lorna Doone*, Sampson, Low, Marston, London, 1869.

Boulton, D'Arcy Jonathan Dacre, *The Knights of the Crown*, Boydell Press, London, 1987.

Brawer, Michael K., and Kirby, Roger, *Fast Facts: Prostate Specific Antigen*, Health Press, Abingdon, 1997.

Breasted, J H., *The Dawn of Consciousness*, Charles Scribner's Sons, New York, 1934.

Brennan, J. H., *An Occult History of the World*, Futura Publications, London, 1976.

Brenner, Sydney (ed.), *Telomeres and Telomerase*, Ciba Foundation and John Wiley, New York, NY, 1997.

Brier, Bob, *The Murder of Tutankhamen*, Berkley Books, New York, NY, 1998.

Brumby, Robin, *Doctor John Dee – The Original 007*, Academic Board of Dacorum College, Hemel Hempstead, 1977.

Bull, Norman J., *The Rise of the Church*, Heinemann , London, 1967.

Butler, Elizabeth M., *Ritual Magic*, Cambridge University Press, Cambridge, 1949.

Byock, Jesse (ed.), *The Saga of the Volsungs*, Penguin, Harmondsworth, 1999.

Carpenter, Clive, *The Guinness Book of Kings, Rulers and Statesmen*, Guinness Superlatives, Enfield, 1978.

Carpenter, Humphrey, *J. R. R. Tolkien*, Harper Collins, London, 1987.

Carus, Dr. Paul, *The History of the Devil and the Idea of Evil*, Gramercy Books, New York, 1996.

Castries, Duc de, *The Lives of the Kings and Queens of France*, (trans. Anne Dobell for Académie Francaise), Weidenfeld & Nicolson, London, 1979.

Cavendish, Richard, *The Black Arts*, Perigee, New York, NY, 1983.

Cernenko, Dr. E. V. and McBride, Angus, *The Scythians 700-300 BC*, Osprey—Men at Arms, London, 1986.

Chadwick, Nora K., *Early Brittany*, University of Wales Press, Cardiff, 1969.

Charles, R. H. (trans.) *The Book of Enoch*, (Revised from Dillmann's edition of the Ethiopic text—1893) Oxford University Press, Oxford, 1906 and 1912.

Chrétien de Troyes, *le Conte del Graal*, (trans. Ruth Harwood Cline), University of Georgia Press, 1985.

Church, Rev. Leslie F. (ed.), *Matthew Henry's Commentary on the Whole Bible*, Marshall Pickering, London, 1960.

Clarke, G. W. (trans.), *The Octavius of Marcus Minucius Felix*, Newman Press, New York, 1974.

Clayton, Peter A., *Chronicle of the Pharaohs*, Thames & Hudson, London, 1994.

Clébert, Jean-Paul, *The Gypsies*, (trans. Charles Duff), Visita Books, London, 1963.

Coghlan, Ronan, *The Illustrated Encyclopaedia of Arthurian Legends*, Element Books, Shaftesbury, 1993.

Cohen, J. M., and Phipps, J-F, *The Common Experience*, Rider, London, 1979.

Coleman, Christopher B., *The Treatise of Lorenzo Valla on the Donation of Constantine*, University of Toronto Press, Toronto, 1993.

Cowan, David R., and Silk, Anne, *Ancient Energies of the Earth*, Thorsons, London, 1999.

Cruden, Alexander, *Complete Concordance to the Old and New Testament and the Apocrypha*, Frederick Warne, London, 1891.

Cummins, W. A., *The Age of the Picts*, Alan Sutton, Stroud, 1995.

Day, David, *Tolkien's Ring*, Harper Collins, London, 1994.

Deacon, Richard, *A History of the British Secret Service*, Grafton Books, London, 1982.

Devereux, Paul, *Secrets of Ancient and Sacred Places*, Brockhamptom Press, London, 1992.

Dewar, James, *The Unlocked Secret*, William Kimber, London, 1966.

Dixon, Karen R., and Southern, Pat, *The Roman Cavalry*, Routledge, London, 1997.

Doresse, Jean, *The Secret Books of the Egyptian Gnostics*, Hollis & Carter, London, 1960.

Douglas, George, *Scottish Fairy and Folk Tales*, Walter Scott, London, 1901.

Dunn, Waldo Hilary, *R. D. Blackmore – a Biography*, Robert Hale, London, 1956.

Ehler, Sidney Z., and Morral, John B. (eds.), *Church and State through the Centuries*, Burns & Oates, London, 1954.

Encyclopaedia Judaica Decannial, Keter Publishing, London, 1997.

Eusebius, *The History of the Church from Christ to Constantine*, Penguin, Harmondsworth, 1989.

Farmer, David, *Dictionary of Saints*, Oxford University Press, Oxford, 1997.

Farrar, Janet and Stewart, *A Witches Bible*, Phoenix, Custer, WA, 1996.

Fergusson, John, *Basic Heraldry*, The Herbert Press, London, 1993.

Fideler, David (ed.), *Alexandria No.2*, Phanes Press, Grand Rapids, MI, 1993.

Fleming, Fergus, with Husain, Shahruckh; Littleton, C. Scott, and Malcor, Linda, *Heroes of the Dawn – Celtic Europe*, Duncan Baird/Time Life, London, 1996.

Florescu, Radu, and McNally, Raymond, *Dracula*, Robert Hale, London, 1973.

Frankfort, Henri, *Kingship and the Gods*, University of Chicago Press, Chicago, 1948.

Frazer, Sir James George, *The Golden Bough*, Papermac, London, 1987.

Freese, J. H. (trans.), *The Octavius of Marcus Minucius Felix*, Macmillan, New York, 1919.

French, Peter J., *John Dee – The World of an Elizabethan Magus*, Routledge & Kegan Paul, London, 1972.

Gardner, Barry, *Lorna Doone's Exmoor*, Exmoor Press, Dulverton, 1990.

Gardner, Gerald B., *Witchcraft Today*, I-H-O Books, Thame, 1954.

Gardner, Laurence, *Bloodline of the Holy Grail*, Element Books, Shaftesbury, 1996.

Genesis of the Grail Kings, Bantam Press, London, 1999, and Element Books, Boston 2000.

Gerber, Pat, *Stone of Destiny*, Cannongate, Edinburgh, 1997.

Gibson, Michael, *The Symbolists*, Harry N. Abrams, New York, 1988.

Gimbutas, Marija, *The Gods and Goddesses of Old Europe*, Thames & Hudson, London, 1974.

Grant, Kenneth, *Aleister Crowley and the Hidden God*, Frederick Muller, London, 1973.

Outside the Circles of Time, Frederick Muller, London, 1980.

The Magical Revival, Skoob Books, London, 1991.

Nightside of Eden, Skoob Books, London, 1994.

Graves, Robert, *The White Goddess*, Faber & Faber, London, 1961.

with Patai, Raphael, *Hebrew Myths* – The Book of Genesis, Cassell, London, 1964.

Green, Miranda, *The Gods of the Celts*, Alan Sutton, Stroud, 1986.

Gregor, Walter, *Notes on the Folk-lore of the North East of Scotland*, Folk-lore Society, London, 1881.

Gregory of Tours, *A History of the Franks* (trans. Lewis Thorpe), Penguin, Harmondsworth, 1964.

Grimm, Jacob, *Teutonic Mythology*, Routledge – Thoemmes Press, London, 1999.

Gustafson, Fred, *The Black Madonna*, Sigo Press, Boston, 1991.

Hall, Manly P., *The Lost Keys of Freemasonry*, Macoy Publishing and Masonic Supply, Richmond, VA, 1976.

The Secret Teachings of all Ages, The Philosophical Research Society, Los Angeles, 1989.

Hall, Nor, *The Moon and the Virgin*, Harper & Row, New York, 1980.

Hallam, Elizabeth (ed.), *The Plantagenet Chronicles*, Guild Publishing, London, 1986.

Harry, Rev. George Owen, *The Genealogy of the High and Mighty Monarch, James*, Simon Stafford, London, 1604.

Harvey, John, *The Plantagenets*, B. T. Batsford, London, 1948.

Hastings, James, *Dictionary of the Bible*, T. & T. Clark, Edinburgh, 1909.

Herodotus, *The Histories*, (trans. Robin Waterfield), Oxford University Press, Oxford, 1998.

Heidel, Alexander, *The Babylonian Genesis* (*Enûma elish*), University of Chicago Press, Chicago, IL, 1942.

The Gilgamesh Epic and Old Testament Parallels, University of Chicago Press, Chicago, IL, 1949.

Henderson, Ernest F. (trans.), *Select Historical Documents of the Middle Ages*, G. Bell, London, 1925.

Hervey, Thomas K., *The Book of Christmas*, Frederick Warne, London, 1888.

Higgins, Godfrey, *The Celtic Druids*, Rowland Hunter, London, 1827.

Higham, N. J., *The Kingdom of Northumbria*, AD 350-1100, Alan Sutton, Stroud, 1993.

Hocart, A. M., *Kingship*, Oxford University Press, Oxford, 1927.

Holt, J. C., *Robin Hood*, Thames & Hudson, London, 1982.

Hutton, Ronald, *The Pagan Religions of the British Isles*, Basil Blackwell, Oxford, 1991.

Huxley, Aldous, *The Doors of Perception – Heaven and Hell*, Flamingo, London, 1994.

Jacobsen, Thorkild, *The Sumerian King List* (Assyrialogical Studies No.11), University of Chicago Press, Chicago, 1939.

James, Montague R. (ed.) , *The Apocryphal New Testament*, Clarendon Press, Oxford, 1924.

Jaynes, Julian, *The Origin of Consciousness in the Breakdown of the Bicameral Mind*, Houghton Mifflin, Boston, MA, 1976.

Jennings, Hargrave, *The Rosicrucians – Their Rites and Mysteries*, Routledge, London, 1887.

Jones, Steve, *In the Blood – God, Genes and Destiny*, Harper Collins, 1996.

Josephus, Flavius, *The Works of Flavius Josephus – The Antiquities of the Jews, The Wars of the Jews* and *Against Apion*, (trans. William Whiston), Milner & Sowerby, London, 1870.

Jullian, Philippe, *The Symbolists*, Phaidon Press, London, 1973.

Keating, Geoffrey, *The History of Ireland*, (trans. David Comyn and Rev. P. S. Dinneen), 1640, reprinted Irish Texts Society, London, 1902-14.

Kenney, James F., *The Sources for the Early History of Ireland,* Four Courts Press, Dublin, 1966.

King, John, *The Modern Numerology*, Blandford / Cassell, London, 1996.

Kipling, David, *The Telomere*, Oxford University Press, 1995.

Knappert, Jan, *The Encyclopedia of Middle Eastern Religion and Mythology*, Element Books, Shaftesbury, 1993.

Koltuv, Barbara Black, *The Book of Lilith*, Nicolas-Hays, York Beach, Maine, 1986.

Kramer, Heinrich, and Sprenger, James, *The Malleus Maleficarum*, (trans. Rev. Montague Summers), Dover Publications, NY, 1971.

Krishnamurti, Jiddu, *First and Last Freedom*, Victor Gollancz, London, 1961.

Kuhn, Alvin Boyd, *The Lost Light*, Academy Press, Elizabeth, NJ, 1940.

Ladas, Alice Kahn, with Whipple, Beverly, and Perry, John D., *The G Spot*, Dell Publishing, New York, NY, 1993.

Lang, Andrew, *The Red Fairy Book*, Longmans Green, London, 1890.

Leland, John, *The Itinerary of John Leland in or about the Years 1535-1543*, (5 vols., ed. L. Toulmin Smith), London, 1906-10.

Lewis, H. Spencer, *The Mystical Life of Jesus*, Ancient and Mystical Order Rosae Crucis, San Jose, CA, 1982.

Littleton, C. Scott, and Malcor, Linda A., *From Scythia to Camelot*, Garland Publishing, New York, 1994.

Macaulay, Lord Thomas Babington, *The History of England*, Penguin, Harmondsworth, 1986.

MacDari, Conor, *Irish Wisdom*, The Four Seas, Boston, MA, 1923.

MacDougall, James, *Folk Tales and Fairy Lore in Gaelic and English*, John Grant, Edinburgh, 1910.

Macmillan Encyclopedia, The, Macmillan, London. 1983.

MacNeill, E., *Celtic Ireland*, Academy Press, Dublin, 1981.

Maddox, Donald and Sturm-Maddox, Sara (eds.), *Mélusine of Lusignan*, University of Georgia Press, Athens, GA, 1996.

Major, John, *A History of Greater Britain As Well England and Scotland*, (trans. Archibald Constable), Scottish History Society, Edinburgh University Press, Edinburgh, 1892.

Malory, Sir Thomas, *Mort D'Arthur*, New York University Books, New York, 1961.

March, Jenny, *Dictionary of Classical Mythology*, Cassell, London, 1998.

Marie de France, *Lays*, (trans. Eugene Mason), J. M. Dent, London, 1954.

Martin, Malachi, *The Decline and Fall of the Roman Church*, Secker & Warburg, London, 1982.

Mathers, S. L. MacGregor, *The Key of Solomon the King*, Routledge & Kegan Paul, London, 1972.

Matthews, W. H., *Mazes and Labyrinths*, Dover Publications, New York, NY, 1970.

McBeath, Alastair, *Tiamat's Brood*, Dragon's Head Press, London, 1999.

Melton, J. Gordon, *The Vampire Book*, Visible Ink Press, Farmington Hills, MI, 1999.

Michelet, Jules, *Satanism and Witchcraft*, Citadel Press, New York , 1992.

Miller, Elizabeth, *Dracula: The Shade and the Shadow*, Desert Island Books, Westcliff-on-Sea, 1998.

Dracula: Sense and Nonsense, Desert Island Books, Westcliff-on-Sea, 2000.

Mills, Watson E. (ed.), *Lutterworth Dictionary of the Bible,* Lutterworth Press, Cambridge, 1994.

Moncreiffe, Sir Iain of that Ilk, Bt., *Royal Highness Ancestry of the Royal Child,* Hamish Hamilton, London, 1982.

Moore, Clement C., *The Night Before Christmas,* Harper Collins, London, 1997.

More, Dr. Henry, *Antidote Against Atheism,* London, 1653.

Morris, William, *Sigurd the Volsung,* Thoemmes Press, Bristol, 1994.

Murray John (7th Duke of Atholl), *Chronicles of Atholl and Tullibardine Families,* Ballantyne, London, 1908.

Murray, Margaret A., *The God of the Witches,* Oxford University Press, Oxford, 1970.

The Witch Cult in Western Europe, Oxford University Press, Oxford, 1971.

Nederlander, Munin, Kitezh—*The Russian Grail Legends,* (trans. Tony Langham), Aquarian Press, London, 1991.

Newark, Tim, and McBride, Angus, *Barbarians,* Concord Publications, Hong Kong , 1998.

Newsome, David, *The Convert Cardinals,* John Murray, London, 1993.

Norgate, Kate, *England Under the Angevin Kings,* Macmillan, London, 1887.

Norris, Pamela, *The Story of Eve,* Picador, London, 1998.

O'Brien, Christian and Barbara Joy, *The Shining Ones,* Dianthus, Cirencester, 1997.

The Genius of the Few, Dianthus, Cirencester, 1999.

Oldenbourg, Zoé, *Massacre at Montségur,* (trans. Peter Green), Pantheon, New York, NY, 1961.

Osen, Lynn M., *Women in Mathematics,* Massachusetts Institute of Technology, Cambridge, MA, 1997.

Osman, Ahmed, *Out of Egypt,* Century, London, 1998.

Ovid, *Metamorphoses,* (trans. A. D. Melville), Oxford University Press, Oxford, 1986.

Pagels, Elaine, *The Origin of Satan*, Random House, New York, 1995.

Patai, Raphael, *The Hebrew Goddess*, Wayne State University Press, Detroit, 1967.

The Jewish Alchemists, Princeton University Press, New Jersey, 1994.

Pennick, Nigel, *The Pagan Book of Days*, Destiny Books, Rochester, Vermont, 1992.

Phillips, Graham and Keatman, Martin, *The Shakespeare Conspiracy*, Century, London, 1994.

Piggott, Stuart, *Ancient Europe*, Edinburgh University Press, Edinburgh, 1965.

Planché, J. R., *The Conqueror and his Companions*, Tinsley Bros., London, 1874.

Porter, J. R., *The Illustrated Guide to the Bible*, Duncan Baird, London, 1995.

Potter, Jeremy, *Good King Richard*, Constable, London, 1983.

Ravenscroft, Trevor, *The Cup of Destiny*, Rider, London, 1981.

The Spear of Destiny, Samuel Weiser, York Beach, ME, 1982.

(with Wallace-Murphy, Tim), *The Mark of the Beast*, Samuel Weiser, York Beach, ME, 1997.

Reiter, Russel J., and Robinson, Jo, *Melatonin*, Bantam Books, New York, 1996.

Robinson, James M. (ed.), *The Nag Hammadi Library*, Coptic Gnostic Library: Institute for Antiquity and Christianity, E. J. Brill, Leiden, 1977.

Roney-Dougal, Serena, *Where Science and Magic Meet*, Element Books, Shaftesbury, 1993.

Roux, Georges, *Ancient Iraq*, George Allen & Unwin, London, 1964.

Russell, Jeffrey B., *A History of Witchcraft*, Thames & Hudson, London, 1980.

Saint-Yves, Leonard de, *Selected Writings of De Sade*, Peter Owen, London, 1963.

Schrödter, Willy, *A Rosicrucian Notebook*, Samuel Weiser, York Beach, Maine, 1992.

Scholem, Gershom G., *On the Kabbalah and its Symbolism*, Schocken Books, New York, NY, 1965.

Schonfield, Hugh J., *The Passover Plot*, Element Books, Shaftesbury, 1985.

Scot, Reginald, *The Discoverie of Witchcraft*, London, 1584 and 1665.

Sevely, Josephine Lowndes, *Eve's Secret*, Bloomsbury, London, 1987.

Shapiro, Debbie, *The Body Mind Workbook*, Element Books, Shaftesbury, 1990.

Shepard, Odell, *The Lore of the Unicorn*, George Allem & Unwin, London, 1967.

Shoemaker, Alfred L., *Christmas in Pennsylvania*, Stackpole Books, Mechanicsburg, PA, 1999.

Shu'al, Katan, *Sexual Magick*, Mandrake, Oxford, 1995.

Siefker, Phyllis, Santa Claus, *Last of the Wild Men*, MacFarland, Jefferson, NC, 1997.

Silverman, David P., *Ancient Egypt*, Piatkus, London, 1997.

Sitchin, Zecharia, *The 12th Planet*, Avon Books, New York, NY, 1978.

Skene, William Forbes (ed.), *Chronicles of the Picts and Scots*, HM General Register, Edinburgh, 1867.

Spenser, Edmund, *The Fairy Queen*, Everyman—J. M. Dent, London, 1996.

Speiser, E. A., *The Anchor Bible*, (trans. from Hebrew text), Doubleday, Garden City, New York, 1964.

Starbird, Margaret, *The Woman With the Alabaster Jar*, Bear, Santa Fe, NM, 1993.

Stein, Walter Johannes, *The Ninth Century*, Temple Lodge, London, 1991.

Stokes, Whitley (ed.), *Félire Óengusso Céli Dé*, (*The Martyrology of Oengus the Culdee*), Dublin Institute for Advanced Studies, Dublin, 1984.

Stoyanov, Yuri, *The Hidden Tradition in Europe*, Arkana-Penguin, Harmondsworth, 1994.

Summers, Montague, *The History of Witchcraft and Demonology*, Castle Books, Edison, NJ, 1992.

The Vampire, Dorset Press, New York, 1996.

The Vampire in Europe, Bracken Books, London, 1996.

Sutherland, Elizabeth, *In Search of the Picts*, Constable, London, 1994.

Tacitus, *The Annals of Imperial Rome*, (trans. Michael Grant), Cassell, London, 1963.

Tatar, Maria (ed.), *The Classic Fairy Tales*, W. W.Norton, London, 1999.

Taylor, Gladys, *Our Neglected Heritage*, Covenant Books, London, 1969-74.

Taylor, J. W., *The Coming of the Saints*, Covenant Books, London, 1969.

Thiering, Barbara, *Jesus the Man*, Doubleday, London, 1992.

Tolstoy, Count Nikolai, *The Quest for Merlin*, Hamish Hamilton, London, 1985.

Tudor-Craig, Sir Algernon, Melusine and the Lukin Family, Century House, London, 1932.

Turner, P. F. J., *The Real King Arthur*, SKS Publishing, Ankhorage, Alaska, 1993.

Unterman, Alan, *Dictionary of Jewish Lore and Legend*, Thames & Hudson, London, 1991.

Voragine, Jacobus de, *The Golden Legend*, (trans. William Caxton. ed. George V. O'Neill), Cambridge University Press, Cambridge, 1972.

Waddell, L. A., *The British Edda*, Chapman & Hall, London, 1930.

The Phoenician Origin of the Britons, Scots and Anglo-Saxons, Luzac, London, 1931.

Waite, Arthur Edward, *The Hidden Church of the Holy Grail*, Rebman, London, 1909.

Alchemists Through the Ages, Steiner Books, New York, (reprint) 1988.

Walji, Hasnain, *Melatonin*, Thorsons, London, 1995.

Walker, Barbara G., *The Women's Encyclopedia of Myths and Secrets*, Harper & Row, New York, 1983.

Wallace-Hadrill, J. M., *The Long Haired Kings*, Methuen, London, 1962.

Warner, Marina, *From the Beast to the Blonde*, Chatto & Windus, London, 1994.

Watson, W. J., *The History of the Celtic Place Names of Scotland*, William Blackwood, Edinburgh, 1926.

Wigoder, Geoffrey (ed.), *Encyclopaedia Judaica Decannial*, Keter Publishing, Jerusalem, 1997.

Wilken, Robert L., *The Christians as the Romans Saw Them*, Yale University Press, New Haven, Conn., 1984.

Williamson, John, *The Oak King, the Holly King and the Unicorn*. Harper & Row, New York, 1986.

Wilson, Colin, *From Atlantis to the Sphinx*, Virgin Books, London, 1996.

Wood, David, *Genisis – The First Book of Revelations*, Baton Press, Tunbridge Wells, 1985.

with Campbell, Ian, *Geneset – Target Earth*, Bellevue Books, Sunbury upon Thames, 1994.

Wood, Michael, *In Search of the Dark Ages*, BBC Books, London, 1981.

Legacy – A Search for the Origins of Civilization, BBC Network Books, London, 1992.

In Search of England, Viking-Penguin, Harmondsworth, 1999.

Woodroffe, Sir John (Arthur Avalon), *The Serpent Power*, Dover Publications, New York, NY, 1974.

Woolley, Sir C. Leonard, *Ur of the Chaldees*, Ernest Benn, London, 1929.

Coronation Rites, Cambridge University Press, Cambridge, 1915.

The Sumerians, W. W. Norton, London, 1965.

Yates, Frances A., *The Rosicrucian Enlightenment*, Routledge & Kegan Paul, London, 1972.

Yatri, *Unknown Man*, Sidgwick & Jackson, London, 1988.

Yeats, W. B., *The Celtic Twilight*, Colin Smythe, Gerrards Cross , 1981.

Zuckerman, Arthur J., *A Jewish Princedom in Feudal France*, Columbia University Press, New York, NY, 1972.

INDEX

REALM OF THE RING LORDS

THE MYTH AND THE MAGIC OF THE GRAIL QUEST

The contents of this book are also available in other formats:

E-book in Acrobat PDF and Rocket formats

The complete cassette edition set read by Laurence Gardner

Realm of the Holy Grail—Volume II CD Rom
(MP3 audio read by Laurence Gardner)

Other releases in 2001 (In hardback and colour illustrated editions):

Bloodline of the Holy Grail (Author's special edition)
Genesis of the Grail Kings (Author's special edition)

Information is available on all Laurence Gardner's books and formats from the MediaQuest Site at:

http://www.mediaquest.co.uk/lgardner.html

Also, for more on Laurence Gardner's work, lectures and updates visit:
laurencegardner.com

MEDIAQUEST